T0299329

Research Methods for Operations and Supply Chain Management

Research Methods for Operations and Supply Chain Management, third edition, is a toolkit of research approaches primarily for advanced students and beginner researchers, but also a reference book for any researcher in operations and supply chain management (OSCM).

Many students begin their careers in research limited by the one or few approaches taken by their department. The concise, accessible overviews found here equip them with an understanding of a variety of methods and how to use them, enabling students to tailor their research project to their own strengths and goals. The more seasoned researcher will find comprehensive descriptions and analyses on a wide variety of research approaches.

This updated and enhanced edition responds to the latest developments in OSCM, including the growing prominence of services and production of intangible products, the complete supply chain, and the increasing use of secondary data and of mixed approaches. Alternative research approaches are included and explored to help with the planning of research. This edition also includes expanded literature reviews and analysis to guide students towards the next steps in their reading, and more detailed step-by-step advice to tie theory with the research.

Including contributions from an impressive range of the field's leading thinkers in OSCM research, this is a guide that no one embarking on an OSCM research project should be without. Previous editions of this book were published under the title *Research Methods for Operations Management* and *Researching Operations Management*.

Christer Karlsson is an Emeritus Professor of Innovation and Operations Management at Copenhagen Business School, Denmark. He is also an Emeritus Professor at the Stockholm School of Economics, Sweden, and a Professor at the European Institute for Advanced Studies in Management (EIASM) in Brussels, Belgium.

Research Methods for Operations and Supply Chain Management

Third Edition

Edited by Christer Karlsson

Routledge
Taylor & Francis Group

LONDON AND NEW YORK

Cover image: © Getty Images

Third edition published 2024
by Routledge
4 Park Square, Milton Park, Abingdon, Oxon OX14 4RN

and by Routledge
605 Third Avenue, New York, NY 10158

Routledge is an imprint of the Taylor & Francis Group, an informa business

© 2024 selection and editorial matter, Christer Karlsson; individual chapters, the contributors

The right of Christer Karlsson to be identified as the author of the editorial material, and of the authors for their individual chapters, has been asserted in accordance with sections 77 and 78 of the Copyright, Designs and Patents Act 1988.

All rights reserved. No part of this book may be reprinted or reproduced or utilised in any form or by any electronic, mechanical, or other means, now known or hereafter invented, including photocopying and recording, or in any information storage or retrieval system, without permission in writing from the publishers.

Trademark notice: Product or corporate names may be trademarks or registered trademarks, and are used only for identification and explanation without intent to infringe.

First edition published by Routledge 2008
Second edition published by Routledge 2016

Previous editions of this book were published under the title *Research Methods for Operations Management* and *Researching Operations Management*.

British Library Cataloguing-in-Publication Data
A catalogue record for this book is available from the British Library

Library of Congress Cataloguing-in-Publication Data
Names: Karlsson, Christer, editor.
Title: Research methods for operations and supply chain management / edited by Christer Karlsson.
Other titles: Researching operations management.
Description: Third edition. | Abingdon, Oxon; New York, NY: Routledge, 2024. | Earlier edition published as: Researching operations management. | Includes bibliographical references and index. |
Identifiers: LCCN 2023025495 (print) | LCCN 2023025496 (ebook) | ISBN 9781032324364 (hardback) | ISBN 9781032324340 (paperback) | ISBN 9781003315001 (ebook)
Subjects: LCSH: Industrial management--Research. | Production management--Research. | Operations research.
Classification: LCC HD30.4.R478 2024 (print) | LCC HD30.4 (ebook) | DDC 658.5/7--dc23/eng/20230525
LC record available at https://lccn.loc.gov/2023025495
LC ebook record available at https://lccn.loc.gov/2023025496

ISBN: 978-1-032-32436-4 (hbk)
ISBN: 978-1-032-32434-0 (pbk)
ISBN: 978-1-003-31500-1 (ebk)

DOI: 10.4324/9781003315001

Typeset in Times New Roman
by MPS Limited, Dehradun

Contents

Figures

Tables

Contributors

This book is written by leading scholars in the field describing how to carry through research at the very highest level with the aim of getting published. The authors have been chosen from scholars who have considerable experience in doing and managing research, getting research published and reviewing research in the field of operations and supply chain management. They are, in order of appearance, the following:

Christer Karlsson holds an MSc and a PhD degree from Chalmers University of Technology, Gothenburg, Sweden, in the area of Industrial Management. He is a Professor Emeritus of Innovation and Operations Management at Copenhagen Business School, a Professor Emeritus at the Stockholm School of Economics, and a Professor at the European Institute for Advanced Studies in Management (EIASM) in Brussels. He is a laureate of the Royal Swedish Academy of Engineering Sciences (IVA). For over fifteen years he has been Director of the nationwide Swedish applied research institute, Institute for Management of Innovation and Technology (IMIT). He is the Founder, appointed Fellow, and lifetime board member of the European Operations Management Association (EurOMA), Honorary Fellow of EIASM, and Fellow of the Product Development Management Association (PDMA), He is fellow of the University of Cambridge Industrial Policy Forum. He is a member of several editorial boards of professional journals, including *International Journal of Operations and Productions Management, Journal of Product Innovation Management,* and *International Journal of Innovation Management.*

Pär Åhlström holds an MSc and a PhD degree from the Stockholm School of Economics in Sweden. He is currently Torsten and Ragnar Söderberg Professor of Operations Management at Stockholm School of Economics, where he is also Vice President Degree Programs. He is a Research Fellow at the Institute for Management of Innovation and Technology (IMIT), a member of the Royal Swedish Academy of Engineering Sciences (IVA), and a fellow of the European Operations Management Association (EurOMA). Previous positions include Professor of Operations Management at Chalmers University of Technology, Gothenburg, Sweden, and Research Fellow at London Business School. His research interests are in the areas of operations strategy, service operations management, and innovation management. He has published in several journals, among others the *International Journal of Operations and Production Management,* the *European Management Journal,* the *Journal of Product Innovation Management, Technovation,* and the *International Journal of Services Technology Management.*

Cipriano Forza holds an MSc and a PhD degree from the University of Padova. He is a Professor of Management and Operations Management at the University of Padova, where he served as coordinator of the PhD course in Management Engineering and Real Estate Economics. He teaches research methods at the European Institute for Advanced Studies in Management (EIASM) in Brussels and has been visiting scholar at Minnesota University, London Business School, and Arizona State University. He served on the board of the European Operations Management Association (EurOMA) and he is a Fellow EurOMA. He acted as an associate editor for the *Journal of Operations Management* and *Decision Sciences Journal*. Currently, he is a reviewer for several scientific journals and he is a member of the scientific committee of the Academic Journal Guide. He has participated in the international survey-based research 'High Performance Manufacturing' since 1990. He published in various journals including the *Journal of Operations Management*, the *International Journal of Operations and Productions Management*, the *International Journal of Production Research*, the *International Journal of Production Economics*, and *Production Planning and Control*.

Enrico Sandrin holds a PhD in Operations Management from the University of Padova and is an Assistant Professor in the Department of Management and Engineering at the same university. Formerly, he worked as a knowledge engineer for product configuration, as a buyer, and as a controller in a firm operating in the machinery industry, where he also contributed to many business transformation projects sometimes collaborating with leading consulting companies. His research activity revolves around the study of product variety and customization management, product configuration, organization design, and human resource management for mass customization. His research has been published in international journals such as the *International Journal of Operations & Production Management*, the *Journal of Manufacturing Systems*, the *International Journal of Production Economics*, *Computers in Industry*, *Industrial Management & Data Systems*, and the *Journal of Systems & Software*. One of his survey-based papers was awarded the Harry Boer Highly Commended Award at the EurOMA conference 2016.

Chris Voss gained a BSc(Eng) at Imperial College London, and an MSc and PhD at London Business School. He is Professor of Operations Management at Warwick Business School and Emeritus Professor at London Business School, where he has also held the post of Deputy Dean. Professor Voss was the founder, and for many years chairman, of the European Operations Management Association (EurOMA) and is a Fellow EurOMA, of the Production and Operations Management Society (POMS), The British Academy of Management and the Decision Science Institute. He was president of the POMS service management college and is on the editorial advisory board of a number of journals, including the *International Journal of Operations and Production Management*, the *Journal of Product Innovation Management*, the *Journal of Operations Management, the Journal of Service Research* and the *British Journal of Management.*

Mark Johnson holds an EngD and an MSc from the University of Warwick. He is currently a Professor of Operations Management at Warwick Business School. He was previously at Cranfield School of Management where he was the leader for the Servitization theme of the University's EPSRC-funded Innovative Manufacturing Research Centre (IMRC). He is an Associate Editor for the *Journal of Operations Management* and Senior Associate Editor for the *International Journal of Physical Distribution and Logistics*

Management. His research has been published in *Research Policy*, the *Journal of Supply Chain Management*, the *International Journal of Operations and Production Management*, the *International Journal of Production Economics* and the *International Journal of Physical Distribution and Logistics Management* among others.

Jan Godsell gained an MEng Management with Japanese from the University of Birmingham and an EMBA and PhD from Cranfield University. Following a career in industry with organizations including ICI, Zeneca and Dyson, Jan started her academic career at Cranfield University. She is currently Dean of Loughborough's School of Business and Economics. Jan is a Chartered Mechanical Engineer and member of the Institution of Mechanical Engineers, Manufacturing Industries Division Board. She is also a member of the Manufacturing Advisor Group for the UK Department for Business Innovation and Skills and of the European Management Association Board and she serves on the editorial advisory board of a number of journals, including the *International Journal of Operations and Production Management.*

Paul Coughlan is a Professor in Operations Management at the Trinity Business School, Trinity College Dublin, Ireland. He is a Fellow of the College and an Honorary Fellow of the European Operations Management Association (EurOMA). He has published in the *International Journal of Operations and Production Management, British Journal of Management, Creativity & Innovation Management, Systemic Practice and Action Research,* and *Action Learning: Research and Practice.* His co-authored book with David Coghlan, *Collaborative Strategic Improvement through Network Action Learning: The Path to Sustainability,* was published by Edward Elgar (2011). He holds a PhD from the University of Western Ontario, Canada, and MBA and BE degrees from University College, Cork, Ireland. He has been President of the board of the European Institute for Advanced Studies in Management (EIASM), Chair of the board of the Innovation & Product Development Management Conference (IPDMC), and a member of the board of EurOMA.

David Coghlan is a Professor Emeritus at Trinity Business School, Trinity College Dublin, Ireland, and is a Fellow Emeritus of the college. He specializes in organization development and action research and is active in both communities internationally. He has published over three hundred articles and book chapters. Recent co-authored books include *Collaborative inquiry for Organization Development and Change* (Edward Elgar, 2021). He is the co-editor of *The Handbook of Methods in Organizational Change Research* (Edward Elgar, 2023). He is currently on the editorial boards of the *Journal of Applied Behavioral Science, Action Research* and *Action Learning: Research and Practice* among others.

J. Will M. Bertrand gained an MSc and a PhD at Eindhoven University of Technology in the Netherlands. He is an Emeritus Professor of Production and Operations Management at the Department of Industrial Engineering and Innovation Sciences of Eindhoven University of Technology. He held a visiting position at Rutgers University in the United States and has worked in managing positions for ASML and for Philips in the Netherlands. He has served as a member of the board of the Dutch Society for Logistics Management (VLM), and has been the Scientific Director of the BETA Research School for Operations Management and Logistics in the Netherlands. He served as a member of the editorial board of the International Journal of Operations and Production Management, and the International Journal of Production Research.

Jan C. Fransoo is a Professor of Operations and Logistics Management in the School of Economics and Management at Tilburg University. He further holds courtesyappointments at Eindhoven University of Technology and Massachusetts Institute of Technology. Fransoo's current research studies operations and decision-making in retail supply chains and transport operations, and his past research has studied this in the chemical, pharmaceutical, and food industry. He is method-agnostic and conducts model-based, econometric, experimental, and qualitative work. He has been the advisor of more than 30 doctoral students and more than one hundred Master's students. He has published about 130 papers across a wide variety of journals, including all Operations Management journals on the FT50 list. He serves as associate editor of *Operations Research* and of *Production and Operations Management*, and served on the editorial board of multiple other journals including *Journal of Operations Management, Decision Sciences, OR Spectrum, and Flexible Services and Manufacturing Journal.* He has served as editor of leading books including *Behavioral Operations in Planning and Scheduling, Sustainable Supply Chains: A Research-Based Textbook on Operations and Strategy,* and *Reaching 50 Million Nanostores: Retail Distribution in Emerging Megacities.* Fransoo frequently collaborates in research and in consulting with major corporations, tech startups, national and regional governments, and intergovernmental organizations. He has held senior leadership positions at Eindhoven University of Technology and Kuehne Logistics University, and served on the board of the *European Operations Management Association* and *Production and Operations Management Society.*

Maximiliano Udenio is an Associate Professor of Operations Management in the Research Center for Operations Management of the Faculty of Economics and Business of the KU Leuven, in Belgium. He teaches supply chain management and operations strategy at the bachelor and master level of the business engineering program. His research is in the field of Operations Management; mainly studying inventory dynamics, the evolution of the structure of supply chain networks, and issues related to supply chain sustainability. In terms of methodology, his work is strongly model-based – analytical and empirical. He collaborates with top international researchers in the field and has published research in journals such as*Journal of Operations Management* and *European Journal of Operational Research.*

Acknowledgements

This book is based on a European Doctoral Educational Network (EDEN) programme by the European Institute for Advanced Studies in Management (EIASM) in collaboration with the European Operations Management Association (EurOMA), with the editor as creator and first coordinator, the other first authors, and in later versions, others as faculty. Some of the material has been published previously in a special issue of the *International Journal of Operations and Production Management*, 22(2), 2002, with this book's editor as guest editor.

We acknowledge the following:

EIASM for its development of the EDEN concept and for providing the opportunity to develop and run this EDEN workshop on research methodology. The workshop has, at the time of publication of this book, had its 30th anniversary.

EurOMA who have supported the development and operation of this workshop by providing faculty and making the event known in the EurOMA network as well as promoting its role as a compulsory PhD programme in many business schools and universities.

The *International Journal of Operations and Production Management*, which published the first research versions of a couple of the chapters in this book; hence making the workshop the key reference for research methodology in operations and supply chain management.

Finally, Routledge should be acknowledged for their support in bringing the wide scope of thoughts of these authors together in a comprehensive research methodology textbook of this kind.

1 Introduction to the book

Christer Karlsson

Chapter overview

This book is both a textbook and a reference. It is especially aimed at PhD candidates, Master's thesis writers, and young researchers, but the more experienced researcher will also find the wide scope of research approaches helpful.

The book can be used as a complete text on research methodology in operations and supply chain management (OSCM) and adjacent areas, or for consideration of general research issues combined with a deeper focus only on the specialized chapter with the most relevant method. It can even be a lexicon of all the main approaches to OSCM research, suitably contained in one text.

The book is structured with the following principle. First, research philosophy is discussed in Chapter 2. Then methodology is discussed, and research is planned in Chapter 3. Different research approaches and the methods they use are discussed in Chapters 4–9.

After the introduction, the book starts in Chapter 2 with research philosophy, which includes worldview, what is real, what knowledge is, reasoning, logic, roles, and outcomes of research. What research is and what good research is are both discussed. Chapter 3 focuses on key activities in the early parts of the research process that are generic in so far as they cut across the different research approaches. Chapter 4 is about surveys using questionnaires, but also covers many general issues on sampling, validity, reliability, and other issues common to all approaches. Chapter 5 addresses case research, from single to multiple cases. The importance of rigor and how to achieve it in case research is underlined. Chapter 6 is on longitudinal field studies, in-depth studies of change processes inside organizations. Chapter 7 is on action research where the researcher enters the organization with the combined aim of making changes in the organization while studying it. Chapter 8 is on clinical research where the researcher is a clinician called upon by the organization to help solve a problem. Chapter 9 discusses modelling and simulation with the possibilities of analysing more or less holistic perspectives and trying out 'what-if' analyses; that is, examining the effect of different managerial interventions.

DOI: 10.4324/9781003315001-1

1.1   Introduction

The aim of this book is to be a comprehensive textbook and reference for how-to-do good research in the fields of operations and supply chain management. First, the book is intended as a core textbook for Master's and PhD candidates and young researchers. Second, it is a comprehensive textbook and handbook for researchers in the field, providing basic knowledge about the different research approaches.

The primary focus of the book is to support PhD students in their first or second year of study as well as Master's thesis writers and students on higher-level courses that contain some research methodology. However, the book is aimed not only at young researchers. More experienced researchers can benefit from a comprehensive description of all the most common research approaches in operations and supply chain management (OSCM). All the authors involved in this book have benefited from repeated acquaintance with each other's deeper knowledge of the different approaches. Several faculty members have participated in the series of methodology seminars on which this book is based, indicating that not even faculty members can be experts in the entirety of the wide range of research methodology knowledge represented here.

A particular problem, especially for PhD candidates and young researchers, is that many departments tend to specialize in one or only a small number of approaches to research, and so they are not exposed to the breadth of possible research methods. The book covers enough of each of the most important research approaches to allow students at least to practice different approaches and set them in relation to other approaches, but this is not intended to be a specialized text on any single approach or method. Thus, it gives a platform that few research settings can provide, that enables the individual researcher to choose appropriate and complementary approaches and helps them to develop a stronger argument for their own research choices.

The subject of the book is the different research methods frequently used in studies on OSCM as well as adjacent applied management areas such as management of innovation, product development, research and development (R&D), logistics, and so on. Typical courses the title is intended for would incorporate the topics of research methodology, research methods, and thesis writing. Typical course levels are the final part of Bachelor's programmes, Master's programmes, and the first or second year of PhD programmes.

1.2   How to use the book

The chapters of the book have a logical sequence but can also be used as standalone references. The second chapter is aimed at developing the reader's capability for enhancing the level of scientific contribution in their research, and the necessary skills in positioning it. The third chapter gives a hands-on approach to planning a research project in a way that is 'complete'. Six chapters on different research approaches follow with descriptions, discussions, and cases with references and analytical comments. Research methods and tools are defined, described, and demonstrated with examples. Substantial references to published articles and sometimes a brief bibliography are annotated at the end of each chapter. Each chapter is summarized, with the most important points made in bullet-pointed listing. At the end of the book, there is an extensive index with subjects, issues, and authors.

There are at least three different ways of using this book. First, it can be used as a complete text on research methodology in OSCM and adjacent areas. Chapter 2 sets out to help with considerations of what research is, what it produces, issues to consider before and during conducting research, and what quality of research is. Then the reader moves on to Chapter 3 to be assisted in planning research and considering the appropriate research approaches and methods to use. Chapters 2 and 3 are intentionally written in a dialectic style with the purpose of helping researchers consider all of the issues in the research planning phase. Chapter 4 and onwards are more specialized in tone, with a less dialectic but still practice-oriented style. Chapter 4 in particular not only describes survey research, but also goes into detail regarding how research questions are formulated, how data are selected and gathered, and the important issues of validity and reliability. Subsequent chapters follow the same format with different research approaches and methods, as presented in more detail next. A second way of using the book, especially for the reader who has already started a research project and has chosen a main method, can be to study the general parts and then focus only on the specialized chapter with the most relevant method. In addition, other chapters can be used as references, remembering the strength of combining approaches. Third, the book can be a lexicon of all the main approaches to OSCM research, suitably contained in one text. The logic of the structure is such that it should be easy to navigate. The text is structured and formatted in a manner intended to allow searching and referencing and with a certain intended sequence of research methods.

1.3 Overview of the book chapters

To give the reader assistance in seeing the whole book in a comprehensive way, all chapter abstracts follow here.

1.3.1 Chapter 2 abstract

Fundamental standpoints are that research aims at the creation and development of knowledge and that research must be of a high quality in terms of validity and reliability. Research contributions consist of additions to pre-existing knowledge, deal with phenomena not previously observed, or may contradict earlier knowledge. Research can be explorative, descriptive, analytical, causal, and normative relative to the state of existing knowledge. A general research process contains Identification of a problem or issue, Literature review, Aim, objective, or purpose of the research, Research question, Research approach and methods, Conceptual framework, Data collection, Analysing and interpreting data, Synthesizing and concluding, Evaluating the research and suggesting further research, Reporting and communicating. Researcher roles include observer, surveyor, analyst, communicator, sounding board, actor, consultant, and clinician. Depending on how knowledge is created the three perspectives of deductive, inductive, and abductive argument are applied. Demonstrate the contribution by relating results to earlier existing knowledge, make claims for generalizability and discuss forms of generalization. The key issue in research quality is credibility or trustworthiness, which request validity and reliability. The research must be done rigorously (which is not rigid). For many researchers, it is 'publish or perish'. Plan for publication early during the research process.

1.3.2 Chapter 3 abstract

This chapter concerns the research process – the sequence of activities that takes you from the start of a research project to publication. The focus is on a set of activities taking place in the early parts of the research process, before data are collected and analysed. The activities are generic and apply to all the different research approaches described in the remainder of the book. The first activity regards the importance of contributing to knowledge. To properly understand the research process, an understanding of its goal is necessary, which is to contribute to existing knowledge. The second activity is choosing a research topic, as any contribution to knowledge starts with finding a suitable research topic. The third activity is the literature review and various ways of using and misusing literature. The fourth activity is developing research questions, which are a fundamentally important part of any research process. The final activity regards some key considerations in choosing a research approach. In this the final part of the chapter three considerations in selecting a research approach are discussed: the achievement of methodological fit, the impact of the researcher's philosophical position and practical considerations.

Following the overview provided by Chapters 2 and 3, subsequent chapters deal with individual research approaches in specific detail.

1.3.3 Chapter 4 abstract

Chapter 4 is about surveys using questionnaires. It takes a processual view, moving from the theoretical model to hypothesis development to empirical investigation, and covers many general issues on sampling, validity, reliability, and other issues common to all research approaches. Because of this, Chapter 4 is important not only in itself, but also because of many fundamental issues valid across the subsequent chapters on specific approaches. It takes as a starting point conceptualization of the research issue through the development of a theoretical model and discusses the unit of analysis and definitions. The reader is then taken through the steps of detailed research planning, paying particular attention to the development of measures. Before going to present the survey execution activities the chapter deepens advanced issues regarding the interdependences between the theoretical aspects (e.g. monadic/polyadic constructs) and survey design choices (e.g. single/multiple respondents). Special care is then given to how to analyse and interpret data, further discussing validity issues. Commonly used and advanced data-analysis methods are presented. Finally, emerging issues and techniques in data collection, management, and analysis are presented such as data integration from multiple sources and data visualization. Along this chapter, the reader can see the evolution of OSCM survey research in the last forty years.

1.3.4 Chapter 5 abstract

Chapter 5 addresses when, why, and how to use case research. It sets out the choices open to the researcher and describes the approaches needed to conduct case research with rigour. It addresses how case research can be used for theory development, theory testing, theory elaboration, and the relationship with inductive, deductive, and abductive research. Important elements are the criteria for choosing cases and sample controls. Research can be based on single cases, but mostly multiple cases; the choices in case selection and on what basis should these choices be made is set out. Data is usually based on interviews and analysis of documentation, but triangulation is important and many other data sources can be used. The need for rigour and how to achieve it in case research is emphasized. An important approach is developing a research framework with clearly defined constructs and research questions. Case research should not just be visits to organizations, rigour is achieved through research instruments and protocols. The analyses should be well structured and systematic, both within and across cases. A common result of case studies is generation and/or testing of hypotheses; how to achieve this in a reliable manner is examined.

1.3.5 Chapter 6 abstract

Longitudinal field studies are in-depth studies of change processes. They are case studies studying a phenomenon over time and often involve real-time studies of organizational phenomena, with the researcher being present in the organization. Research questions often concern how organizational change emerge, develop, grow, or terminate over time. Before entering the field, a framework for data gathering is critical. Longitudinal field researchers rely heavily on participant observation. To avoid going native, the researcher regularly withdraws from the field back to the academic environment. Analysing longitudinal field data is a challenging task due to the large amounts of data. Central to data analysis is data reduction. It starts with the writing of a narrative of the process. The narrative is divided into basic units of information, using explicit decision rules. The third step is to code incidents. The incidents are finally sorted and recoded. Generation of theory starts while the researcher is still in the field. The starting point for building theory is the incidents, but the interest is in the mechanisms underlying them. The analysis requires identifying sequences and patterns in the events. The theory developed needs to be constantly compared with existing theory.

1.3.6 Chapter 7 abstract

Chapter 7 introduces action research which, as the term suggests, has a dual focus. The action intention aims to address a practical concern of individuals, groups, organizations, or communities. The research intention aims to generate practical or actionable knowledge for use beyond the immediacy of the specific situation. A distinctive feature of action research is that it is undertaken in collaboration with those who are stakeholders in the practical issues, making them co-researchers rather than subjects. This combination of action and research in a single paradigm distinguishes action research philosophically from those forms of research that focus on generating knowledge only. It marks action research as a most relevant approach to organizational, societal, and global transformation in how it addresses real issues with those who care about them, and cogenerates useful, actionable knowledge for researchers and practitioners. In the context of today's challenges to operations and supply chain management, action research provides a rich philosophy, methodology and methods for relevant and impactful action and research. The chapter provides a grounding in action research in the context of operations and supply chain management and discusses issues relating to design, planning, implementation, theory development, quality, ethics, and required skills.

1.3.7 Chapter 8 abstract

This chapter describes clinical approaches to management research and positions them in relation to other field research approaches. The researcher is asked to intervene in a diagnostic relationship and concurrent development. The researcher intervenes to help the organizational patient and concurrently does research on that organization. There is a parallel process of helping the client and developing scientific results. The researcher may for a period intervene in the organization and for a next period withdraw for analysis. The researcher inquires with a client and problem-solving focus. Pure inquiry has a mapping purpose. Diagnostic inquiry has the purpose of searching for causalities. Action-oriented inquiry has the purpose of searching for both past and future causalities. Confrontative inquiry has the purpose of influencing not only the thought process but also the actual content of the dialogue.

In clinical management research, much data come from client needs and perspectives while the inquiry comes from the clinical researcher's theory. There are several client relations issues to consider such as the client pays a fee, many sensitive issues must be kept confidential, and ethical and legal issues must be handled. Concluding clinical research enables learning about causal relations in organizational development.

1.3.8 Chapter 9 abstract

Chapter 9 discusses model-based research in OSCM. Starting with a historical overview of how modelling research evolved from scientific management, management consulting, and military applications. The differing philosophies that gave rise to operations research in the United States and operational research in the United Kingdom are discussed as is their impact on current model-based research in OSCM.

The focus then turns to the main methodologies used in the field. The emphasis here is on quantitative models and causal relationships between the variables of the model. These can be descriptive as well as prescriptive and are valuable in both understanding and solving OSCM problems. Axiomatic research is primarily driven by the mathematical model (itself an abstraction of reality); the main concern of the researcher is to provide insights into the structure of the problem as defined within the model. Empirical research, on the other hand, is driven by data. In this class of research, the primary concern of the researcher is to ensure that there is a model fit between the observations made of reality and the model made of that reality. In the last twenty years, more and more research combines aspects of both methodologies, embedding axiomatic research in an empirical context and vice versa, with the consequence that researchers require understanding across research methods, leading to larger and more multi-disciplinary author teams.

Finally, setting up models based on these quantitative research strategies is described step by step, including practical examples of model-based research.

1.4 Introduction to the first and second editions

The first edition of this book was published in 2009. It soon became a reference for research methods in both OM and adjacent areas and was widely used in doctoral education. In the second edition the development of the academic fields, research approaches, and what was published was taken into account.

The planning of research was given a new structure and new content. Alternative approaches and surveying and analysing existing knowledge was further developed.

Additional perspectives were added, for example, the use of secondary data, clinical research, and experimental and mixed approaches. There was more on how to conduct the different approaches and ethical issues.

1.5 Introduction to the third edition

This third edition of the book has some considerable developments and extensions. The different approaches to doing research and developing knowledge have been further developed and have comparative analyses in Chapter 2. The field of research has been expanded from mainly OM to cover operations and supply chain management with up-to-date references. This has an effect in all chapters. Additional methods have been added, for example, the use of secondary data, interventionist research, and experimental and mixed methods. Chapter 7 developments cover mode 2 knowledge creation, abductive reasoning, and adding a design science section. Chapter 8 has been expanded with versions of clinical research such as interventionist and collaborative methods. Chapter 9 has been rewritten throughout, substantially expanding the discussion on empirical modelling and its analytical grounding, reflecting the latest trends in the field. All chapters are of course updated with the latest references.

2 Research in operations and supply chain management

Christer Karlsson

DOI: 10.4324/9781003315001-2

2.1 Introduction

This chapter serves as a foundation for the whole book and contains discussions of research philosophy and methodology and introductions to the rest of the book. It is especially targeted at the researcher in the early stage of a PhD program or about to take it on but will also have some tips for the more seasoned researcher. It is followed by Chapter 3, which will focus on the research process and to plan research, after which come the different research approaches.

The chapter starts with a discussion of what research is and what its purposes are, followed by discussions of research outputs, what is typical for research in the areas of operations and supply chain management (OSCM), target groups, what good research is, the role of the researcher, dissemination of research, and ethical aspects. A fundamental standpoint is that research aims at the creation and development of knowledge. A second fundamental perspective is that research must be of high quality in terms of validity and reliability in order for it to be published and so the reader can trust its results.

The book is about research on management. It is a part of the social sciences. Although it focuses on research on management of operations and supply chains, it is largely applicable to the management of other areas. However, it is neither research on humanities nor on formal or natural sciences. The book also focuses on empirical research; that is, approaches that develop knowledge based on observations and experiments. It does not discuss theoretical research.

2.1.1 What is research?

There may be a reasonable consensus that research concerns the creation and development of knowledge, but even so there are variants. The The Organisation for Economic Co-operation and Development (OECD) provides the following definitions:

> Research & development is a term covering three activities: basic research, applied research, and experimental development.
>
> Basic research is experimental or theoretical work undertaken primarily to acquire new knowledge of the underlying foundations of phenomena and observable facts, without any particular application or use in view. Applied research is original investigation undertaken in order to acquire new knowledge. It is, however, directed primarily towards a specific practical aim or objective.
>
> Experimental development is systematic work, drawing on existing knowledge gained from research and/or practical experience that is directed to producing new materials, products, or devices; to installing new processes, systems, and services; or to improving substantially those already produced or installed.
>
> (OECD, 2015)

Key components are that the outcomes or outputs from research are new knowledge and/or new applications. The process of research is common in many definitions, for example:

> Studious inquiry or examination; especially investigation or experimentation aimed at the discovery and interpretation of facts, revision of accepted theories or laws in the light of new facts, or practical application of such new or revised theories or laws.
>
> (Merriam-Webster, 2015)

Research is a process of steps used to collect and analyse information to increase our understanding of a topic or issue. It consists of three steps: Pose a question, collect data to answer the question, and present an answer to the question.

(Creswell, 2007)

Most modern perspectives of research include the purpose of implementation or using knowledge to develop applications. This is described by some researchers as Mode 2 research, as an addition or alternative to traditional pure knowledge creation and development, called Mode 1. Mode 2 was said to be a new form of knowledge production that was context-driven, problem-focused and interdisciplinary. It involved multi-disciplinary teams that worked together for short periods of time on specific problems in the real world (Gibbons *et al.*, 1994). Although the concept of Mode 2 was launched in 1994, it is fair to say that research with the aim of developing applications of knowledge has long been a practice in management and not least in OSCM. We have been doing case and other studies out there in the so-called real world for a long time now. The two modes and several variants, especially of Mode 2, will be dealt with throughout this book.

2.1.2 Why do research?

Before starting a research project, doing research, or, for some individuals, continuing a research career, one should ask oneself several questions. The first and obvious personal question is whether you want to do this at all – which, let us hope, will already have been answered by the reader of this book. However, experience shows that quite a few PhD candidates have chosen to stay in the university environment while others have developed a career in industry. In either case, they may continue to be research active, inquiring into issues in practice. Here, both Mode 1 and Mode 2 research are relevant in management research and not least in management of operations and supply chains. However, it can sometimes be that the researcher who wants an academic career is more inclined to do Mode 1 research while the researcher who thinks of an industrial career often is more interested in doing Mode 2 research. Regardless, the researcher should want to undertake creative work in a systematic way in order to develop new knowledge and new applications of knowledge.

2.1.3 Why do this research?

The specific field we choose within the broad area of management may be selected for very different reasons. Quite often it is something that has interested us during our earlier studies, something we came into contact with. Often, it is just something that was available through grant opportunities or existing or announced research projects. It must be something we really want to dig into, learn more about, and stay focused on for a considerable time in the future, even specialize in.

Unfortunately, or not, opportunism and fashion seem to play important roles. The availability of research grants has a great influence. Other important determining factors should be potentials of research outlets such as academic publications, positions in business schools and universities, and positions and possibilities for employment in companies and other organizations.

A very important aspect of how any study is conducted is that there is a close correlation between the research questions and the suitable method. This book as a whole concerns different approaches, although not all approaches are suitable for a specific issue or research question (we will deal with this more in Chapter 3, which is on the research process and planning). However, the choice may not be a linear process from an interest to a research plan. In a real situation there may be a research opportunity, a project, one or several cases in the form of interested companies, or a call for a research application for a specific purpose. We may end up with a situation in which we know the empirical database and/or the research format better than the precise research question. We may start with a project and plan the research accordingly. We will go deeper into the questions of why to do research and in what way in Sections 2.4–2.6, and then, in a methodology perspective, discuss the appropriateness of different approaches in Chapter 3 that follows.

The target group for which we do the research has implications for how we do research. We may be interested in doing research either in Mode 1 or 2. A combination may also be possible with a focus on theoretical development but with managerial implications. One key factor in the choice lies in personal interest, given that the sponsor or project owner allows it. Doing research in Mode 1 may mean that the personal interest is in knowledge development and that an academic career is the outlook for the future, while doing research in Mode 2 will focus the applicability to working with implementations in organizations or as a consultant. A second key factor is the fit between research questions and approaches. There is no best approach: it is a matter of suitability.

The reason for a researcher to engage in a particular research project is a matter of interest in an issue, availability of opportunities and resources, interest and skills in the research format, potential careers, and an interest and a conviction in gaining and focusing on knowledge.

2.1.4 Research in operations and supply chain management

Research in OSCM covers many issues and is carried out using several different research approaches. Although there is some correlation between the issues and the research approaches, it still leaves us with high, and sometimes confounding, variation within the field. Operations are a transformation activity: transforming resources (machines and people) and converting inputs (materials, people, information) into outputs of goods and services. Within this general definition we all perform operations and operations go on all around us. Operations take place not only in manufacturing but also in supply chains, sales, services, administrative processes, and many more areas. Hence, what is described in this book is applicable to many functions in an organization. However, we often take the production function of either goods or services as a starting point.

The scope of OSCM is wide, is based on the perspective of operations as transformation, and includes the following aspects. First there is the strategic perspective, which focuses on the role of and the objectives for the function of operations. An important aspect here is how operations are related to and play a role in the business model of the organization. Operations play a role in business model innovation and development. The role of operations in the business model leads to a strategy for operations and for how the operations help the firm to compete in the market. Operations systems are designed con- currently with the products and services that the operations system is supposed to produce. Design of the system will include both internal and external systems covering supply, production of goods and service, and distribution. Design involves planning information and material flows as well as layouts and the choice of process technologies for transformation activities. Operations design also involves designing an organization and its processes and structures and staffing it with human resources. There is a need to choose and develop planning and control of capacity, inventory, and transformation activities in the internal as well as the external production and service systems, and to design and build different support systems for quality assurance, system maintenance, and system improvements.

There are some characteristics of the OSCM field that influence how we deal with it. It is an applied field with a managerial character. It deals with issues and problems encountered in the so-called real world. It is cross-disciplinary, drawing on disciplines such as economics, finance, accounting, organizational behaviour, marketing, mathematics, and more.

In each of the areas we find research on different issues conducted with different research approaches and with the perspectives of different disciplines. There are surveys with questionnaires and interviews, there are single and multiple case studies, there are longitudinal field studies, there is action research, and there is modelling and simulation. We address each of these important research approaches in the following chapters of this book.

2.2 Research outputs and targets

As researchers in the field, we have concurrent target groups, and we address issues relevant to both academics and practitioners. We direct our results primarily to the academic world, but also to practitioners.

The aims of research in management are often related to good practice. The close connection to practice makes relevance a major criterion for good management research. Since research also needs to contribute to the academic world in management research, we often face the problem of concurrent needs for practical relevance and academic contribution.

A fundamental characteristic of good research is that there is significant contribution to knowledge. New knowledge may be significant in different ways. Typically, research contributions consist of additions to pre-existing knowledge. Research results can also be more or less significant in terms of the size of their contribution to theory or practice. For example, results may deal with phenomena not previously observed, or they may contradict earlier knowledge. Another important factor is the potential value that can be created when applying the research results. How to consider the potential contribution and plan it is further developed in Chapter 3.

The choice of target group has particular significance. At whom are the contributions to knowledge aimed? There is a range of targets, from the individual firm to OSCM practitioners, to OSCM researchers, as well as other management researchers and policymakers. A common risk for the young researcher is formulating the aim and research questions too generally and not framing a researchable question. But there is also the converse risk of being too narrow. For example, the problem may have no general value beyond the studied case. Solving a specific problem for an individual organization using existing well-established knowledge may be of limited value both to the research community and to the practitioner community. It risks being consultancy rather than research.

The most significant characteristic of good research is that, methodologically, it is well done. Research is expected to provide trustworthy knowledge, since it is done by independent knowledgeable scholars trained to develop knowledge using rigorous processes. The quality of research is dealt with in Section 2.7.

2.2.1 *The aims and scope of research*

The aim of research is the creation and development of knowledge, and the output is the contribution to knowledge. Research output is published and presented mainly in the form of research articles in professional scientific journals, as well as in books, especially anthologies and more applied texts. Student textbooks seldom contain previously unpublished knowledge but may combine and transfer pre-existing knowledge in new and accessible ways.

Research may have different purposes, in broad terms, confirmation, falsification, and exploration. Often the initial thought of purpose would be confirmation. Building on existing research is one obvious path to follow. Previous findings may be confirmed in other organizational, industrial, technological, or cultural settings. One reason for choosing confirmation may be a quest to find truths. Another reason may be that management research models are often based in the natural sciences with facts based on physical phenomena. However, general truths are hard to reach in behavioural research. The second purpose, falsification, offers many more opportunities. While confirmation will need a rather extensive study, falsification only needs to identify the rejection of an earlier hypothesis or theory. This is not to say that it is easy to achieve falsification, but there are many alternatives in studying different activities, business environments, or cultures. The third purpose, exploration, offers endless opportunities. There are always issues and problems from different empirical situations that have not been studied before. Organizational and contextual contingencies will influence the scope and, for example, the extent to which it applies to industries, the maturity or size of an organization, or geographical or cultural setting. However, generalizing the conclusions may be difficult and the researcher should ensure that the research contribution is substantial and not too specific to one unique situation.

2.2.2 *The triad targets of academia, practice, and society*

A challenge that will often occur for the management researcher is to create contributions and value not only for academia but also for practice. This challenge will promote the often empirically based research approaches used in OSCM. The field of OSCM deals to a large extent with applied and cross-disciplinary issues and research is often carried out in close relation to industry. However, the practice should be seen in a wider perspective than the firm. OSCM research has the potential to contribute on many levels: society, industry, organization, group, and individual.

Even if researchers in OSCM face a quest for contributions both to the academic's and to the practitioner's world, the degree and extent of involvement in practice may vary substantially from gathering data to taking action. For example, there are low degrees of involvement when mailing questionnaires or modelling processes on a computer. With interviews there is somewhat more, but still a small amount of interaction. Staying a bit longer in the field and observing what is going on in practice enables observations which may be more or less participative and longitudinal. The researcher may have an objective to improve the studied object and, therefore, to engage in action research. The researcher may even intervene, taking on a helping and treating role in relation to the studied object, leading to clinical research such as collaborative and interventionist research approaches.

The role of research is, however, not limited to supplying the target groups of academia and direct practitioners with new knowledge. In addition to the basic roles of research and teaching, researchers are responsible for the dissemination of their research output to society. Knowledge should be interpreted together with practitioners and the implications developed. Researchers are also expected to participate in 'next tier' activities. For example, through research parks, incubators, and other organizational forms researchers are increasingly required to observe and facilitate knowledge coming into action.

The demand on universities and, correspondingly, their demand on researchers is increasingly rooted in the economic context of the research. More and more, universities are requested to contribute to economic growth in general as well as to regional and business development. Research-funding applications often include a section on relevance in terms of possibilities for commercialization. This requirement is derived from shorter development time scales for impact in industry, leading in particular to shorter cycle times in research.

2.3 Roles of the researcher

Since research is performed in quite different ways depending on the aim and format of the research, the researcher's role has many connotations. A researcher may be seen as just the person doing research, but since there are many different types of research there are also many different types of researchers. Here we limit our discussion to the academic researcher or research candidate doing research in a university or other academic institution such as a business school.

2.3.1 Type of research

The researcher will have different roles depending on the type of research, the research approach, methodology, the used methods, the intended product and contribution, and the target group or groups. We have already made a distinction between Mode 1 research, aiming at knowledge development, and Mode 2 research, aiming at application of knowledge. Further, research is done differently depending on the aim and research questions and the state of existing knowledge. We differentiate between research that is explorative, descriptive, analytical, causal, or normative. The last of these may mean direct intervention, such as in action and clinical research with collaboration and interventions. The role of the researcher will then have many differences.

2.3.2 Different roles for a researcher

As researchers, we often refer to ourselves as scholars. This indicates an educated person and can encompass everything from a student to a teacher, to a scientist. It means that we have certain knowledge, but we continuously want to develop it further. To do this we have to be competent at running the research process. This is developed in Section 2.4. There are several functions we have to fulfil. During those research activities, and especially in relation to the researched object, we have several roles, including the following.

2.3.2.1 Observer

Whether the researcher uses questionnaires, interviews, or participation, the researcher is supposed to be skilled in observing, which is key for collecting empirical data. Directly related to this, the researcher must be good at recording the data that can be observed and it must be done in a systematic way.

2.3.2.2 Surveyor

The researcher needs to be able to grasp large amounts of data and review it in a systematic way. Importantly, the researcher must be able to get a good understanding of the existing body of knowledge in the relevant areas.

2.3.2.3 Analyst

It is paramount that the researcher has analytical skills. This means abilities to break down data and classify it in categories. These should be systematized in an orderly way, so they turn into information.

2.3.2.4 Communicator

Especially in interview situations, but even more as a participative observer, the researcher must be skilled in communicating. Concepts and constructs need to be explained to the theoretical not-so-well-versed practitioner. Communicating demands listening skills even more than talking skills in order to hear what the person wants to say in addition to what they are saying and to make the person want to speak their mind.

2.3.2.5 Sounding board

In participatory roles, from being an observer to a clinician, it is expected that the researcher can contribute with knowledge and comment on situations in the studied object. It calls for an ability to listen, analyse, and then relate to models and theories that can inform the practitioner.

2.3.2.6 Actor and other partner roles

The study object may want help with doing certain things as a consequence of what is learnt in the ongoing research. This calls for a skill in the researcher and 'how-to' knowledge, not only 'what' knowledge.

2.3.2.7 Consultant

Based on the identified problems and developed knowledge, the researched object is likely to ask the researcher for advice on what should, or at least could, be done. The researcher will here be helped if s/he has knowledge that is not only conceptual and descriptive but is also about causalities.

2.3.2.8 Clinician

The most advanced interventionist role is when the researcher is called for help. The whole idea is to cure the researched object while at the same time use it as a database. It is a kind of research in itself, but it is also a role that may come out of a normal research project or at least after the conclusion of the basic research project.

2.4 The research process

A research process goes through many steps and will typically be spun-out over time. In general, it will start with the identification of an issue for research and end up with results published in a report. In reality, the process will have iterative steps and back-loops and it may not even start in step 1, as follows. Planning the actual research process is developed more in Chapter 3. The research process may also vary depending on the research approach and chosen methods, but we can define a generic process as follows:

1 **Identification of a problem or issue to research:** Research often begins with a general statement of a problem, or even better may be an issue or a question to answer. The researcher should also consider the reason and motivation for engaging in the study.
2 **Literature review:** Since research should fill a gap in existing knowledge or add to that knowledge, it is mandatory to know what already exists.
3 **Specifying the aim, objective, or purpose of the intended research:** Again, since research should fill a gap in existing knowledge or add to that knowledge, it is a good idea from the start to be thinking already of what the research could possibly contribute.
4 **Determine specific research questions:** The result of the research should answer some kind of question about what more we want to know. It is important to understand that a research result is different from a textbook. It will not only describe existing knowledge with the purpose of teaching the unknowing student but will also add new knowledge to those who already know the field.
5 **Choice of research approach and methods:** We now have to consider how the research questions can be answered in a valid and reliable way. Certain methods are appropriate for certain questions. This will be discussed later and in more detail in Chapter 3.
6 **Development of a conceptual framework:** For collecting data and analysing them, we need a conceptual framework. A conceptual framework is like a model of what you study. It can be defined as a visual or written description of the concepts and the relationship between them. We can call it the glasses with which we study the objects we want to research.
7 **Data collection:** The conceptual framework is used for developing questions for questionnaires and interview protocols. In addition to using questionnaires and interviews, we can be observers and participants in the studied object.
8 **Analysing and interpreting the data:** Analysing basically means breaking down the data to understand it and make findings. We will use the conceptual framework to structure the analysis.
9 **Synthesizing and concluding:** This is the creative part. Typically, we will look for patterns and put together findings in new ways. It may be new models, frameworks, or analytical tools. It may also be recommendations for managers.
10 **Evaluating the research and suggesting further research:** The researcher is supposed to discuss the research. Important aspects include discussing how the results fit into earlier research and discussing limitations. Related to that is to suggest what can be done following the results and what has not been answered.
11 **Reporting and communicating the research findings:** The research report is the key product, but it should also be thought where it may be published and otherwise presented.

2.5 Research as contribution to knowledge

In Section 2.2, the role of research was defined as the creation and development of new knowledge and the value of research as the contribution it makes to academia and practice. The concepts of knowledge and contribution and what kinds of contribution there are will now be discussed.

2.5.1 *The concept of knowledge*

The concept of knowledge is a complex concept. It is not the purpose of this book to examine it in depth, and there is a whole range of literature on knowledge and knowledge management. However, a shared understanding of what is meant by knowledge is needed to discuss contribution to knowledge in the context of researching in OSCM. A few definitions of knowledge provide some perspectives. A good overview is given in the United Nations Public Administration Network *Knowledge Management Basics* (UNPAN, 2015). They refer to Plato: 'Plato in his *Meno, Phaedo and Theaetetus* first defined the concept of knowledge as "justified true belief", which has been pre-dominant during the history of western philosophy ever since' (2015). They also cite Turban and Frenzel (1992) 'Knowledge is information that has been organized and analysed to make it understandable and applicable to problem solving and decision making', Wiig (1993) 'Knowledge consists of truths and beliefs, perspectives and concepts, judgment and expectations, methodologies and know-how', and Nonaka and Takeuchi (1995) 'First, knowledge, unlike information, is about beliefs and commit-ment. Knowledge is a function of a particular stance, perspective, or intention. Second, knowledge, unlike information, is about action. It is always knowledge to some end. And third, knowledge, like information, is about meaning. It is context-specific and relational'.

There are many other ways of defining and classifying knowledge. A popular clas-sification in the management area has been the distinction between tacit and explicit knowledge. Explicit knowledge is knowledge that can be captured, documented, transferred, shared, and communicated easily. Tacit knowledge cannot be traced in documents and publications. Polanyi (1966) says that it is personal, context-specific, and therefore difficult to articulate. Nonaka and Takeuchi (1995) refer to tacit knowledge as knowledge that comprises experience and work-knowledge that resides only with the individual. To some extent, one can say that theoretical development in research is about explicit knowledge, while practice involves considerable tacit knowledge.

More distinct perspectives can be found by going further back in history to classical philosophers such as Socrates, Plato, and Aristotle. First, the distinction between knowledge (*epistêmê*) and craft or skill (*technê*)· *epistêmê*, or knowledge, is built on a rational formula or '*logos*'; *technê*, or skill/craft, can be called 'know-how'. An individual can have knowledge without skill or the skill to do something without the (theoretical) knowledge. One may know the law of impact but not possess the skill of playing snooker or possess the skill of playing snooker without knowing the law of impact. Having dis-tinguished craft from scientific knowledge, Aristotle also distinguishes it from virtue (*aretê*) and attitude. By virtue, Aristotle meant the attributes, attitudes, or basic values of an individual. One may have different approaches to the same thing. Playing soccer, one may be a defender or an attacker. Different value systems will guide different behaviour, for example, risk aversion or entrepreneurship. If these three dimensions can exist to any extent with or without the existence of the other, one can say that they are orthogonal. But the existence of each of them will contribute to the competence of the individual. Hence, competence is a more general term and can be said to consist of knowledge, skills, and attributes.

2.5.2 *Philosophy, truths, and realities*

One may think that research is about finding the truths about realities, how things really are. However, from a philosophical perspective, there are different realities and different truths about them. This is especially evident in behavioural sciences and more so than in natural sciences. One individual may find that an organization is structured in one way, while another individual finds that the organization is structured in another way. Before we continue on how to analyse in logical ways, we consider what reality is and what is true about it.

At the base of research philosophy is a view of reality that reflects the researcher's understanding of what exists and what can hence be said to be. The study of what exists and what hence can be said to be is called ontology. It is the science of being. The ontological perspective of the researcher can vary. One researcher can say that there is something called an organization and it can be universally understood, while another can say that an organization is a social construct that exists only in the eyes of the beholder, that is perceived by the individual, and hence that is different from individual to individual. The difference in ontological perspectives will have effects on the researcher and the realities that the researcher sees. A couple of dimensions are worth considering. At one end of the scale the organization is concrete and at the other end it is an abstract conception. Another dimension is whether a concept is universal or is particular; that is, whether it varies from situation to situation. These and other perspectives form a position on the ontological scale. Yes, there are positions along a continuum; it is not only a matter of one extreme or the other. It is critical for the researcher to consider their own ontological perspective. In some situations, a declaration of the taken position can be requested when reporting research results. We will come back to how these influence one's own research in Chapter 3.

Just as there can be different realities there can be different truths. We have already touched upon this in the preceding section on what knowledge is. We call the study of reality ontology and the study of knowledge epistemology. The researcher's ontological perspective may be grounded, for example, in realism with beliefs in universals or in a nominalism that opposes universals with beliefs in particulars. This perspective influences the researcher's epistemology, or how the researcher seeks to know through inquiring into the nature of the world. In the original Greek meaning, it is putting words (logos) to knowledge (epistême). It is a part of philosophy that deals with the philosophical analysis of knowledge or the theory of knowledge. The philosophical question is: How do we know what we know? As we said above, the definition of knowledge as justified true belief has been extant and dominant ever since Plato. This definition means that there must be good (= justified) reasons for believing that something can be verified as absolutely so (= true) regardless of the context. At the other end of the scale, truth depends on the situation and the perspective we have when we observe it. As with ontology a declaration of the taken position in epistemology is critical and can be requested when reporting research results. In Chapter 3 we will come back to how this influences one's own research.

2.5.3 *The logic of reaching a conclusion*

An aspect of particular importance in research is how arguments are built. An argument is a connected series of statements or propositions intended to provide support, justification, or evidence for the truth of another statement or proposition. An argument is said to consist of premises, inferences, and conclusions. A premise of an argument is something that is put forward as a truth, but which is not proven. The conclusion or claim is the statement of the result of the analysis. The inference is the reasoning process between the conclusion and the premises, which translates the premises into the conclusion by formal argument and careful logic.

We differ between three generically different types of reasoning: deductive, inductive, and abductive reasoning. In deductive reasoning, often referred to as top-down logic, the idea is to reach a logically certain conclusion from one or more statements (premises). Logic says that if all of the premises are true then the conclusion must be true. This is based on the assumption that all information is contained in the premises. In inductive reasoning, the premises seek to supply strong but not absolute evidence for the truth of the conclusion. In abductive reasoning, the logical inference goes from a conclusive observation to a theory that can lead to an explanation of the observation.

The logic of all three types of reasoning is built on the same three components or factors. One component is the rule. This concerns how the world is structured and functions. It says that a precondition that can be observed implies a result or conclusion. A second component is a condition that has been empirically observed: the database or the research material. A third component is the result or conclusion. The three ways of arguing differ on where they take their starting point and how the logic proceeds from there. A deductive argument starts by taking a position with a rule, applying it to data to reach a conclusion. An inductive argument starts with something empirically observed, testing conclusions to find the rule. An abductive argument starts with the result or conclusion, testing rules to find out about the precondition. See Figure 2.1.

The difference can be demonstrated by the following brief example:

Deduction: Rule: With low flexibility in the production system, we are not good at make-to-order. Observation: Our production system has low flexibility. Result: Hence, we are not good at make-to-order.

Induction: Observation: Our production system has low flexibility. Result: We are not good at make-to-order. Rule: The reason why we are not good at make-to-order is that our production system has low flexibility.

Logic of argument		
Components		
Rules	Observations	Results
Argumentations		
Deduction	Induction	Abduction
Rule	Observation	Result
⇓	⇓	⇓
Observation	Result	Rule
⇓	⇓	⇓
Result	Rule	Observation

Figure 2.1 The logic of argument.

Abduction: Result: We are not good at make-to-order. Rule: A reason why we are not good at make-to-order is that our production system has low flexibility. Observation: Let us check if our production system has low flexibility.

2.5.4 Deductive, inductive, and abductive research

Deductive, or top-down, research begins with hypotheses based on existing knowledge or literature and seeks to test a hypothesis or an established theory. It follows a process of starting with existing knowledge or assumptions, then formulating a research question or hypothesis based on existing knowledge, theories, or assumptions, then collecting data, and, after analysis, conclusions leading to either confirmation or rejection. In the general model in Figure 2.1 the rule consists of hypothesis or theory, the observation is the data collection, and the result is the support or rejection of the hypothesis.

Inductive, or 'bottom-up', research collects data and observations in order to discern a pattern within them, or to formulate a hypothesis, propositions, or a new theory. In the general model in Figure 2.1, observation is the data gathered through interviews and observations in organizations, often in so-called case research; the result is the analysis done within and across cases analyses looking for patterns in the data; and the rule is the proposition, hypothesis, or even theory that comes out as the conclusion of the research.

Abductive research allows inference as an explanation. In a way, it combines inductive and deductive research. It starts with a real concluded situation. Then it goes to theories that can help explaining the situation or problem. So far it is inductive. The idea is to adduce a hypothetical explanation for the situation by abductive reasoning, claiming that the explanation is reasonable. The process becomes deductive to see if our explanation or theory seems reasonable. The explanation should then not only be logical, but also among the most feasible. This has also been called qualified guessing.

The three perspectives of deductive, inductive, and abductive argument are applicable not only to the whole study, but also to the structure of the research report. They are further discussed in relation to the different research approaches. See for example Chapter 5 for a more extensive development.

2.5.5 Existing knowledge and research contribution

Contributing to knowledge requires that there is an existing field of knowledge to contribute to. To qualify as a contribution, the candidate knowledge shall not have been published anywhere in any respected publication. Thus, it is necessary to know what has already been published. At an early phase research must include a careful mapping and reviewing of the existing published knowledge. There are, of course, at least two more reasons for this review. One is that the research literature gives inspiration to research issues and, in many cases, contains suggestions for further research beyond what has been studied in the individual study. Another reason is that a lot can be built on and used, such as constructs, research protocols, and references to other relevant literature.

The scope of OSCM knowledge, as with almost all areas in the field of management, is almost unlimited. There are different kinds of issues and different perspectives on the area, such as in operations strategy, management, or control. There are disciplines that support OSCM research, such as finance, organizational behaviour, or control theory, that provide different perspectives. With the development of knowledge production and ease of web-based access, relevant areas have had to be narrower, and the knowledge limited to that which is 'most relevant'. Nevertheless, it is a requirement that all relevant adjacent knowledge be covered when mapping and reviewing the literature. Chapter 3 will discuss how to do a relevant review of existing literature depending on the research issue.

That the result of the research is supposed to contribute to existing knowledge does not mean that it has to be a major breakthrough. In the global world of knowledge production, most contributions are, in practice, minor. So what, then, is the size or scope of a contribution?

An important measure of a contribution is how general it is, either in theory or in practice. A theory that applies to many situations is of higher value than a theory specific to one situation. A model that applies to many concrete situations is more valuable the more general the situation is. This is a special challenge in the kind of research that OSCM represents. It may be difficult to generalize at all outside the studied objects and the context. There are many external and internal factors to control for. A study may have been conducted in certain industries, countries, cultures, economic situations, or competitive situations that will limit generalization. Rather than generalization based on statistical evidence, often the researcher will have to make an analytical or theoretical generalization, which will be discussed later under the basis for claims. The planning of research and its process based on the idea of a contribution will be further discussed in Chapter 3.

2.5.6 From exploration to knowing how and why

When contributions to existing knowledge are produced, the field expands and matures. The knowledge base becomes more solid and gradually different development patterns can be observed. Because of the cumulative character of knowledge and the sequential development of the field, different research outputs in different phases of the development of the field of knowledge will be seen. Even when new knowledge is destructive of, or contradicts, existing knowledge, the total knowledge area expands. Studies that show that what was expected (hypothesized) could not be demonstrated also add to existing knowledge. It is said that Edison, when criticized for the thousand unsuccessful experiments he did before he eventually succeeded, responded by saying that they were not mistakes: 'I demonstrated what did not work and why.'

Knowledge development in a field may go through different phases depending on the volume and maturity of existing knowledge. With little to base the theoretical development on, the studies will by necessity take on an explorative character. Hence early-phase research will often be explorative and there will be results in terms of concepts and constructs, classifications, and definitions. A warning can be issued here. If an issue or problem is defined too specifically the field seems to be little researched. However, the possibility of generalization may be meagre, and the result will have little scientific or practical value. Such a narrow definition may signal that the researcher needs to study the area more.

After many explorative studies with different perspectives and approaches, a base or platform identifying components of the field emerges. An increasingly better description of the field is created by more systematic studies covering the explored area. More complete coverage of the field emerges, and the research can be said to have entered a descriptive phase. Descriptive research results will typically identify components, patterns, systems, and structures.

Good descriptive research creates a good foundation for analytical research. Analysing the relations between the pieces starts with a good understanding of components and structures in the field of knowledge. Analytical research finds correlations between variables and identifies how independent variables influence dependent variables. Findings will typically be of the contingent, if–then, character.

Good analytical models create understanding of how one condition or variable will cause a certain effect. The ability to synthesize develops as causal analyses suggest what causes what. If contextual variables and different background variables can be controlled for, there is a possibility of foreseeing and forecasting what will happen in certain situations. Eventually, the research may produce normative models and give advice.

A major reason for discussing the sequence of knowledge development based on a cumulative perspective is that attempts to do everything in one study contain considerable risks. To explore an area, build an analytical model, draw conclusions on causal effects, and eventually provide a set of recommendations may not be possible within a limited scope. Given the pattern of knowledge development, research should typically explore before being able to describe a field of knowledge, know the components before understanding the relations, and know the relations before foreseeing the effects. How to plan a relevant contribution given the state of maturity of the field is further discussed in Chapter 3. The cumulative and sequential development of knowledge creates one possible basis for a classification of knowledge: know what, know how, and know why. Research will initially ask questions about what is in the area. With more knowledge the researchers will try to find out how it is and eventually ask why it is so; that is, what causes this?

2.5.7 *Creating and developing knowledge*

In conducting research, the researcher should consider that there are different levels of knowledge. A comparison may be made with the educational system where the same areas may be studied at different school and university levels, each increasing the individuals' understanding and skills with the help of analytical tools and theory. The empirical base may contain data, information, and knowledge. Data (from *datum*, a figure) are those facts that can be gathered and for which there are measures. When data are put in a system, we say that we form information. With information, somebody can be informed or enlightened. The information can then be put in a context and used, and, as a result, add experience. This experience enables an interpretation of the information, its applicability, effects, and other strengths and weaknesses. As a result, knowledge is developed.

The knowledge development process does not have to proceed with the classic conceptual and theoretical development followed by empirical studies. In 'grounded theory' the researcher starts with collecting data and then tries to find categories through a process of coding. The categories can then be given properties. This enables conceptualization, which enables the researcher to define the different phenomena s/he wants to study and discuss. The developed knowledge gives a framework for describing and reviewing knowledge. Complex structures of concepts can now be built, which can be used for the research. These built-up structures of concepts may be called constructs and can form a base for know-what research.

By considering the concepts or constructs in relation to each other, the possibility for analysing data and information emerges. In analysing the concepts and constructs, the researcher looks at patterns and how they are related to each other. This exploration opens the possibility for understanding, but also a first level of concluding. After breaking down the knowledge, one may also find new ways of putting the pieces together in a process called synthesizing. A way of doing this is to create a model in terms of a representation of a more complex reality. If a model with general validity can be created, it may embody a theory in terms of a systematic statement of principles. A basis for know-how research has been reached. It may, for example, say something about how things work.

An understanding of how things work provides the possibility for studying cause–effect relations. The developed model of how things work may form the basis for hypotheses on what causes what, where the researcher will look for if–then relations. This hypothesizing opens up the possibility for normative conclusions and recommendations. In practice, not actually knowing the causal relations does not always hinder individuals from drawing normative conclusions from just correlations, but this is another discussion. With causal knowledge, a know-why level of knowledge is reached. This will enable further research to build models that managers can use to understand the production system and make informed decisions.

2.6 Research approaches

Research approaches are in the literature often dealt with as quantitative, qualitative, and maybe combined in mixed methods, (occasionally also participatory with interventions such as actions or clinical). This is really simplified since it refers just to alternative data. But both quantitative and qualitative data can be gathered and analysed in different knowledge development approaches. It is more relevant to see research as creation and development of knowledge and then start out from alternative knowledge creation approaches. Deductive, inductive, and abductive are different approaches to knowledge creation and development.

Our scope, our focus, and limitations and delimitations, are the following. We focus empirically based research with objectives of developing practically oriented knowledge for the management of the applied area of Operations and Supply Chains. The Operations Management area includes Innovation and Product Development Management.

Other types of research are for example Theoretical research and Meta Research. Theoretical research involves the development of theory as opposed to using observation and experimentation. As such, non-empirical research seeks solutions to problems using existing knowledge as its source. Meta Research is the study of research using research methods. Can also be called research on research. Focusing the quality of research, it may concern for example biases and methodological flaws.

2.6.1 Knowledge development and research approaches

How do we go about developing new knowledge? We differ between the three generically different types of reasoning: deductive, inductive, and abductive reasoning and analyse what it means for research approaches. Starting in the logic of argument we describe knowledge creation and development and the respective processes and potential contributions. Then we can propose different approaches for research. It should be noted that approaches are sometimes overlapping and can refer to different levels of abstraction. To facilitate comparisons and analyses of different characteristics, this is done in the form of a table. See Table 2.1.

From this we can choose different Research Approaches that will fit the Knowledge creation and development objectives. We will here (in this book in separate chapters) deal with Survey, Case research, Longitudinal field studies, Action research, Clinical including interventionist and collaborative research, and Modelling and Simulation.

Table 2.1 Three types of reasoning

TYPE	Deductive research	Inductive research	Abductive research
Philosophy	In deductive reasoning, often referred to as top-down logic, the idea is to reach a logically certain conclusion from one or more statements (premises). Logic says that if all of the premises are true then the conclusion must be true. This is based on the assumption that all information is contained in the premises	In inductive reasoning the premises seek to supply strong but not absolute evidence for the truth of the conclusion	In abductive reasoning the logical inference goes from a conclusive observation to a theory that can lead to an explanation of the observation
How knowledge is created or developed	Deductive, or top-down, research begins with hypotheses based on existing knowledge or literature and seeks to test a hypothesis or an established theory.	Inductive, or 'bottom-up', research collects data and observations in order to discern a pattern within them, or to formulate a hypothesis, propositions, or a new theory.	Abductive research allows inference as an explanation. In a way it combines inductive and deductive research.
Research process	It follows a process of starting with existing knowledge or assumptions, then formulating a research question or hypothesis based on existing knowledge, theories, or assumptions, then collecting data, and, after analysis, conclusions leading to either confirmation or rejection. In the general model in Figure 2.1 the rule consists of hypothesis or theory, the observation is the data collection, and the result is the support or rejection of the hypothesis.	In the general model in Figure 2.1, observation is the data gathered through interviews and observations in organizations, often in so-called case research; the result is the analysis done within and across cases analyses looking for patterns in the data; and the rule is the proposition, hypothesis, or even theory that comes out as the conclusion of the research.	It starts with a real concluded situation. Then, it goes to theories that can help explaining the situation or problem. So far it is inductive. The idea is to adduce a hypothetical explanation for the situation by abductive reasoning, claiming that the explanation is reasonable. The process becomes deductive to see if our explanation or theory seems reasonable. The explanation should then not only be logical, but also among the most feasible. This has also been called qualified guessing.
Contributions	Hypothesis testing, new theory	Propositions or hypotheses, occasionally theory	Problem solving, Management tools/ models Hypotheses? Or Propositions!
Approaches	Surveys, Modelling, and Simulation Occasional Case research	Case research, multiple and single Longitudinal. Experiments Modelling and Simulation	Interventionist Action and Longitudinal (including Clinical) research Design science Also, Case (maybe single) research

Other research approaches may not have gotten their own chapter but are integrated in this overall chapter structure. Experiments take place both in Action research where theories are tested in organizations and in Longitudinal field studies where new production system designs and product development processes are tested during the project. Interventionist approaches of different kinds are dealt with under Clinical approaches. Multiple methods is sometimes labelled an approach but is dealt with where combinations are especially frequent or relevant such pursuing surveys during a long time longitudinal research project. Even non-empirical research since modelling may not always be empirically based.

2.6.2 Mixed methods

The use of two or more research approaches in the same research project has gotten its own designation as mixed methods. Even if often referred to as mixed methods the researchers really describe and use mixed methodologies, research approaches or designs. The mixing can take place in different relations and sequencing.

a A quantitative deductive study is taken further in a qualitative inductive way looking for explanations.
b A qualitative inductive study is supplemented by a deductive analysis of specific issues looking for some general conditions.
c A quantitative and a qualitative research process are performed in parallel with cross validation for research data quality by triangulation.
d A quantitative and a qualitative research process are performed concurrently with cross influencing for ongoing conceptual and theoretical development.

Mixing takes place in different ways. Versions a and b can also be seen as complementary approaches deepening the results and value of contribution of the research. Alternative c is mainly a methodology for validation enhancing the quality of the results but also the contribution to knowledge. Alternative d can be said to be the full mixing. It is especially applied in interdisciplinary and practice oriented applied research.

2.6.3 Overview of research approaches

Some research approaches have their own chapters; others go across or are integrated. In the history of science of science, we can see dominant approaches, but also some approaches that come and go; some are versions or sub-cultures of more major classes. In Table 2.2., a very condensed characterization with key concepts is summarized to enable comparisons even if details are missing. There are more variants, only the most significant is mentioned. The research approaches are further developed in the respective chapters.

It is important to note and understand that all the research approaches are often used in combinations. Case research and longitudinal field studies may be combined with surveys, action research may turn to clinical, and what started with a survey may become a case project. That will not necessarily denominate the research as mixed methods.

2.7 What to research for academia and practice

The key task in doing research is to make some kind of contribution. Going through a number of steps in building the research contribution will facilitate the process of

Table 2.2 Research approaches overview

Approaches w/ chapters	Concept	Contribution	Process characteristics
Surveys	Deductive	New theory	Questionnaires and interviews
Case research	Inductive	Hypotheses	Questionnaires and interviews
Longitudinal Field Studies	Inductive & abductive	Hypotheses Causality	Interviews, participation
Action Research	Abductive	Theory testing and development	Participation Inquiring
Clinical Research	Abductive	Causal relations	Inquiring Participation
Modelling and Simulation	Deductive & Inductive	Models Theory	Develop models and test
OTHER APPROACHES			
Experiments	Inductive	Theory testing	Interventions
Interventionist	Abductive	Theory development	Inquiring
Design science	Abductive	Theory development	Interventions
Multiple method	Any but typically deductive + inductive	Theory development	Questionnaires and interviews

generating knowledge through research. The discussion here will be conceptual, while the issue of planning the actual research project is dealt with in Section 2.4. The logic and discussion in the next section of this chapter is illustrated in Figure 2.2. When we talk about research we often think of the right-hand side of the figure: a research report that is the outcome and final product of the research. It has a logical sequence starting with the problem and ending with the result. However, from the start we will take a holistic perspective of research and engage in iterative thinking and planning of the intended contribution and how we will get there through analysis, what data will be needed, what method, the precise problem, and the relevant existing literature as described in the left-hand side of the figure.

It is important that the researcher has a mental image of the endpoint so that the research can be planned in a comprehensive way. This task can be compared with project management and its clear goal. The activities that lead to the goal are thought through and the relations between them are considered. This does not mean that the researcher will have to, or can, stick to a detailed plan, but the cohesiveness of the product and process will help and is paramount for quality. So, think holistically and apply a 'logic of and to the end' perspective.

2.7.1 Starting with the intended contribution

Since the researcher is supposed to create a contribution, it is a good idea to start by thinking of the intended contribution. The researcher may not know exactly what the contribution will actually be since that will depend on the outcome of the research. However, an aim is needed and can be expressed in a theoretical model, hypotheses, or other general outcome of the intended research: Approximately what does the researcher envision as the final result or contribution? Furthermore, what is this contribution supposed to do? Will it describe something, find clusters or characteristics,

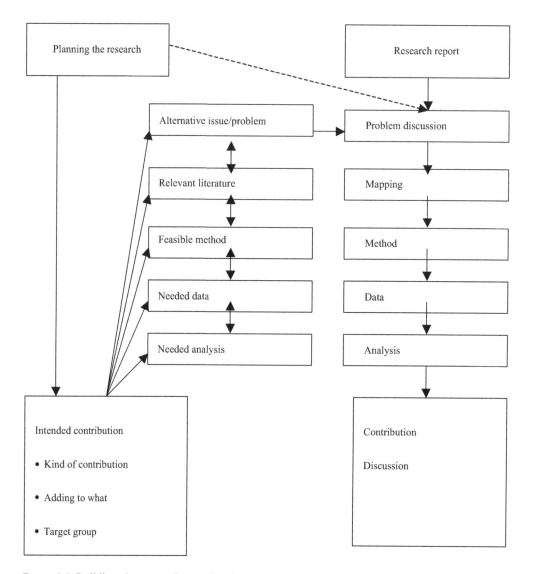

Figure 2.2 Building the research contribution.

explain relations between something, or demonstrate causal effects from something? What kind of contribution is it? What existing knowledge is there to which this contribution will add? To whom is the contribution directed – what are the potential target groups? What kinds of results, conclusions, and discussions of implications can be foreseen?

2.7.2 *Alternative starting points*

The starting point in a real situation may not be the ideal question of where one wants to contribute. Rather, there may be a research project, a project possibility, or an available case or other empirical material on which to do research. So, we start on the left side of the figure with fixed data. These may be possible to analyse in certain ways, which will enable certain kinds of contributions.

Then we can study the literature to see where we can fit in and eventually formulate an appropriate issue or research problem. We still consider an intended contribution and start there in the following logic.

2.7.3 Reverse logic

Having an idea of the intended research contribution, it is practical to follow a form of reverse or backward logic considering what has to be done to reach the intended contribution (see the left side of Figure 2.2). The contribution initiates demands on what to do and how to do it. It is not unusual that the intended research question has to be changed because of a lack of empirical material or resources. When the researcher knows what s/he expects to contribute and to which existing knowledge base, s/he can start the more thorough reviewing of the existing knowledge, analysing the areas of practice and research literature. S/he can then start to find the necessary or feasible way to achieve the knowledge development and plan a study or other effort, for example, simulation, creating a reliable and robust way of doing the research (method), analysing methodology, and creating an empirical and/or theoretical foundation. S/he can also plan how to analyse, synthesize, conclude, and set the contribution in the research field context.

2.7.4 Building the chain of evidence

An important aspect of research quality is that the reader can follow the logic of the study and report (see the right side of Figure 2.2). The logic should ideally allow the reader to be able to repeat the study and arrive at the same results. This is not always realistic outside the natural sciences, such as in OSCM research. There are two important issues to deal with. First, that all the research steps fit together and that it is possible to see how one step follows the other. Second, that the elements of research created in each research step fit so that, for example, the available empirical material will suffice to answer the research question, that the analytical approach will give valid outcomes, and so on.

Although, when planning the research, doing reverse or backward logic planning as described above is helpful, in the report the researcher will and should have a forward chain of evidence. A research report is expected to start with a problem discussion based on the relevant problem from practice and the theoretical formulation. Out of this discussion with reference both to practice and literature, the researcher should develop a clear problem definition. Then there should be a thorough review of the literature to develop a picture of the relevant knowledge and gaps in the knowledge. The researcher should then be able to formulate the research questions. These may be explorative, hypothesis-generating, hypothesis testing, or whatever. In this connection, one would expect a theoretical development resulting in a conceptual framework of what will be studied. Miles and Huberman (1994) defined a conceptual framework as a one that 'explains, either graphically or in narrative form, the main things to be studied – the key factors, concepts, or variables – and the presumed relationships among them'.

This model, or framework, will then be used in data gathering and analysis. This brings us to considerations of methodology. What should be studied and with what methods can the researcher do the study in order to achieve valid results. In reality, the researcher will often find that s/he has to reformulate the research question here because of available resources, but this may or may not be seen in the final report. In the considerations of methodology, it should also be made clear how the analysis is intended to be done. A discussion that integrates the research question, the theoretical and empirical base, data gathering, analysis, and the kind of expected results is especially expected here. Following this, the data and the analysis will be presented. Finally, after the analysis, a synthesis can be made, and conclusions can be reached.

To make the study repeatable and able to be followed, it is an advantage to separate data analysis and creative thinking by the researcher in a following synthesis. On the other hand, research approaches such as action research are built upon an ongoing sequence of observation, analysis, and making changes, so it is hard to separate the analysis from the synthesis. The sequence of analysis, synthesis, and conclusions may not exactly fit all research approaches, but should be seen as a general target. Details of the different approaches are discussed in the following chapters.

2.7.5 The problem–method–contribution fit

Not all research questions can be answered by all research methods and one particular method cannot answer all types of research questions. A wish to find out about common practice in an industry is not well answered by an action research project in one firm, and a mailed questionnaire survey may not give deep insight into causal relations in implementation projects.

There are some typical situations we may consider. We may want to study a rather unexplored issue. For that purpose, we will search rather openly among the available data in practice as well as in the literature that can give meaning to the issue. We will identify patterns and come up with hypotheses or propositions or, in the best of cases, generate theory. An opposite situation and research aim is when we test more precise research questions and hypotheses. Typically, large sample surveys through questionnaires, possibly triangulated with interviews, are used to reach statistically significant validation or falsification of hypotheses. One approach is not in itself better than the other, but there should be a fit between what we want to contribute, what study we should and can do, and the formulated research aim.

The fit between problem, method, and contribution is often reached in an iterative manner. It may turn out that the research question was not possible to answer with the available data and research resources or the data may turn out to be suitable for answering another and more interesting research question than was first defined. Often a research project, especially for a young researcher, will start with a given methodology or even method. There may be a school of thought at the institution or there may be certain available data and nothing more.

The feasible type of research question, and hence method, is related to the advancement of the research field. Early-stage research will be explorative and inductive, while mature-stage research will be focused and deductive (Edmonson and McManus, 2007). Developing the fit between research questions, methods, and data can start with either. Conventional thinking may start in problem definition, followed by choice of method, analysis, synthesis, and generated results. As an alternative, empirical studies may also start with the data and choosing it to enable sense-making and theorization. It is a matter of the connections between the pieces in the problem definition, method, data, and conclusion that gives quality to the research (Van Maanen *et al.*, 2007). A prerequisite for getting it right may be that we are aware of our own view on epistemology and ontology, something we will discuss in Chapter 3.

2.7.6 *Value of the contribution: Generalizability*

The desired outcome of the research is to reach a possibility of claiming that both the researcher and the reader have learnt something in general rather than only the particular researcher in relation to the particular situation. This means that the researcher will in some way or another generalize around what has been found. Generalizability is a standard aim in all research but will mean different things in different approaches and related research issues. In quantitative research, generalization is achieved by statistical sampling. Adequate sampling will increase the representativeness of the empirical base and broaden the area for which the researcher can claim validity. The question is of course: Generalizable in relation to what? Is it a matter of industry, organization size, geographical location, or what? In qualitative research the issue is different, and the sampling or selection of cases will have the aim of finding cases of particular interest for the research issue. The researcher can either do a purposive sampling, if the research question is related to a certain population, or theoretical sampling, finding cases that are specific in relation to the theory area in which the research is grounded. Generalization can then be done by comparisons with similar cases and with theory in what is called analytical generalization. The demand for generalizability will vary with the perspective: if positivist, this will mean that there is a presumption of an objective reality; if constructivist, then that reality is socially constructed by interpretation. For more positivistic case studies there is some need for generalizability, while interpretative studies often do not have this requirement. See further discussions on contributions in Chapter 3.

2.7.7 *A comprehensive view on contribution*

The ultimate criteria for assessing the research will be the value of the contribution and the quality of the research. The final part of a research report should discuss the contribution and relate it to earlier existing knowledge. It should also discuss the approach and qualities of the study. There are always limitations and shortcomings, and it is important for the demonstration of quality that the researcher shows ability to discuss these issues.

2.8 Research quality

Demands on research have many dimensions related both to content and to form. Sometimes in the discussion of research quality, there is only a focus on how well the study is done. However, the content and its relevance should not be forgotten.

A first question any producer may ask themselves is whether there is a need for the product and whether it will be demanded. For the researcher, this means asking whether the research on OSCM deals with issues that are important to operations managers or those involved in managing operations, and/or the results are valuable for the research community so that knowledge is taken forward and the results can be built on further. Even if the issue is of importance, the researcher should ask themselves whether this is an issue that needs to be researched or that is suitable for research. The issue may be trivial and hence without need for either practitioners or academics (except for the researcher).

Then there are all the questions about the form or how well the research has been done. Research quality will be discussed further in each chapter, because what is good research is partly approach dependent. Here, only some general aspects are mentioned that are well known to readers of research methodology. A deeper discussion of these concepts will be dealt with in the following two chapters on planning research (Chapter 3) and survey research (Chapter 4).

The reader should be able to evaluate whether the research has been done in a reliable way. A general but hard to fulfil aim is that the reader should be able to repeat the study and see if the same results are achieved. This is, of course, much more difficult in behavioural sciences with their unique and context-specific cases than in natural sciences, but the principle is worth considering. At least the reader should be able to follow the text, understand the chain of logic, and come to the same conclusions or at least understand how they are reached.

For these reasons several questions should be raised. One question is whether appropriate methods of data collection have been used. Another question is whether appropriate methods of data analysis have been used. Are sound and logical conclusions derived and based on the data and the analysis? Are conclusions that are drawn and recommendations that are made thoughtful and reasonable given the study?

2.8.1 The concept of research quality

The general criterion for research quality must be trustworthiness. There are four particular requirements used in social sciences that are of relevance to OSCM research: construct validity, internal validity, external validity, and reliability.

Construct validity means that the operational measures used to measure the constructs actually measure the concepts they are intended to measure. Internal validity means that the study actually measures what it is meant to measure and that demonstrated relationships are explained by the factors described and not by other factors. Similarly, external validity means that the results are valid in similar settings outside the studied objects. Reliability means that the study is objective in the sense that other researchers should reach the same conclusion in the same setting. In positivistic research, this is important for stating that the study demonstrates the 'truth'. Hence, reliability has become the most important criterion in many research communities. Other criteria concerning the quality of the research include systematic, rigorous, repeatable, and ability to follow.

The ultimate objective is to be credible or trustworthy. Research is credible to the extent that appropriate methods for the research aim and questions are used, it is rigorous in its execution, and that it uses appropriate methods for data gathering, analysis, and drawing of conclusions. The role of a methodology section in a research report serves to describe how well the research is done and to convince the readers that they can trust the results. Sometimes methodology chapters seem more aimed at demonstrating that the author has read certain books on research methodology. The methodology section should not be a literature survey but should show that the research is done well. The utmost request is that research, irrespective of approach, is done with rigor. That requirement will be developed throughout this book.

Even if the research is done with utmost rigor, research quality also refers to value. The researcher must clarify how significant the claimed contribution is to the advancement of management knowledge and skills and if the contribution is major or minor.

2.9 Assessing research quality and contribution

In learning what good research is, an effective route is to review what has already been published and submitted for publication. Studying published articles in the targeted publications is mandatory. But one can go further and systematically review them in the way they are reviewed in the double-blind review processes. The present author has run a formal course on reviewing with PhD candidates, and sometimes Master's students. It is, of course, helpful to review our own manuscripts in such a systematic way and even better to do it for each other in a group of researchers or students.

2.9.1 How to review a manuscript

A well-done review should contain both general aspects and careful examination. The general overview should bring up what has been discussed in quality of research and especially analyse the chain of evidence. Start with the title, the abstract, the aim, and then go to the end and see what the actual contribution is. Is there a fit on this level? If so, study the chain of evidence a bit more closely. Is there a problem discussion anchored in practice and theory? Does it end with a clearly defined problem? Is there a solid review of the literature? Are research questions clearly stated? Is there a theoretical development of a research model? Is there a methodology discussion connecting the problem, research question, empirical data, and form for analysis so that the research approach is appropriate for the research question, the empirical data is sufficient for the empirical base, and the analysis is appropriate for answering the research question? Are the data, analysis, and synthesis/conclusion clear and distinct to enable external assessment? Do the conclusions answer the research question? These questions should be addressed in the general overview and then the reviewer can go into detail following the manuscript page by page.

In the next section the questions in the paragraph above are extended and developed into a checklist. The aim is to give researchers a tool for reviewing their own and others' manuscripts by asking most important questions. It may be a good idea to develop a proposal for a manuscript and ask some colleagues to comment on the questions in the checklist in relation to the manuscript.

2.9.2 A checklist for assessing and reviewing research

Theory

a Theoretical foundation

- Are choices of theoretical foundations discussed regarding appropriateness?
- Are all necessary and appropriate concepts included and discussed?
- Are there concepts discussed but not later used? Why?

b Conceptualization

- Which are the key concepts and constructs? Which are the ones used in the aim, research question, hypotheses, and so on?
- Are there theoretical definitions of concepts? There may be different ways of defining a concept.

- Is the meaning of the concepts discussed?
- Are the meanings of concepts used consistently?
- Are there operational definitions of variables?
- Are similar phenomena that could be included in the concepts discussed?
- Are there similar concepts and definitions used by other authors with the same theoretical meaning?

c Characters and consequences of aims and research questions

- What type of questions are the research questions and how can they be answered?
- Is there a discussion of what the research questions imply to delimitations of the study?
- Is there a discussion of what this means to the intended contribution and the possibilities for making different kinds of generalizations?

Method

a Choices concerning methodological approaches

- Are choices well described? They should be in analytical discussions, not only descriptions.
- Are choices discussed and motivated in relation to the aim and research questions?
- Are the choices discussed and motivated in relation to alternative approaches?

b Description of the research process

- Are the different steps and the choices made in the different steps presented and discussed?

c Choice of methods and techniques

- Are chosen techniques for data collection and gathering discussed?

Empirical observations

a Data matrix

- Are the choices of indicators and variables described, discussed, and motivated?

b Alternative empirics

- Are alternative data points, data sources, and empirics discussed?

c Data quality

- Are the qualities of the data in terms of credibility, trustworthiness, reliability, and validity discussed in an adequate manner?

Analysis

a Analytical approach

- Is the chosen way of doing the analysis in line with research question, methodological approach, and available empirics?

b Transparency

- Is the analysis easy to follow? Is it evident which part of the analysis aims at answering which questions and what answers are provided?

c Exhaustiveness

- Does the analysis cover all the essential questions that are possible to respond to with existing theory?
- Is the available empirics used in a way to give exhaustive answers to the questions?
- Are there motivations when essential questions are not discussed, or the analysis is not exhaustive?

Conclusion and discussion

a Generalizations

- Are the conclusions following the analysis logical and sound?
- Are conclusions generalized in a correct way?

b One's own theory

- Do the conclusions and the discussions related to them relate to the theoretical model, framework, and questions that have been stated?

c General theory

- Are the conclusions and the discussions related to them discussed in relation to existing theory and results from other studies?

Format and formalities

a Figures and tables

- Do figures and tables have headings and explanations so they can be understood without reading the text?
- Are figures and tables correctly designed?
- Are figures and tables explained and discussed in the text?

b References

- Are references in the text designed in a correct way according to the publication?
- Do all the references in the text appear in the list of references?
- Is the list of references correctly designed according to the publication?

c Language

- Is it easy to follow the presentation and argumentation?
- Is the text well-structured?
- Is the structure of chapters, sections, and paragraphs linked so the reader can follow from paragraph to paragraph?
- Is there a correct and consequent use of tense?

2.9.3 *Characteristics of good research presentation*

Being able to report on the research is of paramount importance to the researcher. Reporting is important to all studies, but research has an extra strong requirement. What a good research report is differs from discipline to discipline and from area to area, but there are many common characteristics. The requirements are well established in each research community. The standards are also maintained through the peer review process.

2.9.3.1 *Different media and their value and quality*

There are many media or channels through which the researcher can get published, including scientific journals, professional journals, edited books, business journals, research report series, conference proceedings, and working papers. The most prestigious are leading scientific journals and the best professional journals. What determines the value of publication in the various media is to a large extent based on values in the particular research community, not least because of the review processes in which established researchers are reviewers. Important factors that influence the value of a publication are their frequency of appearance in citation indexes or impact factors as well as whether they are included in the business press' ranking systems. For the researcher, the most academically valuable publication will generally be in scientific journals. Within these journals, as within the other channels, there is a more or less established hierarchy of values given to each publisher and specific journal. The following sections focus on journal articles as a medium, though most of the discussion is also relevant for other forms of publication. How to get articles published in scientific journals is then dealt with more in detail in Section 2.10.

2.9.3.2 *How research texts differ from other texts*

Different publications have different purposes and target groups. The research paper has a particular aim in presenting and disseminating a contribution to knowledge to the academic research community in the respective field. The readers, and before that the reviewers, will ask questions such as 'What is the purpose of the research?', 'What is the contribution?', 'What does the author claim?', 'How well is the claim supported?', 'What is the theoretical framework?', 'Does the author know the area well enough?', 'Is the method adequate?', 'Is the report well-structured and easy to follow?', and 'Is it well written?' The criteria the reviewer will use are those established in the publication in question and in the research community. In this respect a researcher is in a different position than a journalist or a novelist. The assessment criteria are much stricter, providing little freedom for innovative forms of presentation.

2.9.3.3 *Common characteristics of good research presentations*

Some criteria regarding the form of the text are more or less common for all media. The report should be written for the reader, not for the author. Remember the target group and that the reader does not know any of the 'extras' from the project that are known by the author. This is one of many reasons why it is so important to present regular outlines to colleagues in the university department or other organizational environment. A report is built from many parts, and it is important that the string of logic is clear to the reader throughout the report. See Section 2.10 on how to build a chain of evidence.

Readability is important in scientific publications. The following questions address this criterion. Is the organization of the manuscript clear, is it well- structured, and is the flow of the argument logical and clear? Is the language appropriate to the target group or groups? Note that in OSCM researchers often address themselves to academics and practitioners simultaneously. How is the style of the text? Is it direct, fresh, and thought-provoking and does it create interest in the reader? Is the length relevant in relation to the contribution and to the format and standards of the publication? How are different kinds of exhibits used? Are figures clear and explained in the text? Does the abstract give a good comprehensive summary of the report, or does it only mention indirectly what the report is about? Does the title give appropriate information about the content and contribution of the report? How is the overall readability?

Following these standards for a report on research is important not only in getting the message through, but also for being accepted in research publications. There is literature on how to write reports and it is helpful to learn from it. For writers submitting texts for publication in academic journals and books, there are also standards from publishers that are normally available from the editor or the publication's website.

2.10 Getting published

Getting published has always been important for a researcher and it is becoming more so. The old saying 'publish or perish' says a lot. Some tend to say, 'If you don't publish you don't exist', at least in the scientific community. It is therefore important to learn how to get published. However, there are many more reasons than just being recognized. Publications and the quality of the publication weigh heavily on academic promotion both internally and when seeking new positions elsewhere. It is also an important factor in popular rankings and hence earns points in the research assessments and accreditation processes that have become important for institutions. Regardless of all these, personal satisfaction may be the most important factor. To see the article printed, to create a domain to be known within, and to have an effect on other research and researchers is rewarding.

2.10.1 Academic publishing

There are many outlets for publishing academic work, but the most important and rewarding from an academic perspective is in scientific journals. International journals count much higher than local or regional ones. This may be unfair to researchers who do not have English as their mother tongue, but it is difficult to get around. There are numerous journals at different levels and it may be difficult to choose. Indexes such as citation indexes and impact indexes are a good indication. A general classification does not exist, but many institutions have journal ranking lists or use well-known lists such as the Academic Journal Guide (AJG) by the Chartered Association of Business Schools (CABS). Search the web for journal rankings and consult your own organization.

A paper will often go through many stages. It may start as a working paper discussed at the department, and after development be presented at a conference, and once developed more be submitted to a journal. Try to find a journal in which there is a reasonable possibility of being accepted, but do not start too low. Good review feedback may help you to get in there or elsewhere later.

2.10.2 Targeting the publication

To get published, there are two basic demands: one on content and one on quality of research. Is the contribution significant enough and relevant for the channel and target group? Is the research quality up to the standards of the research community at which the publication is targeted? In addition to these general questions that were dealt with earlier, under research quality and common characteristics, respectively, it is important to study and carefully analyse the publication policies of the potential publication.

Publications such as journals, books, and reports series for academic research do have publication policies. Get hold of that before you design the manuscript. In scientific journals, policies are mostly published in the journal and on its website together with rules for submitting a manuscript and information about the review process. Normally there are specifications of target groups, types of contributions, and styles of manuscripts. Sometimes there are calls for special issues and then there will be a special definition of the type of contributions expected. Note that special issues do not mean lower levels of standard for acceptance, but the limited focus might make it easier to get in if the submitted manuscript fits the scope.

Additionally, there are some practical points to follow to improve the chances of getting published. Carefully read the publication policy. There are many guidelines and following them will considerably increase the chances of publication. Study some of the published manuscripts. They are not all role models, but they give a good idea of the standards and formats wanted. Read papers authored by members of the editorial board. This gives a very good idea of what they think is good research and what is publishable. Study their references to find out what is important for your literature review. Use references to members of the editorial board. With a more distinct plan, contact the editor or associate editor for your sub-area and find out about plans and additional policies or value systems used by the editor(s).

When targeting, you should not only see the value of your contribution from your perspective. Journals want contributions that fit their mission and they have plans. Look out for announcements of special editions and editors attending conferences.

2.10.3 Publishing process

There is almost always a long path from planning a paper to getting published. A good idea is to envision a few alternatives when planning the paper. For example, when planning the research, you could consider when and where it can be published. The steps mentioned earlier should be thought of: which working papers should be written when, what papers should be submitted to which conferences, and, eventually, what can be published in which journals? Planning the research is the issue in Chapter 3; here we will focus on writing the paper for publication.

Before submitting the paper see to that it is a complete paper with a reasonable chance of being accepted after development. Reviewers can get very annoyed if the author has not done their best. Test your own manuscript against how papers are reviewed. Use the checklist in Section 2.9.2.

2.10.4 Writing the manuscript

There are different kinds of papers. The most common are theory testing and theory development papers. Other alternatives may be conceptual papers, literature reviews, and papers on methodology. The focus of this book is on empirically based papers that are either deductive, testing theory, inductive, generating theory, or abductive, searching for causalities or explanations.

However, this book does not focus on writing reports and dissertations; there is a whole range of literature specializing in that. Each of the following chapters on different research approaches discusses aspects of publishing that type of research, but below follow a few general remarks on writing.

First, write about something interesting, not only to yourself, but to the target group. It should contribute new knowledge and have relevance. A good way to start is by writing a synopsis, which is the whole article in three pages or so. It is a good test of whether there is a real problem or issue, through a research approach that is relevant with an investigation model and plan, empirical data, a framework for analysis, a synthesis leading to the contribution, and results that can be put in relation to existing knowledge. The title must be attractive and mirror the contribution.

In discussing the research problem or issue the author has to make clear that s/he knows what is already published, what s/he wants to contribute, and why it is relevant. Reviewing the literature does not mean a survey but analysing what there is that is relevant. Develop a clear aim for the paper. In the methodology section, remember that it is there to ensure the research is well done, not that the author has read all the popular books on methodology and methods. A fundamental principle is that the reader should be able to follow the article and trust the thought process. Therefore, it is often good to separate the data, analysis, synthesis, and conclusions. Finally, check that conclusions are in line with the aim, explain the importance and relations to earlier research, discuss limitations, and suggest further research. Before submitting the paper to any journal, have it reviewed by colleagues, discussed in seminars, and maybe tested as a conference paper. It is a good idea to have a manuscript proof-read by a professional proof-reader to avoid annoyance because of bad language. Then the paper can be submitted.

2.10.5 Review process and editing

It is the role of peer reviewers and editors to help advance research and its quality. Scientific manuscripts will typically go through several iterations from the submitter via the editor to reviewers and back undergoing continuous improvement. Many manuscripts submitted to journals will be accepted conditionally and accepted after revision. However, they will often require a major revision, which may lead to acceptance if the rewriting is done well or rejected at any stage in the process.

The first step in the review process will be an assessment by one or more editors, one of which may be an area editor. An area editor may cover a sub-field or a geographical area. There are often also invited guest editors, especially for special issues. Many submitted papers are rejected at this stage. With the increasing pressure on researchers to get published and the globalization of management research, it is not uncommon that first-round rejections exceed 50 per cent.

If the paper passes the first screening, it will go for a so-called double-blind review, meaning that authors will not know the identities of the reviewers and the reviewers will not know those of the authors. It may be two or three established researchers who will do the review and respond in anything between two and (in bad cases) six months. The editor will put the reviewers' comments together and hopefully comment on what has to be done and what may be done to the paper. There will be demands such as reworking and resubmitting, major revisions, and minor revisions. Rarely will the response be 'publish as is'.

Then there is time for revisions. Take every comment from the reviewers into careful consideration and do whatever sounds relevant. In most cases, the reviewer will check what is done. Always go through each comment from the reviewer and write clear comments about how you have responded or why you have not. After resubmitting there may be another round if there are some minor issues but see to it that you have done all that you can, or you may be rejected. When you have been accepted and are asked to submit in the standards for manuscripts, it may be wise to have another proof-reading of your manuscript done.

After some time you will be asked to check the typesetting. This may be a boring activity and it must be done in a few days, but it does give a sense of being close to fulfilment. It should be said that several journals have skipped this phase, instead relying on automatic typesetting.

2.11 Research ethics and ethics for researchers

Doing research in a way that is technically of a high standard is not enough. There are also ethical issues a researcher should consider.

2.11.1 What are ethics and morals?

Ethics refers to a system or code of morals. It may contain guiding philosophies and principles of conduct. Moral stands for that which relates to, deals with, or is capable of making the distinction between right and wrong in conduct. Ethical issues may always have been important but have been observed much more in times of concern about humanity, animals, the environment, and the earth as a whole.

2.11.2 Ethics for researchers

Ethical issues for researchers deal with communicating benefits and risks, the protection of identity, privacy, obtaining informed consent, and much more.

There are four areas where the European Commission has defined principles of research ethics for European research: the principle of respect for human dignity, the principle of utility, the principle of precaution, and the principle of justice (European Union, 2010). Some of the important issues for the management researcher may include the following.

- Researchers should exercise strict requirements for consent procedures. Justification for involvement of vulnerable individuals or groups must be made. Data must be fairly and lawfully processed for limited purposes, and be adequate, relevant, and not excessive, accurate, not kept longer than necessary, processed in accordance with the data subject's rights, secure, and not transferred to countries without adequate protection. Each participant in a research project should be informed clearly of its goals, any possible adverse effects, and their ability to refuse to enter or to retract their involvement at any time with no consequences. Moreover, no inducement should justify participation in a research project (European Union, 2010). Although this principle is developed with research on individual human beings, the same can be said for individuals and groups of individuals forming an organization. Especially in such situations, it should be taken into account that not all individuals are able to understand a contract with such rules. An explanation in terms suitable for the targeted individuals should follow.

- Researchers should exercise strict requirements for utility. The researcher must be able to prove that the benefit from the research justifies the burden put on the population. This is especially sensitive if the rights of human individuals are affected.
- Researchers should exercise strict requirements for precaution. Each research project should be preceded by a careful assessment of predictable risks and burdens in comparison with the foreseeable benefits for the subject to others. A specific issue is the issue of dual use; for example, a research output may serve peaceful as well as aggressive aims.
- Researchers should exercise strict requirements for justice. There should be an analysis of benefits sharing. Intellectual property rights issues should be considered, identified, and inducements to research participants, empirical data sources, and researchers justified. Compensation for negative effects on participants and issues of equality should be considered.

For these ethical considerations, with whom should the researchers make contracts and who will follow up on it? There are reasons why the researcher should make a contract with the world, humanity, the environment, and each concerned individual. There is a lack of contracting partners, but each governing body, be it the university or the granting body, should develop and demand a contract with at least some of the points mentioned above. Increasingly research granting organizations include articles on ethics in their contracts.

A checklist of what to consider may be of help. The following checklist is based on a document from the National Institute of Environmental Health Sciences (NIEHS) (Resnik, 2011; Shamoo and Resnik, 2009).

- Honesty: Strive for honesty in all scientific communications. Honestly report data, results, methods and procedures, and publication status. Do not fabricate, falsify, or misrepresent data. Do not deceive colleagues, granting agencies, or the public.
- Objectivity: Strive to avoid bias in experimental design, data analysis, data interpretation, peer review, personnel decisions, grant writing, expert testimony, and other aspects of research where objectivity is expected or required. Avoid or minimize bias or self-deception. Disclose personal or financial interests that may affect research.
- Integrity: Keep your promises and agreements; act with sincerity; strive for consistency of thought and action.
- Carefulness: Avoid careless errors and negligence; carefully and critically examine your own work and the work of your peers. Keep good records of research activities, such as data collection, research design, and correspondence with agencies or journals.
- Openness: Share data, results, ideas, tools, and resources. Be open to criticism and new ideas.
- Respect for intellectual property: Honour patents, copyrights, and other forms of intellectual property. Do not use unpublished data, methods, or results without permission. Give credit where credit is due. Give proper acknowledgement or credit for all contributions to research. Never plagiarize.
- Confidentiality: Protect confidential communications, such as papers or grants submitted for publication, personnel records, trade or military secrets, and interviewee records.

- Responsible publication: Publish in order to advance research and scholarship, not to advance just your own career. Avoid wasteful and duplicative publication.
- Social responsibility: Strive to promote social good and prevent or mitigate social harms through research, public education, and advocacy.
- Non-discrimination: Avoid discrimination against anybody on the basis of sex, race, ethnicity, age, or other factors that are not related to the research.
- Legality: Know and obey relevant laws and institutional and governmental policies.
- Protect human subjects: When conducting research on human subjects, minimize harm and risks and maximize benefits; respect human dignity, privacy, and autonomy; take special precautions with vulnerable populations; strive to distribute the benefits and burdens of research fairly.

2.12 Summary

2.12.1 What is research and why is it done?

There may be a reasonable consensus that research concerns the creation and development of knowledge, but there are variants. Most modern perspectives of research include the purpose of implementation or use of the knowledge to develop applications, sometimes described as Mode 2. Before going about it, the potential researcher should ask oneself a couple of questions. Why do the research I am thinking of? If I am going to do research, in what field, on what issue, with what research approach, in what way, for which targets, and why me? What is my possibility of making a contribution?

2.12.2 Research outputs and targets

Research aims at the creation and development of knowledge. Operations concern transforming human, physical, and information resources into products and services and exist in, and apply to, all functional areas of a company or other organization. Research in OSCM can concern both pure knowledge and application and addresses both academics and practitioners. There are often concurrent needs for practice relevance and academic contribution. Research can have different aims, such as exploration, confirmation, and rejection. The degree and extent of the involvement of the researcher varies not only with the research project but also with the research approach. Research is increasingly expected to have economic impact.

2.12.3 Roles of the researcher

Research is done differently depending on aim and research questions and the state of existing knowledge. Roles that the researcher will have to, or may be asked to, take on include observer, surveyor, analyst, communicator, sounding board, actor and other partner roles, consultant, and clinician.

2.12.4 The research process

The research process will go through many steps and will typically start with the identification of an issue to research and end up with results published in a report. A generic process may look like this. 1) Identification of a problem or issue to research; 2) Literature review; 3) Specifying the aim of the intended research; 4) Determining specific research questions; 5) Choice of research approach and methods; 6) Development of a conceptual framework; 7) Data collection; 8) Analysing and interpreting the data; 9) Synthesizing and concluding; 10) Evaluating the research and suggesting further research; 11) Reporting and communicating the research findings.

2.12.5 Research as contribution to knowledge

Competence can be said to consist of knowledge, skills, and attributes. We differ between deductive, inductive, and abductive research depending on what logic we follow. The result of the research should be to contribute to existing knowledge. This means adding something that was not known in the research community. Research can be explorative, descriptive, analytical, causal, and normative relative to the state of existing knowledge. There are different levels of knowledge in terms of know-what, know-how, and know-why. Results will be constructs, system descriptions, analytical models, forecasts, and recommendations.

2.12.6 What to research

The first question to ask is whether there will be a demand for the research results. Will academics find that it advances knowledge and is worth considering? Will practitioners be helped in understanding and dealing with the issues they face? The key task in doing research is to make a contribution to knowledge. To plan the research, apply a holistic and 'final logic' perspective on the whole research. Start with the intended research contribution and enter a form of reverse logic. In many situations the starting point may be the studied object or data, which will imply both possibilities and limitations to the research aim and format.

2.12.7 The problem-method-contribution fit

There must be a fit between research issue, method, data, and results. A chain of evidence should be clear. Make claims for generalizability and discuss forms of generalization. Check that the contribution matches the aim. Demonstrate the contribution by relating results to earlier existing knowledge.

2.12.8 Research quality

The key issue in research quality is that of credibility or trustworthiness. There are requests for validity and reliability. The demands vary with research approach. The research must be done rigorously (which is not rigid).

2.12.9 Assessing research quality and contribution

In learning what good research is, an effective route is to review what is already published and submitted for publication. Systematically review the literature in the way it is reviewed in the double-blind review processes. Journals have schemes for reviewing; submitters can also learn a lot from these schemes. Use checklists and maybe develop your own.

2.12.10 Characteristics of good research presentation

There are many outlets; international scientific refereed journals are the crown. Remember to make a contribution, not only a text. Keep the target group in mind and remember that the reader does not know any of the 'extras' from the project that are known by the author. The line of thinking must be clear through- out the report; consider the chain of evidence. Readability is important for reaching out.

2.12.11 Getting published

For many researchers, it is 'publish or perish'. Plan for publication early during the research process. Target the publication or possible alternatives. Start by writing a comprehensive synopsis. That will make you think of the whole article. Repeatedly present to, and get reviews from, colleagues; use your research group or network. The review process will probably be long with several steps but getting published is worth the effort.

2.12.12 Research ethics and ethics for researchers

Ethics refer to a system of codes of morals. There are ethical issues about humanity, animals, environment, and the earth. Research ethics include respect for human dignity, utility, precaution, and justice. Check yourself against criteria lists. Even if you do not come to judgement, having your value system clear makes you stronger.

References

Creswell, J. W. (2007) *Qualitative Inquiry and Research Design: Choosing among Five Approaches*, 2nd edn. Thousand Oaks, CA: SAGE Publications.

Edmonson, A. C. and McManus, S. E. (2007) Methodological fit in management field research. *The Academy of Management Review*, 32(4), 1,155–1,179.

European Union (2010) *European Textbook on Ethics in Research*. Luxembourg: Publications Office of the European Union.

Gibbons, M., Limoges, C., Nowotny, H., Schwartzman, S., Scott, P. and Trow, M. (1994) *The New Production of Knowledge: The Dynamics of Science and Research in Contemporary Societies*. London: Sage Publications.

Merriam-Webster (2015) *Research*. Available online at www.merriam-webster.com/dic-tionary/research (accessed 17 November 2015).

Miles, M. B. and Huberman, A. M. (1994) *Qualitative Data Analysis: An Expanded Source Book*, 2nd edn. Thousand Oaks, CA: Sage Publications.

Nonaka, I. and Takeuchi, H. (1995) *The Knowledge-creating Company: How Japanese Companies Create the Dynamics of Innovation*. New York, NY: Oxford University Press.

OECD (2015) Glossary of Statistical Terms. Available online at https://stats.oecd.org/glossary (accessed 17 November 2015).

Polanyi, M. (1966) *The Tacit Dimension*. Chicago, IL: University of Chicago Press.

Resnik, D. B. (2011) *What Is Ethics in Research and Why Is It Important?* Available online at www.niehs.nih.gov/research/resources/bioethics/whatis/ (accessed 17 November 2015).

Shamoo, A. E. and Resnik, D. B. (2009) *Responsible Conduct of Research*, 2nd edn. New York: Oxford University Press.

Turban, E. and Frenzel, L. E. (1992) *Expert Systems and Applied Artificial Intelligence*. New York: Macmillan Publishing.

UNPAN (2015) *Knowledge Management Basics: Concepts, Objects, Principles, and Expectations*. Available online at http://unpan1.un.org/intradoc/groups/public/documents/un/unpan031578.pdf (accessed 17 November 2015).

Van Maanen, J., Sørensen, J. B. and Mitchell, T. R. (2007) The interplay between theory and method. *The Academy of Management Review*, 32(4), 1,145–1,154.

Wiig, K. M. (1993) *Knowledge Management Foundations: Thinking about Thinking – How People and Organizations Create, Represent, and Use Knowledge*. Arlington, TX: Schema Press.

Further reading

Alvesson, M. and Sköldberg, K. (2010) *Reflexive Methodology: New Wistas for Qualitative Research*, 2nd edn. London: Sage Publications.

Becker, H. S. (1998) *Tricks of the Trade: How to Think about Your Research While You're Doing it.* Chicago, IL: University of Chicago Press.

Bickman, L. and Rog, D. J. (eds) (2000) *Handbook of Applied Research Methods.* Thousand Oaks, CA: Sage Publications.

Boyatzis, R. E. (1998) *Transforming Qualitative Information: Thematic Analysis and Code Development.* Thousand Oaks, CA: Sage Publications.

Burgess, K., Singh, P.J., and Koroglu, R. (2006) Supply chain management: A structured literature review and implications for future research. *International Journal of Operations & Production Management*, 26(7), 703–729.

Carter, C.R., Sanders, N.R., and Dong, Y. (2008) Paradigms, revolutions, and tipping points: The need for using multiple methodologies within the field of supply chain management. *Journal of Operations Management*, 26(6), 693–696.

Coughlan, P., Draaijer, D., Godsell, J., and Boer, H. (2016) Operations and supply chain management. *International Journal of Operations & Production Management*, 36(12), 1673–1695.

Craighead, C. W. and Meredith, J. (2008) Operations management research: Evolution and alternative future paths. *International Journal of Operations & Production Management*, 28(8), 710–726.

Eisenhardt, K. M. (1989) Building theories from case study research. *The Academy of Management Review*, 14(4), 532–550.

Fawcett, S.E., and Waller, M.A. (2013) Considering supply chain management's professional identity: The beautiful discipline (or, "We don't cure cancer, but we do make a big difference"). *Journal of Business Logistics*, 34(3), 183–188.

Ghauri, P. N. and Grønhaug, K. (2002) *Research Methods in Business Studies: A Practical Guide*, 2nd edn. Harlow: Pearson Education.

Hedrick, T. E., Bickman, L. and Rog, D. J. (1993) *Applied Research Design: A Practical Guide.* Newbury Park, CA: Sage Publications.

Jorgensen, D. L. (1989) *Participant Observation: A Methodology for Human Studies.* Thousand Oaks, CA, USA: SAGE Publications.

Koufteros, X. A., Babbar, S., Behara, R. S., and Baghersad, M. (2021) OM research: Leading authors and institutions. Decision Sciences, 52(1), 8–77.

Kouvelis, P. et al. (2006) Supply chain management research and POM: Review, trends, and opportunities. *Production and Operations Management*, 15(3), 449–469.

Lee, A. S. (1995) Reviewing a manuscript for publication. *Journal of Operations Management*, 13, 87–92.

Maxwell, J. A. (2013) *Qualitative Research Design: An Interactive Approach*, 3rd Thousand Oaks, CA, USA: SAGE Publications.

Roh, J., Krause, R., & Swink, M. (2016) The appointment of chief supply chain officers to top management teams: A contingency model of firm-level antecedents and conscquences. *Journal of Operations Management*, 44(1), 48–61.

Sachan, A., and Datta, S. (2005) Review of supply chain management and logistics research. *International Journal of Physical Distribution & Logistics Management*, 35(9), 664–705.

Silverman, D. (2000) *Doing Qualitative Research: A Practical Handbook.* Thousand Oaks, CA: SAGE Publications.

Simpson, D., Meredith, J., Boyer, K., Dilts, D., Ellram, L.M., and Leong, G.K. (2015) Professional, research, and publishing trends in operations and supply chain management. *Journal of Supply Chain Management*, 51(3), 87–100.

Strauss, A. and Corbin, J. (1998) *Basics of Qualitative Research: Techniques and Procedures for Developing Grounded Theory*, 2nd edn. Thousand Oaks, CA: SAGE Publications.

Sutton, R. I. and Staw, B. M. (1995) What theory is not. *Administrative Science Quarterly*, 40(3), 371–384.

Taylor, A. and Taylor, M. (2009) Operations management research: Contemporary themes, trends, and potential future directions. *International Journal of Operations & Production Management*, 29(12), 1,316–1,340.

Thomas, R., Defee, C., Randall, W., and Williams, B. (2011) Assessing the managerial relevance of contemporary supply chain management research. *International Journal of Physical Distribution & Logistics Management*, 41(7), 655–667.

Vallet-Bellmunt, T. et al. (2011) Supply chain management: A multidisciplinary content analysis of vertical relations between companies, 1997–2006. *Industrial Marketing Management*, 40, 1347–1367.

Voss, C.A. (1995) Operations management – from Taylor to Toyota – and beyond? *British Journal of Management*, 6(Supplement S1), S17–S29.

Wagner, B., and Fearne, A. (2015) 20 years of supply chain management: An International Journal. *Supply Chain Management*, 20(6). doi: 10.1108/SCM-09-2015-0378

Wieland, A. et al. (2016) Mapping the landscape of future research themes in supply chain management, *Journal of Business Logistics*, 205–212, doi: 10.1111/jbl.12131

Wieland, A. (2021) Dancing the supply chain: Toward transformative supply chain management. *Journal of Supply Chain Management*, 57(1), 58–73.

Yin, R. K. (1981a) The case study as a serious research strategy. *Knowledge: Creation, Diffusion, Utilization*, 3(1), 97–114.

Yin, R. K. (1981b) The case study crisis: Some answers. *Administrative Science Quarterly*, 26(1), 58–65.

3   The research process

Pär Åhlström

Chapter overview

This chapter concerns the research process – the sequence of activities that takes you from the start of a research project to publication. The focus is on a set of activities taking place in the early parts of the research process, before data are collected and analysed. The activities are generic and apply to all the different research approaches described in the remainder of the book. The following five activities are discussed in this chapter:

1 **Contributing to knowledge.** To properly understand the research process, an understanding of its goal is necessary, which is to contribute to existing knowledge.
2 **Choosing a research topic.** Any contribution to knowledge starts with finding a suitable research topic.
3 **Using literature to develop the research topic.** The third part of the chapter addresses the literature review and various ways of using and misusing literature.
4 **Developing research questions.** Research questions are a fundamentally important part of any research process, but are notoriously difficult to formulate.
5 **Considerations in choosing a research approach.** The final part of the chapter discusses three considerations in selecting a research approach: the achievement of methodological fit, the impact of the researcher's philosophical position and practical considerations.

3.1 Contributing to knowledge

As discussed in Chapter 2, the key outcome or product of the research process is a new contribution to knowledge. If there is no original contribution, a thesis will not be accepted for a PhD and a paper will not be accepted for publication. But what constitutes a contribution? This question can puzzle new and experienced researchers alike. Chapter 2 made the important point that the more general a contribution is the better. But how and in what way can a general contribution to knowledge be made?

Making a contribution means contributing to the general body of knowledge of a particular topic. This statement may sound trivial, but it means that you must contribute to more than your own personal knowledge. The fact that you, the researcher, know more than you did previously is a necessary but not a sufficient condition for a research contribution.

DOI: 10.4324/9781003315001-3

In their article, aptly titled "Making a meaningful contribution to theory", prominent operations and supply chain management scholars present six different and complementary views on the role of theory in making contributions (Boer et al., 2015). They conclude that theory is the fundamental engine that drives the creation of knowledge. Theory is the currency in which researchers trade, so just doing empirically interesting work or solving a problem that an organization faces is not enough. But they also stress that there is no one right way to make a contribution.

Making a general contribution is often linked to theory. At times the term *theoretical contribution* is used. We will therefore start the task of understanding how to make a contribution to knowledge by defining theory. However, there are also other ways to make a contribution, as will be discussed later.

3.1.1 What is theory?

If contributing to knowledge is related to theory, we must understand clearly what theory is. A theory can be defined as a set of interrelated constructs, definitions and propositions that present a systematic view of phenomena by specifying relationships among variables, with the purpose of explaining and predicting the phenomena. Theories explain facts and provide stories as to why phenomena work as they do. They can and should be used to make predictions (Schmenner and Swink, 1998).

Not surprisingly perhaps, there are slightly different views of the constituent elements of a theory. However, these viewpoints share a few common denominators. For instance, both Whetten (1989) and Wacker (1998) include the following three constituent elements in a theory:

1 conceptual definitions of the theory's constructs;
2 defined relationships between constructs; and
3 a limitation of the theory's domain, i.e. the boundary conditions within which the proposed relationships hold.

Both authors also discuss a fourth element, though in slightly different ways. Whetten (1989) stresses the importance of explaining why constructs relate to one another as the theory claims they do. Wacker (1998) also mentions the *why* but focuses primarily on the theory's predictive ability.

Theories are not built; they are invented (Schmenner et al., 2009). Theories cannot be systematically constructed or deduced from facts, but require inspiration and creativity. Furthermore, they cannot be proved, but only disproved by findings that run counter to their predictions or explanations. In disproving theories, hypothesis testing is critical. When hypotheses are tested, we gain facts with which we can confront theory.

Theories are not purely academic exercises, in the sense of being unrelated to the real world. On the contrary, it is often said that nothing is quite so practical as a good theory (Van de Ven, 1989). In fact, the very definition of theory provides guidelines to answer common questions that occur in managerial practice (Wacker, 1998). First, theory defines all variables by answering the common questions of *who* and *what*. The domain specifies the conditions where the theory is expected to hold, thus answering the common questions of *when* and *where*. The relationship-building stage specifies the reasoning by explaining *how* and *why* variables are related. Finally, the predictive claims answer the question of whether a particular event could or should occur.

3.1.2 Research products that are often confused with theory

Having determined what theory is, we should also point out what theory is not, as various concepts are often confused with theory. These other terms could describe research products that constitute contributions to knowledge, but that are not theories (Sutton and Staw, 1995):

1 **References are not theory.** Listing references to existing theories and mentioning their names is not the same as explicating the causal logic that they contain. Thus, using references as a smoke screen to hide the absence of theory is a practice that should be avoided.
2 **Data are not theory.** Data describe which empirical patterns were observed, whereas theory explains why empirical patterns were observed or can be expected to be observed. Thus, prior findings cannot by themselves motivate hypotheses; a theory is needed.
3 **Lists of variables or constructs are not theory.** A theory must explain why variables or constructs are connected. A predicted relationship must be explained to provide theory.
4 **Diagrams are not theory.** Although figures that show causal relationships may be an important part of a theory, they by themselves are not theory. Some verbal explication of the logic is needed to explain why the portrayed relationships will be observed.
5 **Hypotheses are not theory.** Hypotheses make explicit how the variables and relationships that follow from a logical argument will be operationalized. But hypotheses are concise statements about what is expected to occur, not why it is expected to occur.

Apart from these five, additional terms are used to describe various research products that could constitute valid contributions but should not be confused with theory. The first such term is *proposition*. There is a relationship between propositions and hypotheses. Both are related to theory but are not theory in themselves. The difference is that hypotheses require measures whereas propositions involve concepts (Whetten, 1989). In that sense, propositions can be more loosely formulated than hypotheses. Any good theory should lead to a number of propositions.

A model is a way to operationalize a theory for empirical testing. For this reason, the term *model* is sometimes used synonymously with theory (Whetten, 1989), although models do not always meet the requirements placed on theories. A distinction can be made between variance models and process models and thus, by extrapolation, between variance and process theories (Markus and Robey, 1988). Variance models (or theories) are concerned with predicting levels of outcomes based on levels of predictor variables; they are thus concerned with cause and effect. Process models (or theories) are concerned with explaining how outcomes develop over time.

The term *conceptual model*, although sometimes used quite loosely, has a specific meaning, particularly when applied to modelling and simulations (see Chapter 9). Here the starting point is a particular problem as observed in the real world (Mitroff et al., 1974). The conceptual model sets out in broad terms the definition of the particular problem to be solved, and it specifies the variables that will be used to define the nature of the problem. It is thus a conceptualization of reality and of a practical problem, but as such it may not be testable.

Taxonomy is at times used in connection with contributions. This term comes from the Greek words for *arrangement* and *method*. Taxonomies are used to classify things according to their similarities. They originated as a means of classifying organisms in biology but are also created in other disciplines. In operations and supply chain management, for instance, Miller and Roth's (1994) taxonomy of manufacturing strategies is a prominent example. Taxonomies are not theories, although they may represent excellent contributions to knowledge.

The final term frequently used in connection with contributions is *framework*. There are different ways of seeing frameworks. Miles and Huberman (1994), in their hugely influential book on qualitative data analysis, use the term *conceptual framework* to describe something that exists prior to the start of a study. The framework "explains, either graphically or in narrative form, the main things to be studied – the key factors, concepts, or variables – and the presumed relationships among them" (Miles and Huberman, 1994, p. 18).

Frameworks can also be the end product of a research process. They can help us to grasp phenomena or to see them in a certain perspective and can create an overall understanding. Frameworks may, but they usually do not, address the issue of causality. Frameworks can be expressed in many forms, such the 2 × 2 matrices that are often used as a way of simplifying and expressing complex organizational phenomena. They can also be expressed as checklists. Although frameworks resemble theory, they do not contain all the elements required of theories. Still, frameworks can make important contributions to knowledge.

3.1.3 Making theoretical contributions

If contributions are linked to theory, does this mean that every researcher needs to invent a new theory? Luckily, this is not the case. Developing theory is difficult; hence new theories do not come along every day. We should not expect every journal or PhD thesis to come up with a theory. Far from every research process needs to, can or perhaps should end up in a new theory. In fact, Roger Schmenner has suggested that there may indeed be a risk of having too many theories and too little understanding (Schmenner et al., 2009).

If new theories are not necessary to make a contribution, how can researchers make theoretical contributions? Based on his role as editor of a top general management journal, the *Academy of Management Review*, David Whetten (1989) proposed several ways in which theoretical contributions can be made:

- Researchers can make theoretical contributions by *adding or subtracting factors from an existing theory*. However, this requires that the proposed additions or deletions are of sufficient magnitude to substantially alter the core logic of the existing theory. One way to demonstrate the value of a proposed change in a list of factors is to identify how this change affects the accepted relationships between the variables. Simply adding a new variable to an existing list is not sufficient to constitute a theoretical contribution.
- One fruitful way, but the most difficult, to develop theory is to address the why of the theory, that is, to *find alternative explanations for the occurrence of a phenomenon*.
- Researchers can also *address the domain limitations of the theory*. Beyond identifying the limitations of a theory's range of application, it is also necessary to explain why this anomaly exists, so that the theory can be revised to accommodate this new information. Conversely, applying a theory to a new setting and finding that it works as expected is not instructive by itself. This conclusion has theoretical merit only if something about the new setting would have suggested that the theory shouldn't work under those conditions.

Whetten (1989) concludes by stating that three broad themes underlie theoretical contributions. First, it is not sufficient to propose improvements addressing only a single element of an existing theory. Critiques should focus on multiple elements of the theory. Second, theoretical contributions should marshal compelling evidence, be it logical or empirical. Third, making theoretical contributions involves proposing remedies or alternatives.

3.1.4 Contributing to operations and supply chain management knowledge

It should be clear by now that making a theoretical contribution is a rather tall order. To suggest that all research needs to make theoretical contributions following the guidelines suggested above would be unreasonable. There are other ways of contributing to knowledge. Christopher A. Voss suggests that, since developing a new theory is difficult, research tends to contribute to existing theory, or to use existing theory to explain phenomena (Boer et al., 2015). One of the most common ways of contributing to existing knowledge, he states, is through contingency approaches (Sousa and Voss, 2008), which address such questions as what processes and practices apply in which contexts, what relationships hold or do not hold in which contexts, and where methods do or do not work or how they vary in different contexts.

Voss also indicates that another widely used way to contribute to existing knowledge is to examine and test relationships between variables (Boer et al., 2015). Since most relationships are complex, it is often fruitful to explore the moderators of these variables. Moderators are factors that influence the strength of the direct effect between two variables. Moderating effects inform our understanding of the theories underlying relationships and their contingencies.

Roger Schmenner highlights the neglected role of discovery as another type of contribution to knowledge (Boer et al., 2015). Researchers can and should advance our understanding by doing discovery and not simply by trying to advance one or another theory. In discovery, facts are important. Although a distinction is commonly made between theory-building and theory-testing research, most existing research is neither of these, as Mark Pagell has argued (Boer et al., 2015). Generally, we either identify important new facts (fact building) or test the validity of previously identified facts (fact testing). Important facts, discovered in a robust manner, constitute an important contribution and deserve publication, Pagell contends. Over time, facts accumulate and contribute to the development of new theory or the falsification of existing theory. Hence, facts can contribute to knowledge.

Wacker (1998) argues, similarly, that an important general objective of research can be fact-finding. The purpose of fact-finding research is to build a lexicon of facts that are gathered under specified conditions. Good fact-finding research carefully defines concepts, stipulates domains, gathers evidence (facts) and then uses the evidence to discover whether relationships exist. Strictly speaking, fact-finding research is not theory building, since evidence is gathered before the relationships are explained and predicted. But it can provide facts that can later be integrated into a theory. To do so, it needs to involve precise definitions and well-defined domains.

Contributions can also be less formal in nature, such as pointing out flaws in an existing theory when it is applied to a new or different context (even without necessarily proposing a better one), or identifying important and relevant issues that the existing literature fails to address (Boer et al., 2015). Challenging, critiquing, or refuting existing theory constitutes a valid and valuable contribution to knowledge. Thus, testing existing theory, building new theory, criticizing existing theory, or simply describing a new phenomenon observed in the real world are all valid forms of research and can make a meaningful contribution to knowledge.

Of course, it is always necessary to convince other researchers that you have in fact made a contribution. Papers submitted to journals must be persuasive to reviewers and editors. PhD theses need to satisfy supervisors and examiners. Thus, judgements of the proposed contribution are in the eye of the beholder (Boer et al., 2015). Ultimately, the value of any contribution will be determined by its utility in informing practice and/or future research.

Two contingencies can impact judgements as to whether a particular research effort constitutes a substantial contribution to knowledge: 1) how mature the knowledge of the topic or phenomenon is and 2) the view taken on fundamental issues of philosophy of science. We will turn to these two contingencies now.

3.1.5 Linking contributions to the maturity of knowledge

Chapter 2 pointed out that there are different types and levels of knowledge. One way of expressing this notion has to do with how mature the knowledge of a particular topic or phenomenon is. Edmondson and McManus (2007) have proposed that theory in management research falls along a continuum from nascent to mature:

- Nascent theory proposes tentative answers to novel questions of how and why, often merely suggesting new connections among phenomena in situations where little or no previous theory exists.
- Mature theory presents well-developed constructs and models that have been studied over time with increasing precision by a variety of researchers, resulting in a body of knowledge that contains points of broad agreement.

Between these two endpoints in the continuum, Edmondson and McManus describe an area called *intermediate theory*, which presents provisional explanations of phenomena, often introducing a new construct and proposing relationships between it and established constructs. Although the research questions may allow the development of testable hypotheses, as in mature theory research, one or more of the constructs involved is often still tentative, similar to nascent theory research.

This differentiation between levels of maturity is important because the nature of the research being conducted tends to determine the nature of possible contributions. The maturity of knowledge in a research area affects whether researchers engage in either theory building or theory testing. The link between maturity of knowledge and contribution has also been articulated in an operations and supply chain management setting. Boer et al. (2015) suggest that there are two fundamental and equally valid ways in which research contributes to theory:

- Through exploratory studies, observing and identifying interesting, relevant and potentially counterintuitive phenomena that cannot be explained well enough by existing theory, and thus proposing these for further testing.
- Through confirmatory studies, empirically testing propositions in a given context so as to refute, amend, expand or confirm them as new theory and to define the realm of the theory's applicability. These studies seek to test theory and describe its application in practice.

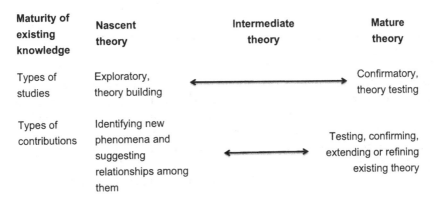

Figure 3.1 Linking contributions to the maturity of knowledge.

The relationship between the maturity of knowledge, types of studies and types of contributions is illustrated in Figure 3.1.

3.1.6 *Linking contributions to research philosophy*

Contributing to knowledge, finally, requires being mindful of the fundamental issues of meaning and knowledge, because what one considers a contribution depends on the position taken on fundamental issues of ontology and epistemology (Burrell and Morgan, 1979), concepts that were introduced in Chapter 2.

- Ontology refers to assumptions about the very essence of the phenomena under investigation. The basic question here is whether the reality to be investigated is external to the individual or the product of individual consciousness. Is reality a given, existing out there in the world, or the product of one's mind?
- Epistemology refers to assumptions about the nature and status of knowledge, and about how one might begin to understand the world and communicate this understanding as knowledge to fellow human beings. These assumptions entail ideas about what forms of knowledge can be reliably obtained and how one can sort out what is to be regarded as "true" from "false".

To put these philosophical ideas in more practical terms, first, do you think that scientific theories represent reality or not (the ontological question)? Second, do you think that scientific theories get closer and closer to the truth over time (the epistemological question)? Based on your answers to these two questions, Martin Kilduff suggests the following two extreme positions (Boer et al., 2015):

- If you answer yes to both questions, meaning that you think scientific theories represent reality and that these theories move ever closer to the truth, you are termed a *realist*. For a realist, a contribution consists of a better or more inclusive explanation of a phenomenon.
- If you answer no to both questions concerning ontology and epistemology, meaning that you accept no claims concerning theory's correspondence with reality or its approach to the truth, you are termed an *instrumentalist*. This means that you think

theories are useful instruments in helping to predict events and that a contribution involves providing a better predictive framework, model or theoretical tool that helps to solve an empirical problem, even if the framework incorporates wildly inaccurate representations of reality.

Considering the applied nature of operations and supply chain management, which stems from its dual heritage in both industrial engineering and the social sciences (Boer et al., 2015), it is possible to assume that many scholars take a realist perspective on the meaning of a contribution. Nevertheless, realism is not the only valid perspective on what a research contribution entails. In action research, for instance, where the philosophical perspective on research is different from that prevalent in realism, an important part of the contribution is actionable knowledge, as will be discussed in Chapter 7.

3.2 Choosing a research topic

Having discussed the nature of the outcome of the research process – the contribution – we can now turn to the start of the research process. Research often starts with a research topic. But we do not perform research on research topics, because research topics are too wide to be amenable to research. The topic provides the starting point; the research itself will be performed to answer more narrowly stated research questions. But before discussing research questions, let us start by discussing the nature of good research topics.

3.2.1 On the nature of research topics

Many research projects, especially PhD projects, start from a general area of interest: "I am doing research on supply chains in luxury fashion industries" or "I am interested in maintenance of rolling stock". It is natural to start out at this broad level. However, research topics must be more narrowly specified than a general area of interest. They should be stated with enough specificity that the researcher can become the leading expert on that topic (Booth et al., 2008).

One common source of research topics, particularly in operations and supply chain management, is practical problems. The real-life problems faced by organizations and managers drive much of our research, as discussed in Chapter 2. However, It is necessary to make a critical distinction between practical problems and research problems. Practical problems are *not* research problems. Practical problems are solved by action, by doing something that eliminates the cause of the problem. Research problems are defined by what you do not know or understand about something (Booth et al., 2008). We solve research problems by answering research questions that help us to understand the problem better. This is how we add to scholarly knowledge.

From this observation, it follows that practical problems *in themselves* do not form the basis for good research. A common mistake among PhD students, particularly those whose research is closely connected to one or several organizations, is to use a practical problem as the starting point for research. This approach is *not* sufficient to enable high-quality research.

Practical problems are an important input to research topics, but they need to be combined with literature. We may, for example, already know the answer to the practical problem an organization is facing. If that is the case, tying the research too closely to the practical problem would risk the contribution to knowledge to suffer. Only by linking

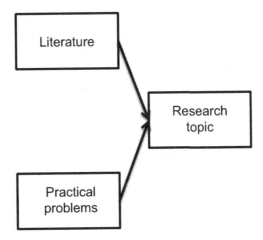

Figure 3.2 Research topics are defined by practical problems and existing literature.

practical problems and the existing research literature can we define research topics. These research topics will then form the basis for research questions, the answers to which contributes to knowledge. At the same time, the research answers should be addressing or perhaps even helping to solve our practical problems.

Practical problems alone can thus not form a basis for good research topics. The current state of knowledge is a fundamentally important basis. Gaining a systematic grasp of the relevant literature is therefore critically important. This notion is illustrated in Figure 3.2, which indicates that research topics have two sources, literature and practical problems.

Figure 3.2 is not intended to indicate a simple linear relationship between literature, practical problems and research topics. Often one must make several iterations between literature and practical problems in order to arrive at a suitably narrow research topic. This is the important process of funnelling, or moving from a broad area of interest to a narrowly defined research topic.

3.2.2 Sources of research topics

The sources of research topics can of course be many and varied. Often the broad definition of the research topic or area of interest is already given at the outset of a research project. Nevertheless, it is useful to consider where research topics can be generated. The following are merely examples, not an exhaustive list of sources.

- *Industry problems.* Problems experienced by practitioners can be an important source of both research topics and funding, as industry may wish to sponsor research towards solving these problems.
- *Industry trends.* Apart from specific problems, industry trends, or general areas of concern to managers and organizations, can be a fruitful source.
- *Literature studies.* Research topics can of course emerge directly from a literature review.
- *Previous research.* Some PhD students base their research on a topic that arose during their MSc work. Similarly, many experienced researchers find that new research topics emerge from ongoing research.

- *Personal experience.* The researcher's previous experience may also help to identify good research topics. One reason for initiating research may be a desire to learn how to deal with problems that one has experienced.
- *Networking.* Research topics can emerge from social networks and activities – friends, colleagues, conference presentations, supervisors, etc.
- *Funding bodies.* Numerous entities fund research studies, and often their calls for proposals can be a fruitful source of research topics, as they are directly linked to funding opportunities.

3.2.3 Characteristics of good research topics

In considering the suitability of a research topic, it is important to keep in mind that research needs to achieve the dual objectives of applied use and advancing fundamental understanding (Van de Ven & Johnson, 2006). This is particularly so in operations and supply chain management research, which generally has the twin aim of contributing to both research and practice. On the research contribution side, the fundamental question is whether the topic needs to be researched. To answer this question, we must review existing literature to determine whether knowledge of the topic is well developed and if there are opportunities for contributing new knowledge. On the practical side, we should consider whether the topic is of concern to practitioners, such as managers, policy leaders, and funding bodies.

If the research topic clears these two hurdles, there remains the question of whether the topic is suitable for research. On a general level, you must determine whether it is feasible to design a study that allows the topic to be researched. More specifically, do *you*, as an individual researcher, have the ability, access, and resources to design and carry out a study that would enable you to address the research topic in a suitable way?

Finally, the researcher's own interest is crucial. The research process involves living with a research topic for extended periods of time. Therefore, it is advisable that you yourself find the research topic interesting. For PhD students, it is helpful if your supervisor is interested in the topic. Finally, although this can be very difficult to judge, you may wish to consider whether the research topic will be of interest to the wider research community when you have completed your work and are ready to publish it.

3.3 Using literature to develop the research topic

A systematic grasp of existing literature is critical to contribute to knowledge, which means that reviewing literature is essential. Reviewing literature takes place throughout the research process, although it is usually more heavily emphasized during the early stages of research. There is often a need to continue searching the literature several times during the research process, particularly since the body of knowledge is growing at an increasingly rapid pace and new studies relevant to your work may be appearing.

This section will discuss several reasons for reviewing the literature thoroughly, along with strategies for finding literature, reading it, and managing the literature materials. These tasks may seem mundane, but they are critical to the quality of the research process. Finally, there is a discussion of various ways of using (and misusing) literature.

3.3.1 Reasons for conducting a literature review

Performing a literature review is important for several reasons. First, the literature helps to *define a researchable topic*. As already discussed, to understand whether there is an opportunity to make a contribution, we must review existing literature and identify what knowledge already exists. Our research must rest on a firm grasp of existing literature.

Second, existing literature can *inform our research*. It can provide inspiration for research topics, or concepts and constructs that we can reuse. We can learn from the methods employed in prior research and borrow from existing research protocols. Finally, we can find theories, models, and frameworks that we can use in our own research.

Last but not least, reviewing literature helps to *build critical researcher skills*. Reviewing large numbers of studies hones a researcher's ability to handle and classify large amounts of information. A good literature review also trains the researcher in critically evaluating existing knowledge, which is an important research skill.

3.3.2 Strategies for finding literature

In searching for literature, a strategy is often needed since accessing literature is getting increasingly easy, as technology develops, and as the rate at which literature is produced is increasing. There are several strategies. Probably the most obvious approach is to use one or more of the various databases of scientific literature that can be found online and in university libraries. However, other approaches can also be effective, especially at the outset when the literature search is still quite broad. Leading textbooks often point to the key literature in particular topic areas. Journals publish literature reviews on various topics. You may be able to locate PhD theses related to your research interest; if their authors have done their job well, their reference lists will direct you to useful literature. Colleagues, supervisors, and other researchers can also recommend key references.

Another useful source of assistance is librarians, who are experts in how to search for and find literature. And while you are at the library, browsing the shelves may cause you to discover some interesting books. Browsing can also be used with journals, whether in physical or electronic form. With help from colleagues, you will quickly identify the major journals that address your research topic. Going through the table of contents of these journals can often help to uncover important references.

Once you have become generally familiar with the literature and have narrowed your research topic, you will most likely find that a few individuals stand out as publishing key literature related to your topic. Scanning their CVs and personal homepages and perhaps contacting them to see what they are currently working on can be a fruitful way of staying up to date with the latest developments. Academic conferences are also valuable, as they feature research on which people are currently working and that has not yet been published. Even with the increasingly common practice of pre-publishing accepted journal papers, years can pass between first submission and the accepted final paper's appearance online.

Finally, once you have started to identify a number of important references, you can employ citation searches, either electronically through search engines and databases or by browsing the reference lists of the most important sources. Citation searches are an important way of refining the literature review.

3.3.3 Reviewing the literature systematically

The importance of systematic literature reviews is increasing in the management field (Tranfield et al., 2003). The systematic literature review was originally developed in medicine for the purpose of giving policy recommendations based on existing literature, through the application of a replicable, scientific, and transparent process for searching for and reviewing literature. There are clear advantages in following the practices employed in conducting a systematic literature review. The keywords to describe these practices are "rigorous" and "transparent".

Being systematic starts with planning the review. At this stage, having a review protocol is critical (Tranfield et al., 2003). The review protocol contains information on the search strategy for identifying relevant studies, along with the criteria for including or excluding studies considered for review. As flexibility is often necessary when you are conducting a literature review in a management discipline, it is important to explicitly state any changes in the search strategy and the rationale for these changes. The key point is that the protocol should not limit the researcher's creativity, but should accurately reflect the literature search activities conducted, so that other researchers can replicate the search.

During the actual search, rigor and transparency are again critical. A systematic search begins with identifying the keywords, search terms and search strings that are most appropriate for the study. The search strategy must be reported in sufficient detail to permit replication. It is also important to specify the sources used in the search. As for deciding what literature to include or exclude, it is very beneficial if multiple researchers can make these judgements independently. If this is not possible, the inclusion decision should be based on a set of predetermined criteria and checklists.

Finally, the need for rigor and transparency continues during the extraction of data from the literature. To reduce human error and bias, systematic reviews employ data extraction forms (Tranfield et al., 2003), which include essential source information (e.g. title, authors, journal, publication details) and any other features of the study that are considered important, such as the study context and an evaluation of the study's quality. The data extraction process requires documentation of all steps taken. Preferably, a double extraction process is employed, in which two independent assessors analyse a study, after which their findings are compared and, if necessary, reconciled.

3.3.4 Reading for a literature review

Your literature search will probably uncover hundreds of relevant papers and books. These all need to be read; but how? Start from the beginning and read until the end? Maybe not – unless you want to spend several years just reading, and probably you don't.

There is actually an important point in this whimsical comment. Beginner researchers often spend far too much time reading literature as part of their review. The key here is to be both effective and efficient. Developing speed-reading skills will greatly enhance your efficiency; the time you spend acquiring these skills will be saved multiple times over. But you do not want to miss anything important whilst reading, and hence you must also be effective.

With time and practice, you will develop your own way of reading effectively and efficiently. One suggestion, though, is to start by browsing the title and abstract, introduction, and conclusions of an article. Then speed-read to identify the most important parts for your research, the ones that you will go back and read in more detail. In this way, with experience, you can develop a good sense of an article in a surprisingly short time.

Reading for a literature review is a distinctive process. Conducting a literature review requires becoming familiar with large amounts of literature, to see the big picture and the trends in the literature. It also involves evaluating the research that you are reading, which is an important skill to spend time developing. Furthermore, reviewing literature generally involves several iterations, as you will discover new things along the way and may need to go back and review sources that you read earlier, but with a different purpose in mind.

A final important point on reading literature is that some key works will have to be read much more carefully, perhaps even several times. During your literature review, you will find that certain sources are absolutely critical to your research. They may be the ones closest to your own topic, or they may deal with important methodological issues or form important parts of your theoretical framework.

3.3.5 Managing the literature materials

Some wise person once said, "Research is 5% inspiration and 95% perspiration." This is certainly true at the literature review stage. Once you have successfully located and read the hundreds of papers and books that relate to your research, you now have to manage this vast source of information. Managing your literature database is a relatively mundane component of research but a very important one, as your bibliography represents a critical basis for your research.

The management of literature materials starts with note taking. As you read literature, you must apply a clear method of note taking. Most likely, your method will develop over time and will be highly personal. The important thing is to find a note-taking method that suits you and your needs. Nevertheless, a few pieces of advice may be useful.

First, be sure to separate the facts contained in the reference from your own interpretation of these facts, particularly since your interpretation may change over time. It is also important to keep eclectic notes, particularly at the beginning of the research process, as it will take some time before you have a clear idea of the key issues in the existing literature. These notes can be written directly on the source document, or they can be kept separate. Exactly how you do this may vary, but it is useful to keep notes that can be separated from the original reference, as doing so will simplify your process of analysing the literature.

Your method for managing the literature materials should also include a system for classifying the literature. Various items of information can be included, such as the author, title, keywords, date read, purpose, research methods employed, specific subject, key references, conclusions, and your analysis of the reference.

Whatever method of note taking and classification you employ, managing your literature materials is critical. It is thus essential to choose a software package to assist your management of materials early in the research process, learn how it is used, and ensure that all data records are properly maintained. As you continue to read and review literature, there will be times when you cannot remember where you found particular information. It is frustrating to know that you have read something but be unable to figure out where. You need to know the *where* in order to compile your own reference list. The investment you make in keeping your literature materials in order will prove very worthwhile.

There are many software packages for managing literature. When this chapter was written, some popular ones were the following:

- EndNote
- JabRef
- Mendeley

- Reference Manager
- RefWorks
- Qiqqa
- Zotero

Software for managing literature changes quickly, so it makes no sense here to offer specific recommendations. Talk to colleagues and other researchers and do some research on your own to find a package that suits your needs

3.3.6 The various ways to use existing literature

Existing literature can be used in many different ways, some of which are appropriate whilst others are not. Also, some ways of using literature are generic, whereas some depend on the research approach chosen.

A first use of existing literature, which cuts across research approaches, is to *motivate and position the research*. The importance of this activity was highlighted above when discussing the importance of combining practical problems with existing literature to arrive at research topics. The suggested research is motivated by reviewing the existing literature with a focus on understanding what research has already been conducted and what additions to this knowledge are needed. Reviewing literature to motivate the research is primarily an early-stage activity, although it can continue throughout the research process. In your final research product (your paper or thesis), the motivation and positioning of the research topic will always appear in an early section.

A second use of literature is to *create a framework for the research*. The framework can be seen as analogous to a pair of eyeglasses that the researcher puts on to study the chosen research topic. It is the theoretical toolbox that helps you study and understand the research problem, through determining what will be studied. The exact nature and application of the framework will vary.

In theory-developing research, the framework is usually less formal and can take on various forms. Nevertheless, the framework is likely to contain the main dimensions to be studied during data collection and analysis. The framework may also specify possible or suggested relationships between the dimensions. It can be useful, even in theory-developing research, to attempt to articulate the research focus by drawing a conceptual model, to illustrate the concepts and the relationships between them. Recognize, however, that your formulation of the conceptual model is likely to change during the research process, as your understanding of the research topic increases.

The research framework can be used to help you choose what data to collect. In this regard, it is important to keep the framework flexible. In case research, for instance, one needs to develop a framework before going into the field to collect data. Without a focus on what data to collect and where, there is a risk of missing important data. But the framework must also be flexible enough to permit adjusting the focus as the under-standing of the research topic develops. See Chapter 5 for further detail on this point.

The framework can also be used in the data analysis stage in theory-developing research. In that sense, existing literature is used as lenses to focus the actual analysis. This analysis process can be difficult to codify and explain, but the framework may, for instance, be used to define the concepts and the relationships between them during the analysis phase. Chapter 5 also contains more information on the data analysis stage in theory-developing case research.

In theory-testing research, the framework will be quite formal, with the concepts and the relationships between them often expressed as a research model accompanied by a series of hypotheses, which are tested using data. In theory-testing research, the research model is critical, since it is the foundation for construct development and for the data collection. If a survey is used to collect the data, the questions are designed based on the research model, which thus dictates what data are collected. In theory-testing research, the framework also acts as a guide for the data analysis. By having pre-defined constructs and relationships between these constructs, the analysis of the data is highly determined by the initial framework.

A third use of literature is to *support more hands-on "action" in the research*. In action research, for instance, existing literature can guide efforts to understand a system through actively trying to change it. More information on action research is provided in Chapter 7. In both theory-developing and theory-testing research, we can use existing constructs from literature. It is often very useful to spend time searching for existing constructs rather than reinventing the wheel yourself. This can help to ensure the quality of the research, as well as building cumulatively on previous research.

A fourth use of literature is for *interpreting and explaining research findings*. This use is particularly important in theory-developing research, for instance case research. Although researchers conducting case studies must go into the field with a clear idea of what they are looking for (based on their framework as discussed earlier), a new set of literature may be needed to understand and explain the findings that emerge from the research. You will find more information on how to do this in Chapters 5 and 6.

Finally, it is important to *discuss the research findings in relation to existing literature*. This step is critical in articulating and highlighting what the research contributes to the existing body of knowledge. In doing so, we should return to the same literature we used to motivate and position the research. At the start of the research process, we justified the need for our research by referencing existing literature; at the end of the research process, we need to return to this literature and explain what new knowledge our research has added. If you have specified your research specifically enough, you may find yourself clearly oriented towards making comparisons with a handful of key references at this stage.

3.3.7 *Ways of misusing literature*

Having discussed how literature can be properly used in multiple ways, depending in part on the research approach employed, the discussion now turns to ways of misusing literature. One common mistake is to *only describe literature and not analyse it*. A literature review involves more than merely describing and citing literature. The literature should be critically analysed, addressing such questions as what has been done, how and why. A literature review should also include discussions of what in current literature is good or less good and (most importantly) what is missing.

Another mistake is to *simply review literature without using it*. For instance, one student wrote, "My research touches on different literature", and then went on to describe various theories, but without making any connection between these theories and the proposed research. In other words, the literature was not put to any use. A literature review is not just an occasion to show that you have read certain literature; you must also show *how* you will draw on this literature in your own research. Researchers often refer to literature reviews as providing a theoretical foundation for their research, but this makes no sense unless the theory reviewed actually is used.

Table 3.1 Ways of using and misusing literature

Using literature	Misusing literature
Motivating and positioning the research.	Only describing literature and not analysing it.
Creating a framework for the research.	Reviewing literature without using it.
Borrowing existing concepts and constructs.	Employing too many (perhaps even
Interpreting and explaining the research findings.	incompatible) grand theories.
	Citing high-level theories as a guise for
Discussing the research findings in relation to existing literature	contributing to theory

Another pitfall is to *employ too many (perhaps even incompatible) grand theories*. It has become increasingly common for operations and supply chain management researchers to borrow theory from other disciplines – referring, for instance, to dynamic capabilities, transaction cost economics, or network theory. This is not necessarily a problem in itself, but it is important to realize that although grand theories can be useful, it is generally not possible to use more than a few (or perhaps even more than one) at a time. Theories can be both empowering and constraining, as they come with a set of assumptions regarding methods, constructs, worldviews, and explanations. Some of these features in different theories may not even be compatible. It is important to be a critical consumer of theory and not refer to certain grand theories just because everyone else does. Dynamic capabilities may be important, but that does not mean that all researchers can or should attempt to use it.

Another particularly problematic misuse of literature occurs if the *usage of high-level theories is taken as a guise for contributing to theory*. Commonly this error results in researchers attempting to contribute to high-level theories, rather than focusing on the mid-range theories that are more specific and possibly more relevant to the problem at hand. It is virtually impossible to make a significant contribution to those high-level theories that are so fundamental in explaining how businesses operate as to be almost tautological (Boer et al., 2015). There is also a risk that importing theory from outside of the discipline risks going beyond the boundaries of validity of these particular theories.

Table 3.1 summarizes the discussion on the various ways of using, and misusing, literature.

3.4 Developing research questions

If you have only a research topic to guide the research, you may find endless data and never know when you have enough (Booth et al., 2008). This is where research questions are important. Research questions help you narrow your search to the data that you need to answer the question. They bring focus to a study and narrow the research topic to a meaningful and manageable size (Edmondson and McManus, 2007). Therefore, the formulation of research questions is an important activity in the research process. But formulating research questions, and particularly good ones, is also a challenging task, particularly for a PhD student. In fact, there is no surer way to make a PhD student sweat than by asking, "So what is your research question?" This part of the chapter will help you develop your research question.

The first and most important thing to note about research questions in operations and supply chain management is that, like the research topics from which they follow, they tend to be grounded in both practical problems and literature (see Figure 3.3).

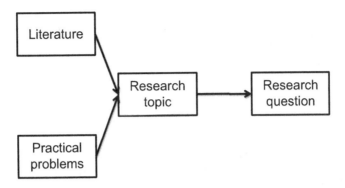

Figure 3.3 Research questions are motivated by practical problems and existing literature.

3.4.1 *What research questions are not*

To better understand the nature of research questions, it is useful to understand what research questions are not. Research questions are fundamental in bringing focus to research. Other mechanisms that help to achieve this focus are referred to with the terms *purpose, aim, propositions,* and *hypotheses.* All of these are important too, but they do not replace the need for clearly specified research questions.

First, a research purpose is not the same thing as a research question. You answer a research question through your research. At the same time, the research also has a purpose, which typically comprises a statement of what the research is trying to achieve and how this end is to be achieved.

Here is the purpose statement from my own PhD thesis: "The purpose of the present study is to determine sequences of Lean production principles through an examination of the patterns of issues in the adoption process." I do not mean to present this rather complex sentence as an exemplar, but simply as an example of how a purpose statement is formulated. It is clearly not a research question, although the two are related. Somewhere underlying this purpose is a research question.

What about a "research aim"? According to the Oxford Advanced Learner's Dictionary, an aim is "the purpose of doing something; what somebody is trying to achieve". The similarity between aim and purpose is readily apparent. According to the Oxford Advanced Learner's Dictionary, purpose is "the intention, aim or function of something; the thing that something is supposed to achieve". The two words thus seem virtually identical. Indeed, the terms *research purpose* and *research aim* are used interchangeably by many researchers. However, they are not always expressed in the same way, and this can be confusing. As a possible, albeit slight, distinction, *research aim* may be used to express the desired end of the research, or what the research seeks to deliver. *Research purpose*, on the other hand, can be used to describe what the research intends to achieve and how.

Research propositions and hypotheses are the last two terms that should not be confused with research questions. Propositions and hypotheses are both related to theory, but propositions involve concepts whereas hypotheses require measures and specify in greater detail than propositions the relationships to be tested. Both propositions and hypotheses can be the starting point for research, particularly theory-testing research. Propositions can also be where the research ends up, for instance in case research. Nevertheless, research questions are still needed.

3.4.2 Types and forms of research questions

The range of potential research questions is virtually endless, but they can generally be categorized into four types:

1 Exploratory
2 Descriptive
3 Explanatory
4 Prescriptive

Regardless of the type, a research question has both substance and form (Yin, 2003). Substance refers to the focus of the study – what the study is about. With regard to form, there are six basic questions: *who, what, where, when, how,* and *why.* The first two forms of research questions (who and what) can come in two derivative forms, through adding the questions "how many" and "how much".

There is a relationship between the type and form of research questions. The first four forms of research questions (who, what, where, and when) can be both exploratory and descriptive. The final two questions (how and why) are more explanatory, in that they deal with links between concepts, rather than with mere frequencies or incidences.

Since the possibilities for legitimate research questions are so vast, it is impossible to stipulate any general guidelines on their exact formulation. However, it is easier to describe examples of research questions that should be avoided (Booth et al., 2008):

- Avoid research questions to which you could simply look up the answer. Research questions that ask *how* and *why* invite deeper thinking than *who, what, when* or *where* questions, and deeper thinking tends to lead to more interesting answers.
- Avoid research questions whose answers could only be speculative; if you cannot find data, you cannot answer the question.
- Avoid research questions of a dead-end nature, i.e. questions that, when answered, would likely cause readers to think "so what?"

The precise research question is often formulated quite late in the research process. As the research question helps to focus the research and particularly the data collection, it is of course necessary to have a general idea of the question early on, but the exact formulation may come much later. This decision will depend in part on the research approach selected and the inherent flexibility contained in the research approach for developing the question as the research process moves on. Case research, longitudinal field studies, action research and clinical research are all research approaches in which the exact formulation of the research question can take place later in the research process.

3.4.3 Research questions depend on maturity of knowledge

It was noted earlier that the maturity of knowledge of a particular topic tends to determine the nature of the possible contribution. Since there is a natural link between research questions and contributions, as the answers to the questions posed determine the contribution, research questions also tend to depend on the maturity of knowledge. Using the same gradations of knowledge maturity as previously, Figure 3.4 illustrates the relationship between the type of research question and the maturity of existing knowledge.

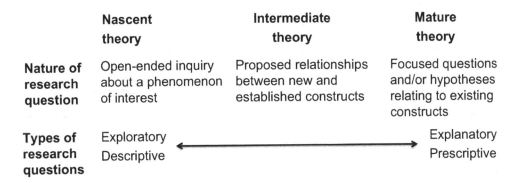

	Nascent theory	Intermediate theory	Mature theory
Nature of research question	Open-ended inquiry about a phenomenon of interest	Proposed relationships between new and established constructs	Focused questions and/or hypotheses relating to existing constructs
Types of research questions	Exploratory Descriptive	⟵⟶	Explanatory Prescriptive

Figure 3.4 Research questions depend on maturity of knowledge.

Source: Adapted from Edmondson and McManus (2007).

3.4.4 Framing: using literature to construct the research question

Existing literature provides key input into the formulation of a research question. By positioning the research question in relation to existing literature, the researcher can construct an argument as to why the particular research question is worth the effort. There are various methods of making this argument, or framing the research question. The clearly dominant way of constructing research questions is "gap spotting" (Sandberg and Alvesson, 2011). Jörgen Sandberg and Mats Alvesson describe three main ways in which researchers can justify their research question by articulating gaps in existing literature. The three are not mutually exclusive. They are summarized in Table 3.2 and explained below.

3.4.4.1 Neglect spotting

Here the researcher identifies a research topic where no (good) research has been carried out. The aim is to find a white spot on the knowledge map, a gap that can be filled by answering the research question posed by the researcher. More specifically, the researcher can search for areas in existing literature that have been *overlooked* or *under-researched* or that *lack empirical support*.

3.4.4.2 Confusion spotting

Here the researcher identifies some kind of confusion in existing literature by identifying previous research on the topic and concluding that available evidence is contradictory. Typically, constructing research questions in this way entails describing *competing explanations* in existing literature. The research question aims to sort out the identified confusion in the literature and to explain it.

3.4.4.3 Application spotting

Here the researcher identifies a new application in existing literature. It involves searching for a shortage of a particular theory or perspective in a specific research area, arguing that the literature needs to be *extended* or *complemented* in some way. The researcher's task is then to provide an alternative perspective to further our understanding.

While these means of identifying gaps in existing literature provide the justification for the vast majority of research, Sandberg and Alvesson (2011) also suggest an alternative approach, problematization. They argue that problematization is particularly relevant for

Table 3.2 Ways of constructing research questions through gap spotting

Basic gap spotting modes	Specific versions of basic gap spotting modes
Neglect spotting	Looking for areas in existing literature that are overlooked or under-researched or that lack empirical support
Confusion spotting	Looking for competing explanations in existing literature
Application spotting	Extending and complementing existing literature

Source: Adapted from Sandberg and Alvesson (2011).

theory building. It involves identifying and challenging the assumptions that underlie existing theory and, based on that challenge, seeking to formulate more informed and novel research questions.

3.5 Considerations in choosing a research approach

The last general consideration in the research process is to choose a research approach. One underlying and very important message of this book is that research approaches are not good or bad in themselves. Different approaches have different strengths and weaknesses. George Homans expressed this truth very well already in 1949: "People who write about methodology often forget that it is a matter of strategy, not of morals. There are neither good nor bad methods but only methods that are more or less effective under particular circumstances" (Homans, 1949, p. 330).

Subsequent chapters of this book will describe in detail the characteristics of different research approaches and what is necessary to execute each of them with excellent quality. Each chapter will give also the reader a good understanding of when to choose a particular approach. Here, I will focus on describing three overall considerations in deciding on a research approach: first, the notion of methodological fit and how it should guide this decision; second, the importance of the philosophical position that the researcher takes; and third, some practical considerations that can play an important role in the selection of a research approach.

3.5.1 Methodological fit

The core of the notion of methodological fit is that there should be internal consistency among all the main elements of a research project – i.e. research question, maturity of existing knowledge, research approach and contribution (Edmondson and McManus, 2007). The notion of methodological fit was introduced in Chapter 2, where the need to find a fit between the problem, method, and contribution was discussed. The aim here is to develop this discussion and also to link it to some of the ideas presented earlier in this chapter. The notion of methodological fit is illustrated in Figure 3.5.

The key theme of Figure 3.5 is internal consistency. The double-headed arrows signify that all the different elements should fit together. Chapter 2 pointed out that the research process may start at different places, particularly for a beginning PhD student. Perhaps there already exists a dataset collected as part of an ongoing research project. If so, the research approach may already have been decided. In this case, it is still necessary to ensure that the research question asked fits the research approach and the data collected as part of the approach, as well as the maturity level of existing knowledge and the possible contribution that can be made.

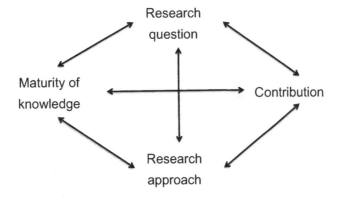

Figure 3.5 Methodological fit – internal consistency between key elements of a research project.

Figure 3.5 does not imply that any of the four elements included takes temporal precedence over the others. Methodological fit is often achieved in an iterative manner, as explained in Chapter 2. However, in any research, a thorough grasp of existing literature on the chosen research topic is absolutely critical. Only through understanding what research already exists on a topic can a researcher develop and refine effective research questions (Edmondson and McManus, 2007).

Consistency among the elements in Figure 3.5 involves six different dyadic relationships. Two of these have already been addressed, namely the relationship between maturity of knowledge and both (a) types of contributions and (b) types of research questions. The focus here is on the relationship between maturity of knowledge and the research approach, as this is an important relationship that links the research approach to the research questions and contributions. The following discussion of this relationship is based on Figure 3.6, which illustrates the notion that different research approaches tend to be used at different levels of maturity of knowledge.

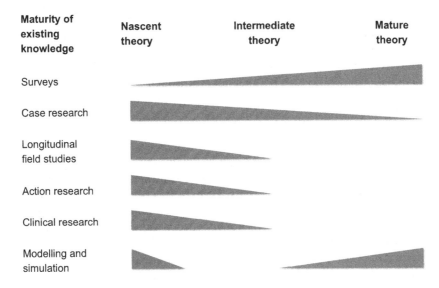

Figure 3.6 The relationship between existing knowledge and research approach.

The shaded areas in Figure 3.6 illustrate when a particular research approach is likely to be used. For instance, surveys may be used when the existing knowledge of a phenomenon has developed beyond the nascent stage and is entering the intermediate stage. At this point, there are provisional explanations of phenomena and some constructs have been defined. But most often, surveys are employed in the theory-testing stage, where the existing knowledge of a phenomenon is mature. Surveys can also be used in the development of knowledge – Chapter 4 discusses their use for descriptive and exploratory purposes – but this is less common.

Subsequent chapters will describe how and when different research approaches are most applicable. As shown in Figure 3.6, each research approach can be used at different levels of maturity of knowledge, but the use of each approach tends to follow particular patterns. Case research, to take a second example, can be used for testing and refining theory, as discussed in Chapter 5; however, case research tends to be used for more exploratory and theory-building purposes.

The three approaches of longitudinal field studies, action research, and clinical research share a common characteristic. The very nature of these approaches and the in-depth data that they provide make them suitable at the early stages of the development of knowledge of a particular phenomenon. This fact does not rule out their applicability at more mature stages of knowledge development, but they are much less frequently used in such situations.

Finally, simulation and modelling are used when the existing knowledge of a phenomenon is fairly mature, although their application does depend on the type of model developed and it is also possible to use modelling at an early stage of knowledge development, as illustrated in Figure 3.6.

3.5.2 *Philosophical position*

The choice of research approach also needs to reflect the researcher's position with regard to the fundamental issues of ontology and epistemology, or what can be termed one's "philosophical position". Based on the view taken of the world and how knowledge of the world is won, it is possible to develop a notion of different philosophical positions (Burrell and Morgan, 1979). There are different ways of expressing these positions, but for the sake of simplicity, we can use a continuum with two endpoints: the positivist researcher and the interpretative researcher.

The positivist researcher sees reality as objective (Gephart, 2004): the world is external to the individual. This reality can be understood through research. The emphasis is on observable facts, derived from valid and reliable measurement. The goal is to discover objective truth, providing results and conclusions that are replicable, verifiable, and generalizable.

The positivist philosophical position tends to be highly prevalent in operations and supply chain management research, although the reason for this dominance is hard to pin down. Perhaps it is related to the history of the discipline, with its firm basis in industrial engineering, apart from its social science roots. Perhaps it is because the nature of what we study often involves socio-technical systems that consist of both social actors and technical artefacts. Regardless, the term *positivist* is not intended in any derogatory sense, but merely as a descriptive representation of the views taken with regards to ontology and epistemology.

The interpretative researcher, on the other hand, assumes that reality is socially constructed (Berger and Luckmann, 1967). Reality is not objective or "out there" but exists as multiple local, intersubjective realities composed from subjective and objective meanings (Gephart, 2004). The researcher's task is to produce descriptions of organizational members' meanings and definitions of a situation and to understand how they construct their reality. Research therefore becomes dependent upon the researcher as a participant. All observation and analysis is considered to be socially constructed, and research is concerned with providing an interpretation of the research phenomenon.

There is of course a question whether these two philosophical positions represent distinct, irreconcilable positions with no possible middle ground or endpoints of a continuum. On a philosophical level, this is probably a very hard question to answer. On a more practical level, the question may not be so important, particularly for a PhD student. Trying to address one's own philosophical position can cause much confusion early in the research process. Insufficient experience in research makes it hard for a young scholar to settle on any one specific philosophical position. Usually, only after one has conducted extensive research does it become possible to define one's own position. One may also feel uncomfortable with both extremes, believing that one's own perspective on ontology and epistemology may not fit well with either endpoint.

The importance of raising the issue of one's philosophical position in relation to the research approach is related to the notion of "fit". The message is not that you must find a philosophical label to place on your research. Rather, it is crucial to ensure consistency between the philosophical position and the research approach. This consistency has many facets, but primarily it involves how data are gathered and analysed. There is no "right" philosophical position; the important thing is to make up your mind on how you view the world and how knowledge of it can be gained, and then conduct your research in a way that is consistent with the implications of this position.

3.5.3 *Practical considerations in choosing a research approach*

Finally, there are several practical considerations in choosing a research approach. Three such factors will be considered here: (a) access, (b) institutional factors, and (c) skills and interests. These can at times be very important in determining a research approach or can at least put clear boundaries on what research approaches are feasible.

3.5.3.1 *Gaining access to data*

You may think that you have spotted a wonderful opportunity to make a splendid contribution to knowledge, but making the contribution requires access to data. Access must be considered early in study design, as lack of access can ruin the best research plans. But access to data can also be a starting point for good research. Perhaps you are fortunate enough to gain access to data not normally open for research. This opportunity may help you design a study that makes a valuable contribution to knowledge. Unfortunately, however, access to data is more often a constraining rather than an empowering factor.

All research approaches are subject to various kinds of access issues. For example, the use of surveys poses the challenge of eliciting a sufficient response rate, as discussed in Chapter 4. Researchers using the case study method will need to gain access to suitable cases. Chapter 5 discusses strategies for gaining access to cases, particularly in situations when the cases are chosen based on the research questions and not (as unfortunately is sometimes the practice) based on convenience.

Researchers conducting longitudinal field studies, action research, or clinical research tend to face even larger difficulties with regard to access to organizations. This is because these three research approaches tend to demand longer periods of interaction with organizations and hence demand more of their time. Moreover, action research and clinical research are built on the premise that the researcher will make a contribution to the organization. This feature, paradoxically, can become a clear threat to gaining access, as well as an incentive encouraging access. Issues of access in relation to these more interactive research approaches are discussed in Chapters 7 and 8.

Simulation and modelling can also present difficulties in gaining access to data. Clearly, there are no such problems if the researcher works entirely in the conceptual domain. However, if the researcher wishes to develop and/or test the model using real data, these data must be available. Even if one has successfully negotiated the needed access to information from one or more organizations, there remains the issue of getting suitable data without confounding "noise". Finally, for extensive computations and model-building scenarios, access to sufficient computing power may be a challenge.

3.5.3.2 Considering institutional factors

Institutional factors related to the research environment may also affect the selection of research approach. You may be working on a project as part of a research group or a larger department. You are certainly associated with a university or another type of research institution and may be working more or less closely with one or more colleagues. At all these levels, there may be different views with regard to such questions as the following:

• What is good research?
• What research approaches are appropriate?
• What kinds of research questions should be pursued?
• What types of industries should be researched?

The preferred answers to these questions may be more or less explicit. But even if they are only implicit, they do exist, perhaps as taken-for-granted assumptions that are part of the culture of the research project, research group, or academic department.

Institutional factors can have a positive impact by cultivating an aspiring researcher's understanding of how to do research. Also, you may have intentionally chosen your research environment because of your alignment with that setting's answers to the questions listed above. There is a certain amount of self-selection here; people tend to choose a research environment that they find well-suited to their interests.

However, institutional factors can become problematic if one wants to do research that is seen as deviating too far from the norm. Imagine, for example, what would happen if you wanted to do action research in a group where everyone is doing surveys, or clinical research in a setting where mathematical modelling is the norm?

I am exaggerating for the point of emphasis. Still, the problem can be real; if your research approach is seen as deviating too much from the norm, there can be issues. These issues may not (or at least they should not) arise due to any ill intent, particularly if the research environment scores high on intellectual curiosity. But there may simply not be enough competence and experience in that environment to support your interests properly. It is of course hard to give advice on how to act in such a situation, but the important message here is that institutional factors can greatly affect one's latitude as to selection of a research approach and that therefore these factors may need to be anticipated and managed.

3.5.3.3 Considering your own interests and skills

The final practical consideration in choosing a research approach is to consider your own interest and skills. This advice may sound fairly obvious, but it should not be underestimated. The research process is long and can be very uncertain. Just as your interest in the research topic is important to sustain your motivation, so is your interest in executing the chosen research approach. If you are not particularly keen on your research approach at the outset, you will not like it any better at the end.

Your skills are equally important because once you have chosen a particular research approach you will need to learn how to execute it. Especially if this research is your PhD project, your choice may be driven in part by your desire to learn. Nevertheless, it is important for you to understand what skills are needed to execute a given approach, if for no other reason than self-preservation reason if you do not want to subject yourself to performing tasks that lie far outside your comfort zone. The chapters in this book on the various research approaches will provide more information on the skills required to execute each approach. Here I will merely outline the key skills involved.

To conduct high-quality survey research, you must be patient, structured, and systematic. High-quality survey development demands repeated iterations between existing literature and survey design, and this process takes time and requires the researcher to remain up-to-date on pertinent literature. It is misleadingly easy to compose a survey and send it out, only to find that the data collected are nowhere near robust enough to be publishable. Thus, the design must be painstakingly systematic. You also need patience and a certain amount of social and people skills to solicit good responses, particularly if conducting face-to-face interviews. Finally, strong statistical skills are needed to analyse the data.

The case researcher first of all needs to be able to negotiate access to organizations. There is also a need for social and people skills, not only for initial access but also because much of the success in gathering data rests on building relationships with people. Since the main (though not the only) method of data collection in case research tends to be interviews, excellent interviewing skills are essential, including the ability to ask relevant questions, listen actively to answers and be flexible enough to both follow and guide the interviewee. The case researcher needs to be a bit like a journalist, both in collecting the data and writing up the results. There are few standard formats for writing up case research, so the researcher faces the challenge of convincing readers that the conclusions reached are trustworthy. In terms of conducting the analysis, the case researcher must have a high tolerance for ambiguity and must be able to perceive patterns, often in massive amounts of unstructured data. This requires a well-developed analytical ability.

The action researcher needs skills similar to those of the case researcher. Since the action researcher needs to develop relationships with organization members to an even larger extent than the case researcher, people, and social skills are crucial. What sets the action researcher's role apart is the need for political and interventionist skills in order to identify and pursue appropriate action. Taking such action also requires making ethical judgements, excelling in communication and collaboration, and being able to reflect on your own actions and their consequences. Considerable knowledge of the particular problem area being addressed is also necessary. These traits presume a high level of personal and intellectual maturity. In terms of data collection, systematic journal keeping is crucial. Finally, the action researcher needs a very high tolerance for uncertainty and ambiguity, as the research process is very hard to control and evolve in unanticipated directions.

The clinical researcher needs very similar skills to those of the action researcher, as the two research methods share many features in terms of the researcher's role and how data are collected, even though the approaches are distinct as explained in Chapter 8.

The longitudinal field researcher needs to blend the skills of the case researcher and the action researcher. As explained in Chapter 6, the defining feature of longitudinal field research is that the researcher studies an evolving phenomenon, often a change process, longitudinally and in real time. The study often takes place over an extended period of time. Given the long-term interpersonal relationships involved, the need for social and people skills becomes pronounced. Even if the researcher is not personally involved in taking action, just spending long periods of time in an organization will require good political skills. In terms of data analysis, high tolerance for ambiguity is again essential. Since the extended period of time spent in the organization tends to generate large amounts of unstructured data without any pre-defined methods for analysing the data, the level of ambiguity tends to be very high.

Finally, the researcher interested in using simulation and/or modelling as a research approach needs superior skills in mathematics, programming, and simulation. To construct good models, the ability to abstract reality into a model is crucial. Sufficient understanding of the practical problem that forms the basis for the research is also needed.

3.6 Chapter summary: Completing the research cycle

This chapter has focused on a set of key activities in the early parts of the research process. The first activity was *understanding the nature of contributions,* the end product of the research process. The contention was that it is possible to contribute to knowledge in ways other than the daunting task of developing theory. Several terms that are often confused with theory were presented and defined, such as propositions, models, taxonomies, and frameworks. All of these can constitute important contributions. Other ways of making contributions to knowledge include the following:

- Adding or subtracting factors from an existing theory.
- Addressing the domain limitations of the theory by addressing questions such as what practices and methods apply in which contexts.
- Finding facts through discovery, employing precise definitions and well-defined domains.

It was observed that contributions are linked to the maturity of knowledge and to one's research philosophy, implying that the judgement of what constitutes a contribution is ultimately in the eyes of the beholder.

The second part of the chapter focused on *choosing a research topic*, the start of the research process. It was stressed that the research topic should be formulated quite narrowly. Although research topics in operations and supply chain management often originate from practical problems, these problems need to be combined with literature to create a good basis for research. The current state of knowledge on the topic is critical. There are many potential sources of research topics. In choosing a topic, it is important to understand whether there is a need for research on the topic and whether the topic is suitable for research.

The third part of the chapter addressed the *literature review and the various ways of using (and misusing) literature*. Strategies for finding, reading, and managing literature were presented. Particular emphasis was placed on the need to review the literature systematically, with rigor and transparency. Common ways of both using and misusing literature were described.

The fourth part of the chapter considered the task of *developing research questions*, which helps to bring focus to a study and narrows the research topic to a meaningful and manageable size. Research questions have both substance (the focus of the study) and form (who, what, where, when, how, and why). Four types of research questions were identified: exploratory, descriptive, explanatory, and prescriptive. The type of research questions appropriate for a given project was found to depend, in part, on the maturity of knowledge. Finally, various ways of using literature to motivate research questions were discussed. They were all versions of spotting a gap in existing literature, such as identifying areas that have been overlooked or under-researched, that lack empirical support or where there are competing explanations in existing literature.

The final part of the chapter addressed three *considerations in choosing a research approach*. The first consideration was the importance of achieving methodological fit, or internal consistency among the following elements: research question, maturity of existing knowledge, research approach, and contribution. Particular emphasis was paid to the relationship between maturity of existing knowledge and the research approach. Second, the importance of the researcher's philosophical position was highlighted. Third, several practical considerations in choosing a research approach were discussed: access to data, institutional factors, and the researcher's own interests and skills.

Having discussed the five general activities in the research process, it is now possible to complete the depiction of the "research cycle", as illustrated in Figure 3.7. The figure portrays the relationship between key concepts and activities in the research process.

The starting point in Figure 3.7 is the intersection between practical problems and literature, from which we define research topics in operations and supply chain management. Practical problems alone are not enough to undergird high-quality research; we

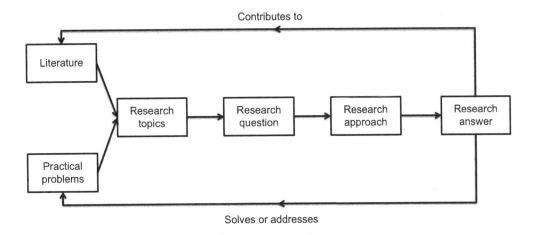

Figure 3.7 Completing the research cycle.

need a systematic grasp of existing literature to define suitable research topics. Although research topics are the starting point, they are too wide to be amenable to research. Therefore, good research involves answering research questions, which are constructed to help us narrow our search to those data that we need to answer our question.

Based on the research question, we then select a research approach. Here it is important to ensure internal consistency between the research approach, the research question, the maturity of existing knowledge, and the potential contribution. The execution of the research approach, particularly data collection and analysis, leads to answering the research question we posed.

The research answer forms the basis for a contribution. Now that we have an answer to the question, we need to close the loop, or complete the research cycle. The contribution need to be positioned against and related to existing literature. Ideally, the contribution should also contribute to solving or addressing the practical problems that initially motivated the research.

References

Berger, P. L. and Luckmann, T. (1967), *The social construction of reality: A treatise in the sociology of knowledge*, Garden City, NY: Doubleday.

Boer, H., Holweg, M., Kilduff, M., Pagell, M., Schmenner, R. and Voss, C. A. (2015), 'Making a meaningful contribution to theory', *International Journal of Operations and Production Management*, 35(9): 1231–1252.

Booth, W. C., Colomb, G. G. and Williams, J. M. (2008), *The craft of research* (3rd edition), Chicago: University of Chicago Press.

Burrell, G. and Morgan, G. (1979), *Sociological paradigms and organisational analysis*, London: Heinemann.

Edmondson, A. C. and McManus, S. E. (2007), 'Methodological fit in management field research', *Academy of Management Review*, 32(4): 1246–1264.

Gephart, R. P. (2004), 'Qualitative research and the Academy of Management Journal', *Academy of Management Journal*, 47(4): 454–462.

Homans, G. C. (1949), 'The strategy of industrial sociology', *American Journal of Sociology*, 54: 330–337.

Markus, M. L. and Robey, D. (1988), 'Information technology and organizational change: Causal structure in theory and research', *Management Science*, 34(5): 583–598.

Miles, M. B. and Huberman, A. M. (1994), *Qualitative data analysis: An expanded sourcebook*, Thousand Oaks, CA: Sage.

Miller, J. G. and Roth, A. V. (1994), 'A taxonomy of manufacturing strategies', *Management Science*, 40(3): 285–304.

Mitroff, I. I., Betz, F., Pondy, L. R. and Sagasti, F. (1974), 'On managing science in the systems age: Two schemas for the study of science as a whole systems phenomenon', *Interfaces*, 4(3): 46–58.

Sandberg, J. and Alvesson, M. (2011), 'Ways of constructing research questions: Gap-spotting or problematization?' *Organization*, 18(1): 23–44.

Schmenner, R. W. and Swink, M. L. (1998), 'On theory in operations management', *Journal of Operations Management*, 17(1): 97–113.

Schmenner, R. W., Van Wassenhove, L., Ketokivi, M., Heyl, J. and Lusch, R. F. (2009), 'Too much theory, not enough understanding', *Journal of Operations Management*, 27(5): 339–343.

Sousa, R. and Voss, C. A. (2008), 'Contingency research in operations management practices', *Journal of Operations Management*, 26(6): 697–713.

Sutton, R. I. and Staw, B. M. (1995), 'What theory is not', *Administrative Science Quarterly*, 40(3): 371–384.

Tranfield, D. R., Denyer, D. and Smart, P. (2003), 'Towards a methodology for developing evidence-informed management knowledge by means of systematic review', *British Journal of Management*, 14: 207–222.

Van de Ven, A. H. (1989), 'Nothing is quite so practical as a good theory', *Academy of Management Review*, 14(4): 486–489.

Van de Ven, A. H. and Johnson, P. E. (2006), 'Knowledge for theory and practice', *Academy of Management Review*, 31(4): 802–821.

Wacker, J. G. (1998), 'A definition of theory: Research guidelines for different theory-building research methods in operations management', *Journal of Operations Management*, 16(4): 361–385.

Whetten, D. A. (1989), 'What constitutes a theoretical contribution?', *Academy of Management Review*, 14(4): 490–495.

Yin, R. K. (2003), *Case study research: Design and methods*, Thousand Oaks, CA: Sage.

4 Surveys

Cipriano Forza and Enrico Sandrin

Chapter overview[1]

4.1 When to use survey research
4.2 The survey research process
4.3 What is needed prior to survey research design

- The theoretical model
- Defining the unit of analysis
- Developing and testing the operational definitions
- Stating the hypotheses

4.4 Designing a survey

- Considering constraints and information needs
- Planning the activities
- Designing the sample
- Choosing the data collection method
- Developing the measurement instrument
- Defining how to approach companies and respondents

4.5 Pilot testing the questionnaire

- Handling non-respondents and non-response bias
- Inputting and cleaning data
- Assessing the measurement validity and reliability

4.6 Advanced issues in theory formalization and survey design
4.7 Survey execution
4.8 Data analysis and interpretation of results
4.9 What information should be reported in research articles
4.10 Ethical issues in survey research

DOI: 10.4324/9781003315001-4

4.1 Introduction

A comparison of contemporary research in operations management (OM) and supply chain management (SCM) with that conducted in the early 1980s reveals an increase in the use of empirical data (derived from field observation) to supplement mathematics, modelling and simulation in order to develop and test theories (Craighead and Meredith, 2008). Many authors have called for this empirical research since OM became an established field of study (such as marketing, management information systems, etc.) within the management discipline (Meredith et al., 1989; Flynn et al., 1990; Filippini, 1997; Scudder and Hill, 1998). The rationale was to reduce the gap between management theory and practice, to increase the usefulness of operations and supply chain management (OSCM) research to practitioners and, more recently, to increase the scientific recognition of the OSCM fields. Survey research is one of the methods widely used to perform this empirical research in OSCM.

4.1.1 *What survey research is and for what purposes it can be used*

In OSCM, as in other fields of business, research can be undertaken to solve an existing problem in a work setting. This chapter focuses on survey research conducted for a different reason: to contribute to the general body of knowledge in a particular area of interest. In general, a survey involves the collection of information from individuals (through the web or mailed questionnaires, telephone calls, personal interviews, etc.) about themselves or about the social units to which they belong (Rossi et al., 1983). Usually, information is collected only about a subset (a sample) of elements belonging to an entire group of people, firms, plants or things that the researcher aims to investigate. The selection of the sample is made according to certain rules so that the researcher can obtain information with a known level of accuracy about large populations (Rea and Parker, 1992).

Survey research, like other types of field studies, can contribute to advancing scientific knowledge in different ways (Kerlinger, 1986; Babbie, 1990). Accordingly, researchers often distinguish between exploratory, confirmatory (theory testing) and descriptive survey research (Pinsonneault and Kraemer, 1993; Filippini, 1997; Malhotra and Grover, 1998).

Exploratory survey research takes place during the early stages of research on a phenomenon when the objective is to gain preliminary insight into a topic, and provides the basis for more in-depth survey research. Usually, there is no model and the concepts of interest need to be better understood and measured. In the very preliminary stages of inquiry, an exploratory survey can help researchers determine which concepts to measure in relation to the phenomenon of interest, the best way to measure them, and how to discover new facets of the phenomenon under investigation. Subsequently, an exploratory survey can be used to uncover or provide preliminary evidence of associations among concepts. Later, it can help researchers explore the validity boundaries of a theory. In the last two cases, models and measures are clearly more advanced than in the first case.

In OSCM, new topics continuously arise that have been scarcely researched or have not been researched at all in the past, thus requiring exploratory research. Configuration of products and services is an example of such an issue that has been brought to the attention of the OM, SCM, and marketing communities in the early 2000s. In framing exploratory survey research on this issue, and in specifying its intended contribution, Salvador and Forza (2004: 276, 289) wrote as follows:

As a whole, the examples present in the literature suggest that engineering a company's operations in order to get the maximum potential benefits out of product configuration might be a challenging task for a company. We do not know, however, where and to what extent the issues reported in individual cases may be generalized to a larger population of companies [...] Because of the embryonic stage of published research on the impact of product configuration on operations, the nature of our empirical inquiry is exploratory [...] we chose to run a large-scale survey in order to assess whether or not the case-based information present in the literature can be generalized to companies facing the customization-responsiveness squeeze [...] This allowed us to collect evidence of widely perceived managerial issues relating to product configuration [...] Future works may build on the insights we provided, articulating a theory of the interdependency between a company's operations and the adoption of configurable product structures. Based on theoretical advances, multi-items measures tapping some relevant constructs underlying the studied phenomenon may be developed.

Sometimes exploratory survey research is carried out using data collected in previous studies in order to gain new insights into a topic at low cost before embarking on a new ad-hoc survey. In such cases, survey research may be used to explore associations between concepts or the boundaries of validity of these associations. For example, Corbett and Whybark (2001: 967, 978), in presenting their research on the relationship between manufacturing practices and performances, stated:

The first objective of this paper is to explore the relationship between a manufacturing practice index and a performance index using data gathered by the Global Manufacturing Research Group (GMRG) to see if the results are the same as found in the other data [surveys] The larger the number and intensity of the practices used, the greater the performance of the firm. When the entire GMRG data set is used, however, there is still a great deal of scatter in the data; more than in the results of some of the other researchers [...] It was possible to identify two groups of firms that differed significantly on their performance indices, but that had the same practice scores [...] Still, it is clear that the managers in some firms extract greater performance from a given set of practices than other managers can. Finding out why should be a high research priority.

Confirmatory (or theory testing or explanatory) survey research takes place when knowledge of a phenomenon has been articulated in a theoretical form using well-defined concepts, models and propositions. Some established OSCM subfields have been researched extensively, in part through survey research, and the corresponding bodies of knowledge have been developed enough to allow researchers to engage in theory-testing survey research (Handfield and Melnyk, 1998; Soni and Kodali, 2012; Chatha et al., 2015). Here, data collection is carried out with the specific aim of testing the concepts developed in relation to the phenomenon, the linkages hypothesized among the concepts and the validity boundaries of the model. Correspondingly, all of the potential sources of error have to be carefully considered. Narasimhan and Kim (2002: 304) in a typical example of OSCM theory-testing survey research, clearly presented the theory that they were going to test and maintained a tight connection between each part of their work and this theory:

The focus and thrust of this paper mirrors what has been said in the literature. The premise [...] is that coordination between marketing strategies (diversification) and SCI [supply chain integration] strategies will lead to better performance than when the two strategies are pursued independently [...] In short, most empirical studies have either ignored or failed to fully address how diversification strategy affects performance. This paper posits that SCI moderates the relationship between diversification and performance, by potentially reducing the importance of interaction effect between product diversification (PD) and IMD [international market diversification] on performance [...] The remainder of the paper is organized as follows. The next section discusses the literature review leading to the development of a research model to be tested. The following section discusses the sampling frame, measures and data collection. This is followed by a discussion of the results of model testing. In the final section we present implications and conclusions.

Sometimes, before embarking on a confirmatory survey to test a theory, OSCM researchers use secondary data to expose a theory to empirical tests that can allow for theory refinement and better design of the survey. This approach is different from exploratory survey research based on available data because, in this case, the theory is already well formalized. Even so, secondary data usually have a number of limitations that the researchers should mention openly (Kiecolt and Nathan, 1985; Roth, 2007). Anderson et al. (1995: 638) made exemplary use of this kind of survey research:

Only recently has such a theory of quality management to describe and explain the effectiveness of the Deming Management Method been articulated by Anderson, Rungtusanatham, and Schroeder [...]. In this paper, the proposed theory [...] is empirically examined. The constructs [...] are operationalized using measurement statements developed by the World-Class Manufacturing research project team [...]. It is important to note that this paper does not claim to present formal conclusive tests of the proposed theory; the secondary nature of both the construct's operationalization and the data limits the ability to do so.

The use of secondary data can range from exploration to theory testing. They can be used alone or in combination with primary data. Some examples can be useful. Blindenbach-Driessen and van den Ende (2014) used Dutch Community Innovation Survey (CIS) data, collected by Statistics Netherlands (Centraal Bureau voor de Statistiek), to test their hypotheses on the locus of innovation in manufacturing and service firms. The CIS is an instrument of the European Union that assesses and compares the innovativeness of firms in the countries of the European Union. In their study, Gardner et al. (2015) combined primary and secondary data collected in hospitals in 2008, 2009 and 2010.

It should be noted that generating and testing a hypothesis can be achieved through the process of deduction (i.e. develop the model, formulate testable hypotheses, collect data, then test hypotheses) and through the process of induction (i.e. collect the data, formulate new hypotheses based on what is known from the data collected and test them). This chapter deals with the first approach. However, these two approaches can be combined. Bagozzi and Phillips (1982), for example, stated that deductive and inductive approaches could be applied in the same research. They proposed a new methodological paradigm for organizational research, termed *holistic construal*. This approach 'is neither rigidly deductive (or formalistic) nor purely exploratory. Rather it subsumes a process by which theories and hypotheses are tentatively formulated deductively, tested on data and, later, reformulated and retested until a meaningful outcome emerges' (Bagozzi and Phillips, 1982: 460). This approach 'is intended to encompass aspects of both the theory-construction and theory-testing phases' (Bagozzi and Phillips, 1982: 461). Therefore, in research following this approach, we can observe a starting model and a refined model, as illustrated by Forza and Filippini's (1998) article on total quality management (TQM).

Descriptive survey research is aimed at understanding the relevance of a phenomenon and describing the incidence or distribution of the phenomenon in a population. The primary research objective is not theory development, although it can provide useful hints for both theory building and theory refinement through the facts it describes (Dubin, 1978; Malhotra and Grover, 1998; Wacker, 1998). Many issues that are interesting to practitioners, policymakers and academics can be researched through descriptive surveys. Examples include the level of adoption of best practices or an investigation of the performance objectives pursued by companies in different sectors or countries. Consider, for instance, the following excerpt from Husseini and O'Brien's (2004: 126–127, 129, 142–143, 145) article:

> This paper aims to investigate manufacturing strategies and practices in [...] newly industrialising countries (NICs) [...]. A vast amount of literature exists in the manufacturing strategy area. We review those related to our discussions [...]. Data from the first round of the International Manufacturing Strategy Survey (IMSS) [...] constitutes the main source for our study [...]. We consider a comparative analysis of manufacturing strategy and practice data between a group of NICs, referred to as Group 1, and the two benchmarks which we define for this purpose [...]. Group 1 consists of four countries: Argentina, Brazil, Chile and Mexico, which are the four largest economies in Latin America [...]. Benchmark 1 represents average data for the two industrially leading countries, Japan and USA [...]. Benchmark 2 represents the average IMSS data for the UK, Germany and Italy [...]. The results [...] help in identifying some general characteristics for the firms in NICs as compared to those in more developed countries [...] [Firms operating in NICs] are facing a considerable amount of under-investment in process technology, [...] diseconomies of scale due to their much limited markets [...]. Due to the complexity of manufacturing strategy formulation for the kind of less stable and or less supportive environment, and also due to its particular difficulties in implementation, we believe a hybrid use of both planning and adaptive (or incremental) modes for manufacturing strategy process could be more appropriate for the firms in NICs. However, such a hybrid approach needs to be more elaborated.

Over the time, more OSCM research has been conducted in contexts and topics that have previously received limited attention, such as services (hospitals, hotels, etc.), some specific manufacturing sectors (agriculture, construction, etc.), some developing countries and so on. In these contexts, we can observe a flowering of exploratory and descriptive surveys. See, for example, the articles on service supply management (Ellram et al., 2007), sustainable procurement in the public sector (Brammer and Walker, 2011), drivers and obstacles of product recovery in Greece (Kapetanopoulou and Tagaras, 2011) and causes of lack of demand for eco-efficient services by business customers (Anttonen et al., 2013).

4.1.2 *When to use survey research*

Theoretical constraints associated with the state-of-the-art knowledge on a researched issue, and practical constraints associated with the kind of contribution the researcher intends to make, may limit survey applicability. As a consequence, survey research may be not the best choice or may need to be combined with other methods.

When the available knowledge on a research issue is very limited, then concepts are not well defined, measures are not available, lessons from previous empirical research may not be available, associations between concepts and explanations of these associations may be unknown and so on. Exploratory survey research and, to a certain extent, descriptive survey research are the available survey choices. They provide new insights on the phenomenon of interest, its relevance, the contexts in which it takes place and on how to measure the involved concepts. These kinds of surveys complement the knowledge gained though case studies, overcoming the limited generalizability of cases and pushing towards the development of measures that can be used in different contexts. However, the highly structured questionnaires and the limited presence of open questions, which are necessary to perform good quantitative analyses, limit the exploration capability in comparison with case studies. Therefore, case studies and surveys should be seen as complementary in exploratory and theory-building research.

When knowledge on a topic is widely available and theory-testing research is to be carried out, then theory-testing survey research should be considered. Survey is one of the preferred methods in this situation, as it allows for testing whether the hypothesized relationships or differences hold in different contexts. This generalization capability is one of the main strengths of the survey method, together with the relatively limited effort required to collect and analyse data compared to other methods. However, if the aim of the researcher is to investigate the mechanisms that explain the hypothesized relationships, then survey research may present some limitations on its own, so using it in combination with case studies may represent a better methodological alternative. Likewise, if the researcher aims to give detailed prescriptions for practice, for example, to implement a postponement initiative in order to reduce inventory costs, then survey research falls short on precision or simply may not be feasible due to the need for detailed information on the context and the relevant variables. In this case, simulation or mathematical modelling is preferable, although a survey may help provide parameters or other empirical data for use.

Therefore, a survey is a suitable method when knowledge of the phenomenon under investigation is not too underdeveloped, when generalization is an important intended contribution, when the variables and the context can be detailed and when the empirical evidence sought concerns 'how variables are related', 'where the relations hold' and 'to what extent a given relation is present'. When research needs depart from these conditions, survey research should be complemented by other methods.

4.1.3 *Which OSCM topics have been researched by means of survey*

Survey research has been used (sometimes in combination with other methods) to investigate phenomena in different OSCM subfields (see Table 4.1). The researcher interested in a given OM subfield can gain valuable insights into the possibility of survey use by considering whether survey research has been previously employed in that subfield. No previous use of survey research may suggest the existence of severe constraints, while previous use may suggest that survey research is applicable, albeit with careful scrutiny of previous experience.

Table 4.1 Survey research in OSCM subfields

OSCM subfields	Survey	Modelling and survey	Theoretical conceptual and survey	Case study and survey	Simulation and survey	Total survey	Total topic	Survey percentage (per cent)
Strategy	77	3	6	2		88	213	41
Quality	51	2	5			58	222	26
Process design	33	3	2			38	221	17
Inventory control	16		1	1		18	317	6
Purchasing	15					15	39	38
Scheduling	13	1				14	500	3
Services	11	1		1		13	53	25
Distribution	7					7	61	11
Facility layout	2	3				6	149	4
Project management	3				1	3	34	9
Aggregate planning	3					3	13	23
Work measurement	3					3	10	30
Quality work life	3					3	4	75
Maintenance	2					2	40	5
Facility location		1				1	21	5
Forecasting	1					1	20	5
Capacity planning						0	41	0
Count total	240	14	14	4	1	273	1,958	14
Article total	206	11	10	3	1	231	1,754	13
Double count number	34	3	4	1	0	42	204	21

Source: Adapted from Pannirselvam et al. (1999: 104).

Note: The review considered 1,754 OM articles, which appeared in the period 1992–1997 in the following journals: Decision Sciences Journal (DSJ), IIE Transactions (IIE), International Journal of Operations and Production Management (IJOPM), International Journal of Production Research (IJPR), Journal of Operations Management (JOM), Management Science (MS), Production and Operations Management (POM).

Quality management, operations strategy and SCM (in particular, purchasing) are three OSCM subfields that have been traditionally widely researched through surveys. More recently, some service aspects (e.g. service quality, new service development) and environmental issues have also been widely researched through surveys. Even though surveys are widely used in these OSCM subfields, there are ongoing discussions concerning the appropriateness of survey research to these subfields, and how survey research should be designed in specific subfields. Some researchers address these points in a systematic way, thus paving the way to a better understanding of the possible contributions and shortcomings of each research method applied to a specific research issue. For example, Barnes (2001: 1079–1080, 1085–1087) while discussing the use of surveys to investigate the manufacturing strategy process, wrote:

> It is also extremely doubtful whether survey research would provide the rich data set required. [...] Survey research risks superficiality, and may be unreliable if reliant on a single respondent from one organisation (Bowman and Ambrosini, 1997). This problem might be particularly acute when investigating the strategy process, as the perceptions and interpretations of events by individuals are likely to play a key role. [...] Surveys seem best suited to large scale data gathering, especially where factually based data is required, as would be the case when investigating the content of operations strategy (e.g. Flynn et al., 1997) [...] Notwithstanding Hill et al.'s (1999) criticisms of their use in operations management research, questionnaires have been used to investigate aspects of the operations strategy process (e.g. Anderson et al., 1991; Tunalv, 1990). Questionnaires invariably have the benefit of greater efficiency for the researcher. Key issues in their use centre on what questions to ask, in what form and of whom. It is generally agreed that questionnaires are best suited to asking specific rather than general questions, and for closed rather than open questions (Robson, 1993). As such they are best aimed at collecting data to test theories, hypotheses or propositions [...]. The effectiveness of the method depends entirely on the quality of the questionnaire responses obtained. This in turn relies on the diligence, goodwill and level of understanding of respondents. Foregoing the opportunity of personal contact with respondents is less time-consuming for the researcher. However, it prevents respondents from seeking clarification from the researcher and the researcher from responding to non-verbal communications. Interviewing a key respondent in the organisation might alleviate these dangers, but this reduces efficiency.

4.1.4 *How survey research has been used in OSCM*

Recognition of the value of empirical research in OSCM has led to an increase in both the number and the percentage of studies based on empirical research and, especially, on survey research (Rungtusanatham et al., 2003). The number of survey-based articles increased steadily from the mid 1980s to the early 1990s, and then increased sharply from 1993. By 1996, empirical research-based articles accounted for approximately 30 per cent of the research published in the main OM outlets, and survey-based articles accounted for 60 per cent of this empirical subset. The use of surveys in OSCM empirical research has remained high over time (see, for example, Soni and Kodali (2012) for empirical research on SCM). As survey research has become more widely used, rigour has also increased. A number of studies have helped the discipline achieve this outcome. In the late 1980s and again in the late 1990s, a number of articles contrasted the use of survey and other research methods in OM, providing insights into when and why survey research can be used (see Table 4.2). In 1990, Flynn *et al.* provided general indications on how to use surveys in OM and, subsequently, in the second half of the 1990s, a number of studies analysed how survey research both had been and should be used in OSCM (see Table 4.3). Since 2000, a number of articles have focused on very specific aspects of survey research in OSCM and on its application to specific OSCM subfields (see Tables 4.3 and 4.4). More recently, a number of articles have been published that have identified specific methodological weaknesses of OSCM survey-based articles and have provided valuable suggestions on how to deal with such weaknesses (see Table 4.3). All of these articles constitute a valuable body of knowledge and capitalize on the experience of survey research in OSCM. Collectively and progressively, they set and re-set the standards of survey-based research in OSCM.

Yet, in spite of the progress that has been made, there are still many opportunities to improve the application of survey research. These opportunities are noted in the papers summarized in Tables 4.2, 4.3 and 4.4. In particular, it should be avoided to quote methodological articles without implementing their indications, which is unfortunately sometimes the case. In addition, top OSCM journals are going to require not only proper use of survey methodology, but also evidence of a true understanding of the specific aspects of this method (see, for example, what Guide and Ketokivi, 2015, said on commonly accepted thresholds and rules of thumb).

Improvement opportunities relate to several aspects of survey research and increase in number, detail and required effort as time passes. However, they may be grouped around the following general issues:

• Framing the survey research in terms of theoretical contributions (thorough use of available theoretical background, clear statement of the intended theoretical contribution, use of clearly defined concepts, clear consideration of the boundaries of validity of the results, etc.).
• Use of scientific (i.e. reliable and valid) measurement instruments, possibly shared across OSCM researchers (if a measure cannot be trusted, no empirical result deriving from that measure can be trusted).
• Rigour in the survey design and in the execution phases (sampling, administration, data analysis, etc.).
• Clarity and explicitness in reporting information on the survey execution (these are basic requirements if comparison, replication and critical use of the results are to be possible).

The rest of this chapter is devoted to presenting the overall structure of a survey research process (Section 4.2) as well as detailed prescriptions on how to conduct it (Sections 4.3 to 4.10), and to illustrate the properties of well-done survey research (Section 4.11) in order to reduce the shortcomings that OSCM survey research is likely to encounter. The chapter should help OSCM researchers, especially those engaging in survey research for the first time, by providing an overview of the survey research process.

4.2 The survey research process

Survey research is a long process, which requires a pre-existing theoretical model (or conceptual framework). It includes a number of related sub-processes: the process of

Table 4.2 Survey research usage in OSCM compared to the usage of other methods

Article	Content related to survey research
Amoako-Gyampah and Meredith, 1989	They analyse (in terms of research content and methods) the papers published in 10 journals in the period 1982–1987 and papers that were in the pipeline (published in the *Proceedings of the Annual Meeting of the Decision Sciences Institute*, 1986 and 1987).
Meredith et al., 1989	They present and discuss alternative research paradigms in OM. Subsequently, they classify the articles published in DSJ and MS in 1977 and the articles published in the same journals plus JOM in 1987. The incidence of survey-based articles was 0 per cent in 1977 and 4 per cent in 1987.
Wacker, 1998	He discusses what a good theory is, compares different approaches (including survey) to contribute to theoretical development and analyses the application of these approaches across *JOM, MS, IJPR, IJOPM, POM, Harvard Business Review (HBR), DSJ, Product Innovation Management (PIM)* in the period 1991–1995.
Scudder and Hill, 1998	They review and classify empirical research in OM by considering 13 journals (traditional outlets of OM research) in the decade 1986–1995. They provide evidence of the growing use of survey research in OM.
Pannirselvam et al., 1999	They assess the state of research in OM by examining the research topics addressed and the methodologies used. The articles considered were published in *DSJ, IIE, IJOPM, IJPR, JOM, MS, POM* in the period 1992–1997. They provide detailed information about the use of survey research (eventually in combination with other methods) to study the various OM topics.
Gupta et al., 2006	They review and evaluate more than 150 empirical research papers published in *POM* over the period 1992–2005. They classify the empirical research articles based on their primary purpose, data collection approach, data analysis technique and operations topics.
Roth, 2007	She provides a brief history of the empirical tradition in OM with reference to both manufacturing and service management.
Sousa and Voss, 2008	They examine and critique how current OM research investigates the contextual conditions under which best practices are effective. They reflect on the use of different methods for best practice contingent research, including survey research.
Soni and Kodali, 2012	They provide a comprehensive assessment of empirical research methods in SCM. They consider the 21 journals that cover 75 per cent of the SCM articles published between 1980 and 2009, thus identifying 619 empirically based papers. They find that empirical research in SCM is predominantly based on surveys (55.54 per cent of articles), focuses more on theory building than on verification, rarely uses triangulation of data and longitudinal data collection, is scanty in developing countries, is mainly written at the firm level and does not examine several industrial sectors, including construction, retail and agriculture.
Pagell and Shevchenko, 2014	They reflect on some limits of current research on sustainable supply chain management (SSCM). Some of their reflections are helpful in thinking critically on OSCM survey research.
Van Weele and Van Raaij, 2014	They reflect on what can be done to increase the relevance and rigour of purchasing and supply management (PSM) research. They suggest that, to foster its rigour, future research should allow for an increase in the number of replication studies, longitudinal studies and meta-analytical studies. Future PSM research designs should reflect a careful distinction between informants and respondents and careful sample selection. When discussing the results of quantitative studies, future PSM research should report on effect sizes and confidence intervals, rather than on *p*-values.

Table 4.3 Specific analyses of survey research in OSCM

Article	Content related to survey research
Flynn et al., 1990	They provide the foundation of empirical research in OM. They present various empirical research designs with a special focus on the survey. They provide several useful prescriptions and tools for survey research. A list of scales usable in OM surveys is provided, along with examples of their applications to OM concepts, and discussed. A list of empirical research in OM is provided, including the specifications of topics investigated and the analytical method used in each study.
Verma and Goodale, 1995	They discuss the importance of statistical power analysis in field-based empirical research in OM and related disciplines. They analyse the statistical power of 28 survey-based articles published in *JOM* and *DSJ* in the period 1989–1992. They draw implications for OM survey research.
Filippini, 1997	He traces the evolution of OM topics and research approaches in the period 1986–1996. He analyses the *Proceedings of the Annual Meeting of the Decision Sciences Institute*, 1996, and compares the results with those of Amoako-Gyampah and Meredith (1989). He draws attention to the need for improving the quality of survey research in OM.
Flynn et al., 1997	They provide an overview of the first round of the survey-based World Class Manufacturing (WCM) research project. This project, in the subsequent rounds, has been conducted at an international level. It is characterized by great attention to the measurement issue and by wide coverage of OSCM issues. This project is currently in its fourth round.
Whybark, 1997	He provides a detailed view of the Global Manufacturing Research Group's (GMRG) survey research. This is one of the longest established survey research programmes in OSCM. This project involved many countries and provided knowledge on the use of manufacturing practices in those countries.
Van Donselaar and Sharman, 1997	They present the details of the survey process and procedure in a successful survey of the transportation and distribution sector. Such detailed information is usually not reported in survey-based articles due to space constraints.
Collins and Cordon, 1997	They identify and discuss methodological issues surrounding the design and administration of large-scale surveys. They compare the design and execution of two survey research studies on manufacturing strategy that led to insights concerning sample selection, respondent preparation, bias, etc.
Forza and Di Nuzzo, 1998	They analyse the possibility of combining results of different surveys and provide suggestions to allow future meta-analyses on OM issues.
Forza and Vinelli, 1998	They present the opinions of 89 OM scholars on the desirable characteristics of survey research as well as the expected contribution of future survey research.
Malhotra and Grover, 1998	In order to bridge the gap between survey research and theory development, they provide a normative perspective on what constitutes 'good' survey research and develop a list of 17 ideal survey research attributes. They then apply these 17 attributes to evaluate 25 survey-based OM papers from four journals between 1990 and 1995 to evaluate OM survey research and provide suggestions for improving it.
Rungtusanatham, 1998	He draws attention to content validity. This is one of the first articles that addresses this topic in OSCM.
O'Leary-Kelly and Vokurka, 1998	They provide an in-depth review of different methods available for assessing the construct validity of measures. They provide some examples taken from OM research on manufacturing flexibility.

Handfield and Melnyk, 1998	They reflect on the theory-building process of an empirical OM study. They exemplify their reflections by means of OM research on TQM. They provide indications on how to assess empirical theory-driven research.
Hensley, 1999	He focuses specifically on the development and use of reliable and valid measurement scales in OM research. He reviews six studies in terms of their approaches to the development and validation of multiple-item measurement scales. He identifies and discusses the strengths and weaknesses of these six studies in order to evaluate methods of scale development used in OM, discusses why OM researchers encounter difficulties in developing scales and offers advice regarding when and why OM researchers may want to develop scales.
Klassen and Jacobs, 2001	They assess the different effectiveness of post, fax, PC disk-by-post and web mail surveys (combined with e-mail notification). They use a total sample of 118 respondents from both small and large companies and from both manufacturing and service companies. They compare the different surveys against cost, coverage error, response rate, item completion rate and systematic respondent bias.
Forza, 2002	He presents in detail the survey research process in the OM research context. He provides indications for each phase of the survey research process in order to improve the research quality and efficiency.
Frohlich, 2002	He analyses the 233 single-manager surveys published in *DSJ, IJOPM, IJPR, JOM, MS, PIM* and *POM* in the period 1999–2000. He analyses answer rates and their dependence upon survey planning decisions. He reviews techniques to improve answer rates in OM surveys.
Boyer et al., 2002	Through a controlled experiment, they compare print versus electronic surveys.
Ho et al., 2002	They address several issues relevant for SCM survey research, such as construct definition, construct validity and modelling choice.
Rungtusanatham et al., 2003	They consider six major OM journals (*DSJ, MS, JOM, IJPR, IJOPM, POM*) and analyse in detail all the survey-based articles published in these journals over 21 years (1980–2000), for a total of 285 articles. The historical analysis provides an overview of the issues researched through surveys and of several methodological issues.
Ketokivi and Schroeder, 2004	They conduct a multitrait–multimethod analysis of perceptual performance measures to investigate item-specific trait, method and error variance.
Tsikriktsis, 2005	He discusses the research implications of missing data and types of missing data. He provides recommendations on which techniques should be used under different circumstances to improve the treatment of missing data in OM survey research.
Shah and Goldstein, 2006	They review applications of structural equation modelling (SEM) in *MS, JOM, DSJ and POM* from the earliest applications of SEM in studies published in these journals in 1984 through August 2003 and provide guidelines to improve the use of SEM in OM research.
Rungtusanatham et al., 2008	They discuss when it is appropriate to pool data provided by key informants with transparently different demographics across units of analysis in order to create a single larger data set for statistical manipulations. They provide guidelines for pre and post data collection actions to assure measurement equivalence.
Roth et al., 2008	They provide a compilation of multi-item scales and objective items derived from empirical OSCM articles published since 1990 in *JOM, MS, POM, Manufacturing & Service Operations Management (MSOM), DSJ, Journal of Service Research (JSR), IJPR* and *IJOPM*. Each measure is presented in detail, providing descriptions of the construct, of the measure and of its validity and reliability. Examples of questionnaires are provided.

(Continued)

Table 4.3 (Continued)

Article	Content related to survey research
Craighead et al., 2011	They analyse survey-based articles published between 2001 and 2009 in *IEEE Transactions on Engineering Management (IEEE-TEM)*, *JOM* and *POM* to assess if and how scholars address common method variance (CMV). They provide recommendations and examples on remedies for CMV to be applied in the design and data analysis phases.
Brusco et al., 2012	They provide an overview of some alternative clustering procedures (including advantages and disadvantages), identify software programs for implementing such procedures and discuss the circumstances where they might be employed gainfully in OM research.
Peng and Lai, 2012	They present a practical guideline for evaluating and using partial least squares (PLS) in OM research. They explain when and how to use PLS in OM, provide OM research examples, and review and summarize the use of PLS in the recent OM literature.
Wowak et al., 2013	They perform a meta-analysis of 35 studies in the supply chain knowledge (SCK)–performance relationship that collectively include more than 8,400 firms. They conclude that the SCK–performance relationship is stronger when (i) examining operational performance, (ii) gathering data from more than one supply chain node, (iii) gathering data from multiple countries, (iv) examining service industries and (v) among more recently published studies. They use a multidimensional operationalization of both SCK and performance, and multiple operationalizations for performance.
Roh et al., 2013	They empirically investigate whether neglecting the multi-sided nature of certain constructs (such as supplier–customer integration) can affect the research validity and reliability and may invalidate research inferences and results. They offer practical guidance regarding assumptions routinely made in single rater research and propose when single rater data may be appropriate for multi-stakeholder research.
Malhotra et al., 2014	They review OM studies that test for mediation, published in *DSJ, JOM, MS, MSOM* and *POM* in the 2002–2012 time period. They identify four commonly used mediation approaches. They evaluate the existing methodologies and make recommendations on how to improve the rigour of mediation testing in OM. They provide OM examples to illustrate the relevance and advantages of these recommendations as well as their ease of use.
Rungtusanatham et al., 2014	They synthesize literature in different disciplines to provide an accessible tutorial for the mathematical foundation of mediation effects and the various methods available to test for these effects. They provide procedural guidance to SCM scholars in the form of eight recommendations aimed at improving the theorizing, testing and drawing of conclusions about mediation effects. They also review 81 SCM articles involving mediation processes that were published between 2008 and 2011 in *Journal of Business Logistics (JBL)*, *JOM* and *Journal of Supply Chain Management (JSCM)*.
Knoppen et al., 2015	They provide a comprehensive framework for treating equivalence both prior to data collection and during subsequent analyses. They assess the extent to which equivalence is considered in survey research in *DSJ, IJOPM, IJPR, JOM, MS* and *POM* between 2006 and 2011, by analysing 465 survey-based articles. They provide suggestions on how to deal with lack of full equivalence.
Guide and Ketokivi, 2015	They redefine some methodological criteria for *JOM*. They spot a number of misunderstandings about some of the key methods used in manuscripts submitted to *JOM* and discourage authors from using some outdated practices in their manuscripts. In order of importance, they state that it is time to investigate causality more seriously, to limit the use of

Helmuth et al., 2015	rules of thumb and to show an understanding of which rules have a basis in formal statistical inference and which do not, to understand the tools that a researcher uses and to justify their use, to use both ex ante and ex post methods to address common method bias and to stay abreast of methodological developments. They review empirical SCM articles published in *JOM, POM, DSJ, MS, MSOM, JBL, International Journal of Logistics Management (IJLM), International Journal of Physical Distribution and Logistics Management (IJPDLM), JSCM and Journal of Purchasing and Supply Management (JPSM)* in the years 2002–2012, by examining 4,235 statistical tests that appear in 217 unique studies. They examine: (1) effect size, (2) statistical power and (3) reliability and controls.
Schoenherr et al., 2015	They examine the risks and benefits of using survey research firms for data collection. While this approach has some history in other disciplines, it is still relatively new in OSCM. They conclude that the use of survey research firms for empirical data collection can be a viable, alternative approach to self-administered surveys. However, care should be taken in its application and they provide useful hints based on their experience.
Abbey and Meloy, 2017	Researchers would like to identify and eventually discard respondents that do not pay enough attention in answering. This paper presents various forms of attention checks, discusses the advantages and disadvantages of different methods, highlights the objectivity of implementation and underscores the potential outcomes from their use. It is focused on primary data collection from undergraduate student populations. It is particularly useful for behavioural OM research and for online data collection that pays respondents.
Flynn, et al., 2018	They discuss issues related to using single respondents to provide perceptual information and a single source to address polyadic constructs (i.e. constructs that include relationships, multiple entities, or attributes that cannot be characterized by a single objective description). They consider both common method bias and respondent bias. They describe potential ways to address these issues, providing opportunities to improve survey research designs in SCM when an optimal design is not possible.
Ketchen, et al., 2018	They claim that the theory should drive the design of a survey without excessive compromise. In SCM research this means, for example, involving both customers and suppliers and only customers or only suppliers in informing on customer-supplier relationships. Additional examples are the use of respondents actually informed in what they are asked, the use of higher granularity to take into account the heterogeneity of plants within a company and the consideration of the temporal dimension.
Kull, et al., 2018	They present arguments for why single-respondent designs can be more appropriate in the small and medium-sized enterprise (SME) setting, particularly when considering the various facets of SCM and the untapped potential of SCM-SME research
Montabon, et al., 2018	They propose that single respondent surveys continue to be a viable SCM research method, under the condition that necessary care is taken in its design and implementation. By reviewing single respondent survey-based articles published in *DSJ, JBL, JOM* and *JSCM* in the last 10 years, they recommend to use multimethod research design, careful informant selection and better documentation.
Krause, et al., 2018	They summarize the main challenges that survey research in SCM faces when dealing with single respondents and argue that having multiple respondents does not necessarily represent a cure-all solution. They explore the characteristics of research questions that can be addressed through single key informants.

(Continued)

Table 4.3 (Continued)

Article	Content related to survey research
Edwards, 2019	He moves from the consideration that answering a survey question is actually a complex process. The characteristics of the individual (e.g. ability, motivation), of the instrument (e.g. instructions, length), and the method (e.g. administered online, paper-and-pencil format) influence the validity of the emitted responses, i.e. the extent to which the provided scores reflect the thoughts and beliefs of respondents. He provides methods to analyse response validity and remedies for this issue. The main focus is on behavioural OM.
Ketokivi, 2019	He focuses on how individual-level responses can provide information on system-level traits. He highlights that understanding the multilevel essence of theoretical concepts is crucial and that confounding levels may lead to inferences that are not only biased but even fallacious.

Table 4.4 Survey research in specific subfields of OSCM

Article	Content related to survey research
Boyer and Pagell, 2000	They investigate a number of methodological issues regarding measures used in operations strategy and advanced manufacturing technology.
Barnes, 2001	He reviews the methodological options for the empirical investigation of the operations strategy process, including survey. The advantages and disadvantages of each, together with the circumstances in which they might best be used, are identified. He focuses on the practical implications for researchers.
Dangayach and Deshmukh, 2001	They examine manufacturing strategy articles published in refereed journals until January 2001. They provide some information on the use of the survey in the manufacturing strategy topic.
Davies and Kochhar, 2002	They address methodological issues (several related to survey) that can improve the quality of findings from manufacturing best practice and performance studies.
Zhang et al., 2011	They review survey-based papers focused on the relationship between information and communication technology (ICT), SCM and supply chain (SC) performance to detect explanations for similarities and differences in reported findings. They consider articles published in *MS, JOM, DSJ, IJOPM, POM, IJPR, International Journal of Production Economics (IJPE), MIS Quarterly (MISQ), ISR, JMIS, IM, JBL, IJPDLM, IJLM* and *JSCM* between 1995 and mid 2010.
Chatha et al., 2015	They systematically review manufacturing strategy literature published between 1966 and 2010 in 34 journals. They investigate developments in research design, data collection methods, countries where data are collected, sample size, respondent types, statistical techniques used and the time horizons of the studies.

translating the theoretical domain into the empirical domain; the design and pilot-testing processes; the process of collecting data for theory testing; the data-analysis process; and the process of interpreting the results and writing the report. The survey research process is illustrated in Figure 4.1.

The required level of sophistication of the conceptual model differs among the different types of survey research. Exploratory survey research, in the most exploratory fashion, can be carried out without a theoretical model. However, defining a sketchy framework that at least classifies the variables measured (for example, levers and performance) will improve the quality of the survey and will increase the contribution of the subsequent data analysis and interpretation. Theory-testing survey research puts great importance on the model, since, by definition, it is not theory testing if it is not based on a theoretical model from the outset. Any flaw in the modelling undermines the contribution of such theory-testing survey research. Descriptive survey research does not necessarily require a model: only a rigorous definition of the concepts to be measured is required. However, again in this case, the availability of a model will facilitate a meaningful presentation of the results, and a reduction in the length of the questionnaires, and will improve the usability of the resulting data for other purposes. Therefore, the rule is 'the more well developed the model, the better' for any kind of survey research, although the minimum acceptable level of development differs.

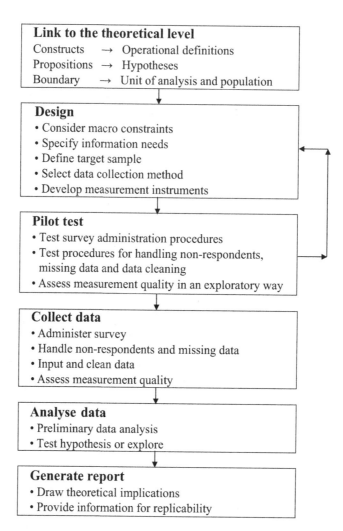

Figure 4.1 The survey research process.

The analyses performed when data are available differ among the different types of survey research. Exploratory survey research uses more descriptive analyses and less model-based analyses (for example, it uses exploratory factor analysis instead of confirmatory factor analysis). Furthermore, it may perform many different trials to gather new insights from the available data. A proposed model can be the result of the data analysis. Theory-testing survey research carries out previously planned analyses and even post-hoc analyses to better interpret the obtained results. Relational analyses are used more than descriptive analyses in theory-testing survey research. Eventually, the tested model can be modified and retested. Descriptive survey research uses descriptive analyses; however, it can also use data reduction techniques (such as factor analysis) to present a more parsimonious view of the phenomenon being described.

The care and rigour with which the various steps of survey research are performed varies across survey research types. Exploratory survey research does not put stringent constraints on measurement. Single-item perceptual measures may be acceptable if knowledge on that issue is limited. Theory-testing survey research requires extreme rigour in all analyses. For example, the measures must satisfy all the requirements of good measurement. Descriptive survey research requires rigour in representing the population under study, but less rigour than theory-testing survey research in terms of measurement.

In summary, different types of surveys place different emphasis on the model, require different levels of rigour in their measures, entail different levels of sophistication in data analysis, require different degrees of theoretical effort, etc. All of these differences may result in differing emphases on the various phases of the overall survey research process, even though all of the different phases are present.

The following sections focus on theory-testing survey research, as it is the most demanding type of survey research. In this way, it is easier to increase awareness both of possible shortcomings and of useful preventative actions that can be taken. However, in the various sections, some consideration is given to the other types of survey research as well, especially in Section 4.9, where the main differences between theory-testing survey research and other types of survey research are synthesized.

4.3 What is needed prior to survey research design?

Before starting survey-based research, the researcher should have taken the steps previously recalled in this text by Karlsson (Chapter 2) and Åhlström (Chapter 3). First, the researcher should have a clear idea of what the problem is about and should discuss it in depth. Second, the researcher should map the problem in the existing literature in order to be cognizant of what is already known and what is still unknown. This activity might reveal that the researcher's original idea is infeasible or has already been pursued by somebody else. Third, the researcher should clarify the intended contribution of the research. For all of these points, a thorough literature review is crucial.

The contribution of a survey research project depends on how well it is based on existing knowledge, since in survey research, as distinct from case studies or action research, the structured and specific data collection procedures make it difficult to recover missing information. In exploratory survey research, a careful consideration of the available knowledge allows the researcher to perform the most rigorous survey permitted by the state-of-the-art knowledge on the phenomenon of interest. In theory testing, this facilitates the reuse of measures, explanations and previous results, thus enabling surveys that do not suffer the limitations encountered in previous studies. To clarify this point, consider the differing motivations of both exploratory and theory-testing survey-based research.

Exploratory survey research may pose several problems with regard to framing the research, as little support is provided by the available literature. Appropriate framing and positioning of the research is important to focus the research and to open up a discussion, thus paving the way to further research. This effort clearly emerges in the Salvador and Forza (2004: 288–289) exploratory survey-based article, where they wrote:

> The management scholar addressing the topic of product configuration has to confront two key issues: (1) is product configuration really a management topic, or should be left to knowledge engineers and design theorists? (2) in case it has some managerial implications, how much relevant are these implications in the business world? In addressing the first question, we defined an appropriate operational context for product configuration, i.e. the customization-responsiveness squeeze. Then, we synthesize what

product configuration is from a technical standpoint, by drawing on past research by Artificial Intelligence and Design Theory scholars. Finally, we conceptually explained why it is relevant from a management standpoint. We addressed the second question by means of a hybrid quantitative–qualitative exploratory research design.

In contrast, theory-testing survey research is based on more established knowledge and, therefore, the focus of the research is easier to communicate clearly. This excerpt from Anderson et al. (1995: 638) illustrates the positioning of theory-testing survey research:

Only recently has such a theory of quality management to describe and explain the effectiveness of the Deming Management Method been articulated by Anderson, Rungtusanatham, and Schroeder [...] In this paper, the proposed theory of quality management underlying the Deming Management Method is empirically examined.

4.3.1 The theoretical model

Before starting a survey-based research, it is necessary in a theory-testing survey (and it is convenient in an exploratory or descriptive survey) for the researcher to establish the conceptual model. Several works (Dubin, 1978; Bacharach, 1989; Sekaran, 1992; Wacker, 1998) agree that this can be achieved by providing:

1 *Construct names and nominal definitions*: clear identification, labels and definitions of all the constructs (i.e. 'theoretical concepts' or, in somewhat looser language, 'variables') considered relevant.
2 *Propositions*: presentation and discussion of the role of the constructs (independent, dependent, intervening, moderating), the important linkages between them and an indication of the nature and direction of the relationships (especially if available from previous findings).
3 *An explanation*: a clear explanation of why the researcher would expect to observe these relationships and, eventually, linkages with other theories (within or outside OSCM; e.g. Amundson, 1998).
4 *Boundary conditions*: definition of the conditions under which the researcher might expect these relationships to hold; these include the identification of the *level of reference* of the constructs and statements of their relationships (i.e. where the researcher might expect the phenomenon to exist and manifest itself: individual, group, function or organization).

Developing good nominal definitions (sometimes called 'formal conceptual definitions') is a major issue in advancing OSCM theories. In this field, there are concepts that have been defined ambiguously and whose scope has so widened in use that they are vague and overlap with other concepts. This is the case for terms such as *world-class manufacturing, lean production, agile production, lean-agile production* or *dynamic manufacturing*. These concepts have been used for a long time with some overlap in their meanings. Are they really different things? What do they have in common and what differentiates them? A different problem is represented by terms that are used with different meanings. Take, for example, the term *form postponement*. In some cases, it is used to refer to a specific process configuration, while in others, it refers to a change in a process configuration; sometimes it refers to physical activities, while other times to decisions. Different meanings lead to different operationalizations and different relationships to other concepts.

Table 4.5 A summary of the rules for a good formal conceptual definition

Rule 1: Definitions should be formally defined using primitive and derived terms. Formal conceptual definitions should differentiate between formal concepts and non-formal measurable terms. All definitions should follow the 'rule of replacement'.

Rule 2: Each concept should be uniquely defined. It should exclude (as many as possible) terms shared with other definitions to reduce confusion with related concepts. This rule (Rule 2) means that the formal conceptual definitions denotation matches as closely as possible match its connotation.

Rule 3: Definitions should include only unambiguous and clear terms. Put another way, do not use vague or ambiguous terms.

Rule 4: Definitions should have as few terms as possible in the conceptual definition to avoid violating the parsimony virtue of 'good' theory.

Rule 5: Definitions should be consistent within the production/operations management field. That is, formal conceptual definitions should be as similar as possible between studies.

Rule 6: Definitions should not make any term broader. New definitions should not expand a concept to make it broader and less exclusive.

Rule 7: New hypotheses cannot be introduced in the definitions. In production/operations management, the definitions should not include instances where only 'good' events happen.

Rule 8: Statistical tests for content validity must be performed after the terms are formally defined. These empirical tests are not tests of the conceptual validity of a concept but, rather, are used to test if the formally defined concepts sample the conceptual domain.

Source: Wacker (2004: 638).

A considerable part of past and, to a lesser extent, also current OSCM research has paid insufficient attention to developing good formal conceptual definitions. It is crucial to understand that, without a clear and unambiguous definition of a concept, the content validity of a measure of the concept cannot be assessed since the content has not been yet been determined. Without an agreement regarding what a concept means, it is meaningless to assess face validity (in this case, face validity assessment would be used as a tool to develop concepts instead of as a tool to develop a measure of a concept). Further, if there are two concepts that overlap, it would be meaningless to test for discriminant validity between the corresponding measures. Finally, if a performance outcome is placed within the definition of a practice, then it is meaningless to test the predictive validity of a measure of this practice by using the same performance as a criterion variable. Fortunately, there are now some guidelines (see Table 4.5) on how to provide a good formal conceptual definition (Wacker, 2004) and there are some examples of articles devoted to identifying the domain of a specific concept as a preliminary step of measure development (see, for example, the work of Koste and Malhotra (1999) on manufacturing flexibility).

Very often, the theoretical framework is depicted through a schematic diagram. While not being a requirement, it may be useful to facilitate clear communication. The researcher can find valuable support for this task in methodological books in social sciences (such as Dubin, 1978; Kerlinger, 1986; Emory and Cooper, 1991; Miller, 1991; Sekaran, 1992) or in OSCM (e.g. Anderson et al., 1994; Flynn et al., 1994), and in methodological articles in OSCM (e.g. Meredith, 1998; Wacker, 1998).

Theory-testing survey-based articles must be particularly clear in presenting the theoretical model. Anderson et al. (1995: 639–641), for example, recalled the theoretical model that they were going to test in the following way:

[There are] seven constructs or the 'Whats' of a theory [...]. The seven constructs are: (1) Visionary Leadership, (2) Internal and External Cooperation, (3) Learning, (4) Process Management, (5) Continuous Improvement, (6) Employee Fulfillment, and (7)

Customer Satisfaction [...]. Nominal definitions for the seven constructs are shown in Table [...]. [Visionary Leadership, for example, is defined as] the ability of management to establish, practice, and lead long-term vision for the organization, driven by changing customer requirements, as opposed to an internal management control role [...]. The formal statement [that specifies the relationships among the seven constructs] is depicted as a path diagram in Figure [...] and can be stated as follows: 'The effectiveness of the Deming Management Method arises from leadership efforts toward the simultaneous creation of a cooperative and learning organization to facilitate the implementation of process-management practices, which, when implemented, support customer satisfaction and organizational survival through sustained employee fulfilment and continuous improvement of processes, products, and services'. In the final stage of theory development, Anderson [...] juxtaposed the resulting set of relational elements and statements shown in Figure [...] in order to determine the level of support for the proposed constructs and relationships, essentially responding to the question of 'Why' – 'Why are the constructs related as proposed?' [...] A second comment concerns the generalizability of the proposed constructs and relationships [...] [The validity of the proposed theory] across different national cultures [is debated] [...] the empirical study reported in this paper marks a beginning towards addressing this issue by exploring the validity of the articulated theory using both American-owned and Japanese-owned plants in the US.

Sometimes, OSCM surveys are carried out with multiple purposes so that several papers – some descriptive, others theory testing and others exploratory – can be derived from a single data collection initiative. In this case, the researcher may rely on several theoretical models to design the survey. Whybark's (1997: 687–688) comments, below, with reference to the GMRG survey make this point well.

There is no single, specific theory, hypothesis, or process model behind the GMRG surveys. Instead, much of what is included was suggested because it is associated with one or more general operations management theories. These theories were not pulled together into a specific meta-theory for guiding the design, however. This general descriptive design is consistent with the objective of the project, yields results that permit some theory testing and serves as the basis for some theory building. Many operations management theories have been tested with the GMRG data, but the concepts that guided the development of the questionnaire were very broad. One of these concepts was that there would be differences in manufacturing practices among the countries in which the survey was administered. Thus one of the objectives was to develop a questionnaire that could be used to document manufacturing practices in many countries. More narrowly focusing on specific hypotheses might unnecessarily restrict the opportunity to gather general data. [...] Another concern that broadly guided the GMRG project was the need to control for potential industry differences. There was a strong a priori assumption that there would be fairly significant differences between industries that could mask country differences if they were not controlled [...] Literature and consultants have suggested that certain practices are associated with good performance. These contentions did influence the design of the questions in the second questionnaire so that some of these hypotheses on the relationships between practices and performance can be tested.

To maintain clarity, however, it is recommended that a single piece of research that uses data collected through a multipurpose survey pursue only one objective, either exploratory or descriptive or theory testing. It is also recommended that theory testing and descriptive purposes be investigated in depth before the survey is designed so that the sample and the operationalizations of the variables are satisfactory.

Unfortunately, the formal theory for several OSCM topics is underdeveloped. For many years, OSCM has developed implicit theories, and the lack of explicitness has hindered the testing of these theories. As a consequence, before embarking on theory-testing survey research, the OSCM researcher is often obliged to develop a theoretical framework. This development activity itself can be publishable (as, for example, Anderson et al., 1994; Flynn et al., 1994; Forza, 1995).

4.3.2 *From the theoretical model to the hypotheses*

Once the constructs, their relationships and the boundaries of validity of these relationships have been articulated, then the propositions that specify the relationships among the constructs have to be translated into hypotheses that relate empirical indicators. For example, the researcher might propose the following: 'The adoption of TQM in organizations would have positive effects on organizational performance'. Such a statement is at the conceptual level. At the empirical level (i.e. at the level of the hypotheses), the following hypothesis might be tested: 'The return on investment (ROI) is positively correlated with the degree of TQM adoption'. In this hypothesis, the 'degree of TQM adoption' is an empirical and numerically based measure of how extensive the adoption of TQM is or how committed the organization is to TQM. In other words, before the researcher can talk about how to collect data, it is necessary to:

1 Define the unit of analysis corresponding to the level of reference of the theory.
2 Provide and test the operational definitions for the various constructs.
3 Translate the propositions into hypotheses.

4.3.2.1 *Defining the unit of analysis*

The empirical parallel of the 'level of reference' of the theory is the 'unit of analysis'. The unit of analysis refers to the level of data aggregation during the subsequent analysis. The unit of analysis in OSCM studies may be individuals, dyads, groups, plants, divisions, companies, projects, systems and so on (Flynn et al., 1990). Operations management and SCM researchers should pay greater attention to specifying clearly both the level of reference and the unit of analysis. Unfortunately, many empirical works do not clearly state the level of reference and, subsequently, do not defend the choice of the unit of analysis. However, attention to the unit of analysis is increasing (e.g. Paulraj et al., 2008; Peng et al., 2013).

It is necessary to determine the unit of analysis when formulating the research questions. Data collection methods, sample size and even the operationalization of constructs may sometimes be determined or guided by the level at which the data will be aggregated at the time of analysis (Sekaran, 1992). Not defining the unit of analysis in advance may mean that later analyses, appropriate for the study, cannot be performed.

When the level of reference is different from the unit of analysis, the researcher will encounter the cross-level inference problem, that is, the problem of collecting data at one level and interpreting the result at a different level (Dansereau and Markham, 1987). For example, if data are collected, or analysed, at a group level (for example, at the plant level), and conclusions are drawn at an individual level (for example, at the employee level), the researcher will encounter the ecological fallacy problem (Robinson, 1950;

Babbie, 1990). The issue of cross-level inference becomes more important when more than one unit of analysis is involved in a study (Babbie, 1990). Discussion of methodological problems associated with the level of analysis (plant, strategic business unit (SBU), company) can be found in Boyer and Pagell (2000), with reference to operations strategy and advanced manufacturing technology; and in Vokurka and O'Leary-Kelly (2000), with reference to manufacturing flexibility.

The definition of the unit of analysis is not obvious in some research. Defining it at a theoretical and empirical level is important to avoid the cross-level inference problem and even the possibility that a reader might fail to understand the level to which the research refers. Rungtusanatham (2001: 664–665) provided an exemplary definition of the unit of analysis:

> The unit of analysis in this study is, at a theoretical level, a transformation process, and, at an empirical level, a process operator. The job of a single process operator in a manufacturing environment is, itself, a transformation process, complete with inputs and outputs. Therefore, one can arguably equate, as Cantello et al. (1990, p. 62) did, a process operator's job to a transformation process. As such, individual-level data about the deployment of SPC [statistical process control] with respect to an individual's job and the individual employee's perceptions about, and affective reactions to, his or her job would be appropriate for conducting empirical examinations of Proposition 1 and 2.

4.3.2.2 Developing and testing the operational definitions

This section focuses mainly on the 'what' part of an operational definition (the list of observable elements), while leaving the 'how' part (the specific questions, etc.) to Section 4.4.5.

4.3.2.2.1 DEVELOPING THE OPERATIONAL DEFINITIONS

The first problem that the researcher faces is to translate the theoretical concepts into observable and measurable elements. If this work is not done well, the nominal definitions will not match the operative definitions. In this case, the rest of the research cannot be trusted. Some articles are well done in terms of data processing and present their results clearly, but show considerable misalignment between nominal definitions and operative definitions (sometimes they do not even provide a clear nominal definition). These articles may be considered as examples of garbage in, garbage out, diminishing any contribution provided by the empirical analysis.

If the theoretical concept is multifaceted, then all of its facets have to find corresponding elements in the operational definition. The following excerpt from Sekaran (1992: 156–157) well illustrates this issue:

> Operationally defining a concept does not consist of delineating the reasons, antecedents, consequences, or correlates of the concept. Rather, it describes the observable characteristics of the concept in order to be able to measure it. [...]
>
>   Learning is an important concept in educational setting. [In order] to measure the abstract concept [...] [of] learning we need [...] to break it down to observable and measurable behaviors. [...] The dimensions of learning may well be as follows: 1. Understanding, 2. Retention, 3. Application. [...] Terms such as understanding, remembering, and applying are still abstract [each dimension can be further decomposed in observable elements. Understanding is decomposed in] [...] answer questions

correctly, give appropriate examples. [...] [Retentions is specified in] recall material after some lapses of time. [...] [Application is decomposed in] solve problems applying concepts understood and recalled, and integrate with other relevant material.

The list of observable elements in each construct facet should be developed before writing the items/questions that constitute the measure. Separating the two tasks will help the researcher focus on the content instead of on the wording. A careful literature review, a collection of all the measures previously used for the concept under investigation and a conceptual analysis of the content must be performed. The works of Koste and Malhotra (1999) and Koste et al. (2004) provide good examples of this practice.

This action of reducing abstract constructs so that they can be measured (i.e. construct operationalization) presents several challenges: aligning the theoretical concepts and the empirical measures, choosing between objective and perceptual questions and choosing the number of questions for the construct, for a dimension of a construct or for an observable element. These problems can be alleviated by using operational definitions that have already been developed, used and tested. The availability of such operational definitions is increasing rapidly in OSCM and articles recently published in top OSCM journals have been collected in a handbook (Roth et al., 2008). In spite of that improvement, the researcher may be forced to develop new measures or to improve existing ones: here, research that reports previous experiences and gives suggestions on measure development may be useful (see, for example, Converse and Presser, 1986; Hinkin, 1995; Hensley, 1999).

The translation from theoretical concepts to operational definitions can be very different from construct to construct. While some constructs lend themselves to objective and precise measurement, others are more nebulous and do not lend themselves to such precise measurement, especially when people's feelings, attitudes and perceptions are involved. When constructs such as 'customer satisfaction' have multiple facets, involve people's perceptions or feelings, or are planned to be measured through people's perceptions, it is recommended that operational definitions that include multiple elements be used (Lazarsfeld, 1935; Payne, 1951; Malhotra and Grover, 1998; Hensley, 1999). In contrast, when objective constructs are considered, a single direct question would be sufficient.

Sometimes, constructs can be measured through both perceptual and objective measures. In this case, the properties of the two methods should be compared. One important case is that of operational and financial performance, which, in OSCM surveys, are investigated through perceptual measures. Ketokivi and Schroeder (2004) showed that this approach is acceptable, but requires caution.

The process of identifying the elements to insert in the operational definition, as well as the items (questions) in the measure, may include both contacting those in the population-of-interest to gain practical knowledge of how the construct is viewed in actual organizations, and identifying important features of the industry being studied. 'The development of items using both academic and practical perspectives should help researchers develop good preliminary scales and keep questionnaire revision to a minimum' (Hensley, 1999: 348).

4.3.2.2.2 TESTING THE OPERATIONAL DEFINITIONS FOR CONTENT VALIDITY

When the operational definition has been developed (i.e. when the set of items in a multi-item measure has been developed), the researcher should test it for content validity. The content validity of a construct measure can be defined as the degree to which a measure's items represent a proper sample of the theoretical content domain of a construct (Nunnally and Bernstein, 1994). The concept of 'content validity' has been controversial in social indicators research (Sireci, 1998). Stated otherwise, it is the degree to which the measure spans the domain of the construct's theoretical definition (Rungtusanatham, 1998).

Two conditions are to be satisfied by a measure's items in order to confirm content validity. First, each item should fall within the concept's theoretical domain. Second, the set of items should capture the different facets of a construct in a balanced way. If the items are too similar to each other, then important facets of the constructs are probably not covered. If the items touch only one aspect of a multifaceted construct, then the measure does not span the entire domain of the construct.

Evaluating the face validity of a measure (i.e. assessing whether the measure 'at face value' seems like a good translation of the theoretical concept) can indirectly assess its content validity (Rungtusanatham, 1998). Face validity is a matter of judgement and must be assessed before data collection. In order to highlight the importance of making such an assessment before heavy data collection, Menor and Roth (2007) presented, and performed, the development of a new measurement instrument as a two-stage process. In stage 1, they performed item generation and purification refinement prior to developing their questionnaire and field study. In stage 2, they focused on the survey instrument, data collection, confirmatory analyses and item refinement. They iterated the first stage four times in order to reach enough agreement between experts.

The assessment of face validity in OSCM surveys is quite rare, but it has increased over the years. Even in more established disciplines such as marketing, however, the assessment of face validity has involved various approaches, procedures and metrics (see Hardesty and Bearden, 2004).

One possible approach to assessing face validity involves a panel of subject-matter experts who are exposed to individual items and are asked to judge the degree to which these items are representative of the construct's conceptual definition. Subsequently, for each ith candidate item in the measure, Lawshe's (1975) content validity ratio (CVR_i) is calculated. Mathematically, CVR_i is computed as follows:

$$CVR_i = \frac{n_e - \frac{N}{2}}{\frac{N}{2}}$$

where n_e is the number of subject-matter experts indicating the measurement item i as 'essential' and N is the total number of subject-matter experts in the panel. Lawshe (1975) has also established a minimum CVR_i for different panel sizes. For example, for a panel size of 25, the minimum CVR_i is 0.37). As an alternative to CVR_i, other metrics/criteria are available (see Hardesty and Bearden, 2004).

Another approach to assessing face validity is to give judges both the list of items and the definition of each construct or construct dimension. Subsequently, judges are asked to map the items into the construct definitions or, for multifaceted constructs, into the construct dimension definitions (Hardesty and Bearden, 2004). Cohen's (1960) κ index, as well as other inter-rater agreement indexes, is also used to assess face validity and to improve it, if necessary, through identifying which items to discard. An interesting example of an application of this approach to new service development research can be found in Menor and Roth (2007). A combination of the two approaches was adopted by Rungtusanatham et al. (1999: 307–308):

> Assessing face validity [...] can be accomplished by having the constituent measurement items evaluated by subject-matter experts, under the condition that the experts have been briefed as to the dimension's research definition [...] For this research, seven subject-matter-experts on SPC volunteered to participate in evaluating the face validity of the 66 measurement items for the 14 SPC implementation/practice dimensions [...] Each expert was asked to complete [...] two tasks [...] For task A [attributing each item to the closest dimension for the meaning], we provided the seven experts with the operational definitions for each of the 14 dimensions and a random listing of the 66 measurement items. The sorting results from task A were then used to compute Cohen's (1960) κ, an index [...] [of] the overall degree of inter-expert agreement as to the placement of the measurement items [...] We then asked the subject-matter-experts to evaluate, in task B, how adequately each measurement item measures the dimension to which it has been assigned. For each measurement item, the experts were asked to respond to a seven-point scale with '1' anchored as 'barely adequate' and '7' anchored as 'almost perfect'. [...] From the experts' input for task B, we computed and evaluated the average adequacy score and the standard deviation of adequacy scores for each individual measurement item.

This phase of preliminary checking for content validity may prevent subsequent problems with reliability and convergent/discriminant validity (see Section 4.5). The researcher has the opportunity to identify and to modify ambiguous or difficult-to-interpret items, which, in turn, improves reliability. If multiple constructs are investigated, the use of a Q-sort procedure may help to identify the convergent/discriminant capability of a given set of items. If an item is mapped by some experts into one construct and by others into another, it means that the item does not contribute to discriminating between the two constructs. If the researcher adds an additional category, named 'other constructs', and an item is mapped into this category by some experts, then the item may be problematic for the assessment of convergent validity, which will be performed after data collection.

A researcher who has devoted enough effort to testing items and constructs before data collection can make the same claim as Oliveira and Roth (2012: 167) did when they developed the measurement instrument for service orientation: 'Thus, we have evidence that the constructs and their associated items exhibited tentative reliability and validity'. Please note that tentative reliability and validity need further assessment after data collection.

4.3.2.3 *Stating hypotheses*

A hypothesis is a logically conjectured relationship between two or more variables (measures), expressed in the form of testable statements. A hypothesis can also test whether there are differences between two groups (or among several groups) with respect to any variable or variables. These relationships are conjectured on the basis of the network of associations established in the theoretical framework and formulated for the research study. Hypotheses can be set in either the propositional or the if-then statement form. If terms such as 'positive', 'negative', 'more than', 'less than' and 'alike' are used in stating the relationship between two variables or in comparing two groups, the hypotheses are directional. When there is no indication of the direction of the difference or relationship, they are called non-directional. Non-directional hypotheses can be formulated either when the relationships or differences have not been explored previously, or when there are conflicting findings. It is better to indicate the direction when known.

The null hypothesis is a proposition that states a definitive, exact relationship between two variables. For example: a) the correlation between two variables is equal to zero; or b) the difference between the means of two groups in the population is equal to zero. Sekaran (1992: 81–83) explained the null hypothesis as follows:

> In general the null statement is expressed as no (significant) relationship between two variables or no (significant) difference between two groups. [...] What we are implying through the null hypothesis is that any differences found between two sample groups (or any relationships found between two variables based on our sample) is simply due to random sampling fluctuations and not due to any 'true' differences between the two population groups (or relationship between two variables). The null hypothesis is thus formulated so that it can be tested for possible rejection. If we reject the null hypothesis, then all permissible alternative hypotheses related to the tested relationship could be supported. It is the theory that allows us to trust the alternative hypothesis that is generated in the particular research investigation. [...] Having thus formulated the null H_0 and alternative H_a hypotheses, the appropriate statistical tests, which would indicate whether or not support has been found for the alternative, should be identified.

A clear example of how to pass from a theoretical model to hypotheses is provided by Rungtusanatham et al. (1998: 79, 83). In their work, the difference between propositions and hypotheses as well as the difference between constructs are clearly expressed:

> Proposition 1: Visionary leadership enables the simultaneous creation of a cooperative and learning organization [...]. The theoretical constructs [i.e. visionary leadership, cooperative organization and learning organization] were operationalized as multi-item measurement scales [...]. Stated in standard null form, Proposition 1 suggests the following two hypotheses [...]. Hypothesis 1: Visionary Leadership [intended as the specific measure of the construct] is not positively related to Internal and External Cooperation [idem] [...]. Hypothesis 2: Visionary Leadership [idem] is not positively related to Learning [idem].

In formulating a hypothesis on the links between two variables, an OSCM researcher should be conscious of the type of relation being tested. For example, if the researcher tests a relation between two variables by means of Pearson's r coefficient, a linear relationship is implicitly assumed. If results are not statistically significant, the researcher cannot conclude that there is no association. It can only be stated that, in the sample, there is no evidence of a linear relationship between the two variables considered. However, an exponential relation could exist and, if tested, could emerge. In summary, when stating the hypotheses, and later, when choosing the appropriate test, the researcher should think carefully about the kind of link being assumed/tested. Narasimhan and Kim (2002: 309) were very clear on that point, as demonstrated in the following:

> Hypothesis 3a. The moderating effect of IMD [international market diversification] on the curvilinear relationship between PD [product diversification] and performance is insignificant, as the level of internal integration across the supply chain increases.

4.4 How a survey should be designed

Survey design includes all of the activities that precede data collection. In the following presentation of this phase of the survey research process, it is assumed that the researcher has already performed all of the activities recalled in Section 4.3; namely, problem focusing, literature review, etc. In this stage, the researcher should consider all the possible shortcomings and difficulties and should find the right compromise between rigour and feasibility. Planning all the future activities in a detailed way and defining documents to keep track of the decisions made and the activities completed are necessary to prevent subsequent problems.

4.4.1 Considering constraints and information needs at the macro level

Before embarking on a survey, the researcher should consider the suitability of the survey method and the overall feasibility of the research project. If a well-developed model is not available, then the researcher should consider how much time and effort will be required to develop such a model. Time, costs and general resource requirements can constrain a survey project, forcing a less expensive type of survey or, in the extreme, making it infeasible. Other possible constraints are the access to the population and the feasibility of involving the right informants.

In survey research, there is a trade-off between time and cost constraints, on the one hand, and minimization of four types of error, on the other hand:

- *Sampling error*: A sample with no (or unknown) capability of representing the population (because of inadequate sample selection or because of self-selection) excludes the possibility of generalizing the results beyond the original sample.
- *Measurement error*: Data derived from the use of measures that do not match the theoretical dimensions, or are not reliable, make any test meaningless.
- *Statistical conclusion error*: When performing statistical tests, there is a probability of concluding that the investigated relationship does not exist even when it does exist.
- *Internal validity error*: When the explanation given of what has been observed is less plausible than rival explanations, then the conclusions can be considered erroneous.

While dissatisfaction with the above-mentioned constraints could halt the survey research, failure to minimize all of the above four errors 'can and will lead to erroneous conclusions and regression rather than progress in contribution to theory' (Malhotra and Grover, 1998: 415).

To evaluate the tightness of the constraints adequately, the researcher should identify the main information needs (such as the time horizon, nature of the information, etc.), which flow from the stated hypotheses and, ultimately, from the various purposes of the study. For example, if the study aims at a very rigorous investigation of causal relationships, or if the theoretical model implies some dynamics, then longitudinal data may be required (i.e. data on the same unit at different points in time). Boyer and Pagell (2000) have called for such an extended time horizon when researching operations strategy issues. Similarly, if the study requires information that is considered confidential by the respondents, then the cost and time required to obtain the information is probably high and a number of survey design alternatives are not viable. Finally, a study may aim to not only test a theory but also to perform additional exploratory analyses, while reducing the cost of the research and increasing the speed of generating knowledge. In this case, the problem is to satisfy questionnaire length constraints: classifying information items by priority can be helpful in subsequently choosing which questions to eliminate (Alreck and Settle, 1985; Babbie, 1990).

It is useful, at this point, to give an example of what it means to consider a survey project at the macro level. Collins and Cordon (1997: 703, 706) while reporting on and comparing their survey experiences, clearly highlighted the importance of macro-level choices for a survey project:

> A comparison of the different approaches taken in the two studies, and indeed the differences in approach taken by the IMD and IBM researchers in the 'Made in Switzerland' study raises a number of [methodological] issues [...] sample (sector) selection, respondent preparation, quality assurance for data input, the elimination of bias and the gathering of data complementary to that of survey instrument. The first study, 'Manufacturing strategies in western Europe', included an initial set of interviews with 16 companies followed by a mailed questionnaire answered by 121 companies. The second study, 'Made in Switzerland', while also obtaining data from 116 manufacturing site/plants, was conducted exclusively by interviewing company executives. While the second approach requires more resources, it has [...] the following advantages: a) the preparation of the respondents seems more rigorous, b) higher quality and more consistent data – furthermore, apparent inconsistencies point out interesting new hypotheses, c) blatant bias is eliminated, d) the gathering of complementary data to that of the questionnaire allows for the testing of face validity and the testing of hypotheses that were not made explicit at the beginning of the study, e) much higher response rate.

4.4.2 Planning activities

Survey research is a process with a series of steps that are linked to each other (see Figure 4.1). Carefully planning this process is crucial to preventing problems and assuring the quality of the research process. For this reason, the design phase should be detailed and should be followed by a pilot-testing phase aimed at assuring that the survey instrumentation and procedures are adequate.

However, in planning the research activities, it should be recognized that the decisions made during the early steps affect the choices available at later steps (see Figure 4.2). For

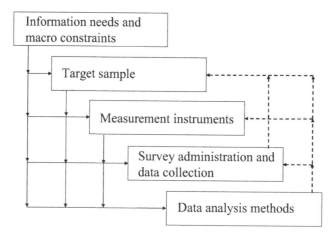

Figure 4.2 Linkages between decisions in survey planning.

Source: Adapted from Alreck and Settle (1985: 26).

example, if the researcher decides to use a phone survey, this choice will subsequently limit the number and the sophistication of the measures that can be employed.

It is not possible to proceed step by step: constraints and limitations in the later steps should be considered in the earlier steps. For these reasons, major decisions about data collection (telephone, interview, web and mail) and the time horizon (cross-sectional, longitudinal) must always be made prior to selecting a sample and designing and constructing the questionnaire and other material. It is important to match the capabilities and the limitations of the data processing methods with the sampling and instrumentation. For more details on project planning, see Alreck and Settle (1985).

4.4.3 The sample

Before discussing the sample, the following terms should be defined: *population, population element, population frame, sample, subject* and *sampling. Population* refers to the entire group of people, firms, plants or things that the researcher wishes to investigate. A *population element is* a single member of the population. The *population frame* is a list of all the elements in the population from which the sample is to be drawn. A *sample* is a subset of the population: it comprises some members selected from the population. A *subject* is a single member of the sample. Finally, *sampling* is the process of selecting a sufficient number of elements from the population so that by studying the sample, and understanding the properties or the characteristics of the sample subjects, the researcher will be able to generalize the properties or characteristics to the population elements. Sampling overcomes the difficulties of collecting data from the entire population, which can be impossible or prohibitive in terms of time, costs and other human resources.

Sample design is a step that is often overlooked in OSCM surveys (Forza and Di Nuzzo, 1998; Rungtusanatham et al., 2003). Many articles do not report adequately how their sample was constructed and do not provide sufficient information on the resulting sample. The majority of survey-based OM articles (approximately 88 per cent) do not rely on a probabilistic sampling approach (Rungtusanatham et al., 2003). Poor sample design can constrain the application of more appropriate statistical techniques and the generalizability of the results.

Two issues should be addressed when designing the sample: randomness and sample size. Randomness is associated with the ability of the sample to represent the population of interest. Sample size is associated with the requirements of the statistical procedures used for assessing the measurement quality and testing the hypothesis.

4.4.3.1 Population frame

The population frame should be drawn from widely available sources (e.g. Rungtusanatham et al., 2005; Schoenherr and Swink, 2012) to facilitate the replication of studies. The classification of the industry/industries under investigation (frequently specified through International Standard Industrial Classification (ISIC) codes) is an important aspect of defining the study population. Even though ISIC codes can provide a useful starting point, they were not designed for OSCM research. Therefore, the classification may need to be modified to fulfil the needs of an OSCM researcher (Flynn et al., 1990). Additionally, in some countries, ISIC codes are not available, the list of companies and their ISIC codes are too expensive and other classifications, if available, cannot always be trusted. The GMRG survey has solved these problems by using product descriptions as the industry selection criterion (Whybark, 1997). To facilitate control of industry effects, a good practice is, therefore, to consider four-digit ISIC codes when building the population frame and then the research sample. This issue should not be underestimated, since 'controlling for industry effects can compensate for variability between industries, in terms of processes, work force management, competitive forces, degree of unionisation, etc.' (Flynn et al., 1990: 260).

There are other justifiable ways of choosing a sample, based on specific features (for example, common process technology, position in the supply chain, etc.), which should be controlled for in the investigation of the phenomenon under study. For example, Dun & Bradstreet's databases are useful sources, since they provide information (in some countries at the plant level) such as products made, number of employees, addresses and so on (see www.dnb.com). Other than industry, another important variable to control for is company size: the number of employees and sales are easily available and can be incorporated in the sample selection process.

Sometimes it is difficult to identify and/or reach the population elements that have certain characteristics. Other times, a researcher can reach only one part of the population. Therefore, in a number of cases, the researcher has to be creative in identifying/reaching the population elements and in describing the considered population. Some examples can be helpful. Swink and Jacobs (2012) used multiple sources – web searches, books, practitioner journals and academic journals – to identify a preliminary list of Six Sigma adopters (both manufacturing and service companies). Mollenkopf et al. (2007) worked closely with five Internet retailers to select customers who had returned a product in the previous 2–3 months. Lai et al. (2008) took two lists of third-party logistics (3PL) providers registered with the Ministry of Communications of China and the China International Freight Forwarders Association. Chen et al. (2011) effectively presented the sample they used to explore the influence of business-to-business co-production on service innovation in the information technology (IT) industry. Llach et al. (2013) well justify the importance of the chosen population, based on personal interviews with the managers of 374 establishments in the food and beverage services subsector. Finally, the motivation for using a sample of students when studying e-quality provides interesting reading in Wen et al. (2014).

4.4.3.2 Sample design

There are several sample designs, and they can be grouped into two families: probabilistic and non-probabilistic sampling. In probabilistic sampling, the population elements have some known probability of being selected, differently from non-probabilistic sampling. Probabilistic sampling is used to assure the representativeness of the sample when the researcher is interested in generalizing the results. When time or other factors are considered by the researcher to be more important than generalizability, then non-probabilistic sampling is usually chosen. Table 4.6 shows some basic types of sampling approaches (for more details, see Babbie, 1990).

Stratified random sampling is a very useful type of sampling, since it provides more information for a given sample size. Stratified random sampling involves the division of the population into strata and a random selection of subjects from each stratum. Strata are identified on the basis of meaningful criteria like industry type, size, performance or other categories. This procedure ensures high homogeneity within each stratum and heterogeneity between strata. Stratified random sampling allows the comparison of population subgroups and allows control for factors like industry or size, which very often affect results.

Table 4.6 Sampling approaches

Representativeness	Purpose is mainly	Type of sampling
Essential for the study => probabilistic sampling	Generalizability	Simple random sampling; systematic sampling
	Assessing differential parameters in subgroups of a population	Proportionate stratified random sampling (for subgroups with an equal number of elements) Disproportionate stratified random sampling (for subgroups with a different number of elements)
	Collecting information in localized areas	Area sampling
	Gathering information from a subset of the sample	Double (or multistage) sampling
Not essential for the study => non-probabilistic sampling	Obtain quick – even if unreliable – information	Convenience sampling
	Obtain information relevant to and available only from certain groups	Judgement sampling (when looking for information that only a few experts can provide) Quota sampling (when the responses of special-interest minority groups are needed)

4.4.3.3 Sample size

Sample size is the second concern when designing the sample. It is a complex issue and is linked to the significance level and the statistical power of the test, and also to the size of the researched relationship (for example, the association strength or amount of difference).

When making a statistical inference, the researcher can make either a Type I error (reject the null hypothesis H_0 when it is true) or a Type II error (H_0 is not rejected when the alternative hypothesis H_a is true). The probability of making a Type I error (α) is called the *significance level*. Typically, in most social sciences (OSCM included), α is taken to be 0.05; however, in several cases $\alpha = 0.01$ and $\alpha = 0.001$ are used. The null hypothesis is rejected if the observed significance level (*p*-value) is less than the chosen value of α (McClave and Benson, 1991). The probability of a Type II error is β, and the *statistical power* is equal to 1-β. A high statistical power is required to reduce the probability of failing to detect an effect when it is present. A balance between the two types of errors is needed because reducing any one type of error increases the probability of the other type of error. Low statistical power leads to a study that is not able to detect large size effects, while high power leads to committing unnecessary resources in order to detect only trivial effects. Methodologists consider a power of about 0.8 as a reasonable and realistic value for research in social/behavioural sciences (e.g. Verma and Goodale, 1995). This means that only 20 per cent of the repeated studies will not yield a significant result, even when the phenomenon exists.

Even though the power of a statistical test depends on three factors (α, effect size and sample size), from a practical point of view, only the sample size is used to control the power. This is because the α level is effectively fixed at 0.05 (or some other value) and the effect size (for example, the size of the difference in the means between two samples or the correlation between two variables) can also be assumed to be fixed at some unknown

Table 4.7 Effect size and statistical power and sample size

Effect size	Stat. Power = 0.6		Stat. Power = 0.8	
	α = 0.05	α = 0.01	α = 0.05	α = 0.01
Large effect (e.g. strong association)	12	18	17	24
Medium effect (e.g. medium association)	30	45	44	62
Small effect (e.g. small association)	179	274	271	385

value (the researcher may wish not to change the effect, but only to detect it). The required sample sizes, with desired statistical powers of 0.8 and 0.6, are shown in Table 4.7 as a function of effect size (and significance levels). One can see that the required sample size increases while increasing the statistical power, and/or decreasing the significance level, and/or decreasing the size of the effect researched. Verma and Goodale (1995) have provided more details (and a selected bibliography) on this issue. They have also provided some figures for the statistical power evident in OM articles published in the *Journal of Operations Management (JOM)* and *Decision Sciences Journal (DSJ)* in the period 1990–1995. Their study is complemented by Helmuth et al. (2015), who showed that there is only a 38 per cent likelihood that SCM articles published in the years 2002–2012 correctly identify statistical relationships with small effect sizes.

4.4.4 Data collection method

Data can be collected in a variety of ways, in different settings and from different sources. In survey research, the main methods used to collect data are interviews and questionnaires. Interviews may be structured or unstructured. They can be conducted either face-to-face or over the telephone. Questionnaires can be administered personally, by telephone (in person or through interactive voice responding systems) or through the web, and can be posted or e-mailed to the respondents.

Each data collection method has merits as well as shortcomings. The best method cannot be chosen without taking into account the needs of the specific survey as well as the time, cost and resource constraints. Different methods can be used in the same survey to compensate for the weaknesses of each method. However, the use of mixed approaches may raise difficult issues, the most important of which is represented by the fact that a same respondent may give different answers to the same question administered through different methods. Problems and possible solutions are discussed by Dillman (2007: 217–244) and Dillman et al. (2014: 398–449).

In a postal survey, questionnaires are printed and sent by post. The respondents are asked to complete the questionnaire on their own and to send it back. Posted questionnaires have the following advantages: they are inexpensive; they can be completed at the respondent's convenience; they can be prepared to give an authoritative impression; they can ensure anonymity; they can reduce interviewer bias; and the respondent has more time to consider his/her responses. On the other hand, posted questionnaires have a lower response rate than other methods, involve longer time periods and are more affected by self-selection, lack of interviewer involvement and lack of open-ended questions.

In a face-to-face survey, the interviewer solicits information directly from a respondent during personal interviews. The advantages are: flexibility in sequencing the questions,

Table 4.8 Comparison of data collection methods

Factors influencing coverage and secured information	Mailed	Personal interview	Telephone survey	E-survey
Lowest relative cost	2	4	3	1
Highest response rate	4	1	2	3
Highest accuracy of information	2	1	4	3
Largest sample coverage	1	4	3	2
Completeness, including sensitive materials	3	1	2	4
Overall reliability and validity	2	1	3	4
Time required to secure information	4	2	1	3
Ease of securing information	1	4	3	2

Source: Adapted from Miller (1991: 168).

details and explanation; the possibility of administering highly complex questionnaires; improved ability to contact hard-to-reach populations; higher response rates; increased confidence that data collection instructions are followed. On the other hand, disadvantages include: higher costs; interviewer bias; the respondent's reluctance to co-operate; greater stress for both respondents and interviewer; less anonymity. An interesting example is Yee et al. (2010), where employee loyalty, service quality and firm performance in the service industry were investigated by visiting 300 shops in Hong Kong.

Telephone surveys involve collecting information through the use of telephone interviews. The advantages are: rapid data collection; low costs; anonymity; large-scale accessibility; higher confidence that instructions are followed. The disadvantages are: less control over the interview situation; less credibility; lack of visual materials.

In the 2000s, a new way to approach companies and administer questionnaires appeared. The researcher can send a questionnaire through e-mail or ask respondents to visit a website where the questionnaire can be filled in without the need to return the questionnaire physically, since data input is done directly by the respondent. One advantage of these methods is the minimal cost compared with other means of distribution (Dillman, 2007). However, potential problems lie in sampling and controlling the research environment (Birnbaum, 1999; Dillman, 2007).

Table 4.8 summarizes the relative strengths of the different methods. Here, '1' indicates that the method has the maximum strength and '4' represents the minimum with respect to each factor considered. Dillman (1978: 74–76) and Rea and Parker (1992) provide more detailed comparisons.

Electronic surveys have been developing rapidly since the late 1990s, even though there was some debate on their use at the beginning. Klassen and Jacobs (2001: 726–727) reported the first systematic experimentation and comparison of electronic surveys in OM (of web-based, e-mail, fax and PC disk-by-mail technologies), providing many insights into this issue:

If a survey was to be conducted only using the Web-based technology, respondents are unlikely to be truly representative of the population. [...] Moreover, if Web surveys become commonplace, reviewer expectations for response rates may need to be adjusted downward from 20 per cent (Malhotra and Grover, 1998) to possibly 10 per cent (i.e. Web response rate was approximately half that of other technologies). Second, while the return rate of the Web survey was lower than other survey technologies, the item completion rates of surveys completed using Web, fax and disk-by-mail technologies were significantly higher than with the mail survey. Third, the limited evidence of systematic bias with the application of computing technology in forecasting characteristics can be viewed as either a threat to data validity or an opportunity to collect data from a different subgroup [...] This finding indicates that a sub-sample of best practice users in operations management can be tapped who otherwise might be underrepresented. At the present time, a combined approach of using Web and fax technologies to survey managers offers significant benefits over the sole use of mail for establishment-level, self-administered surveys.

Boyer et al. (2002: 370–371) provided further research on the properties of electronic surveys in OM:

In general, our study confirms the findings of Klassen and Jacobs (2001) [...] and extends their findings [...] electronic surveys offer important capabilities in terms of contingently coding questions [...] Electronic surveys are much more challenging to develop [...] require different handling procedures [...] but lead to] greater efficiency [in data entry] and greater data accuracy [...] Both methods [electronic and mail surveys] had statistically similar response rates, scale/construct means and inter item reliabilities [...] Electronic surveys have substantially fewer missing responses [...] Electronic surveys provide an important capability to design surveys in a contingent manner.

The web survey technique has made impressive improvements in the last decade. On the one hand, researchers have gained a better understanding of web survey requirements in terms of visual design and consideration of computer logic (constraints and opportunities) (see Dillman, 2007 and Dillman et al., 2014). At the same time, respondents' confidence continues to increase as web instruments and communication technologies improve their speed and (user) friendliness. All of these changes together make web-based surveys much less problematic in terms of response rate and non-response bias. These improvements lead to a need to reassess the findings of Klassen and Jacobs (2001) and Boyer et al. (2002) included above. One important issue to investigate is the possibility of having multiple respondents from the same organization by using a web-based survey.

4.4.5 *The measurement instrument*

One of the main characteristics of the survey is that it relies on structured instruments to collect information. Once the researcher has decided on the content of a measure (the specific empirical aspects that have to be observed), several tasks remain in order to develop the measurement instrument, namely:

• Defining how the questions are to be formulated to collect the information on a specific concept (see Subsection 4.4.5.1).
• For each question, deciding the scale on which the answers are to be placed (see Subsection 4.4.5.2).
• Identifying the appropriate respondent/s for each question (see Subsection 4.4.5.3).
• Putting the questions together in questionnaires that facilitate and motivate responses from the respondent/s (see Subsection 4.4.5.4).

The main issues related to each task are discussed in the following subsections. It should be noted, however, that the actual design of the survey questionnaire depends on whether the questionnaire is to be administered by telephone interview, on-site interview, on-site using pen-and-paper or by post using pen-and-paper.

4.4.5.1 Wording

In formulating survey questions, the researcher should ensure that the language of the questionnaire is consistent with the respondents' level of understanding. If a question is not understood or is interpreted differently by respondents, the researcher will get unreliable responses to the question, and these responses will be biased. The researcher also has to choose between open-ended (allowing respondents to answer in any way they choose) or closed questions (limiting respondents to a choice among alternatives given by the researcher). Closed questions facilitate quick decisions and easy information coding, but the researcher has to ensure that the alternatives are mutually exclusive and collectively exhaustive. Another choice in formulating the questions is a mix of positively and negatively worded questions in order to minimize the tendency in respondents to circle the points mechanically towards one end of the scale.

The researcher should replace double-barrelled questions (i.e. questions that have different answers to its subparts) with several separate questions. Ambiguity in the questions should be eliminated as much as possible. Leading questions (i.e. questions phrased in a way that leads the respondent to give responses that the researcher would like or comes across as wanting to elicit) should be avoided as well. In the same way, loaded questions (i.e. questions phrased in an emotionally charged manner) should be eliminated. Questions should not be worded to elicit socially desirable responses. Finally, a question or a statement should not exceed 20 words or a full line in print; for further details on wording, see, for example, Horst (1968), Converse and Presser (1986) and Oppenheim (1996).

4.4.5.2 Scaling

A second task in developing the measurement instrument concerns the scale that will be used to measure the answers. The scale choice depends on the ease with which the respondent can respond to items and the ease with which the subsequent analyses can be performed. There are four basic types of scale: nominal, ordinal, interval and ratio (see Table 4.9).

Table 4.9 Scales and scaling techniques

Basic scale type	What it highlights	Scaling technique
Nominal	Difference	Multiple choice items, adjective checklist, staple scale
Ordinal	Difference, order	Forced ranking scale, paired comparison scale
Interval	Difference, order, distance	Likert scale, verbal frequency scale, comparative scale, semantic differential scale
Ratio	Difference, order, distance with 0 as meaningful natural origin	Fixed sum scale

The sophistication of the application for which the scales are suited increases with the progression from nominal to ratio. As the sophistication increases, so also does the information detail, the ability to differentiate the individuals and the flexibility in using more powerful tests. For a more detailed treatment of the use of scales in OSCM, see Table 4.10 and Flynn et al. (1990).

When addressing data analysis later in this chapter, we will note the importance of considering two basic kinds of data: nonmetric (qualitative) and metric (quantitative). Hair et al. (1992: 5) clearly characterised these two kinds of data:

> Nonmetric data includes attributes, characteristics, or categorical properties that can be used to identify or describe a subject. Nonmetric data differs in kind. Metric data measurement is made so that subjects may be identified as differing in amount or degree. Metrically measured variables reflect relative quantity or distance, whereas nonmetrically measured variables do not. Nonmetric data is measured with nominal or ordinal scales and metric variables with interval or ratio scales.

4.4.5.3 Respondent identification

Frequently, the unit of analysis in OM research is the plant, or company. However, the plant (company) cannot give the answers: it is the people who work in the plant (company) that provide information on that plant (company).

Due to the functional specialization and hierarchical levels in organizations, some people are knowledgeable about some facts, while others know only about others. The researcher should therefore identify the appropriate informants for each set of information required. Increasing the number of respondents, however, increases the probability of receiving only some completed questionnaires, leading to incomplete information, which can impact the results of relational studies. On the other hand, answers from respondents who are not knowledgeable cannot be trusted and increase random or even bias error.

Further, if perceptual questions are asked, one can gather a perception that is personal to that respondent. In order to enhance confidence in the findings, the researcher can use some form of triangulation, such as multiple respondents for the same question or multiple measurement methods (for example, qualitative and quantitative). These strategies reduce the common method/source variance; that is, the potentially inflated empirical relationships that can occur when the data have been collected using the same method or have been provided by the same single source (Rungtusanatham et al., 2003). Vokurka and O'Leary-Kelly (2000) and Boyer and Pagell (2000) discussed this issue in relation to research on manufacturing flexibility, operations strategy and manufacturing technology.

4.4.5.4 Rules of questionnaire design

Once the questions have been developed and their associations with the respondent(s) have been established, the researcher can put together the questionnaire (Converse and Presser, 1986). There are some simple things that the researcher should keep in mind. Some basic rules of courtesy, presentation and readability are essential for successful data collection. An attractive and neat questionnaire with an appropriate introduction, clear

Table 4.10 Scaling techniques in OSCM

Scaling technique	Example	When to use	Benefits	Limitations
Multiple choice items	Which of the following philosophies concerning quality are used by your plant? Please check *all* that apply. ___ Total quality control by all employees ___ Continuous improvement of quality ___ Statistical process control ___ Zero defects as a goal for all employees.	Entire range of responses should be classifiable into a limited number of discrete, mutually exclusive categories.	Simple, versatile. Can be used to obtain either a single response or several.	Respondents may not always follow directions when a single response is desired. Should not be used for numeric (continuous) data, where a direct question is more appropriate. Limited statistical analysis is possible due to nominal data.
Forced ranking scale	Please rank the importance of the following objectives or goals for manufacturing at your plant over the next five years. Rank #1 the most important objective, #2 for the next most important and so on. You may rank several objectives the same if they are of equal importance. ___ Low unit cost. ___ Ability to rapidly introduce new products or make design changes ___ Ability to make rapid volume changes ___ Consistent quality ___ High performance products ___ Fast deliveries ___ Dependable delivery ___ Low manufacturing cycle time.	Used when researcher seeks to obtain the standings of the items relative to each other.	Obtain most preferred item, as well as the sequence of the remaining items. Relativity between items is measured.	Absolute standing of an item is not measured, nor is the interval between items. Response task rapidly becomes tedious for respondents if more than a few items are included.
Likert scale	We emphasise good maintenance as a strategy for achieving schedule compliance. ___ Strongly agree ___ Agree	Use when it is necessary to obtain people's position on certain issues or conclusions.	More readily analysed and interpreted than open-ended attitude questions. Flexible, economical and easy	Respondents may be lulled into marking the same response for each item; therefore, care should be taken that some of the

(Continued)

Table 4.10 (Continued)

Scaling technique	Example	When to use	Benefits	Limitations
	— Neither agree nor disagree — Disagree — Strongly disagree.		to compose items. Can obtain a summated value in order to measure a more general construct.	items are inclined towards the pro side of the issue and the rest towards the con side.
Ratio scale	— How many engineering change orders occurred last year?	Used when exact figures on objective (as opposed to subjective) factors are called for.	Permit identification of not only the magnitude of the differences but also of the proportion of the differences.	Precise figures may not be available to respondents and may be more likely to be perceived as confidential information. Different respondents may respond using different units of measures due to habit.

Source: Adapted from Flynn et al. (1990: 275–281).

instructions and a well-formatted set of questions will make it easier for the respondents to answer the questions.

For both the researcher and the respondent, closely placed related questions facilitate cross checks on the responses (for example, 'what is the percentage of customer orders received by electronic data interchange (EDI)?' and 'what is the percentage of customer order value received by electronic data interchange (EDI)?'). Mixing items that belong to different measures contributes to avoiding stereotype answering. The presence of reversal questions keeps attention high. The length of the questionnaire affects the response rate and attention in filling in the questionnaire. Finally, codes can facilitate subsequent data input.

In the 2000s, questionnaire design has introduced the so-called principles of visual design. These principles consider the appearance of the questionnaire not only as a manifestation of care and professionalism, but also as a communicating instrument whose importance is close to that of wording. The underlying reason is the observation that respondents, before reading a question, make a number of visual interpretations based on visual processing, which may lead them to skip a question or to misinterpret instructions on how to answer. Even when they are reading a question, they do not put equal attention on each word of the question, thus risking misinterpretation of the question. Visual aids greatly reduce this kind of error. Dillman (2007) and Dillman et al. (2014) illustrated the principle of visual design and provided a number of useful examples.

4.4.6 Approaching companies and respondents

To increase the probability of successful data collection, the researcher should plan the execution of the survey research carefully and should provide detailed instructions on the following: a) how the sampling units are going to be approached; and b) how the questionnaires are going to be administered. In other words, the protocol to be followed in administering the developed questionnaire has to be developed.

Increasingly, companies and respondents are being asked to complete questionnaires and are becoming more reluctant to collaborate. Researchers, therefore, must find ways to obtain the collaboration of companies and specific respondents. Dillman (1978, 2007) and Dillman et al. (2014) emphasized that the response to a questionnaire should be viewed as a social exchange, suggesting that the researcher should:

- *Reward the respondent* by showing positive regard, giving verbal appreciation, using a consulting approach, supporting his or her values, offering tangible rewards and making the questionnaire interesting.
- *Reduce costs to the respondent* by making the task appear brief, reducing the physical and mental efforts that are required, eliminating chances for embarrassment, eliminating any implication of subordination and eliminating any direct monetary costs.
- *Establish trust with the respondent* by providing a token of appreciation in advance, identifying with a known organization that has legitimacy and building on other exchange relationships.

A peculiar problem of OSCM survey research is the difficulty in reaching the right respondents. Researchers often send a questionnaire to a company without knowing the name of the respondent. In this case, there is a high probability that the questionnaire will be lost or delivered to a person who is not interested (or knowledgeable) on the subject.

The contact strategy should take this problem into account and the approach should vary based on such influencing variables as, for example, the company size, which can influence the presence of certain professional/managerial positions.

In OSCM, Flynn et al. (1990, 1997, 1999) suggested, and also successfully implemented, a contact strategy based on contacting potential respondents and obtaining their commitment to questionnaire completion prior to distribution. Flynn et al. (1999: 259), for example, wrote:

> The plant manager of each sampled plant was contacted by telephone to solicit the firm's participation. Participating plant managers each appointed a plant research coordinator to serve as liaison with the research team. The packet of questionnaires was sent to the plant research coordinator. It included 21 questionnaires, targeted at various respondents in the plant. For example, the accounting questionnaire requested performance information, while the direct labor questionnaire contained a set of scales designed to determine workers' perceptions of practices and culture at the plant. The research coordinator distributed the questionnaires to the named managers and a random sample of 10 direct laborers. Respondents were asked to return their questionnaires to the plant research coordinator in sealed envelopes. When the entire set had been received, the plant research coordinator returned the packet of sealed envelopes to the research team. [...] In return for participating, each firm was provided with a detailed profile of its practices and performance, as well as benchmark data on practices and performance in its industry. This yielded a response rate of 60 per cent of the firms that were contacted. Analysis of the industry, size and location of responding and nonresponding firms did not indicate any significant differences; although it was not possible to question non-respondents on items more relevant to the hypotheses, there was not a respondent bias indicated in this basic analysis.

McFadden et al. (2009) successfully used a similar contact strategy when investigating patient safety in hospitals. When respondents understand the purpose of a study, lack of anonymity may not be as problematic. This approach allows for the provision of feedback to respondents, which may serve as an incentive to participate. This method also establishes personal contacts, which reduces the possibility of missing data.

Approaching companies and respondents is a process. The number and sequence of the steps, the means used at each step and the decisions made at each step all have an effect on the answer rate and the reliability of the data. The experience of Collins and Cordon (1997: 701) provides a good example:

> The approach used by IMD and IBM in contacting the companies/sites differed and is worthy of comment [...] The initial contact with a prospective respondent was made by phone. The project was described in detail, with a particular emphasis being placed on the benefits accruing to the company/division/site/executive through participation as well as the time commitment that was required. The executive was finally asked if he or she would agree to receiving a letter, essentially summarizing the telephone conversation, together with copies of the questionnaire in the desired language or languages. It was only after the receipt of the letter and questionnaires that the executive was asked to decide whether or not to participate. A few days after receipt of the letter, the executive was contacted to determine his/her reaction and, in the case of an affirmative response, to fix a date for the plant tour and interview. An affirmative response

solicited a letter to the executive confirming the time and date of the visit as well as designating those members of the research team who would participate. Additional questionnaires were forwarded if necessary. Of the 36 individuals contacted whose sites met the a priori criteria for participation, 35 agreed to participate in the study – a response rate of 97.2 per cent [...] Of the 35 executives ultimately interviewed by the IMD team, 26 were known beforehand to the IMD researchers [...] The others were referred to the researchers by individuals in the aforementioned group.

Even though reference contact procedures such as those presented above, and others summarized by Frohlich (2002), do exist in OSCM, the researcher has to rely on his or her experience and knowledge of the context being investigated. An adaptation of the contact procedures described in the literature is needed. This is consistent with the tailored approach proposed by Dillman (2007) and Dillman et al. (2014).

Due to the increasing difficulty of obtaining responses via traditional forms of survey administration, even in OSCM, some researchers are using survey research firms for data collection and it is expected a strong increase in this practice (Schoenherr et al., 2015). Among the various issues related to this practice, one, in particular, should receive greater attention from researchers, i.e. the response rate (Schoenherr et al., 2015: 291).

The response rate may thus be very small, or – even worse – may be indeterminate if the survey research firm does not provide information on how many invitations were sent out (and for that matter, how many of these were actually delivered to the recipient and did not bounce back or got routed to a spam folder). Depending on what information is or is not provided by the survey research firm, it might be impossible to calculate a traditional measure of nonresponse bias, challenging the representativeness of the sample and the generalizability of the results. We also note that in our experience [...] the response rate that we computed was based on the number of individuals that accessed the survey, and not the total number of email invitations sent out by the survey firm (since the information was not provided to us).

4.5 Pilot testing the questionnaire

4.5.1 Purpose and modality of pilot testing

Once the questionnaires, the protocol for administering these questionnaires and the identity of the sample units are defined, the researcher has to examine the measurement properties of the survey questionnaires and the viability of the administration of these surveys. In other words, the researcher has to test what has been designed. The number of problems that testing can highlight is remarkable, even when all the previous steps have been followed with maximum attention.

The pre-test of a questionnaire should be done by submitting the 'final' questionnaire to three types of people: colleagues, industry experts and target respondents. The role of colleagues is to test whether the questionnaire accomplishes the study objectives (Dillman, 1978). The role of industry experts is to prevent the inclusion of some obvious questions that might reveal the investigator's ignorance in some specific areas. The role of target respondents is to provide feedback on everything that could affect whether and how the targeted respondents answer the questions. The target respondents can pre-test the questionnaire separately or in a group. If the questionnaire is to be mailed, it can be sent to a small pre-test sample. Telephone questionnaires must be tested by telephone as some details cannot be tested in a face-to-face situation (Dillman, 1978). This type of questionnaire is easy to test and the researcher can modify and use the revised questionnaire on the same day.

Experience has shown that the best way to pre-test a self-administered questionnaire is to proceed in two phases, each with completely different but complementary objectives. In the first phase, the researcher fills in the questionnaire with a group of potential respondents (Fowler, 1993) or when visiting three or four potential respondents. The respondents should complete the questionnaire as they would if they were part of the planned survey. Meanwhile the researcher should be present, observing how respondents fill in the questionnaire and recording their feedback. Subsequently, the researcher can ask: a) whether the instructions were clear, b) whether the questions were clear, c) whether there were any problems understanding what kinds of answers were expected or in providing answers to the questions posed and d) whether the planned administration procedure would be effective.

In the second phase (not always performed in OSCM surveys), the researcher carries out a small pre-test sample (for example, 15 units) to test the contact-administration protocol, to gather data for performing an exploratory assessment of the measurement quality and to obtain information to better define the sample and the adequacy of the measures in relation to the sample. In this phase, the researcher can also carry out a preliminary analysis of the data in order to investigate: a) whether the answers to certain questions are too concentrated due to the choice of scale, b) whether the content of the answers differs from what was expected and c) whether the context modifies the appropriateness of the questions (for example, a question can be meaningful for B2B companies but not for B2C companies, or can be appropriate for medium-sized companies but not for very small or large companies). Furthermore, it may be possible to observe the effects of missing data and non-response bias in order to define appropriate countermeasures. This pilot study can help to better define the sample and to plan for a 'controlled sample' instead of the 'observational sample', which is generally more problematic but, unfortunately, more common in OSCM studies. In sum, this pilot test should resemble as closely as possible the actual survey that will be conducted for theory testing.

4.5.2 Handling non-respondents and non-response bias

Non-respondents alter the sample frame and, therefore, can lead to a sample that does not represent the population, even when the sample was adequately designed for that purpose. Non-respondents, as such, can limit the generalizability of the results. In the pilot-testing phase, the researcher should identify a way to address this problem.

From 1995 to 2000, the answer rate in the top seven OM journals typically varied from 20 per cent to 40 per cent, with an average of 32 per cent (Frohlich, 2002). Some OSCM scholars have stated that it is important to reach a response rate of greater than 50 per cent (Flynn et al., 1990), as found in the other social sciences. Other researchers have set the limit at 20 per cent (Malhotra and Grover, 1998). This point is much debated, as many researchers find it hard to agree on these response rate percentages. However, especially for theory-testing survey research, response rate in combination with non-response bias is a major issue. The example provided by Fowler (1993: 43), reported in Table 4.11, is instructive.

Table 4.11 Effect of biased non-response on survey estimates

Response rate (per cent)	Bias level (Percentage of non-respondents with characteristics (blond hair))						
	(10)	(20)	(25)	(30)	(40)	(50)	(75)
90	27	26	25	24	23	22	19
70	31	27	25	23	19	14	03
50	40	30	25	20	10		
30	60	37	25	13			

Source: Fowler (1993: 43).

Fowler estimated the presence of blond-haired persons in a population of 100 persons with 25 blond-haired individuals. If the response rate is 70 per cent, and 75 per cent of non-respondents have blond hair, it means that out of the 30 non-respondents, $0.75 \times 30 \approx 22$ have blond hair and therefore only 25–22 = 3 blond-haired individuals responded. Therefore, the estimate is three blond-haired persons in the population while, in reality, there are 25 such individuals. Table 4.11 shows that when there are major biases (e.g. non-respondents have characteristics, such as blond hair, that are systematically different from the respondents) even studies with response rates of approximately 70 per cent produce considerable errors in estimates. When response rates are lower, estimates are not very good, even when bias is modest. The problem is that 'one usually does not know how biased non-response is, but it is seldom a good assumption that non-response is unbiased' (Fowler, 2013: 49).

Operations management and SCM researchers could consider articles from other disciplines in order to increase their awareness of non-respondent causes (see Roth and Bevier, 1998; Greer et. al., 2000) and effects (see Wilson, 1999, who underlined the resulting lack of external validity). To calculate the response rate, the researcher can refer to Dillman (1978: 49–52).

The non-response effects on results can be addressed in two ways: a) by trying to increase the response rate and b) by trying to identify the non-respondents in order to control whether they are different from the respondents.

Response rates can be increased considerably when a subsequent follow-up programme is applied. Dillman (1978) proposed that: a) after one week, a postcard is sent to everyone (it serves as a reminder and as a thank you), b) after three weeks, a letter and a replacement questionnaire are sent only to non-respondents, c) a final mailing is done, similar to the previous one (or even a telephone call). Dillman (2007) also suggested a combination and tailoring of modalities for approaching respondents and reminding them to fill out the questionnaire and return it. A phone call is often more useful, since it makes it possible to: a) confirm that the target respondent has received the questionnaire, b) establish a personal contact, c) take some time to explain the research, d) help the respondent and e) gather some information on non-respondents.

Researchers should at least keep track of the non-respondents. They should survey some of them (even using a condensed questionnaire or a telephone call) to understand whether and how much bias has been introduced (see, for example, Ward et al., 1994). A researcher can investigate reasons that prevent target respondents from responding when calling respondents to solicit for answers. In addition, a researcher can also check for differences between the first wave of respondents and later returns (Lambert and Harrington, 1990). Even though this second approach provides useful information and is widely used, the researcher should keep in mind that he or she is still comparing the respondents that, in the end, provided a response.

The researcher could trade sample size for sample representativeness. He or she can follow two opposite strategies: a) devote great effort for a limited number of contacts or b) devote little effort for a great number of contacts. The former strategy leads to a higher response rate, a known sample bias and higher data reliability and completeness. The latter may lead to larger samples, but with unknown representativeness and data quality.

Since OSCM tends to rely on small sample sizes, it would be useful at this point to check the credibility of the available sample. Sudman (1983) provided a scale to evaluate the credibility of a small sample. This scale, reported and commented on by Forza (2002), is based on the following considerations. Usually, a sample taken from a limited geographic area represents the population less than a sample taken from multiple locations. Articles that discuss possible sample bias are more credible than those that do not. The use of a special population, in some cases, is a powerful tool to test a theory, but if it is used for convenience, it can introduce obvious biases. It is possible that sample sizes are satisfactory when the total sample is considered, but, after breakdowns, the resulting sub-samples may not be adequate in size for more detailed analyses. When the response rate is poor, it is very likely that some bias has been introduced by self-selection of respondents. Sometimes the researcher is pressed by lack of time or cost or resources; even in this case, some sample designs use the available resources more effectively than do others.

4.5.3 Inputting and cleaning data

The first step in processing data usually entails transcribing the data from the original documents to a computer database. In this process, about 2 per cent–4 per cent of the data can be transcribed incorrectly (Schwab and Sitter, 1974: 13). The errors arise from two situations: a) the transcriber misreads the source document, but correctly transcribes the misinterpreted data (86 per cent of transcription errors are of this type), and b) the transcriber reads the source document correctly, but incorrectly transcribes the data (Karweit and Meyers, 1983). Independent verification of any transcription that involves reading and interpreting hand-written material is therefore advisable.

When an error is detected, the researcher may choose between the following options, singly or in combination, to resolve it (Karweit and Meyers, 1983):

• Consult the original interview or questionnaire to determine if the error is due to incorrect transcription.
• Contact the respondent again to clarify the response or obtain missing data.
• Estimate or impute a response to resolve the error, using various imputation techniques.
• Discard the response or designate it as bad or missing data.
• Discard the entire case.

In the last 20–30 years, progress has been made in the way in which data are collected and cleaned. Optical scanning and web-based questionnaires allow automatic data inputting, thus reducing errors. Computer-assisted personal interviewing (CAPI) or telephone interviewing (CATI) allow interviews to be completed with answers entered directly into databases, thus reducing intermediate steps and errors. The data input programs can perform checks on the data (ensuring, for example, that the values are within a certain range, or that other logical constraints are satisfied). New techniques are available not only for inputting data but also for distributing and even developing questionnaires. Integrated software applications, such as SPSS Data Entry Survey Software or Sphinx Survey, assist in questionnaire development and questionnaire distribution (on the web, for example), as well as in building databases and analysing the collected data. For a quick start with this technology, free access applications such as Survey Monkey[R] are available online. Sometimes, only the basic functionalities are available for free. This kind of technology is particularly effective with single-respondent surveys based on short questionnaires. If a researcher plans to use a long questionnaire or multiple respondents, s/he will have to consider more carefully whether to use this kind of technology or not.

4.5.4 Assessing the measurement quality

4.5.4.1 Importance of ensuring and assessing measurement quality

Section 4.3 has already highlighted the fact that researchers, when moving from the theoretical level to the empirical one, must operationalize the constructs present in the theoretical framework. Carmines and Zeller (1979: 11) noted that 'if the theoretical constructs have no empirical referents, then the empirical tenability of the theory must remain unknown'. When measurements are unreliable and/or invalid, the analysis can lead to incorrect inferences and misleading conclusions. Without assessing the reliability and validity of the measurement instrument, it would be impossible to 'disentangle the distorting influences of [...] [measurement] errors' on theoretical relationships that are being tested (Bagozzi et al., 1991: 421).

Measurement error represents one of the major sources of error in survey-based research (Biemer et al., 1991; Malhotra and Grover, 1998) and should be kept at the lowest possible level. Furthermore, as measurement error affects the results of survey-based research, it should be assessed not only during the research, but also reported in the report or articles derived from the research.

When addressing the issue of measurement quality, the quality of the survey instruments and procedures used to measure the constructs of interest must be considered. However, the most crucial aspect related to measurement quality concerns the measurement of complex constructs by multi-item measures, which is the focus of the remainder of this section. The fundamental aspects of measurement quality assessment are presented throughout this section, with an example taken from OM literature (Ahire and Dreyfus, 2000: 560–561). This example highlights the fact that measurement quality assessment is becoming much more sophisticated in OSCM.

The current research instrument consisting of 30 items [to measure six constructs] was refined prior to testing the proposed model. For this purpose, a confirmatory factor analysis [CFA] of the initial measurement model was conducted using LISREL [...] The initial measurement model with all 30 items resulted in an inadequate fit [...] The initial measurement model was refined using standard CFA refinement procedures [...] as follows. The items with excessive standardized residuals and modification indices were identified and eliminated one at a time [...] we stopped refinement upon attaining generally acceptable model fit thresholds without a substantial reduction in the content validity of constructs. Four items were eliminated from the original 30 items [...] Most of the loadings [of individual retained items on corresponding constructs] are above 0.6 suggesting that the items align well with their respective constructs [...] Thus, considering the large size and heterogeneity of our sample, the model fit indices [...] demonstrate that the refined model fits the data well. [Correlations between scales, i.e. measures of constructs, are reported] [...] Considering the high scale intercorrelations, several reliability and validity indices were computed to ensure that the refined scales represent reliable and valid measurements of the underlying constructs.

4.5.4.2 Measure quality criteria

The goodness of measures is evaluated in terms of validity and reliability. Validity is concerned with whether we are measuring what we intend to measure, while reliability is concerned with stability and consistency in measurement scores. Lack of validity introduces a systematic error (bias), while lack of reliability introduces a random error (Carmines and Zeller, 1979).

4.5.4.2.1 RELIABILITY

Reliability indicates dependability, stability, predictability, consistency and accuracy, and refers to the extent to which a measuring procedure yields the same results in repeated trials (Carmines and Zeller, 1979; Kerlinger, 1986). Reliability is assessed after data collection, although some actions to reduce reliability problems may be taken while assessing face validity (see Section 4.3). The four most common methods used to estimate reliability are: a) test-retest method, b) alternative form method, c) split halves method and d) internal consistency method (see Table 4.12). Fundamental readings on this issue are Nunnally (1978) and Carmines and Zeller (1979).

Table 4.12 Methods to assess reliability

Method	Procedure	Meaning
Test-retest	It calculates the correlation between responses obtained through the same measure applied to the same respondents at different points of time (e.g. separated by two weeks).	It estimates the ability of the measure to maintain stability over time. This aspect is indicative of measure stability and low vulnerability to change in uncontrollable testing conditions and in the state of the respondents.
Alternative form	It calculates the correlation between responses obtained through different measures applied to the same respondents at different points of time (e.g. separated by two weeks).	It assesses the equivalence of different forms for measuring the same construct.
Split halves	It subdivides the items of a measure into two subsets and statistically correlates the answers obtained at the same time to them.	It assesses the equivalence of different sets of items for measuring the same construct.
Internal consistency	It uses various algorithms to estimate the reliability of a measure from measure administration at one point in time.	It assesses the equivalence, homogeneity and inter-correlation of the items used in a measure. This means that the items of a measure should hang together as a set and should be capable of independently measuring the same construct.

The most popular test within the internal consistency method is the Cronbach's coefficient alpha (α) (Cronbach, 1951). Cronbach's α is also the most used reliability indicator in OSCM survey research. Cronbach's α can be expressed in terms of $\bar{\rho}$, the average inter-item correlation among the n measurement items in the instrument under consideration, as follows:

$$\alpha = \frac{n\bar{\rho}}{1 + (n - 1)\bar{\rho}}$$

Cronbach's α is therefore related to the number of items n as well as to the average inter-item correlation $\bar{\rho}$. Nunnally (1978) stated that newly developed measures can be accepted with $\alpha \geq 0.6$; otherwise, $\alpha \geq 0.7$ should be the threshold. With $\alpha \geq 0.8$, the measure is very reliable. These criteria are well accepted in OSCM. Computation of Cronbach's α coefficient is well supported by statistical packages.

4.5.4.2.2 CONSTRUCT VALIDITY

Construct validity refers to the degree to which a measure represents and acts as the concept being measured. While content validity refers to the degree to which the meaning of a set of items represents the domain of the concept under investigation, construct validity refers to the degree to which the scores obtained from using a set of items behave as expected (i.e. load only one underlying factor; correlate quite highly between them; correlate strongly with alternative measures of the same concept; correlate significantly with measures of constructs that are theoretically associated, though less than with measures of the same construct; do not correlate with measures of unrelated concepts; etc.). Obviously, without content validity, it is impossible to have construct validity.

Out of all the different properties that can be assessed concerning a measure, construct validity is the most complex and, yet, the most critical to substantive theory testing (Bagozzi et al., 1991). The notions of construct validity and content validity are sometimes presented in a way that makes it impossible to discriminate between them. This has generated some confusion within the OSCM community and some OSCM researchers have avoided the use of the term 'construct validity', even though they have performed a very thorough measurement validation. Operations management and SCM researchers should take into account recent developments on this issue in other disciplines (see, for example, Strauss and Smith, 2009, and the notion of validity as a unified concept proposed by Messick, 1995).

Construct unidimensionality is the first property to check when assessing construct validity. It should even precede the assessment of reliability. 'It is a matter of logical and empirical necessity that a variable be unidimensional' (Bagozzi, 1980: 126). A multidimensional measure (i.e. a measure comprising of indicators that represent more than one construct) 'cannot, by definition, be considered a variable and hence must not be treated as such in one's theory' (Bagozzi, 1980: 126). From an empirical perspective, 'when a measure of one variable improperly includes empirical indicators that are related to another variable, we are in a sense combining two variables (A and B) to form a new variable (C). Serious problems arise regarding the interpretation of association between C and other variables' (O'Leary-Kelly and Vokurka, 1998: 390).

A measure must satisfy two conditions in order to be considered unidimensional. 'First, an empirical indicator must be significantly associated with an underlying latent variable (i.e. the empirical representation of a construct) and, second, it can be associated with one and only one latent variable (Hair et al., 1992; [...])' (O'Leary-Kelly and Vokurka, 1998: 391).

Assessing unidimensionality is an established practice in OSCM. This may be performed both with exploratory factor analysis (see Saraph et al., 1989; Flynn et al., 1994) and with confirmatory factor analysis (CFA) (see Ahire et al., 1996). Factor analysis can be performed on items belonging to a single summated scale or on items of several summated scales (Birnbaum et al., 1986; Flynn et al., 1990). Ahire and Dreyfus (2000: 561) showed that all the scales of their study 'exhibited high satisfactory unidimensionality' by reporting 'the unidimensionality goodness of fit indexes [which] indicate the extent to which the scale items are associated with each other and represent a single concept'.

Campbell and Fiske (1959) proposed two aspects of construct validity; namely, *convergent and discriminant validity*. *Convergent validity* refers to the degree to which multiple attempts to measure the same concept (e.g. different measures or different items) are in agreement. The idea is that scores obtained by two or more measures of the same thing co-vary highly if they are good measures of the same thing. *Discriminant validity* refers to the degree to which measures of different concepts (or items belonging to different measures) are distinct. The idea is that, if two or more concepts are distinct (i.e. they have content domains that do not overlap), then good measures of these concepts (or items belonging to different measures of these concepts) should not correlate too strongly. O'Leary-Kelly and Vokurka (1998: 399) presented a number of problems caused by the lack of convergent and discriminant validity:

> The use of measures that lack convergent and discriminant validity can lead to numerous problems in the interpretation of the results of a study. For example, the finding of a significant relationship between variables that lack convergent validity might be attributable to the methods used to measure the latent variables, not to any 'true' relationship between them (Fiske, 1982). Similarly, if we use measures of two latent variables, x and y, that fail to demonstrate discriminant validity, we cannot conclude that the measures are reflecting two unique constructs; in this case it would be inappropriate to analyze x and y as separate latent variables.

Convergent and discriminant validity can be tested through the multitrait-multimethod (MTMM) matrix method or the CFA method (for details see Bagozzi et al., 1991; O'Leary-Kelly and Vokurka, 1998).

Increasingly, the practice of testing for convergent and discriminant validity is being applied in OSCM. The trend is to assess them through CFA on items belonging to measures of different constructs (see, for example, Koufteros, 1999). Ahire and Dreyfus (2000: 561) described how they tested for convergent and discriminant validity:

> We report the Bentler-Bonett normed fit index (Δ) as a measure of convergent validity for each scale. All of the scales exceed the threshold of 0.90 for this index.
>
>   Finally, the high scale correlations warranted careful assessment of discriminant validity of the constructs [...] Discriminant validity of constructs can be assessed in different ways. First, adequate discriminant validity is established when the Cronbach reliability coefficient of each of the scales is adequately larger than the average of its

correlations with other constructs. [...] Second, statistically distinct scales exhibit interscale correlations that are adequately different from 1.0 [...] Third, if the percent variance extracted (PVE) by the scale items of a construct is consistently greater than the squared interscale correlations of the construct, additional evidence for the discriminant validity of the construct with respect to all other constructs is established [...] Finally, nested measurement models involving pairs of different constructs (one with a perfect correlation and one with correlation free to vary) can be run and χ^2 difference tested for significance. If the χ^2 difference statistic is significant for 1 *df*, the two constructs are statistically distinct [...] The discriminant validity results [...] confirm that they adequately pass all of the aforementioned tests of discriminant validity.

4.5.4.2.3 CRITERION-RELATED VALIDITY

This aspect of the validity of a measurement instrument is well explained by Nunnally (1978: 111): 'When an instrument is intended to perform a prediction function, validity depends entirely on how well the instrument correlates with what it is intended to predict (a criterion)'.

Criterion-related validity is established when the measure differentiates subjects on a criterion it is expected to predict. Establishing concurrent validity or predictive validity can do this. Concurrent validity is established when the scale discriminates subjects that are known to be different. Predictive validity is the ability of the measure to differentiate among subjects with respect to a future criterion (e.g. the future attainment of a certain 'quality conformance' level that is caused by a change in the level of the 'use of statistical process control').

Rungtusanatham and Choi (2000) showed that in OM, criterion-related validity has been tested using multiple correlations (e.g. Saraph et al., 1989), canonical correlations (e.g. Flynn et al., 1994), and LISREL (e.g. Ahire et al., 1996). Ahire and Dreyfus (2000: 561) described how they tested for criterion-related validity:

> Furthermore, we tested criterion-related validity of the exogenous and intermediate endogenous constructs of the model [...] We assessed the criterion-related validity of the input and intermediate outcome constructs using two additional numerical measures of operational quality, namely, overall rating of product quality within the industry and percentage of repeat customers. The overall rating of product quality [...] exhibits statistically significant correlations [...] with each construct [...] Percentage of repeat customers also indicates statistically significant correlations with each construct.

When a test that is conducted to assess an aspect of construct validity or criterion-related validity does not support the expected result, then either the measurement instrument or the theory could be invalid. It is a matter of researcher judgement to interpret the obtained results.

4.5.4.3 *Steps in assessing validity and reliability*

Developing valid and reliable measures is a process parallel to that of building and testing a theory. Here, measures go through a process of development and testing (see, for example, the framework for developing multi-item measures provided by Malhotra and

Grover, 1998, and Menor and Roth, 2007). The aim is not only to build an instrument that allows for testing a specific theory, but also to have an instrument that is reusable for other theories. Eventually, this instrument can be used in practice for self-evaluation and for benchmarking purposes.

When developing measures in a pilot-testing phase or in exploratory research, cut-off levels (e.g. for Cronbach's α) are less stringent and, due to small sample sizes, assessments (e.g. of unidimensionality) are of an exploratory nature (Nunnally, 1978). However, when testing measures, cut-off levels are set at higher values, confirmatory methods should be used and all of the various relevant aspects of validity and reliability should be considered. If a previously developed measure is used in a modified form, then the quality of the measure should be re-assessed and contrasted with the one of the original measures.

Assessments of measure quality, therefore, take place at various stages of survey research: before data collection; in pilot testing; in ad-hoc analyses to validate the measure; and, finally, after data collection, for hypothesis testing. At all of these stages, measures may be refined and items may be eliminated or modified. The elimination of an item requires the researcher to return to content validity assessment and redo all of the subsequent tests (Rungtusanatham and Choi, 2000). Parasuraman et al. (1988) and Saraph et al. (1989) are interesting examples of measure quality assessment and measure refinement.

4.6 Advanced issues in theory formalization and survey design

4.6.1 Multi-item measures: Reflective versus formative

One important decision in developing and testing a measure is that of conceptualizing and formulating a construct as reflective or formative. If a construct is conceptualized as a reflective construct, then the latent variable determines the construct indicators (i.e. the items that constitute the measure are modelled as being caused by the latent variable). If, conversely, the construct is conceptualized as a formative construct, then the indicators determine the latent variable (i.e. the items are modelled as causing the latent variable). Conceptualizing a construct as formative has a number of implications for measurement development, as discussed by Peng and Lai (2012: 470):

> Unlike reflective constructs, formative constructs 'need a census of indicators, not a sample' (Bollen and Lennox, 1991, p. 307). 'Failure to consider all facets of the construct will lead to an exclusion of relevant indicators [and] thus exclude part of the construction itself, [therefore], breadth of definition is extremely important to causal indicators [i.e. formative indicators]' (Nunnally and Bernstein, 1994, p. 484).
>
> Another potential problem is misspecifying a formative construct as a reflective construct. A review of SEM [structural equation modelling] in OM research suggests that 97 per cent of all studies model latent constructs as reflective (Roberts et al., 2010). The authors argue that the small proportion (3 per cent) of studies that model formative constructs under-represents the true theoretical nature of OM constructs. [...] When a formative construct is specified as a reflective construct, [...] the structural model tends to be inflated or deflated (Jarvis et al., 2003). Jarvis et al. (2003) provide a four-point guideline for determining whether a construct should be reflective or formative: (1) direction of causality, (2) interchangeability of the indicators, (3) covariation among the indicators, and (4) nomological network of the indicators.

We use operational performance as an illustrative example of a formative construct because it is a multi-dimensional concept that typically includes cost, quality, delivery, and flexibility. In the OM literature, operational performance is modeled as reflective constructs in some studies (e.g. Cao and Zhang, 2011 [...]). However, it is more appropriate to model operational performance as a formative construct if one follows the guidelines set by Jarvis et al. (2003) and Diamantopoulos and Winklhofer (2001).

To date, OSCM researchers have mainly adopted covariance-based structural equation modelling (CB-SEM) methods (implemented in software such as LISREL, AMOS and EQS) to assess the measurement quality for reflective constructs. Specifically, Peng and Lai (2012: 471) summarized how construct reliability, convergent validity and discriminant validity are typically assessed when using CB-SEM methods:

Typical measures of construct reliability include Cronbach's alpha and composite reliability. Convergent validity can be assessed by checking whether the average variance extracted (AVE) of the construct is greater than 0.50 (at the construct level) and the item loadings are greater than 0.70 and statistically significant (at the item level). Discriminant validity is usually examined by comparing the square root of AVE with the correlations between the focal construct and all other constructs.

'Because formative indicators need not be correlated, internal consistency, reliability (e.g. Cronbach Alpha), and average variance extracted (AVE) are not appropriate validation criteria' (Hair et al., 2019: 730). More generally, researchers agree that the criteria used to evaluate reflective constructs should not apply to formative constructs (Diamantopoulos and Winklhofer, 2001). Although widely accepted standard procedures for evaluating formative construct properties have not yet emerged, a number of procedures that can be used are available and have been discussed by Peng and Lai (2012).

Some OSCM constructs (e.g. 'lean production' or 'service orientations') are of a multidimensional nature and, in order test them, higher order models must be used. In addition, a reduced measurement model that is able to limit the complexity of their measurement is required. Oliveira and Roth's (2012: 156) study is a useful example of how to develop such a measure:

The authors empirically confirm the nomological network of SO [service orientation] as a third-order latent variable comprised of five combinative service competency bundles: service climate; market focus; process management; human resource policy; and metrics and standards. Together these bundles provide a holistic and integrative representation of the general operating environment's orientation towards customers and a business' general propensity to deliver service excellence. Importantly, the measurement structure of service orientation was found to be invariant for both goods producing and service firms.

4.6.2 Sample heterogeneity and measurement equivalence

Some research deals with samples that exhibit high heterogeneity. For example, they might include both large and small companies, or plants in different countries. International marketing researchers and international business researchers advise that, in these cases, measurement equivalence should be assessed before pooling data or before comparing subgroups. The issue of measurement equivalence has been addressed in some OSCM studies (e.g. Ahire and Dreyfus, 2000; Rungtusanatham et al., 2005). Rungtusanatham et al. (2005) and Knoppen et al. (2015) provided some prescriptions regarding when data can be pooled in the context of highly heterogeneous samples. In particular, Knoppen et al. (2015) provided suggestions on how to deal with lack of full equivalence. Over the coming years, we can expect advancements in this aspect of measurement quality.

4.6.3 Common method bias

Common method bias has been recognized by OSCM scholars for a long time. However, until now, the remedies OSCM researchers have mainly resorted to the use of multiple respondents and some tests after data collection. Recently, it has been recognized that there are several remedies that can be applied both before and after data collection. We can expect that, in the near future, top OSCM journals will be much more demanding in this respect. Guidelines and suggestions have been provided by Craighead et al. (2011) and by Guide and Ketokivi (2015). In particular, OSCM researchers should not claim that there is no common method bias after having performed a weak test.

Literature in OSCM is increasingly recommending to act in the survey-design phase in order to reduce common method bias and not act solely on statistical remedies in the data analysis (Craighead et al., 2011; Guide and Ketokivi, 2015; Flynn et al., 2018). In that respect, Podsakoff et al. (2003; 2012) are fundamental readings. In particular, Podsakoff et al. (2012) recommend obtaining measures of predictor and criterion variables from different sources, having temporal, proximal, or psychological separation between the measures of the predictor and criterion variables, eliminating common scale properties (i.e. scale type, number of scale points, anchor labels, polarity, etc.), eliminating the ambiguity of scale items, reducing social desirability bias in item wording, balancing positive and negative items thus reducing acquiescence or disacquiescence response style biases. Further interventions in the survey-design phase may be needed in order to subsequently be able to apply some statistical remedies they proposed. In particular, these interventions are the inclusion of marker variables, instrumental variables, measures of particular source of method bias (e.g. contaminating factors such as social desirability and positive affectivity).

4.6.4 Theorizing, testing and drawing conclusions with more articulated models

Operations management and SCM are maturing and their theories are becoming more articulated, thus posing new challenges to OSCM survey research (e.g. Squire et al., 2009; Flynn et al., 2010; Turkulainen and Ketokivi, 2012; Feldmann and Olhager, 2013; Wiengarten et al., 2015). Models include, or more often include, more control variables. 'Control variables are extraneous, not directly connected with the main theory and hypotheses but presumably able to confound them. The idea behind control variables is that they essentially remove the variation explained by a predictor variable that has some readily identifiable alternative explanation' (Helmuth et al., 2015: 183). Operations management and SCM researchers are testing theory by employing more complex hypotheses that focus on mediated, moderated or non-linear models in their research designs (Malhotra et al., 2014; Rungtusanatham et al., 2014; Helmuth et al., 2015). In addition to the effect on statistical power (Helmuth et al., 2015), a number of issues have to be taken into consideration while theorizing, testing and drawing conclusions about mediation and moderation, and system effects. Useful guidelines for mediation studies can be found in Malhotra et al. (2014) and Rungtusanatham et al. (2014). For moderation and systems effects, particularly useful are the overall guidelines provided by Sousa and Voss (2008: 697, 707):

> As operations management (OM) best practices have become mature, research on practices has begun to shift its interest from the justification of the value of those practices to the understanding of the contextual conditions under which they are effective—OM practice contingency research (OM PCR). [...] OM PCR scholars should consider the application of configurational research methods (Meyer et al., 1993), an endeavor that has already been embraced by research in operations strategy ([...] Boyer et al., 2000). [In addition], OM PCR scholars may readily draw on work such as Venkatraman's (1989), which provides an overview of analytical methods that can be used to test system forms of fit.

4.6.5 Longitudinal survey

It is known that the cross-sectional survey has some limitations in testing for causality. Notwithstanding its limitations, it has been used, and will continue to be used, for that purpose. However, more professionalism is called for in testing for causality, as clearly stated by Guide and Ketokivi (2015). Alternatively, data collected at different points in time could be used. One interesting example is Swink and Jacob's (2012) study on the impact of Six Sigma adoption in manufacturing and service firms on a year-to-year basis, and over aggregated multi-year periods. Another interesting example is Koufteros et al. (2014), who investigated the effect of performance measurement systems on firm performance by using both a cross-sectional and a longitudinal study, modelling the time dimension in the regressions. A simpler example is that of Orfila-Sintes and Mattsson (2009), where data were collected through personal interviews from hotel establishments (hotels, tourist apartments, campgrounds, etc.) in the Balearic Islands in 2001 and 2004. Other inspiring OSCM articles based on longitudinal studies are Sharma et al. (2016), Durach et al. (2023), Kesidou et al. (2022), Peng et al. (2022), Thirumalai et al. (2022). However, time is not the only issue when testing for causality.

4.6.6 Endogeneity

Endogeneity is another concern that is gaining more and more attention in OSCM (Ketokivi and McIntosh, 2017; Lu et al., 2018). As pointed out by Guide and Ketokivi (2015: v–vi):

> In a nutshell, the problem of endogeneity is this: when a researcher is using non-experimental data to test the hypothesis that X has an effect on Y, it is possible that the variance of X is not exogenous but endogenous to the model. The end result is that the model is misspecified. This in fact applies not just to cross-sectional but even longitudinal research. Even if X is measured at t-1 and Y at t, there could be an unobserved variable Z that affects X at t-1 and Y at t. [...] When arguing that the variance of X gives rise to the variance of Y (causally or otherwise), we expect to see a plausible argument that the direction is indeed from X to Y, not vice versa, or perhaps

caused by an omitted variable. Measurement error can also cause an endogeneity problem: if X and Y have a common measurement error source, X will unavoidably correlate with the error term of Y. Finally, sample selection bias may lead to problems very similar to that of endogeneity (Heckman, 1979).

4.6.7 Measuring polyadic constructs

One key aspect that constrains the design of survey research is whether the investigated constructs are monadic or polyadic. A monadic construct is a construct that focuses 'on a single perspective, such as that of a firm or a department within a firm. For example, a firm's defect rate or the strength of a department's lean practices is monadic constructs' (Flynn et al., 2018: 2). A polyadic construct 'includes relationships, multiple entities, or attributes that cannot be characterized by a single objective description, such as culture, relationship strength, or integration' (Flynn et al., 2018: 3). The term 'polyadic' encompasses 'a continuum of relationships from dyadic (for example, buyer–supplier relationships) to triadic (for example, the buyer–supplier–supplier triads [...]) to network relationships' (Flynn et al., 2018: 3). It is important both to clarify all the parts involved in a construct and to choose respondents accordingly with the observation angle implied by the research question as Roh et al. (2013: 712–713) point out:

> Construct descriptions should explicitly identify all pertinent stakeholders who encompass the unit of analysis under review – whether such analysis is targeted at one focal stakeholder (e.g. a buyer's perspective), a dyadic stakeholder (e.g. a buyer-supplier relationship), or a network of stakeholders (e.g. a buyer and its relationships – direct and indirect – with its tier I and tier II suppliers). For example, the unit of analysis of a study could consider two interacting stakeholders, such as a buyer and supplier. However, the key consideration concerns what the target of the study is: is the goal to understand (i) one party's evaluation of the relationship, (ii) both parties' evaluation of the relationship in isolation; or (iii) both parties' evaluation of the relationship as a true multi-stakeholder dyad? If the goal is either of the first two items, then the construct should explicitly focus on each party's view of the relationship, but conclusions should be limited to that party's perspective only. On the other hand, if the goal is the latter, then the construct should broadly incorporate both parties' perceptions such that conclusions can focus on the multi-stakeholder aspects of the relationship.

The most appropriate way to measure a polyadic construct is to collect data from all of the involved parties. However, practical constraints sometimes preclude it as noted by Flynn et al. (2018: 8):

> As Krause et al. (2018) describe in their commentary, the right key informant can address monadic constructs in their own area of expertise, but no single key informant can provide an unbiased assessment of a polyadic construct, such as integration between functions. Thus, we view the notion of an omniscient, all-knowing key informant as a myth in all but a few very specific situations. As Kull et al. (2018) note, a key informant may be appropriate for a small firm with, say, 43 employees, where the president/owner makes virtually all decisions, and there are no alternative knowledgeable informants [...].

4.6.8 Single or multiple respondentls?

Using either a single respondent or multiple respondents has long been discussed in OSCM. While some researchers highly criticize the choice of a single respondent, others argue for its appropriateness, at least in some cases. It is therefore not surprising that Montabon et al. (2018), by analysing the papers published in *DSJ*, *JBL*, *JOM*, and *JSCM* in the period 2007–2016 found that 34 per cent of the survey-based articles relied on single key informants, 23.8 per cent used multiple informants within each reporting organization (unfortunately, more than one-third of the articles did not report whether single or multiple informants were involved). The fact that *JSCM* in 2018 published an issue with an editorial and 4 articles that discuss the choice of single respondent witnesses that this choice is not a simple one and that the guidelines on it are still evolving. This choice should balance the benefits and the limitations of each option against the specific research question. An appropriate way to approach this decision is to consider what the underlying problems are with respondent choice and how they can be mitigated. Below, some of these problems are recalled showing that the decision is not straightforward:

- Common method bias deriving from the co-presence of the independent and dependent variables in the same questionnaire. In this case, the same informant measures both types of variables thus potentially introducing a bias (e.g. Podsakoff et al., 2012; Flynn et al., 2018). This problem remains even in the case of multiple respondents if the dependent and independent variables are not answered by different respondents.
- Respondent bias. For example, errors can be due to respondents' personal characteristics, traits, and biases (e.g. Flynn et al., 2018; Montabon et al., 2018). Multiple respondents can mitigate this problem but not completely eliminate it. Moreover, 'additional respondents can introduce ambiguity and add complexity to the treatment of data' (Krause et al., 2018: 45).
- Availability of respondents with adequate knowledge and who have the freedom to provide the information (e.g. Montabon et al., 2018; Kull et al., 2018). For example, in entrepreneurial SMEs, very likely, the entrepreneur has these characteristics, wears many hats and his/her answers reflect the views of the firm as a whole.
- Polyadic constructs. If the research question requires considering the views of the various parties involved, it is very likely that multiple respondents are needed to avoid collecting the viewpoint of only one of the various parties (e.g. Roh et al., 2013; Flynn et al., 2018; Krause et al., 2018).
- The opportunity cost to participate in the survey differs more between firms by increasing the number of respondents. For example, in the case of SMEs (Kull et al., 2018), companies with overloaded employees, or companies facing hard times, the requirement of multiple-respondent deters company participation in the survey thus undermining the sample representativeness.

It should be kept in mind that surveys based on single or multiple informants are in the end surveys thus having in common the strengths and weaknesses of the survey method. In order to deeply remove these weaknesses, a researcher should complement surveys with totally different data collection methods. Finally, we should always consider that 'having multiple respondents is less important than having the right respondent' (Krause et al., 2018: 45).

4.6.9 Answering is a complex cognitive process

In designing surveys and in analysing survey-based data it should be kept in mind that answering questions in the OSCM field too is a complex cognitive process. As pointed out by Tourangeau et al. (2000) the answering process progress through the following stages:

• *Experience* (exposure to relevant situations, conditions, and events; attention to aspects of the self; formulation of mental representations; encoding and storing information).
• *Comprehension* (attention to questions and instructions; interpret the meaning of the questions; understand what information is requested; link question content to relevant concepts).
• *Retrieval* (generate retrieval strategy; retrieve specific information; draw from general memories; construct missing details).
• *Judgment* (assess completeness and relevance of information retrieved; integrate information into a unified representation; edit representation as deemed appropriate).
• *Response* (map judgment onto response format; review and edit response; submit response).

The 'manner in which this process unfolds can enhance or undermine the accuracy of the information available to the respondent and increase or decrease the validity of the emitted responses. These complexities apply regardless of whether respondents describe themselves and their personal situations or serve as informants of system level attributes of organizations' (Edwards, 2019: 64). As pointed out by Flynn et al. (2018: 2), this complexity brings many issues in using perceptual measures of organizational phenomena such those involved in OSCM:

> As Ketchen, Craighead and Cheng (2018) describe, reporting on organizational phenomena requires respondents to engage in high-level cognitive processes that require them to work at a high level of abstraction and weight inferences and engage in prediction, interpretation, and evaluation [...]. Even the most competent respondents can experience perceptual and cognitive limitations that result in response inaccuracies [...], particularly for retrospective reports [...], including imperfect recall of past events and coloring of recollections by their implicit theories and biases [...].

The characteristics of the individual (e.g. ability, motivation), of the instrument (e.g. instructions, length), and the method (e.g. administered online, paper-and-pencil format) influence the validity of the emitted responses, i.e. the extent to which the provided scores reflect the thoughts and beliefs of respondents (Edwards, 2019). Research is needed to determine the separate and combined effects of these factors along with the magnitudes of these effects (Edwards, 2019). Edwards (2019), focusing on behavioural OM, provides methods to analyse response validity and remedies for this issue.

4.7 Survey execution

4.7.1 Redoing activities at a larger scale

At the end of pilot testing, the researcher either can proceed with theory testing or will have to revise the survey questionnaires, the survey administration process or both. In the latter case, the researcher would have to go back to the issues raised in Sections 4.3 and 4.4.

It follows that the researcher should move to the survey execution phase only when all relevant issues have been addressed. Ideally, data collection problems and measurement problems should have been reduced to the minimum level by this point. Therefore, at the survey execution stage, the researcher has the opportunity to direct his or her attention elsewhere until the data have been returned.

Fundamentally, in this phase the researcher has to repeat the pilot-testing activities with a large sample:

- Approaching companies/respondents and collecting data.
- Controlling and reducing the problems caused by non-respondents.
- Performing data input and cleaning.
- Treating missing data (recalling respondents, estimating/replacing data).
- Assessing measurement quality.
- Providing feedback to respondents.

Providing feedback to companies/respondents is an ethical obligation (if promised) and should be done to motivate their present and future involvement. This feedback could be a standard summary report, personalised feedback, an invitation to meetings where results are communicated or something else that could be useful to the respondents.

4.7.2 Handling missing data

Handling missing data should be a key concern during data collection. 'When statistical models and procedures are used to analyse a random sample, it is usually assumed that no sample data is missing. In practice, however, this is rarely the case for survey data' (Anderson et al., 1983: 415). Missing data cannot be overlooked, as they have a negative impact on statistical power and may cause biased estimates in several ways (Roth et al., 1999). Useful reviews of how to handle missing data are provided by Anderson et al. (1983), Roth (1994) and, with specific reference to OM, Tsikriktsis (2005).

Two questions must be addressed concerning missing data (Tsikriktsis, 2005). First, how much of the data is missing? As the percentage of missing data increases, not only does the statistical power decrease dramatically, but the different techniques for treating missing data lead to increasingly different results (under 10 per cent, little difference; close to 20 per cent, considerable difference; over 30 per cent–40 per cent, high difference). The second question is whether or not the pattern of missing observations is random. One method of assessing randomness is to split the set of observations into two subsets: one with missing data for the variable, and the other with valid values for the variable. If patterns of significant difference were found between the two subsets on other variables of interest, this would indicate that missing data are not the result of a random process.

The best approach to dealing with missing data is to prevent their occurrence in the first place by increasing respondent involvement, giving clear instructions in the questionnaire and supporting and recalling respondents to ensure completeness after administering the questionnaire. However, in spite of all of these efforts, unavoidably, some data will be missing. Three broad strategies can be adopted: a) deletion, b) replacement based on estimation, c) model-based strategy. Deletion is simply omitting observations with missing data from the analyses. Deletion may be listwise (an entire observation is deleted if it has a missing value in one variable) or pairwise (the observation is deleted only from those statistical analyses that require the missing data). When data are missed randomly, a deletion strategy generally leads to unbiased results but – especially with listwise deletions – decreases statistical power. Replacement based on estimation – the second strategy – involves estimating the missing observation, subsequently replacing the missing data with the estimate and, finally, proceeding with a statistical analysis of the data set. Replacement procedures are of four types: mean-based, regression-based, model-based and hot deck imputation (a missing value is replaced with the actual score from a similar case in the amended data set). The third strategy (model-based) provides explicit modelling of missing data, thus allowing an open analysis and critique. It is the best solution with missing data that are definitely non-random. Tsikriktsis (2005) synthesized the different missing data treatment procedures, presenting advantages, disadvantages, contexts for utilization and references to studies that apply them.

By examining 103 survey-based articles from the *JOM* between 1993 and 2001, Tsikriktsis (2005: 59–61) found that:

> First, 67 per cent of the articles did not mention anything about whether there were missing data and, if there were, how they were treated. [...] Second, authors are not explicit about their treatment of missing data. Only 4 out of 45 articles that were coded as having missing data have clearly stated the technique used (listwise deletion in all four cases). [...] Third, [authors do not mention the presence of missing data, either because they take it for granted or] in order to avoid potential comments from reviewers. [...] Fourth, on average 13 per cent of the data were missing. Such a high percentage of missing data could have catastrophic implications for statistical power. [...] Overall, most advanced methods, such as imputation and model-based procedures, were never used, or, if they have been used, they have not been reported. [...]
>
> Overall, we recommend the following to OM researchers who are dealing with missing data. First, they should understand the reasons that lead to missing data and make an effort to avoid/minimize missing data. [...] Second, researchers should not always fall for listwise deletion that provides a 'quick and easy fix'. Despite the fact that listwise deletion is a 'conservative' technique that results in researchers 'making it harder for themselves' [...], it also reduces statistical power and accuracy more than many other techniques. [...] Finally, authors should be very explicit about how they handle missing data in their manuscripts (method used, why, etc.).

4.7.3 Combining multiple data collections

Survey research in OSCM has always dealt with the issue of data management. This issue, however, is undergoing a number of changes. While the establishment of online data collection and the improved friendliness of statistical packages are facilitating data management, the changing of data sources is making data management harder. Cross-country research brings the need to coordinate data management across different country leaders. The request for multiple respondents as well as the use of multilevel data leads to the need to keep hierarchical information between data. The use of panel data brings the need to manage data that refer to the same item and the same respondent at different points of time, i.e. in different data collection. The use of multimethod many times brings the need to manage data of different types, collected in different ways, likely at different times that refer to the same object. Data (or part of the data used) can be derived from data collection/s performed for different purposes, in other terms they can be secondary data. Both in the case of primary and secondary data we may have the need to integrate survey-based data with data collected in other ways. Finally, these data may derive from texts, videos, audio, etc. (Basole et al., 2022) even in the case of surveys. All these developments pose the problem of data integration and harmonization, a problem that survey researchers have increasingly to face.

Data integration, harmonization, and visualization is a problem that has been faced for a long time by companies and the information sciences have developed approaches that may be useful for OSCM empirical researchers. One inspirational example of the possibilities offered by the integration of different data sources as well as a possible approach to deal with this data integration can be found in Avazpour et al. (2019). They present their integration approach applied in relation to the Australian Urban Research Infrastructure Network which is an 'initiative to make a wide range of demographic, economic, social, cultural and geographic datasets available to geographers, sociologists, government agencies, businesses and ultimately citizens for multi-dataset querying, aggregation and visualization […] [and more specifically they apply it on the example of the] multi-dataset information […] [named] Household Travel Surveys' (Avazpour et al., 2019: 2).

4.8 Data analysis and interpretation of results

Data analysis can be divided into two phases: preliminary data analysis and hypothesis testing. These phases are described below and the most commonly used data-analysis methods are presented briefly. The objective here is to provide some information to complete the overview of the theory-testing survey research process. However, this issue deserves a more extensive discussion, and the reader is encouraged to research this issue in more depth by referring to statistical manuals and consulting with statisticians.

Before getting into the details of the analysis, the kinds of data analyses that have been used in OSCM should be considered. Scudder and Hill (1998) analysed the methods used in 477 OM empirical research articles published during the period 1986–1995 in the 13 main journal outlets for OM research. They found that 28 per cent of articles did not use any statistical data-analysis method (almost all of these articles were based on case studies), while some articles used more than one data-analysis method. Furthermore, they found that 72 per cent of articles used descriptive statistics, 17 per cent used regression/correlation, 9 per cent used means testing, 7 per cent used data reduction (principal component analysis, etc.), 4 per cent used ANOVA and MANOVA, and 3 per cent used cluster analysis. Soni and Kodali (2012) and Chatha et al. (2015) updated these figures with reference to SCM and manufacturing strategy research, respectively. It emerged that more advanced techniques, such as cluster analysis, factor analysis and structural equation modelling (SEM), are increasingly being adopted. It also emerged that top journals are becoming more reluctant to publish survey research that does not apply sophisticated analytical techniques such as the ones mentioned above.

4.8.1 Preliminary data analysis

In order to acquire knowledge about the characteristics and properties of the collected data, some preliminary data analyses are conducted, usually before performing measurement quality assessments or testing the hypotheses. Carrying out such analyses before assessing measurement quality gives preliminary indications of how well the coding and inputting of data have been done, how good the scales are and whether poor content validity or systematic bias should be suspected. Before testing the hypotheses, it is useful to check the assumptions underlying the tests and to get a feel for the data, in order to better interpret the results of the tests.

The discovery of errors, outliers, absence of normality and absence of variance homogeneity leads to a number of actions. These actions may entail modification of the data (error correction, outlier deletion or modification or replacement, observation deletion, variable transformation) to make them suitable for subsequent analyses. Sometimes, however, the problems are so serious that variables should be deleted and the planned analyses should be changed. The need for such actions should not be underestimated. Outliers, for example, bias the mean and inflate the standard deviation and can lead both to Type I and Type II errors.

The knowledge acquired in a preliminary data analysis may influence the discussion of the results and the conclusions. The deletion of certain outliers may introduce a clear restriction on the generalizability of the results, which, in turn, requires a detailed identification and description of these outliers. The description of demographic variables may better characterize the sample under investigation and these characterizations may be important when discussing the generalizability of the results.

Preliminary data analysis is performed by checking central tendencies, dispersions, frequency distributions and correlations. It is good practice to calculate: 1) the frequency distribution of the demographic variables; 2) the mean, standard deviation, range and variance of the other dependent and independent variables; 3) an inter-correlation matrix of the variables. Table 4.13 gives some of the most frequently used descriptive statistics in preliminary data analysis. Table 4.14 presents some of the most common techniques available in statistical packages to perform the preliminary data analysis. Some statistical packages (for example, SAS and SPSS) provide tools for exploratory or interactive data analyses, which facilitate preliminary data-analysis activities through emphasis on visual representation and graphical techniques.

Table 4.13 Descriptive statistics used in preliminary data analysis

Type of analysis	Explanation	Relevance
Frequencies	Refers to the number of times the various subcategories of a certain phenomenon occur.	Generally obtained for nominal variables.
Measures of central tendencies	Mean (the average value), median (half of the observations fall above and the other half fall below the median) and mode (the most frequently occurring value) characterize the central tendency (or location or centre) of a set of observations.	To characterize the central value of a set of observations parsimoniously in a meaningful way.
Measures of dispersion	Measures of dispersion (or spread or variability) include the range, the standard deviation, the variance, and the interquartile range.	To indicate the variability that exists in a set of observations concisely.
Measures of shape	The measures of shape, skewness and kurtosis describe departures from the symmetry of a distribution and its relative flatness (or peakedness), respectively.	To indicate the kind of departures from a normal distribution.

Table 4.14 Techniques used to perform preliminary data analysis

Technique	Explanation	Relevance
Frequency tables	To array data from highest to lowest values with counts, percentages, percentage adjusted for missing values, and cumulative percentages.	Useful to inspect the range of responses and their repeated occurrence. Not particularly informative with interval-ratio scales.
Bar charts and pie charts	To represent graphically the basic information of frequency tables.	Appropriate for relative comparisons of nominal data.
Histograms	To show the frequency of different scores (or score intervals of equal length).	Useful to identify outliers and to get a first feeling of departures from normality. Optimal for continuous variables.
Boxplots	To show graphically the median, spread and interquartile range of scores.	Useful to have a detailed picture of the main body, tails and outliers of the distribution.
Scatterplots	To show relationships between two (or three) variables.	Useful to identify outliers. Useful to get a feeling of the presence and the form of association between variables.
Cross-tabulations	The cells of these tables contain combinations of count, row, column and total percentages.	Useful to perform preliminary evaluation of relationships involving nominally scaled variables.

4.8.2 Analysing data for hypothesis testing

Significance tests can be grouped into two general classes: parametric and non-parametric. Generally, parametric tests are considered more powerful because their data are typically derived from interval and ratio measurements whose likelihood model (i.e. distribution) is known, except for some parameters. Non-parametric tests are used with nominal and ordinal data as well as with interval and ratio data that do not satisfy parametric assumptions. Experts in non-parametric testing claim that non-parametric tests are comparable in terms of power (Hollander and Wolfe, 1999). However, currently in social science, parametric techniques are considered

> the tests of choice if their assumptions are met. Some of the assumptions for parametric tests include: 1) the observations must be independent (that is, the selection of any one case should not affect the chances for any other case to be selected in the sample); 2) the observation should be drawn from normally distributed populations; 3) these populations should have equal variance; 4) the measurement scales should be at least interval so that arithmetic operations can be used with them.
>
> (Emory and Cooper, 1991: 530)

The researcher is responsible for assessing whether or not the assumptions of the chosen test are satisfied and should provide evidence of having performed such checks. It should be remembered, however, that some parametric tests are not affected seriously by violations of assumptions, while, for others, a departure from assumptions may threaten result validity. Non-parametric tests have fewer and less stringent assumptions. They do not require normally distributed populations or homogeneity of variance. Some of them require independent cases, while others are deliberately designed for analyses with related cases. Therefore, when the population distribution is undefined or violates the assumption of parametric tests, non-parametric tests must be used.

According to Emory and Cooper (1991), at least the following three questions should be considered in order to choose the significance test:

1 Does the test involve one sample, two samples or k samples?
2 If two or k samples are involved, are the individual cases independent or related?
3 Is the measurement scale nominal, ordinal, interval or ratio?

Additional questions may arise once answers to these ones are known. For example, what is the sample size? If there are several samples, are they of equal size? Have the data been weighted? Have the data been transformed? The answers can complicate the selection, but once a tentative choice is made, most standard statistics textbooks will provide further details on how to proceed. Decision trees provide a more systematic means of selecting techniques. One widely used guide from the Institute for Social Research (Andrews et al., 1976), starts with a question about the number of variables, their nature and the level of measurement. It continues with more detailed questions, thus providing indications concerning over 130 solutions. Table 4.15 gives examples of some parametric test and Table 4.16 shows non-parametric tests.

In any applied field, such as OSCM, most tools are, or should be, multivariate. If a problem is not treated as a multivariate problem in these fields, it is likely to be treated superficially. Therefore, multivariate analysis (simultaneous analysis of more than two variables) is, and will continue to be, important in OSCM. Table 4.17 presents some of the more established multivariate techniques as well as some of the emerging ones (for more details, see Hair et al., 2019). Exploratory factor analysis and cluster analysis are interdependence techniques, i.e. techniques in which the variables are not divided into dependent and independent; rather, all the variables are analysed simultaneously in an effort to find an underlying structure to the entire set of variables or subjects. Multiple regression, multivariate analysis of variance (MANOVA), multivariate analysis of covariance (MANCOVA), and canonical correlation are dependence techniques, i.e. techniques in which a variable or set of variables is identified as the dependent variable to

Table 4.15 Examples of parametric tests

Test	When to use	Function
Pearson correlation	With interval and ratio data.	Test hypothesis that postulates significant positive (negative) relationships between two variables.
t-test	With interval and ratio data.	To see whether there is any significant difference in the means for two groups in the variable of interest. Groups can be either two different groups or the same group before and after treatment.
Analysis of variance (ANOVA)	With interval and ratio data.	To see whether there are significant mean differences among more than two groups. In order to see where the difference lies, tests like Scheffé's test, Duncan's Multiple Range test, Tukey's test and Student-Newman-Keuls test are available.

Table 4.16 Examples of non-parametric tests

Test	When used	Function
Chi-squared (χ^2)	With nominal data for one sample or two or more independent samples.	Test for equality of distributions.
Cochran Q	With more than two related samples measured on a nominal scale.	Similar function to χ^2, it helps when data fall into two natural categories.
Fisher exact probability	With two independent samples measured on a nominal scale.	More useful than χ^2 when expected frequencies are small.
Sign test	With two related samples measured on an ordinal scale.	Test for equality of the distributions of two groups.
Median test	With one sample.	To test the equality in distribution under the assumption of homoscedasticity.
Mann-Whitney U test	With two independent samples on ordinal data.	Analogue of the two independent sample t-tests, with ordinal data.
Kruskal-Wallis one-way ANOVA	With more than two independent samples on an ordinal scale.	An alternative to one-way ANOVA with ordinal data.
Friedman two-way ANOVA	With more than two related samples on ordinal data.	Analogue of two-way ANOVA with ranked data when interactions are assumed absent.
Kolmogorov-Smirnov	With one sample or two independent samples measured on an ordinal scale.	Test for equality of distribution, with an ordinal scale.

Source: Adapted from Sekaran (1992: 279).

be predicted or explained by other variables known as independent variables, with metric dependent variables. Multiple discriminant analysis and logistic regression (or logit analysis) are dependence techniques with nonmetric dependent variables. Structural equation modelling is a combination of interdependence or dependence techniques that seeks to explain the relationships among multiple variables simultaneously. Covariance-based structural equation modelling (CB-SEM) and partial least squares structural equation modelling (PLS-SEM) are the two techniques of structural equation modelling.

In addition to the methods just presented, a wide variety of regression-based models have been proposed to answer different research questions. For survey research is interesting to draw attention to multilevel/hierarchical models and panel models, which have become increasingly popular. They serve 'to analyze unique types of data structures – nested or hierarchical data for multilevel models and cross-sectional longitudinal data for panel models' (Hair et al., 2019: 322).

Hair et al. (2019: 323) explained multilevel models in a very effective way using the example of student achievement as the dependent variable:

All individuals are embedded within contexts that have an influence on their behavior. Contexts are any external factor outside the unit of analysis that not only impact the outcome of multiple individuals, but also create differences between individuals in separate contexts and foster dependencies between the individuals in a single context. [...] Contexts create data structures that are termed nested, hierarchical or clustered, and have long been acknowledged as a fundamental effect applicable to almost all research

Table 4.17 Main multivariate analysis methods

Multivariate technique	When used	Function
Exploratory factor analysis	When several, metric variables are under analysis and the researcher wishes to reduce the number of variables to manage or find out the underlying factors.	To analyse interrelationships among a large number of variables and to explain these variables in terms of their common underlying dimensions (factors).
Cluster analysis	When metric variables are present and the researcher wishes to group entities.	To classify a sample of entities (individuals or objects) into a smaller number of mutually exclusive subgroups based on the similarities among the entities.
Multiple regression	When a single, metric, dependent variable is presumed to be related to one or more metric, independent variables.	To predict the changes in the dependent variable in response to changes in the several independent variables.
Multivariate analysis of variance (MANOVA) Multivariate analysis of covariance (MANCOVA)	When an experimental situation (manipulation of several nonmetric variables) is designed to test hypotheses concerning the variance in group response on two or more metric-dependent variables.	To simultaneously explore the relationship between several categorical, independent variables (usually referred to as treatments) and two or more dependent metric variables.
Canonical correlation	An extension of multiple regression analysis. When there are several metric dependent variables and several metric independent variables.	To correlate simultaneously several metric, independent variables and several dependent, metric variables.
Multiple discriminant analysis	When the single, dependent variable is dichotomous (e.g. male-female) or multi-dichotomous (e.g. high-medium-low) and, therefore, nonmetric.	To understand group differences and predict the likelihood that an entity (individual or object) will belong to a particular class or group based on several metric, independent variables.
Logistic regression	When the single, dependent variable is nonmetric, dichotomous (binary). It accommodates all types of independent variables (metric and nonmetric) and does not require the assumption of multivariate normality.	To predict the changes in a binary (two-group) dependent variable in response to changes in the several independent variables.
Structural equation modelling	When multiple, separate regression equations have to be estimated simultaneously.	To simultaneously test the measurement model (which specifies one or more indicators to measure each variable) and the structural model (the model that relates independent and dependent variables).

settings […]. Perhaps the most widely used example is student achievement as the outcome measure of interest. We know that student achievement is based to some degree on a number of student attributes, which we define as Level-1, the most fundamental unit of analysis. But we also assume that the context for that outcome (e.g. the classroom setting with the teacher, resources, other students, etc. which is termed Level-2) has an impact. Each level above Level-1 is an aggregation into groups of observations in the lower level (i.e. students into classrooms). The primary objective of any analysis of hierarchical data structure is to accurately assess the effects of each attribute of Level-1 (the student) and characteristic of Level-2 (the classroom) while also determining the extent to which Level-1 and Level-2 collectively impact the outcome. A multilevel model (MLM) is an extension of regression analysis that allows for the incorporation of both individual (Level-1) and contextual (Level-2) effects with the appropriate statistical treatment. […] [However,] the technique can accommodate hierarchical structures with many levels (e.g. students in classrooms in schools in school districts in states).

Furthermore, Hair et al. (2019: 328–329) described also panel models, which have both cross-sectional and time-series dimensions:

In an analysis framework somewhat similar to multilevel models, panel models or panel analysis is a regression-based analytical technique designed to handle cross-sectional analyses of longitudinal or time-series data. In the cross-sectional perspective, it accommodates the typical regression analysis with a series of independent variables being related to an outcome variable. […] But the unique element of panel models is that they also accommodate longitudinal data for both the dependent and independent variables. So instead of having to conduct separate analyses for each year or pool these data across years in some manner, panel models were designed to address the necessary characteristics of this type of data. […] The basic panel model uses a data structure that can be visualized as rows representing an analysis unit (e.g. individual, brand, school, etc.) with both dependent measure and independent variables. This is comparable to a typical regression analysis. But there is one additional variable – a time period indicator. This allows multiple years to be contained in the same dataset so that the complete dataset has all the observations for each analysis unit in each of the time periods.

4.8.3 *Linking measure quality assessment to hypothesis testing*

Section 4.5 emphasized that measurement quality assessment can be done in an exploratory way when pilot testing. Further, it deserves confirmatory analyses when analysing the data that will be used to test the hypotheses. However, this is not enough to assure that the analysis is accurate. Traditionally, in fact, procedures to assess measures of validity-reliability are 'applied independently of statistical procedures to test causal hypotheses. […] [The consequence is that] whereas construct validation procedures typically establish the presence of significant amounts of measurement and/or method error, contemporary hypothesis-testing procedures assume it away entirely' (Bagozzi and Phillips, 1982: 459–460). Measurement and method error can cause 'spurious confirmation of inadequate theories, tentative rejection of adequate theories, and/or distorted estimates of the magnitude and relevance of actual relationships' (Bagozzi and Phillips, 1982: 460). Structural equation modelling provides an instrument to test the measurement quality and to consider it while testing the hypotheses.

Structural equation modelling is a powerful but complex technique. An example of its application in OM can be found in Koufteros (1999). Structural equation modelling is receiving increasing attention within OSCM, but it should be properly applied. Shah and Goldstein (2006) presented the implications of overlooking the fundamental assumptions of SEM and ignoring serious methodological issues. They provided guidelines for improving future applications of SEM in OM research. Operations management and SCM researchers have mainly adopted CB-SEM methods (using software such as LISREL, AMOS and EQS). However, recently, OSCM researchers have started to use PLS-SEM. Peng and Lai (2012) have provided guidelines on when it is appropriate to use PLS-SEM.

4.8.4 Interpreting results

The choice and the application of an appropriate statistical test is only one step in the analysis of data for theory testing. In addition, the results of the statistical tests must be interpreted. When interpreting results, the researcher moves from the empirical to the theoretical domain. This process implies considerations of inference and generalization (Meredith, 1998).

In making an inference on relations between variables, the researcher could incur a statistical error or an internal validity error. The statistical error (see Type I and Type II errors discussion in Section 4.3) can be taken into account by considering the issues of statistical power, significance level, sample size and effect size. An internal validity error mistakenly attributes the cause of a variation to a dependent variable. For example, the researcher could infer that variable A causes variable B while there is an unacknowledged variable C that causes both A and B; therefore, the link that the researcher observes between A and B is spurious. 'POM researchers, in the absence of experimental designs, should try to justify internal validity. This can be done informally through a discussion of why causality exists or why alternate explanations are unlikely' (Malhotra and Grover, 1998: 414).

Even when data-analysis results are consistent with the theory at the sample level, the researcher should be careful about inferring that the same consistency holds at the population level – because of the previously discussed issues of sampling, response rate and response bias. A further aspect of results interpretation concerns the discussion of potential extension of the theory to other populations. The degree to which the study's results can be generalized across populations, settings and other similar conditions constitutes the external validity of the study (Davis, 2005).

4.8.5 Data visualization: Much more than result communication

In performing survey-based data analysis and in presenting the obtained results, OSCM researchers have always taken advantage of the opportunities provided by graphical representations (e.g. by using bar charts and pie charts, histograms, boxplots, scatterplots). Recently, the potential offered by data visualization as well as the availability of large datasets to be examined made visualization an important tool for OSCM researchers. 'Visualization is a scientific approach involving the graphical representation of data in order to allow individuals to see and understand trends, patterns, and outliers in data' (Basole et al., 2022: 172). In OSCM, visualization may help to obtain a holistic interpretation of a complex system such as a supply chain or a healthcare process. Without a holistic view, the investigator risks focusing on the parts, making piecewise considerations and failing fully consider the larger system (Basole et al., 2022).

Data visualization techniques as well as supporting tools are extremely numerous (e.g. Kirk, 2019; Shakeel et al., 2022). Shakeel et al. (2022) surveyed 70 articles from 2017 to 2022 to identify, classify, and investigate the various scopes, aspects and theories of data visualization. They analyse and classify theoretical, analytical, statistical models and techniques for improving the performance of visualization. Kirk (2019) provides practical indications to make appropriate choices in data visualization. In particular, he provides a wide gallery of chart types, including profiles of 49 distinct approaches, to give the reader a sense of the common options that exist. Kirk (2019) organizes the charts into five family groupings, based on what each type is primarily used to show:

- *Categorical*: Comparing categories and distributions of quantitative values (bar chart, clustered bar chart, bullet chart, waterfall chart, radar chart, polar chart, connected dot plot, pictogram, proportional symbol chart, word cloud, heat map, matrix chart, dot plot, beeswarm plot, histogram, density plot, box-and-whisker plot).
- *Hierarchical*: Revealing part-to-whole relationships and hierarchies (pie chart, waffle chart, stacked bar chart, diverging bar chart, Marimekko chart, treemap, sunburst chart, dendrogram, Venn diagram).
- *Relational*: Exploring correlations and connections (scatter plot, bubble plot, network diagram, Sankey diagram, chord diagram).
- *Temporal*: Plotting trends and intervals over time (line chart, bump chart, slope graph, connected scatter plot, area chart, stacked area chart, stream graph, Gantt chart, instance chart).
- *Spatial*: Mapping spatial patterns through overlays and distortions. (choropleth map, isarithmic map, proportional symbol map, prism map, dot map, flow map, area cartogram, Dorling cartogram, grid map).

Visualization may be used through the various stages of research. Focusing on OM, Basole et al. (2022) answer the question: How can visualization help researchers across key stages of empirical research, including theory development, theory testing, and the translation of research results into meaningful practical insights and follow-on discussions? Adding to the previous work of Bendoly (2016) focused on OSCM analytics, their answer highlights the following visualization capabilities (Basole et al., 2022: 179):

- Explore, identify, and portray structures and dynamics in data distributions that may not be encapsulated either in words or by a finite set of numerical summary measures. Reduce the dependency of data examination on preexisting assumptions regarding its structure and behavior. [Visualizations created for the research team in the theory/model development stage].
- Capture the potentially complex structure and dynamics variation from developed theory and model designs. Confirm (or find flaws in) the holistic nature of baseline assumptions central to such theory and model designs. [Visualizations created for the research team in the theory/model testing stage].
- Convert implicit knowledge and analytical experience of researchers regarding prescriptions to external audiences, acknowledging the potentially distinct vantage points held by those audiences. Create opportunity for engagement with those audiences to facilitate feedback. [Visualizations created for practice and research community in the translation/conveyance stage].

Basole et al. (2022) answer also the question: What biases and risks do scholars face when employing visualization techniques in their research? Their answer points out two common misrepresentations (Basole et al., 2022: 180): (1) misrepresentation by omission and (2) misrepresentation by inclusion.

Misrepresentation by omission involves the insufficient portrayal of the systems or subsystems under examination through the exclusion of key features in visual renderings. Clearly such misrepresentation poses a threat to any aspect of the research effort; visualization is no exception. Misrepresentation by inclusion, in contrast, involves the portrayal of superfluous content that distracts from, masks, or distorts key aspects of the systems or subsystems under visual examination. Although often viewed as a lesser concern, such inclusions can nonetheless result in incorrect conclusions as well, and hence, caution must be exerted as to how and when to include various factors during visualization'.

Furthermore, Basole et al., (2022: 183) highlight that visualization research increasingly investigates how to best represent uncertainty graphically,

maximizing the accuracy of scholars' quantitative reasoning while reducing their audiences' cognitive burdens and, subsequently, the chances of misleading interpretation [...] Visualization researchers concerned with representing uncertainty are experimenting with different techniques, including shading, transparency, confidence bands/ellipses, fuzziness, or different graphical markers (dotted versus solid lines). [...] Similarly, temporal changes and evolution of research domains may require researchers to utilize uncommon representations and techniques, including connected plots, multiple snapshots (small multiples), animations, or traces.

Image processing and visualization are advancing also through the use of artificial intelligence (AI). Among the various potential advantages of AI, academics can produce more precise, tailored visualizations, expanding their scope of use and exposing underlying practice-related contingencies. However, using AI in visualization may bring peculiar risks such as data breaches, personal information losses, and explicit data ethics violations. To avoid ethical violations, it could be necessary to set up specialized committees composed of computer scientists, statisticians, and legal experts who can foresee and provide solutions to the involved risks (Basole et al., 2022).

4.9 Information that should be included in articles

In an article reporting the results of a survey-based study, the researcher should provide, in a concise but complete manner, all of the information that allows reviewers and readers to: a) understand what has been done, b) critically evaluate what the work has achieved and c) replicate the work or compare the results with similar studies. To understand what information should be included, one can refer to Verma and Goodale (1995), Malhotra and Grover (1998), Forza and Di Nuzzo (1998), Hensley (1999) and/or Rungtusanatham et al. (2003). The main points to consider are summarized in Table 4.18.

All of the information listed in Table 4.18 is necessary if the purpose of the article has a theory-testing purpose, but this information is also generally useful when the article is of a descriptive or exploratory nature. Providing this information may make evident the

Table 4.18 Information to include in the report

Main issues	Detailed points
Theoretical base	Names and definitions of constructs, conceptualization of constructs (e.g. reflective/formative, monadic/polyadic), relations between variables, consideration of possible endogeneity, validity boundary of the relations, unit of analysis, previous literature on each of these points.
Expected contribution	Purpose of the study (whether it is exploration, description, or hypothesis testing), research questions/hypotheses, types of investigation (causal relationships, correlations, group differences, ranks, etc.).
Sample and data collection approach	Sampling process, source of population-frame, justification of sample frame, a priori sample, resulting sample, response rate, bias analysis. Time horizon (cross-sectional or longitudinal), when and where data has been collected, type of data collection (mail, telephone, web, personal visit), pilot testing, contact approach, kind of recall.
Data pre-treatment	Missing data analysis and treatment, outliers analysis and treatment, data pooling (putting together observations from different sub-populations), scale transformation, data standardization.
Measurement	Description of measure construction process, reference/comparison to similar/identical measures, description of respondents/informants, list of respondents/informants for each measure, description of the data aggregation process (from informants to unit of analysis), measure pre-testing, adequacy to the unit of analysis, adequacy to the respondents/informants, face validity, construct unidimensionality, reliability, convergent and discriminant validity, predictive validity, appendix with the measurement instrument, description of the measurement refinement process including information on techniques used.
Data analysis	Description of the techniques used, evidence that the technique assumptions are satisfied, statistical power, results of the tests including level of significance, interpretation of the results in the context of the hypotheses.
Discussion	Discuss what the substantiation of the hypotheses means in terms of the present research and why some of the hypotheses (if any) may not have been supported. Consider through intuitive but appropriate and logical speculations, how inadequacies in the sampling design, the measures, the data collection methods, control of critical variables, respondent bias, questionnaire design and so on, affect the results, their trustability and generalizability.

shortcomings of the survey. Serious journals and reviewers, however, greatly appreciate those authors who indicate the limitations of their research: a survey-based paper without a serious discussion of research limitations appears somewhat suspect to them. The reason is that while research with fatal flaws cannot be accepted for publication, no research is without limitations. An honest and capable researcher should mention such limitations, thus paving the way to further research and avoiding definitive acceptance of results whose validity is, to some extent, questionable.

Providing all of the required information is difficult and is probably not feasible in a single paper. In fact, with the passing of years, more and more papers have split the outcomes of a survey-based study into two or more articles focused, respectively, on concept formalization, measure development and testing of the main hypotheses. This trend is leading to a more broadly based and stronger theoretical foundation in OSCM survey-based research.

Table 4.19 Requirement differences among survey types

Element/dimension	Survey type Exploratory	Descriptive	Theory testing
Unit(s) of analysis	Clearly defined	Clearly defined and appropriate for the questions/hypotheses	Clearly defined and appropriate for the research hypotheses
Respondents	Representative of the unit of analysis	Representative of the unit of analysis	Representative of the unit of analysis
Research hypotheses	Not necessary	Questions clearly stated	Hypotheses clearly stated and theoretically motivated
Representativeness of sample frame	Approximation	Explicit, logical argument; reasonable choice among alternatives	Explicit, logical argument; reasonable choice among alternatives
Representativeness of the sample	Not a criterion	Systematic, purposive, random selection	Systematic, purposive, random selection
Sample size	Sufficient to include the range of the interest phenomena	Sufficient to represent the population of interest and perform statistical tests	Sufficient to test categories in the theoretical framework with statistical power
Pre-test of questionnaires	With sub-sample of the sample	With sub-sample of the sample	With sub-sample of the sample
Response rate	No minimum	Ideally greater than 50 per cent (pragmatically, see studies on the same topic) and study of bias	Ideally greater than 50 per cent (pragmatically, see studies on the same topic) and study of bias
Mix of data collection methods	Multiple methods	Not necessary	Multiple methods

Source: Adapted from Pinsonneault and Kraemer (1993: 82).

Exploratory, descriptive and theory-testing survey researches are all important and widely used in OSCM. Therefore, an outline of the different requirements of the various types of survey is included below. Obviously, if a particular requirement is relaxed, then there is no longer a need to provide detailed information concerning that requirement. Table 4.19 summarizes the differences in requirements among different survey types.

Even though only a limited part of the above-mentioned information may be reported in an article due to space constraints, researchers have to be prepared to provide them during the review process. It could be necessary to provide them in reply to reviewers or to comply with editor requests. More and more data and process transparency is required by reviewers and editors, sometimes with potential confidentiality implications.

4.10 Ethical issues in survey research

The ethical issues presented in Chapter 2 hold for survey research too. By carefully reading Chapter 2, the OSCM researcher can reassess, from the ethical point of view, what he or she is going to do or is doing. By also following the guidelines provided in this chapter, the researcher can deal with a number of ethical issues presented in Chapter 2 and, in particular, with the issue of carefulness.

However, survey research has some peculiarities that should be taken into account. Gilman (2008), for example, drew attention to some specific ethical issues that survey researchers should consider. According to Gilman (2008: 865–866), the surveyor should:

ensure that survey respondents understand the nature and the purpose of the survey, what is expected of them if they participate, the expected length of time necessary for them to complete the survey [...], how the data will be utilized, and their rights as research participants, including their right to confidentiality

and should also ensure that

potential respondents have the competence to understand why the study is being conducted and what their rights and responsibilities are as respondents in order to participate.

Some of the information needed for OSCM survey research (e.g. costs, quality and time performance) is very sensitive. The implications for the respondents and for the organizations with regard to lack of privacy and/or confidentiality may be very severe. To prevent this risk, the OSCM surveyor should not include the names of the respondents and/or organizations in the data set. If the correspondence between observations and names are to be retained, then they should be kept separate from data files and should not be circulated among the research team.

Trust is essential for collecting good data. Therefore, we should make efforts to increase the trust that respondents have in OSCM surveyors. The OSCM surveyor has a moral obligation to deliver what he or she promises (e.g. a report with the results of the research), within a time frame that is meaningful for the respondents. The behaviour of the OSCM surveyor should communicate that he/she cares about the respondents' privacy and interests. Preventing drawbacks to the respondents and/or their organizations is not enough. The surveyor should also deliver value in exchange for participation in the survey.

4.11 Summary

This chapter has presented and discussed the various steps comprising the survey research process. For each step, the chapter has provided responses to the following questions: a) What is this step about? b) Why should this step be done? c) What are some recommended approaches? Examples of applications in OSCM and more general reference literature are referenced throughout the chapter. Table 4.20 summarizes the questions that the researcher should ask at the various steps of survey research in order to enhance the quality of the process.

By following the guidelines provided in this chapter, the researcher should be able to execute survey research that will meet the main requirements of a scientific research project as outlined by Sekaran (1992: 10–14):

- *Purposiveness*: The researcher has been guided by and communicates a specific aim or purpose for the research.
- *Rigour*: A strong theoretical base and a sound methodology are needed to collect the appropriate information and to interpret it adequately, that is, to do research in a trusted manner.

Table 4.20 Questions to check the quality of an ongoing survey research

Survey phase	Check questions to assure survey research quality
Prior to survey research design	1. Is the unit of analysis clearly defined for the study?
	2. Are the construct's operational definitions clearly stated?
	3. Is it correct to formalize the construct as reflective/formative?
	4. Are mediation and/or moderation effects (if any) identified and correctly formalized?
	5. Is there any endogeneity issue in the theoretical model?
	6. Are research hypotheses clearly stated?
Defining the sample	7. Is the sample frame defined and justified?
	8. What is the required level of randomness needed for the purposes of the study?
	9. What is the minimum sample size required for the planned statistical analyses?
	10. Can the sampling procedure be reproduced by other researchers?
Developing measurement instruments	11. Are already-developed (and preferably validated) measures available?
	12. Are objective or perceptual questions needed?
	13. Is the wording appropriate?
	14. Are all the aspects of the concept considered fairly in the set of items/ indicators?
	15. Does the instrumentation consistently reflect that unit of analysis?
	16. Is the chosen scale compatible with the analyses that will be performed?
	17. Can the respondent/informant place the answers easily and reliably in this scale?
	18. Is (Are) the chosen respondent(s)/informant(s) appropriate for the information sought?
	19. Is any form of triangulation used to ensure that the gathered information is not biased by the respondent(s)/informant(s) or the method?
	20. Are multi-item measures used (in the case of perceptual questions)?
	21. Are the various rules of questionnaire design (see above) followed?
	22. What actions have been taken to prevent common method bias in measurement?
	23. What actions in measurement have been taken to deal with endogeneity?
Collecting data	24. What is the response rate and is it satisfactory?
	25. How much is the response bias?
	26. Are data cleaned from errors or inconsistent answers?
	27. Could missing data affect the results?
	28. Is it possible to pool data or are treatments necessary?
Assessing measure quality	29. Is face validity assessed?
	30. Is field-based measure pre-testing performed?
	31. Is reliability assessed?
	32. Is construct validity assessed?
	33. Is pilot data used for purifying measures or are existing validated measures adapted?
	34. Is common method bias a concern?
	35. Is it possible to use confirmatory methods?
Analysing data	36. Is the statistical test appropriate for the hypothesis being tested?
	37. Is the statistical test adequate for the available data?
	38. Are the test assumptions satisfied?
	39. Do outliers or influencing factors affect the results?
	40. Is the statistical power sufficient to reduce statistical conclusion errors?
Interpretation of results	41. Do the findings have internal validity?
	42. Is the inference (both relational and representational) acceptable?
	43. For what other populations could the results still be valid?

- *Testability*: The researcher can reliably infer whether or not the data support conjectures and he or she has controlled for what can influence the results.
- *Replicability*: It is possible to repeat the study exactly. If controlled repetition of replicable studies is performed, conjectures will be neither supported (or discarded) merely by chance, nor due to differences in method.
- *Precision and confidence*: These refer on the one hand to how close the findings are to 'reality' and, on the other, to the probability that estimations are correct.
- *Objectivity*: The conclusions are based on all the relevant facts and are not influenced by the researcher's subjective values.
- *Generalizability*: refers to the applicability of the research findings to settings different from the studied one.
- *Parsimony*: The use of a small number of variables and relationships among variables to describe and explain a phenomenon generally makes research frameworks more manageable and useful.

Note

1 This chapter is based on Forza, C. (2002) Survey research in operations management: A process based perspective. *International Journal of Operations and Production Management*, 22 (2): 152–194.

Bibliography

Survey and empirical methods in OSCM

Abbey, J. D. and Meloy, M. G. (2017) Attention by design: Using attention checks to detect inattentive respondents and improve data quality. *Journal of Operations Management*, 53–56(November): 63–70.

Amoako-Gyampah, K. and Meredith, J. R. (1989) The operations management research agenda: An update. *Journal of Operations Management*, 8(3): 250–262.

Amundson, S. D. (1998) Relationships between theory-driven empirical research in operations management and other disciplines. *Journal of Operations Management*, 16(4): 341–359.

Barnes, D. (2001) Research methods for the empirical investigation of the process of formation of operations strategy. *International Journal of Operations and Production Management*, 21(8): 1076–1095.

Basole, R., Bendoly, E., Chandrasekaran, A. and Linderman, K. (2022) Visualization in operations management research. *INFORMS Journal on Data Science*, 1(2): 172–187.

Bendoly, E. (2016) Fit, bias, and enacted sensemaking in data visualization: Frameworks for continuous development in operations and supply chain management analytics. *Journal of Business Logistics*, 37(1): 6–17.

Boyer, K. K. and Pagell, M. (2000) Measurement issues in empirical research: Improving measures of operations strategy and advanced manufacturing technology. *Journal of Operations Management*, 18(3): 361–374.

Boyer, K., Bozarth, C. and McDermott, C. (2000) Configurations in operations: An emerging area of study. *Journal of Operations Management*, 18(6): 601–604.

Boyer, K. K., Olson, J. R., Calantone, R. J. and Jackson, E. C. (2002) Print versus electronic surveys: A comparison of two data collection methodologies. *Journal of Operations Management*, 20(4): 357–373.

Chatha, K. A., Butt, I. and Tariq, A. (2015) Research methodologies and publication trends in manufacturing strategy. *International Journal of Operations and Production Management*, 35(4): 487–546.

Collins, R. S. and Cordon, C. (1997) Survey methodology issues in manufacturing strategy and practice research. *International Journal of Operations and Production Management*, 17(7): 697–706.

Craighead, C. W. and Meredith, J. (2008) Operations management research: Evolution and alternative future paths. *International Journal of Operations and Production Management*, 28(8): 710–726.

Craighead, C. W., Ketchen, D. J., Dunn, K. S. and Hult, G. T. M. (2011) Addressing common method variance: Guidelines for survey research on information technology, operations and supply chain management. *IEEE Transactions on Engineering Management*, 58(3): 578–588.

Dangayach, G. S. and Deshmukh, S. G. (2001) Manufacturing strategy: Literature review and some issues. *International Journal of Operations and Production Management*, 21(7): 884–932.

Davies, A. J. and Kochhar, A. K. (2002) Manufacturing best practice and performance studies: A critique. *International Journal of Operations and Production Management*, 22(3): 289–305.

Edwards, J. R. (2019) Response invalidity in empirical research: Causes, detection, and remedies. *Journal of Operations Management*, 65(1): 62–76.

Filippini, R. (1997) Operations management research: Some reflections on evolution, models and empirical studies in OM. *International Journal of Operations and Production Management*, 17(7): 655–670.

Flynn, B., Pagell, M. and Fugate, B. (2018) Survey research design in supply chain management: The need for evolution in our expectations. *Journal of Supply Chain Management*, 54(1): 1–15.

Flynn, B. B., Sakakibara, S., Schroeder, R. G., Bates, K. A. and Flynn, E. J. (1990) Empirical research methods in operations management. *Journal of Operations Management*, 9(2): 250–284.

Forza, C. (2002) Survey research in operations management: A process based perspective. *International Journal of Operations and Production Management*, 22(2): 152–194.

Forza, C. and Di Nuzzo, F. (1998) Meta-analysis applied to operations management: Summarizing the results of empirical research. *International Journal of Production Research*, 36(3): 837–861.

Forza, C. and Vinelli, A. (1998) On the contribution of survey research to the development of operations management theories. In Coughlan, P., Dromgoole, T. and Peppard, J. (eds.) *Operations Management: Future Issues and Competitive Responses*, 183–188. Dublin, Ireland: School of Business Studies.

Frohlich, M. T. (2002) Techniques for improving response rates in OM survey research. *Journal of Operations Management*, 20(1): 53–62.

Guide, V. D. R. and Ketokivi, M. (2015) Notes from the editors: Redefining some methodological criteria for the journal. *Journal of Operations Management*, 37(July): v–viii.

Gupta, S., Verma, R. and Victorino, L. (2006) Empirical research published in production and operations management (1992–2005): Trends and future research directions. *Production and Operations Management Journal*, 15(3): 432–448.

Handfield, R. B. and Melnyk, S. A. (1998) The scientific theory-building process: A primer using the case of TQM. *Journal of Operations Management*, 16(4): 321–339.

Helmuth, C. A., Craighead, C. W., Connelly, B. L., Collier, D. Y. and Hanna, J. B. (2015) Supply chain management research: Key elements of study design and statistical testing. *Journal of Operations Management*, 36(May): 178–186.

Hensley, R. L. (1999) A review of operations management studies using scale development techniques. *Journal of Operations Management*, 17(2): 343–358.

Hill, T., Nicholson, A. and Westbrook, R. (1999) Closing the gap: A polemic on plant-based research in operations management. *International Journal of Operations and Production Management*, 19(2): 139–156.

Ho, D. C. K., Au, K. F. and Newton, E. (2002) Empirical research on supply chain management: A critical review and recommendations. *International Journal of Production Research*, 40(17): 4415–4430.

Ketokivi, M. (2019) Avoiding bias and fallacy in survey research: A behavioral multilevel approach. *Journal of Operations Management*, 65(4): 380–402.

Ketokivi, M. and McIntosh, C. N. (2017) Addressing the endogeneity dilemma in operations management research: Theoretical, empirical, and pragmatic considerations. *Journal of Operations Management*, 52(May): 1–14.

Ketokivi, M. A. and Schroeder, R. G. (2004) Perceptual measures of performance: Fact or fiction? *Journal of Operations Management*, 22(3): 247–264.

Ketchen Jr, D. J., Craighead, C. W. and Cheng, L. (2018) Achieving research design excellence through the pursuit of perfection: Toward strong theoretical calibration. *Journal of Supply Chain Management*, 54(1): 16–22.

Knoppen, D., Ateş, M. A., Brandon-Jones, A., Luzzini, D., van Raaij, E. and Wynstra, F. (2015) A comprehensive assessment of measurement equivalence in operations management. *International Journal of Production Research*, 53(1): 166–182.

Krause, D., Luzzini, D. and Lawson, B. (2018) Building the case for a single key informant in supply chain management survey research. *Journal of Supply Chain Management*, 54(1): 42–50.

Kull, T. J., Kotlar, J. and Spring, M. (2018) Small and medium enterprise research in supply chain management: The case for single-respondent research designs. *Journal of Supply Chain Management*, 54(1): 23–34.

Lu, G., Ding, X. D., Peng, D. X. and Chuang, H. H. C. (2018) Addressing endogeneity in operations management research: Recent developments, common problems, and directions for future research. *Journal of Operations Management*, 64(November): 53–64.

Malhotra, M. K. and Grover, V. (1998) An assessment of survey research in POM: From constructs to theory. *Journal of Operations Management*, 16(17): 407–425.

Malhotra, M. K., Singhal, C., Shang, G. and Ployhart, R. E. (2014) A critical evaluation of alternative methods and paradigms for conducting mediation analysis in operations management research. *Journal of Operations Management*, 32(4): 127–137.

Meredith, J. R. (1998) Building operations management theory through case and field research. *Journal of Operations Management*, 16(4): 441–454.

Meredith, J. R., Raturi, A., Amoako-Jampah, K. and Kaplan, B. (1989) Alternative research paradigms in operations. *Journal of Operations Management*, 8(4): 297–326.

Montabon, F., Daugherty, P. J. and Chen, H. (2018) Setting standards for single respondent survey design. *Journal of Supply Chain Management*, 54(1): 35–41.

O'Leary-Kelly, S. W. and Vokurka, R. J. (1998) The empirical assessment of construct validity. *Journal of Operations Management*, 16(4): 387–405.

Pagell, M. and Shevchenko, A. (2014) Why research in sustainable supply chain management should have no future. *Journal of Supply Chain Management*, 50(1): 44–55.

Pannirselvam, G. P., Ferguson, L. A., Ash, R. C. and Siferd, S. P. (1999) Operations management research: An update for the 1990s. *Journal of Operations Management*, 18(1): 95–112.

Peng, D. X. and Lai, F. (2012) Using partial least squares in operations management research: A practical guideline and summary of past research. *Journal of Operations Management*, 30(6): 467–480.

Roberts, N., Thatcher, J. B. and Grover, V. (2010) Advancing operations management theory using exploratory structural equation modelling techniques. *International Journal of Production Research*, 48(15): 4329–4353.

Roh, J. A., Whipple, J. M. and Boyer, K. K. (2013) The effect of single rater bias in multi-stakeholder research: A methodological evaluation of buyer-supplier relationships. *Production and Operations Management*, 22(3): 711–725.

Roth, A. V. (2007) Applications of empirical science in manufacturing and service operations. *Manufacturing and Service Operations Management*, 9(4): 353–367.

Roth, A. V., Schroeder, R. G., Huang, X. and Kristal, M. M. (2008) *Handbook of Metrics for Research in Operations Management*. Thousand Oaks, CA: Sage Publications.

Rungtusanatham, M. J. (1998) Let's not overlook content validity. *Decision Line*, 29(4): 10–13.

Rungtusanatham, M. J. and Choi, T. Y. (2000) The reliability and validity of measurement instrument employed in empirical OM research: Concepts and definitions. Phoenix, AZ: Arizona State University – Working Paper of Department of Management.

Rungtusanatham, M. J., Choi, T. Y., Hollingworth, D. G., Wu, Z. and Forza, C. (2003) Survey research in operations management: Historical analyses. *Journal of Operations Management*, 21(4): 475–488.

Rungtusanatham, M., Miller, J. W. and Boyer, K. K. (2014) Theorizing, testing and concluding for mediation in SCM research: Tutorial and procedural recommendations. *Journal of Operations Management*, 32(3): 99–113.

Rungtusanatham, M., Ng, C. H., Zhao, X. and Lee, T. S. (2008) Pooling data across transparently-different groups of key informants: Measurement equivalence and survey research. *Decision Sciences*, 39(1): 115–145.

Saraph, J. V., Benson, P. G. and Schroeder, R. G. (1989) An instrument for measuring the critical factors of quality management. *Decision Sciences*, 20(4): 810–829.

Scudder, G. D. and Hill, C. A. (1998) A review and classification of empirical research in operations management. *Journal of Operations Management*, 16(1): 91–101.

Shah, R. and Goldstein, S. M. (2006) Use of structural equation modeling in operations management research: Looking back and forward. *Journal of Operations Management*, 24(2): 148–169.

Schoenherr, T., Ellram, L. M. and Tate, W. L. (2015) A note on the use of survey research firms to enable empirical data collection. *Journal of Business Logistics*, 36(3): 288–300.

Soni, G. and Kodali, R. (2012) A critical review of empirical research methodology in supply chain management. *Journal of Manufacturing Technology Management*, 23(6): 753–779.

Sousa, R. and Voss, C. A. (2008) Contingency research in operations management practices. *Journal of Operations Management*, 26(6): 697–713.

Tsikriktsis, N. (2005) A review of techniques for treating missing data in OM survey research. *Journal of Operations Management*, 24(1): 53–62.

Van Donselaar, K. and Sharman, G. (1997) An innovative survey in the transportation and distribution sector. *International Journal of Operations and Production Management*, 17(7): 707–720.

Van Weele, A. J. and van Raaij, E. M. (2014) The future of purchasing and supply management research: About relevance and rigor. *Journal of Supply Chain Management*, 50(1): 56–72.

Verma, R. and Goodale, J. C. (1995) Statistical power in operations management research. *Journal of Operations Management*, 13(2): 139–152.

Vokurka, R. J. and O'Leary-Kelly, S. W. (2000) A review of empirical research on manufacturing flexibility. *Journal of Operations Management*, 18(4): 485–501.

Wacker, J. G. (1998) A definition of theory: Research guidelines for different theory building research methods in operations management. *Journal of Operations Management*, 16(4): 361–385.

Wacker, J. G. (2004) A theory of formal conceptual definitions: Developing theory-building measurement instruments. *Journal of Operations Management*, 22(6): 629–650.

Whybark, D. C. (1997) GMRG survey research in operations management. *International Journal of Operations and Production Management*, 17(7): 686–696.

Wowak, K. D., Craighead, C. W., Ketchen, D. J. and Hult, G. T. M. (2013) Supply chain knowledge and performance: A meta-analysis. *Decision Sciences*, 44(5): 843–875.

Zhang, X., van Donk, D. P. and van der Vaart, T. (2011) Does ICT influence supply chain management and performance? *International Journal of Operations and Production Management*, 31(11): 1215–1247.

Examples of OSCM articles based on survey research

Ahire, S. L. and Dreyfus, P. (2000) The impact of design management and process management on quality: An empirical investigation. *Journal of Operations Management*, 18(5): 549–575.

Ahire, S. L., Goldhar, D. Y. and Waller, M. A. (1996) Development and validation of TQM implementation constructs. *Decision Sciences*, 27(1): 23–56.

Anderson, J. C., Rungtusanatham, M. and Schroeder, R. G. (1994) A theory of quality management underlying the Deming management method. *Academy of Management Review*, 19(3): 472–509.

Anderson, J. C., Schroeder, R. G. and Cleveland, G. (1991) The process of manufacturing strategy: Some empirical observations and conclusions. *International Journal of Operations and Production Management*, 11(3): 86–110.

Anderson, J. C., Rungtusanatham, M., Schroeder, R. G. and Devaraj, S. (1995) A path analytic model of a theory of quality management underlying the Deming management method. *Decision Sciences*, 26(5): 637–658.

Anttonen, M., Halme, M., Houtbeckers, E. and Nurkka, J. (2013) The other side of sustainable innovation: Is there a demand for innovative services? *Journal of Cleaner Production*, 45(April): 89–103.

Birnbaum, P. H., Farh, J. -L. and Wong, G. Y. Y. (1986) The job characteristics model in Hong Kong. *Journal of Applied Psychology*, 71(4): 598–605.

Blindenbach-Driessen, F. and van den Ende, J. (2014) The locus of innovation: The effect of a separate innovation unit on exploration, exploitation, and ambidexterity in manufacturing and service firms. *Journal of Product Innovation Management*, 31(5): 1089–1105.

Boyer, K. K., Gardner, J. W. and Schweikhart, S. (2012) Process quality improvement: An examination of general vs. outcome-specific climate and practices in hospitals. *Journal of Operations Management*, 30(4): 325–339.

Brammer, S. and Walker, H. (2011) Sustainable procurement in the public sector: An international comparative study. *International Journal of Operations and Production Management*, 31(4): 452–476.

Cantello, F. X., Chalmers, J. E. and Evans, J. E. (1990) Evolution to an effective and enduring SPC system. *Quality Progress*, 23(2): 60–64.

Cao, M. and Zhang, Q. (2011) Supply chain collaboration: Impact on collaborative advantage and firm performance. *Journal of Operations Management*, 29(3): 163–180.

Chen, J. -S., Tsou, H. -T. and Ching, R. K. H. (2011) Co-production and its effects on service innovation. *Industrial Marketing Management*, 40(8): 1331–1346.

Corbett, L. M. and Whybark, D. C. (2001) Searching for the sandcone in the GMRG data. *International Journal of Operations and Production Management*, 21(7): 965–980.

Durach, C. F., Wiengarten, F. and Pagell, M. (2023) The effect of temporary workers and works councils on process innovation. *International Journal of Operations and Production Management*, 43(5): 781–801.

Ellram, L. M., Tate, W. L. and Billington, C. (2007) Services supply management: The next frontier for improved organizational performance. *California Management Review*, 49(4): 44–66.

Feldmann, A. and Olhager, J. (2013) Plant roles. *International Journal of Operations and Production Management*, 33(6): 722–744.

Flynn, B. B., Huo, B. and Zhao, X. (2010) The impact of supply chain integration on performance: A contingency and configuration approach. *Journal of Operations Management*, 28(1): 58–71.

Flynn, B. B., Schroeder, R. G. and Sakakibara, S. (1994) A framework for quality management research and an associated measurement instrument. *Journal of Operations Management*, 11(4): 339–366.

Flynn, B. B., Schroeder, R. G. and Flynn, E. J. (1999) World class manufacturing: An investigation of Hayes and Wheelwright's foundation. *Journal of Operations Management*, 17(3): 249–269.

Flynn, B. B., Schroeder, R. G., Flynn, E. J., Sakakibara, S. and Bates, K. A. (1997) World-class manufacturing project: Overview and selected results. *International Journal of Operations and Production Management*, 17(7): 671–685.

Forza, C. (1995) Quality information systems and quality management: A reference model and associated measures for empirical research. *Industrial Management and Data Systems*, 95(2): 6–14.

Forza, C. and Filippini, R. (1998) TQM impact on quality conformance and customer satisfaction. *International Journal of Production Economics*, 55(1): 1–20.

Gardner, J. W., Boyer, K. K. and Gray, J. V. (2015) Operational and strategic information processing: Complementing healthcare IT infrastructure. *Journal of Operations Management*, 33/34(January): 123–139.

Husseini, M. S. M. and O'Brien, C. (2004) Strategic implications of manufacturing performance comparisons for newly industrialising countries. *International Journal of Operations and Production Management*, 24(11): 1126–1148.

Kapetanopoulou, P. and Tagaras, G. (2011) Drivers and obstacles of product recovery activities in the Greek industry. *International Journal of Operations and Production Management*, 31(2): 148–166.

Kesidou, E., Narasimhan, R., Ozusaglam, S. and Wong, C. Y. (2022) Dynamic openness for network-enabled product and process innovation: A panel-data analysis. *International Journal of Operations and Production Management*, 42(3): 257–279.

Klassen, R. D. and Jacobs, J. (2001) Experimental comparison of web, electronic and mail survey technologies in operations management. *Journal of Operations Management*, 19(6): 713–728.

Koste, L. L. and Malhotra, M. K. (1999) A theoretical framework for analyzing the dimensions of manufacturing flexibility. *Journal of Operations Management*, 18(1): 75–93.

Koste, L. L., Malhotra, M. K. and Sharma, S. (2004) Measuring dimensions of manufacturing flexibility. *Journal of Operations Management*, 22(2): 171–196.

Koufteros, X., Verghese, A. J. and Lucianetti, L. (2014) The effect of performance measurement systems on firm performance: A cross-sectional and a longitudinal study. *Journal of Operations Management*, 32(6): 313–336.

Koufteros, X. A. (1999) Testing a model of pull production: A paradigm for manufacturing research using structural equation modelling. *Journal of Operations Management*, 17(4): 467–488.

Lai, F., Li, D., Wang, Q. and Zhao, X. (2008) The information technology capability of third-party logistics providers: A resource-based view and empirical evidence from China. *Journal of Supply Chain Management*, 44(3): 22–38.

Lambert, D. M. and Harrington, T. C. (1990) Measuring non-response bias in customer service mail surveys. *Journal of Business Logistics*, 11(2): 5–25.

Llach, J., Perramon, J., Alonso-Almeida, M. D. M. and Bagur-Femenías, L. (2013) Joint impact of quality and environmental practices on firm performance in small service businesses: An empirical study of restaurants. *Journal of Cleaner Production*, 44(April): 96–104.

McFadden, K. L., Henagan, S. C. and Gowen, C. R. (2009) The patient safety chain: Transformational leadership's effect on patient safety culture, initiatives, and outcomes. *Journal of Operations Management*, 27(5): 390–404.

Menor, L. J. and Roth, A. V. (2007) New service development competence in retail banking: Construct development and measurement validation. *Journal of Operations Management*, 25(4): 825–846.

Mollenkopf, D. A., Rabinovich, E., Laseter, T. M. and Boyer, K. K. (2007) Managing internet product returns: A focus on effective service operations. *Decision Sciences*, 38(2): 215–250.

Narasimhan, R. and Kim, S. W. (2002) Effect of supply chain integration on the relationship between diversification and performance: Evidence from Japanese and Korean firms. *Journal of Operations Management*, 20(3): 303–323.

Oliveira, P. and Roth, A. V. (2012) Service orientation: The derivation of underlying constructs and measures. *International Journal of Operations and Production Management*, 32(2): 156–190.

Orfila-Sintes, F. and Mattsson, J. (2009) Innovation behavior in the hotel industry. *Omega*, 37(2): 380–394.

Parasuraman, A., Zeithaml, V. A. and Berry, L. L. (1988) SERVQUAL: A multiple-item scale for measuring consumer perceptions of service quality. *Journal of Retailing*, 64(1): 12–40.

Paulraj, A., Lado, A. A. and Chen, I. J. (2008) Inter-organizational communication as a relational competency: Antecedents and performance outcomes in collaborative buyer–supplier relationships. *Journal of Operations Management*, 26(1): 45–64.

Peng, D. X., Verghese, A., Shah, R. and Schroeder, R. G. (2013) The relationships between external integration and plant improvement and innovation capabilities: The moderation effect of product clockspeed. *Journal of Supply Chain Management*, 49(3): 3–24.

Peng, X. D., Ye, Y., Fan, R. L., Ding, X. D. and Chandrasekaran, A. (2022) Cost-quality tradeoff in nurse staffing: An exploration of USA hospitals facing market competition. *International Journal of Operations and Production Management*, 42(5): 577–602.

Rungtusanatham, M. (2001) Beyond improved quality: The motivational effects of statistical process control. *Journal of Operations Management*, 19(4): 653–673.

Rungtusanatham, M., Forza, C., Filippini, R. and Anderson, J. C. (1998) A replication study of a theory of quality management underlying the Deming management method: Insights from an Italian context. *Journal of Operations Management*, 17(1): 77–95.

Rungtusanatham, M., Anderson, J. C. and Dooley, K. J. (1999) Towards measuring the 'SPC implementation/practice construct': Some evidence of measurement quality. *International Journal of Quality and Reliability Management*, 16(4): 301–329.

Rungtusanatham, M., Forza, C., Koka, B. R., Salvador, F. and Nie, W. (2005) TQM across multiple countries: Convergence hypothesis versus national specificity arguments. *Journal of Operations Management*, 23(1): 43–63.

Salvador, F. and Forza, C. (2004) Configuring products to address the customization-responsiveness squeeze: A survey of management issues and opportunities. *International Journal of Production Economics*, 91(3): 273–291.

Schoenherr, T. and Swink, M. (2012) Revisiting the arcs of integration: Cross-validations and extensions. *Journal of Operations Management*, 30(1–2): 99–115.

Sharma, L., Chandrasekaran, A., Boyer, K. K. and McDermott, C. M. (2016) The impact of health information technology bundles on hospital performance: An econometric study. *Journal of Operations Management*, 41(January): 25–41.

Squire, B., Cousins, P. D., Lawson, B. and Brown, S. (2009) The effect of supplier manufacturing capabilities on buyer responsiveness. *International Journal of Operations and Production Management*, 29(8): 766–788.

Swink, M. and Jacobs, B. W. (2012) Six Sigma adoption: Operating performance impacts and contextual drivers of success. *Journal of Operations Management*, 30(6): 437–453.

Thirumalai, S., Lindsey, S. and Stratman, J. K. (2022) You cannot be good at everything: Tradeoff and returns in healthcare services. *International Journal of Operations and Production Management*, 42(3): 357–383.

Tunalv, C. (1990) Manufacturing strategies and decentralisation. *International Journal of Operations and Production Management*, 10(2): 107–119.

Turkulainen, V. and Ketokivi, M. (2012) Cross-functional integration and performance: What are the real benefits? *International Journal of Operations and Production Management*, 32(4): 447–467.

Ward, P. T., Leong, G. K. and Boyer, K. K. (1994) Manufacturing proactiveness and performance. *Decision Sciences*, 25(3): 337–358.

Wen, C., Prybutok, V. R., Blankson, C. and Fang, J. (2014) The role of e-quality within the consumer decision making process. *International Journal of Operations and Production Management*, 34(12): 1506–1536.

Wiengarten, F., Gimenez, C., Fynes, B. and Ferdows, K. (2015) Exploring the importance of cultural collectivism on the efficacy of lean practices. *International Journal of Operations and Production Management*, 35(3): 370–391.

Yee, R. W. Y., Yeung, A. C. L. and Edwin Cheng, T. C. (2010) An empirical study of employee loyalty, service quality and firm performance in the service industry. *International Journal of Production Economics*, 124(1): 109–120.

Research methods in business and social sciences

Avazpour, I., Grundy, J. and Zhu, L. (2019) Engineering complex data integration, harmonization and visualization systems. *Journal of Industrial Information Integration*, 16(December), 100103: 1–13.

Bacharach, S. B. (1989) Organizational theories: Some criteria for evaluation. *Academy of Management Review*, 14(4): 496–515.

Bagozzi, R. P. (1980) *Causal Models in Marketing*. New York, NY: Wiley.

Bagozzi, R. P. and Phillips, L. W. (1982) Representing and testing organizational theories: A holistic construal. *Administrative Science Quarterly*, 27(3): 459–489.

Bagozzi, R. P., Yi, Y. and Phillips, L. W. (1991) Assessing construct validity in organizational research. *Administrative Science Quarterly*, 36(4): 421–434.

Baroudi, J. J. and Orlikowski, W. J. (1989) The problem of statistical power in MIS research. *MIS Quarterly*, 13(1): 87–106.

Bollen, K. and Lennox, R. (1991) Conventional wisdom on measurement: A structural equation perspective. *Psychological Bulletin*, 110(2): 305–314.

Bowman, C. and Ambrosini, V. (1997) Using single respondents in strategy research. *British Journal of Management*, 8(2): 119–131.

Campbell, D. T. and Fiske, D. W. (1959) Convergent and discriminant validation by the multitrait-multimethod matrix. *Psychological Bulletin*, 56(2): 81–105.

Carmines, E. G. and Zeller, R. A. (1979) *Reliability and Validity Assessment*. New York, NY: Sage Publications.

Cohen, J. (1960) A coefficient of agreement for nominal scales. *Educational and Psychological Measurement*, 20(1): 37–46.

Cronbach, L. J. (1951) Coefficient alpha and the internal structure of tests. *Psychometrika*, 16(4): 297–334.

Dansereau, F. and Markham, S. E. (1987) Level of analysis in personnel and human resources management. In Rowland, K. and Ferris, G. (eds.) *Research in Personnel and Human Resources Management*, Vol. 5, 1–50. Greenwich, CT: JAI Press.

Davis, D. (2005) *Business Research for Decision Making*, 6th edn. Belmont, CA: Thomson/Brooks/Cole.

Diamantopoulos, A. and Winklhofer, H. M. (2001) Index construction with formative indicators: An alternative to scale development. *Journal of Marketing Research*, 38(2): 269–277.

Dubin, R. (1978) *Theory Building*. New York, NY: The Free Press.

Emory, C. W. and Cooper, D. R. (1991) *Business Research Methods*. Homewood, IL: Irwin.

Fiske, D. W. (1982) Convergent–discriminant validation in measurements and research strategies. In: Brinberg, D. and Kidder, L. H. (eds.) *Forms of Validity in Research*, 77–92. San Francisco, CA: Jossey-Bass.

Hardesty, D. M. and Bearden, W. O. (2004) The use of expert judges in scale development: Implications for improving face validity of measures of unobservable constructs. *Journal of Business Research*, 57(2): 98–107.

Hinkin, T. R. (1995) A review of scale development practices in the study of organisations. *Journal of Management*, 21(5): 967–988.

Horst, P. (1968) *Personality: Measurement of Dimensions*. San Francisco, CA: Jossey-Bass.

Jarvis, C. B., Mackenzie, S. B., Podsakoff, P. M., Mick, D. G. and Bearden, W. O. (2003) A critical review of construct indicators and measurement model misspecification in marketing and consumer research. *Journal of Consumer Research*, 30(2): 199–218.

Kerlinger, F. N. (1986) *Foundations of Behavioral Research*, 3rd edn. New York, NY: Harcourt Brace Jovanovich College Publishers.

Kirk, A. (2019) *Data Visualisation: A Handbook for Data Driven Design*, 2nd edn. London, UK: Sage Publications.

Lawshe, C. H. (1975) A quantitative approach to content validity. *Personnel Psychology*, 28(4): 563–575.

Lazarsfeld, P. F. (1935) The art of asking why in marketing research: Three principles underlying the formulation of questionnaires. *National Marketing Review*, 1(1): 26–38.

Messick, S. (1995) Validity of psychological assessment. *American Psychologist*, 50(9): 741–749.

Meyer, A., Tsui, A. and Hinings, C. (1993) Configurational approaches to organizational analysis. *Academy of Management Journal*, 36(6): 1175–1195.

Miller, D. C. (1991) *Handbook of Research Design and Social Measurement*. London, UK: Sage Publications.

Nunnally, J. C. (1978) *Psychometric Theory*, 2nd edn. New York, NY: McGraw-Hill.

Nunnally, J. C. and Bernstein, I. C. H. (1994) *Psychometric Theory*, 3rd edn. New York, NY: McGraw-Hill.

Payne, S. L. (1951) *The Art of Asking Questions*. Princeton, NJ: Princeton University Press.

Podsakoff, P. M., MacKenzie, S. B., Lee, J. Y. and Podsakoff, N. P. (2003) Common method biases in behavioral research: A critical review of the literature and recommended remedies. *Journal of Applied Psychology*, 88(5): 879–903.

Podsakoff, P. M., MacKenzie, S. B. and Podsakoff, N. P. (2012). Sources of method bias in social science research and recommendations on how to control it. *Annual Review of Psychology*, 63(January): 539–569.

Robinson, W. S. (1950) Ecological correlations and the behaviours of individuals. *American Sociological Review*, 15(June): 351–350.

Robson, C. (1993) *Real World Research: A Resource for Social Scientists and Practitioners-Researchers*. Oxford, UK: Blackwell.

Roth, P. L., Switzer, F. S. and Switzer, D. M. (1999) Missing data in multiple item scales: A Monte Carlo analysis of missing data techniques. *Organizational Research Methods*, 2(3): 211–232.

Sekaran, U. (1992) *Research Methods for Business*. New York, NY: John Wiley & Sons.

Simon, H. (1980) The behavioral and social sciences. *Science*, 209(4452): 72–78.

Sireci, S. G. (1998) The construct of content validity. *Social Indicators Research*, 45(1–3): 83–117.

Shakeel, H. M., Iram, S., Al-Aqrabi, H., Alsboui, T. and Hill, R. (2022) A comprehensive state-of-the-art survey on data visualization tools: Research developments, challenges and future domain specific visualization framework. *IEEE Access*, 10: 96581–96601.

Straub, D. W. (1989) Validating instruments in MIS research. *MIS Quarterly*, 13(2): 147–169.

Strauss, M. E. and Smith, G. T. (2009) Construct validity: Advances in theory and methodology. *Annual Review of Clinical Psychology*, 5(April): 1–25.

Venkatraman, N. (1989) The concept of fit in strategy research: Toward verbal and statistical correspondence. *Academy of Management Review*, 14(3): 423–444.

Survey in business and social sciences

Alreck, P. L. and Settle, R. B. (1985) *The Survey Research Handbook*. Homewood, IL: Irwin.

Anderson, A. B., Basilevsky, A. and Hum, D. P. J. (1983) Missing data. In Rossi, P. H., Wright, J. D. and Anderson, A. B. (eds.) *Handbook of Survey Research*, 415–494. New York, NY: Academic Press.

Babbie, E. (1990) *Survey Research Methods*, 2nd edn. Belmont, CA: Wadsworth.

Biemer, P. P., Groves, R. M., Lyber, L. E., Mathiowetz, N. A. and Sudman, S. (1991) *Measurement Errors in Surveys*. New York, NY: John Wiley & Sons.

Birnbaum, M. H. (1999) Testing critical properties of decision making on the Internet. *American Psychological Society*, 10(5): 399–407.

Converse, J. M. and Presser, S. (1986) Survey Questions: *Handcrafting the Standardized Questionnaire*. Newbury Park, CA: Sage Publications.

Dillman, D. A. (1978) *Mail and Telephone Surveys: The Design Method*. New York, NY: John Wiley & Sons.

Dillman, D. A. (2007) *Mail and Internet Surveys: The Tailored Design Method*, 2nd edn. Hoboken, NJ: John Wiley & Sons.

Dillman, D. A., Smyth, J. D. and Christian, L. M. (2014) *Internet, Phone, Mail, and Mixed-Mode Surveys: The Tailored Design Method*, 4th edn. Hoboken, NJ: John Wiley & Sons.

Fowler Jr, F. J. (1993) *Survey Research Methods*, 2nd edn. New York, NY: Sage Publications.

Fowler Jr, F. J. (2013) *Survey Research Methods*, 5th edn. Thousand Oaks, CA: Sage Publications.

Gilman, L. M. (2008) Survey ethics. In Lavrakas, P. J. (ed.) *Encyclopedia of Survey Research Methods*, 865–867. Thousand Oaks, CA: Sage Publications.

Greer, T. V., Chuchinprakarn, N. and Seshadri, S. (2000) Likelihood of participating in mail survey research: Business respondents' perspectives. *Industrial Marketing Management*, 29(2): 97–109.

Heckman, J. J. (1979) Sample selection bias as a specification error. *Econometrica*, 47: 153–162.

Karweit, N. and Meyers Jr, E. D. (1983) Computers in survey research In Rossi, P. H., Wright, J. D. and Anderson, A. B. (eds.) *Handbook of Survey Research*, 379–414. New York, NY: Academic Press.

Kiecolt, K. J. and Nathan, L. (1985) *Secondary Analysis of Survey Data*. Newbury Park, CA: Sage Publications.

Oppenheim, A. N. (1996) *Questionnaire Design, Interviewing and Attitude Measurement*. New York, NY: Pinter.

Peter, J. P. (1979) Reliability: A review of psychometric basics and recent marketing practices. *Journal of Marketing Research*, 16(1): 6–17.

Peter, J. P. (1981) Construct validity: A review of basic issues and marketing practices. *Journal of Marketing Research*, 18(2): 133–145.

Pinsonneault, A. and Kraemer, K. L. (1993) Survey research methodology in management information systems: An assessment. *Journal of Management Information Systems*, 10(2): 75–106.

Rea, L. M. and Parker, R. A. (1992) *Designing and Conducting Survey Research*. San Francisco, CA: Jossey-Bass.

Rossi, P. H., Wright, J. D. and Anderson, A. B. (1983) *Handbook of Survey Research*. New York, NY: Academic Press.

Roth, P. L. (1994) Missing data: A conceptual review for applied psychologists. *Personnel Psychology*, 47(3): 537–560.

Roth, P. L. and Bevier, C. A. (1998) Response rates in HRM/OB survey research: Norms and correlates, 1990–1994. *Journal of Management*, 24(1): 97–117.

Sudman, S. (1983) Applied sampling. In Rossi, P. H., Wright, J. D. and Anderson, A. B. (eds.) *Handbook of Survey Research*, 144–194. New York, NY: Academic Press.

Schwab, B. and Sitter, R. (1974) Economic aspects of computer input-output equipment. In House, W. C. (ed.) *Data Base Management*, 10–24. New York, NY: Petrocelli Books.

Tourangeau, R., Rips, L. J. and Rasinski, K. (2000) *The Psychology of Survey Response*. New York, NY: Cambridge University Press.

Wilson, E. J. (1999) Research practice in business marketing: A comment on response rate and response bias. *Industrial Marketing Management*, 28(3): 257–260.

Statistical methods

Andrews, F. M., Klem, L., Davidson, T. N., O'Malley, P. M. and Rodgers, W. L. (1976) *A Guide for Selecting Statistical Techniques for Analysing Social Science Data*. Ann Arbor, MI: Institute for Social Research.

Brusco, M. J., Steinley, D., Cradit, J. D. and Singh, R. (2012) Emergent clustering methods for empirical OM research. *Journal of Operations Management*, 30(6): 454–466.

Hair, J. F., Anderson, R. E., Tatham, R. L. and Black, W. C. (1992) *Multivariate Data Analysis*, 3rd edn. New York, NY: Maxwell MacMillan.

Hair, J. F., Black, W. C., Babin, B. J., and Anderson, R. E. (2019) *Multivariate Data Analysis*, 8th edn. Andover, UK: Cengage.

Hollander, M. and Wolfe, D. A. (1999) *Non-parametric Statistical Methods*, 2nd edn. New York, NY: John Wiley & Sons.

McClave, J. T. and Benson, P. G. (1991) *Statistics for Business and Economics*. New York, NY: Macmillan.

Sharma, S. (1996) *Applied Multivariate Techniques*. New York, NY: Wiley.

5 Case research[1]

Chris Voss, Mark Johnson, and Jan Godsell

Chapter overview

5.1 When to use case research

- Inductive, deductive and abductive research

5.2 Developing the research framework, constructs and questions
5.3 Choosing cases

- How many cases?
- Current or retrospective
- Case selection
- Sample controls

5.4 Developing research instruments and protocols
5.5 Conducting the field research

- Field data collection
- Conducting interviews
- Reliability and validity

5.6 Data documentation and coding
5.7 Data analysis, hypothesis development and testing

- Within case analysis
- Searching for cross-case patterns
- Hypothesis testing and development

References
Further reading

5.1 Introduction

Case research has consistently been one of the most powerful research methods in Operations and Supply Chain Management (OSCM), particularly in the development of new theory (Boer et al., 2015). This is particularly true in today's environment. To cope with the growing frequency and magnitude of changes in technology and managerial

DOI: 10.4324/9781003315001-5

methods, Operations Management researchers have been calling for greater employment of field-based research methods (Lewis, 1998). Pure case research, that is research based on analysis of a limited number of cases to which, at best, only limited statistical analysis can be applied, is widely used in Europe but is less common in North American Operations Management (Drejer et al., 1998). However, there are an increasing number of case research based papers appearing; Barratt, Choi and Li (2011) list over 180 papers published in four top US Operations Management journals that use case research. A recently stated mission of the Journal of Operations Management (JOM) is: 'Highest priority is thus given to studies that are anchored in the real world and build, extend or test generalisable theories or frameworks of managerial significance' (Journal of Operations Management, 2015). This suggests that case research may have a resurgence within the US OM journals.

There are several challenges in conducting case research: it is time consuming, it needs skilled interviewers, and care is needed in drawing generalisable conclusions from a limited set of cases and in ensuring rigorous research. Despite this, the results of case research can have a very high impact. Unconstrained by the rigid limits of questionnaires and models, it can lead to new and creative insights, development of new theory, and have high validity with practitioners – the ultimate user of research. Through triangulation with multiple means of data collection, the validity can be increased further. Many of the breakthrough concepts and theories in Operations Management, from lean production to manufacturing strategy and servitization, have been developed through case research. Finally, case research and other forms of field research described in this book enrich not only theory, but also the researchers themselves. Through conducting research in the field and being exposed to real problems, the creative insights of people at all levels of organisations, and the varied contexts of cases, the individual researcher will personally benefit from the process of conducting the research. Increasingly, new ideas are being developed, not by distant academics, but by those working in close contact with multiple case studies – management consultants! It is important that case research is conducted and published because it is not only good at investigating how and why questions, but also it is particularly suitable for developing new theory and ideas and can also be used for theory testing and refinement. It is also important that case research is conducted well, so that the results are both rigorous and relevant. Case research is a scientific method (Ketokivi and Choi, 2014); it is not an excuse for 'industrial tourism' – visiting lots of organisations without any pre-conceived ideas as to what is being researched.

Operations Management differs from most other areas of management research, in that it addresses both the physical and human elements of the organisation. There is a particular tradition of this kind of research in Scandinavia, where case research is widely used in such research. Case research is widely used in other management disciplines, notably organisational behaviour and strategy. Yin (1994) has described in detail case research design, and Glaser and Strauss (1967) described the grounded theory method. Case research has its roots in the broader field of social sciences, in particular ethnographic studies and anthropology. In this chapter, we will draw on the experience of these disciplines as well as that of researchers in Operations Management. In particular, we will draw on the work of Eisenhardt (1989) and Barratt et al. (2011) who brought together much of the previous work on building theory from case research. Our intention is to provide a roadmap for designing, developing and conducting case-based research and also to describe some recent examples of case-based research in the field of Operations Management.

Most of the research conducted in the field of Operations Management is based on positivist (see Chapter 2) research methods, primarily statistical survey analysis and mathematical modelling. However, since '[...] the explanation of quantitative findings and the construction of theory based on those findings will ultimately have to be based on qualitative understanding' (Meredith, 1998), case research is very important for theoretical advancements in our field. The key steps is conducting case research are shown in the text box on the first page, and are explored in the rest of this chapter.

5.2 When to use case research

A case study is a history of a past or current phenomenon, drawn from multiple sources of evidence. It can include data from direct observation and systematic interviewing as well as from public and private archives. In fact, any fact relevant to the stream of events describing the phenomenon is a potential datum in a case study, since context is important.

(—Leonard-Barton, 1990)

Case research is the method that uses case studies as its basis. A case study is a unit of analysis in case research. It is possible to use different cases from the same firm to study different issues, or to research the same issue in a variety of contexts in the same or different firms. Meredith (1998) cites three outstanding strengths of case research put forward by Benbasat et al. (1987).

1 The phenomenon can be studied in its natural setting and meaningful, relevant theory generated from the understanding gained through observing actual practice;
2 The case method allows the questions of *why*, *what* and *how*, to be answered with a relatively full understanding of the nature and complexity of the complete phenomenon and;
3 The case method lends itself to early, exploratory investigations where the variables are still unknown and the phenomenon not at all understood.

Case studies can be used for different types of research purposes such as exploration, theory building, theory testing and theory elaboration/refinement (cf. Ketokivi and Choi, 2014).

5.2.1 Exploration

In the early stages of many research programmes, exploration is needed to develop research ideas and questions. Many doctoral theses and research programmes begin with one or more case studies in order to generate a list of research questions and areas that are worth deeper investigation.

5.2.2 Theory building

A particular area where case research is strong is theory building. '*Nothing is so practical as a good theory*' (Van de Ven, 1989). Theory can be considered as being made up of four components: definitions of terms or variables, a domain – the exact setting in which the theory can be applied, a set of relationships and specific predictions (Wacker, 1998).

A theory may be viewed as a system of constructs and variables in which constructs are related to each other by propositions and the variables are related to each other by hypotheses (Bacharach, 1989). Without theory, a) it is impossible to make meaningful sense of empirically-generated data, b) it is not possible to distinguish positive from negative results and c) empirical research merely becomes 'data-dredging' (Handfield and Melnyk, 1998). If we are to ground theory on data, then a large and rich amount of primary data is needed, case studies are a prime source of this. Cases are particularly useful when there is uncertainty in the definition of constructs (Mukherjee et al., 2000).

5.2.3 Theory testing

Case research can also be used to test theory (Dul and Hak, 2008; Barratt et al., 2011; Ketokivi and Choi, 2014). Theory testing is deductive in nature and there is a growing understanding that case research can also be used in deductive research (Barratt et al., 2011). The use of a deductive case study approach may make a more appropriate stage in the testing process as opposed to 'leaping' from theory straight to survey research. Despite its limited use for theory testing, case research has been used in the Operations Management field in order to test complicated issues such as strategy implementation (e.g. Pagell & Krause, 1999; Boyer & McDermott, 1999; McLachlin, 1997). When case research is used for theory testing, it is often used in conjunction with survey-based research in order to achieve triangulation, this is the use and combination of different methods and data sources to study the same phenomenon, so as to avoid sharing the same weaknesses (Jick, 1979).

5.2.4 Theory elaboration/refinement

Theory elaboration is similar to theory testing, but the objective is not to test the underlying logic, but to elaborate upon it and refine and/or extend it. The research may also seek to explore the empirical context with more latitude and serendipity. If the research objective is to discover new things rather than confirmation of existing theories, an abductive approach is fruitful (Dubois and Gadde, 2002, p. 559). Inductive and abductive approaches both aim to develop theory. However the focus of abduction is to develop the understanding of a new phenomenon, while induction traditionally aims at generalizing findings from empirical data (Kovács and Spens, 2005). In OM such new phenomena may be those found in practice for which there is no extant theoretical explanation, or where theory may need extending or refining. Abductive reasoning involves modifying the logic of general theory in order to reconcile it with contextual idiosyncrasies (Ketokivi and Choi, 2014). Case research can also be used as a follow-up to survey based research in an attempt to examine more deeply and validate previous empirical results. For example, Meredith and Vineyard (1993) and Hyer et al. (1999a) conducted case research which resulted in extending the fields of AMT and cell system design, respectively.

Inductive, deductive and abductive approaches follow different process sequences. In inductive research, propositions or frameworks are the outcome of the analysis. Deductive research starts with hypotheses which are then empirically tested. In abductive research, an extant theory is identified and explored through an iterative process eventually leading to propositions or frameworks and extension to existing theory. The processes for each are summarised in Figure 5.1. These three processes are ideal types and may not be found in pure form in actual research.

It is important to match the research purpose to the research questions, and in turn match the research structure to the research purpose and questions (Edmondson and

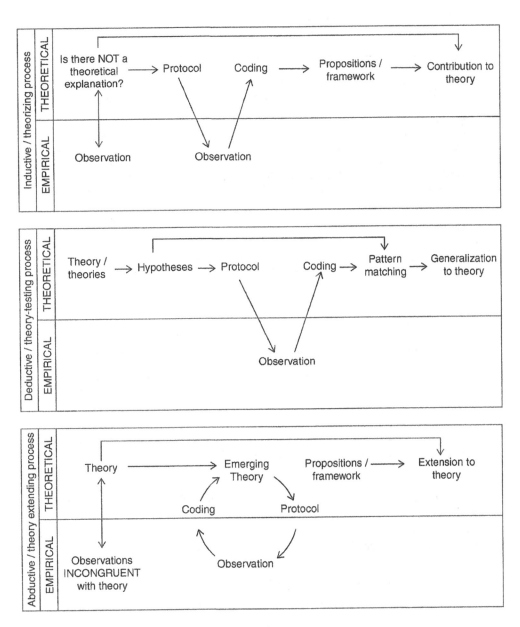

Figure 5.1 Different process paths in case research.

Source: Adapted from Kovács and Spens (2005).

McManus, 2007). Exploration and theory building uses an inductive approach, theory testing requires a deductive approach and abductive approaches are suitable for examining theory elaboration and where empirical observations are incongruent with existing theory. This is summarised in Table 5.1.

Table 5.1 Matching research purpose with methodology

Purpose	Focus of research question	Research structure
Exploration Uncover areas for research and theory development.	Is there something interesting enough to justify research?	Inductive research • In-depth case studies • Longitudinal field study
Theory Building Identify/describe key constructs. Identify linkages between variables. Identify 'why' these relationships exist.	What are the key constructs? What are the patterns or linkages between variables? Why should these relationships exist?	Inductive research • Few focused case studies • In-depth field studies • Multi-site case studies • Best-in-class case studies
Theory Testing Test the theories developed in the previous stages. Predict future outcomes.	Are the theories we have used able to survive the test of empirical data? Did we get the behaviour that was predicted by the theory or did we observe another unanticipated behaviour?	Deductive research • Experiment • Quasi-experiment • Multiple case studies • Large scale sample of population
Theory Extension/Refinement Develop the understanding of a new phenomenon To better structure the theories in light of the observed results.	Are observations incongruent with existing theory? How generalisable is the theory? In what contexts does the theory apply? Refinement of constructs & new structures and relationships between then	Abductive research • Experiment • Quasi-Experiment • Case studies Large scale sample of population

Source: The above is a development of Handfield and Melnyk (1998).

Overall, Operations Management is a very dynamic field in which new practices are continually emerging. Case research provides an excellent means of studying emergent practices. Case research both builds on theory and is an excellent means for the development of theory in Operations Management.

5.3 The research framework, constructs and questions

No matter how small our sample, or what our interest, we have always tried to go into organisations with a well-defined focus.

(—Henry Mintzberg, 1979)

The starting point for case research can be theory or observation (see Figure 5.1), and from this the development of a research framework and questions. Case research has been recognised as being particularly good for examining the *how* and *why* questions (Yin, 1994). Such questions can lead both to theory testing, but more importantly to theory development. In theory building research, no matter how inductive the approach, we need to have a prior view of the general constructs or categories we intend to study, and their relationships. Miles and Huberman (1994) suggest doing this through construction of a *conceptual framework* that underlies the research. Such a framework explains, either graphically or in narrative form, the main things that are to be studied – the key factors, constructs or variables – and the presumed relationships amongst them. Building a conceptual framework will force the researcher to think carefully and selectively about the constructs and variables to be included in the study.

The next vital step in designing case research is the initial research question behind the proposed study. This may precede, or follow directly from the conceptual framework. Even if at this stage the question(s) are tentative, it is important to have as well defined a focus as possible at the start, to guide the collection of data. There is a range of question types, many of which postulate some form of causal relationship (Miles and Huberman, 1994). These include:

Question type	Example of general form
• Causal	• Does X cause Y?
• Non-causal	• What is X?
• Non-causal – policy	• What does 'Y' mean?
• Non-causal evaluation	• What makes W good?
• Non-causal – management	• Is X more cost-effective than Z?

Source: Smith (1987).

The dominant mode for creating a research question is to suggest that the research addresses a gap within the literature. An alternative approach is to 'problematize'; to identify and challenge deeply held assumptions within a field (Alvesson and Sandberg, 2011). The latter approach is may be more risky but can lead to greater theoretical contributions. Problematizing does not mean conducting research devoid of theory, but it can mean the application of previously unused theories from alternative fields in order to explicate phenomena within the OM domain. Case based research is also well suited to respond to 'problems' in the field as these can often emerge directly from the OM context that we seek to serve (Yin, 1994).

Table 5.2 summarises some recent articles in the field of Operations Management using case research. These illustrate the different uses of case research and gives examples of research question. In case research, the amount of data that can potentially be collected is vast; therefore the stronger the research focus, the easier it is both to identify potential cases and to design research protocols.

Underlying the research question is likely to be one or more constructs; a priori specification of constructs is valuable because 'It permits researchers to measure constructs more accurately. If these constructs prove important, then researchers have a firmer empirical grounding for the emergent theory' (Eisenhardt, 1989).

When conducting case-based research it is not uncommon for the research question to evolve over time and for the constructs to be modified, developed or abandoned during the course of the research. This can be a strength, as it can allow the development of more knowledge than if there were just a fixed research question. Again, over time the research may shift from theory building to theory testing. This should be recognised on the one hand, but not used as an excuse for inadequate specification of research questions or constructs. Case research, otherwise risks degenerating into a 'fishing expedition', where the observer is hoping to catch valuable insights that in turn will lead to research questions.

Table 5.2 Examples of case based research in operations and supply chain management

Study	Research question(s)	Purpose	Other data & methods	# of cases	# of interviews
Baines et al. (2020)	What stages of transformation does a manufacturer follow when servitizing .. what contextual factors affect this progression.	Theory Development	Workshops, observation, archival material	14	62
Danese, Mocellin and Romano (2021)	How can BC systems be designed to effectively prevent counterfeiting?	Theory Development	Documentation, web resources, system data	5	20
Done, Voss and Rytter (2011)	What factors influence short-term success and long-term sustainability of best practice interventions?	Theory testing	Documentation and plant tour	8	27
Dube, Van der Vaart, Teunter, and Van Wassenhove, (2016)	Understanding the host government's impact on the logistics performance of international humanitarian organisations?	Theory development	Objective data	6	50
Foerstl et al. (2015)	What are the contextual drivers of PM integration for SSCM? How do they influence the choice of PM integration mechanisms to effectively move beyond sustainability compliance for FT suppliers?	Theory development	Survey, Archival and web data	8	29
Kaipia, Holmström, Småros, & Rajala (2017)	In what situations and how should retail sales data be shared for collaborative S&OP?	Theory development	Design Science/ intervention based research	2	Multiple, with 7 key informants
Kreye (2019)	How does the complexity of the service offering affect the uncertainty during service operations?	Theory Development	Documents, web data	4	56
Oliveira, Argyres and Lumineau (2022)	How does communication style support or hinder adaptation to disruptions and what determines communication style in interorganizational projects?	Theory elaboration	Analysis of 93 meeting minutes and substantial project documentation	7	19 (phone & email exchange)
Polyviou et al. (2020)	What resources or capabilities do medium-sized firms have that enhance their resilience to supply chain disruptions?	Theory Development	Survey, archival data, observation	4	23
de Sá et al. (2020)	How does resilience, built at different nodes of a supply chain, influence supply chain resilience?	Theory Development	Archival data, web data	24	41

Selviaridis and van der Valk (2019)	What are the effects that the framing of contractual performance incentives have on supplier's behavioural and relational responses and on the buyer–supplier relationship?	Theory testing	Document analysis	3	38
Senot, Chandrasekaran and Ward (2016)	How do hospitals promote collaboration between physicians and nurses at the patient level during the delivery of health care?	Theory Development	Observation, objective data, documents and participation	5	49
Sting and Loch (2016)	How do vertical and horizontal coordination interact during the implementation of operations strategy?	Theory Development	Questionnaires, quantitative data on projects	6	16 plus group interviews with 91 informants
van der Valk and Wynstra (2014)	To empirically validate a recently developed typology to demonstrate that services that are similar in terms of technical content,	Theory testing	Documents	1	21
Wu and Jia (2018)	How do the MNEs engage with other institutional actors to overcome the challenge imposed by institutional voids? How does collaboration among institutional actors influence SC localization?	Theory elaboration	Archival data	4	57

5.4 Choosing cases

There is a wide set of choices in conducting case research. These include how many cases are to be used, case selection and sampling.

5.4.1 What is the ideal number of cases?

For a given set of available resources, the fewer the case studies, the greater the opportunity for depth of observation. Single in-depth case studies are often used in longitudinal research (see Chapter 6). Examples include Narasimhan and Jayaram (1998) who used a longitudinal study of a single case to examine reengineering in service operations, and Karlsson and Åhlström (1995) who studied implementation of JIT in a single company over a period of time. Another example of a single case study is Schonberger (1982) whose highly influential book on Japanese manufacturing practices was based on in-depth study of a single Japanese run factory in the United States. There is no clear definition of what is a single case study or unit of analysis. Single cases may sometimes involve the opportunity to study several contexts within the case (Mukherjee et al., 2000). The use of a single case allows for greater depth of exploration, and can be quite powerful both in the early stages of the theory development cycle and when an abductive approach is taken Another common case design is the use of embedded cases (Yin, 1994) where study of a single firm may involve a number of different cases or units of analysis.

Single cases have limitations. The first is the limits to the generalisability of the conclusions, models or theory developed from one case study. When only one case is used, there may also be other potential problems (Leonard-Barton, 1990). These include the risks of misjudging of a single event, and of exaggerating easily available data. These risks exist in all case research, but are somewhat mitigated when events and data are compared across cases. Multiple cases may reduce the depth of study when resource is constrained, but can both augment external validity, and help guard against observer bias. The multi-case studies in Table 5.2 involve 3 to 30 cases.

5.4.2 Current or retrospective cases?

A second choice in case selection is whether to use retrospective or current cases. In many cases this may be an artificial distinction. For example when researching current case studies, it is usually necessary to collect some archival and/or historical data. Retrospective cases allow for more controlled case selection, for example it is possible to identify cases that reflect either success or failure only in retrospect. Longitudinal case research can be particularly valuable, this is discussed in Chapter 6.

One of the most difficult, but most important things we try to identify in research is the relation between cause and effect. The longer the period over which phenomena are studied, the greater the opportunity to observe at first hand the sequential relationships of events. However, as Leonard-Barton (1990) points out there are problems with historical data. For example, participants may not recall important events and even if they do, their recollection may be subject to bias. A particular problem is post-rationalisation, the interpretation of events in a different manner than they would have at the time. For example the respondent may place interpretations on events, or justify decisions with arguments or knowledge that was not available at the time. Similarly, what is described in archive data, such as minutes of meetings may not reflect the whole truth, difficult or controversial items may not be recorded.

The factors governing these choices are summarised in Table 5.3.

Table 5.3 Choice of number and type of cases

Choice	Advantages	Disadvantages
Single cases	Greater depth	Limits on the generalisability of conclusions drawn. Biases such as misjudging the representativeness of a single event and exaggerating easily available data
Multiple cases and embedded cases	Augment external validity, help guard against observer bias	More resource needed, less depth per case
Retrospective cases	Allow collection of data on historical events	May be difficult to determine cause & effect, participants may not recall important events
Current cases	Overcome the problems of retrospective cases	Have long elapsed time and thus may be difficult to do

5.4.3 Case selection and sampling

If case studies are to be used for research, then a vital question is the case selection or sampling. Miles and Huberman (1994) state that sampling involves two actions. The first is setting boundaries that define what you can study and connect directly to the research questions. The second step is creating a sample frame to help uncover, confirm, or qualify the basic processes or constructs that underpin the study.

The traditional way of sampling is to identify a population, and then to select a random or stratified sample from that population. However, in case research we often build a sample of cases by selecting cases according to different criteria (Eisenhardt, 1989, Yin, 1994). When building theory from case studies, case selection using replication logic rather than sampling logic should be used. Each case should be selected so that it either:

- predicts similar results (a literal replication), or
- produces contrary results but for predictable reasons (a theoretical replication).

Miles and Huberman (1994) suggest three kinds of instances have great payoff in case research. First, if you can find a typical or representative case – can you find another one? Second the negative or disconfirming instance and finally, the exceptional or discrepant instance. Another selection criterion is to identify polar types, cases with sharply contrasting characteristics that will highlight the differences being studied. For example, a sample might be constructed of organisations that have high and low performance on certain dimensions, while controlling for performance on others.

An example of theoretical sampling is that of Åhlström et al. (1998), who examined the impact of benchmarking interventions on process improvement. They wished to study the impact of starting point on the outcome of benchmarking. The underlying proposition being that the nature of the process would vary from those firms with high levels of 'best' practice to those with low levels and from those who had high levels of operational performance and low operational performance. From a potential sample set of over 1000 cases on which they had data, they pre-selected a convenience sample of cases where access was likely to be easy. Within this sample they then selected cases based on different starting points at the time of benchmarking. On a matrix of high existing practice and high existing operational performance, they chose cases from each quadrant of the matrix, and a fifth set from companies in the middle. This design facilitated examination of how company context impacts on the effective use of benchmarking. Not all researchers use theoretical or literal sampling in case research. An example in Operations Management research is Pagell and Krause (1999), who studied manufacturing flexibility. They used a convenience sample of 30 case studies.

Sampling plans are likely to evolve over a research project. Miles and Huberman (1994) suggest a number of tests to apply to a sampling plan:

- Is it relevant to the conceptual frame and research questions?
- Will the phenomena to be studied appear? Can they appear?
- Is it one that enhances generalisability?
- Is it feasible?
- Is it ethical in terms of informed consent, potential benefits and risks and relationships with informants?

5.4.3.1 Sample controls

When selecting cases it is also important to consider what are the parameters or factors that define the population and are to be held constant across the sample. Controls rely on the *selection* of the phenomena during the study's experimental design stage for their control. This allows particular factors (e.g. managerial policies, inventory systems) to be, in essence, 'held constant' while others (e.g. costs, defect rates) are left free to vary as they would naturally (Meredith, 1998). For example, Sousa (2000) controlled for quality maturity, Voss (1984) in developing a sample of a single application software area, applied tests of independence to ensure that the software had been developed without input from one of the other organisations. It is important to apply tests to validate the controls and to ensure that each case meets the sample criteria. The researcher should have the courage to discard cases that do not fit their research design and sample structure.

One powerful way of thinking of multi-case research, particularly in the context of theory testing is the distinction between comparative case studies and parallel single case studies where the same proposition is tested independently (replicated) in each of the case study settings. In theory testing we are testing some form of proposition concerning the relationship between concept A and concept B. To be able to test this we must select a sample in which either the dependent or independent concept/variable is held constant between cases (Dul and Hak, 2008).

5.5 Developing research instruments and protocols

Typically the primary source of data in case research is structured interviews, often backed up by unstructured interviews and interactions. Other sources of data can include personal observation, informal conversations, attendance at meetings and events, surveys administered within the organisation, collection of objective data and review of archival sources. The reliability[2] and validity of case research data will be enhanced by a well-designed research protocol (Yin, 1994). A protocol contains, but is more than, the research instrument(s). It will also contain the procedures and the general rules that should be used when deploying the instrument(s), and indicate who or from where different sets of information are to be sought. The core of the protocol is the set of questions to be used in interviews. It outlines the subjects to be covered during an interview, states the questions to be asked, and indicates the specific data required. A commonly used format is the funnel model. This starts with broad and open-ended questions first, and as the interview progresses the questions become more specific and the detailed questions come last. The protocol serves both as a prompt for the interview and as a checklist to make sure that all topics have been covered. In addition, it is often useful to send an outline of the protocol in advance, so that the interviewee(s) are properly prepared. A well-designed protocol is particularly important in multi-case research. When developing the research protocol and instruments it is important to address triangulation as case research data are not just collected by interview. Frequently questionnaires are also used in collecting data within and across cases.

Case research in Operations Management differs from case research in the wider social science field in that researchers are interested in analysing the manufacturing and/or service processes and systems of the unit of analysis. Thus research design in Operations Management should pay attention to what processes and systems are to be studied, the methods for studying them, and the operating data to be collected from them.

As with questionnaires, case research protocols need piloting either in a pilot case or in initial interviews within an organisation.

5.5.1 Single or multiple respondents and viewpoints

In designing case research an important question is what should be the number of respondents? If a set of questions can be reliably answered by one 'key informant' (e.g. a Supply Chain Director), then the research process should focus on identifying these and validating that this person(s) is indeed one. However, when there are questions for which no one person has all the required knowledge, or the events being studied may have different interpretations or viewpoints, how and why questions may be subject to different interpretations. In such cases the researcher may consider interviewing multiple respondents, or using a follow up survey with multiple respondents. In addition, it is also important to recognise that informants are prone to subjectivity and biases. Where this is an issue, the research design should not rely on self-report as the only evidence. In addition, multiple viewpoints provide both triangulation and can enhance validity.

In research design, we must consider the trade-off between efficiency in data collection and richness of data. On the one hand, by asking the same question to a number of people, we may enhance the reliability of our data, and by going beyond formal interviews we can collect much valuable data. On the other hand, it can be very time-consuming. Leonard-Barton (1990) in reporting on a multiple set of case-based research studies found that in a longitudinal in-depth study, she was able to observe many critical events and follow a research thread over a three year period. She also points out that in this sort of research, a large sample size per se may not be as important as in survey research. She gives as an example a pilot study of 25 people followed up with 145 personal interviews. These interviews added bulk, not depth to the research database. One perspective on how many respondents are required is the point at which data (in the case of deductive research) or theoretical saturation (for inductive research) is reached (Strauss and Corbin, 1990). Saturation occurs when the addition of respondents does add any different insights or theoretical advancement. In summary, the researcher should be seeking multiple viewpoints particularly where there is likely to be subjectivity and bias, but be wary of committing too much time and resource.

5.6 Conducting the field research

5.6.1 Who to contact

In researching case based data, it is important to seek out the person(s) who are best informed about the phenomenon and context being researched. This person is often known as the principal informant, and will be one of the key informants who will be those with in-depth knowledge about one or more aspects of what is being studied. However, in gaining access to an organisation, this person may not be known and/or may not be the most appropriate prime contact. An ideal prime contact, should be someone senior enough to be able to open doors where necessary, to know who best to interview to gather the data required and to provide senior support for the research being conducted.

Gaining access is often a sequential process. The first step is writing to or calling a potential prime contact. As case research requires time and commitment from the organisation, it is important that the value and relevance of the research, and the time and resource required is outlined at this stage. In many cases, going through an organisation such as an industry or technical association can provide an accelerated way of doing this, as well as providing the opportunity to select a well-structured and controlled sample. Another route into cases is via social media. Many schools have active alumni networks that have a presence on social media. Using, for example, LinkedIn can be a route to identify cases from a wider population. Pointing out the mutual benefits to potential participants can be helpful. The organisation may find it useful and interesting to have an issue analysed in a systematic way. Thus where organisations have particular problems, access tend to be much easier (see for example Chapter 8, clinical research). Having gained agreement, the next step is to set up the research meetings. For simple research, this can usually be done with a letter outlining the areas that are being investigated, the nature of the people that you would like to interview, and objective and/or archival data that you would like to collect. For more complex case research, set-up visits to the case organisation will probably be necessary. The time required for case research at a site can vary from one or two carefully structured short visits, to a full ethnographic study – in-depth involvement with the organisation over an extended period of time – often years.

In collecting field data, it is important to keep in mind research ethics as discussed in detail in Chapter 2. The main principle in case research is that of informed consent, all interviewees know what use is being made of the data and whether they will be identified in the subsequent output. Feeding back observations and analysis, discussed later is an important way of reinforcing an ethical approach.

5.6.2 Field data collection

As mentioned earlier an underlying principle in collection of data in case research is that of triangulation, the use and combination of different methods to study the same phenomenon. Such methods can include interviews, questionnaires, direct observations, content analysis of documents, and archival research. Reliability of data will also be increased if multiple sources of data on the same phenomenon are used. Two examples in Operations Management research illustrate this. Boyer and McDermott (1999), studied strategic consensus in operations strategy. They performed semi-structured interviews on-site in seven plants, with either the Plant Manager, Vice President of Operations or President of each firm. Issues relating to the historical development of the firm, its main competition, main markets, structural (e.g. AMT) and infrastructural (e.g. worker training) investments were explored in these discussions. Interviews typically ranged from one to two hours in duration. In addition, the survey questions were discussed and elaborated upon, and any questions relating to the content of the survey were answered. Discrepancies between survey responses and interview discussion were noted and clarified. To augment the on-site interviews and surveys, tours of the manufacturing facility were arranged. These tours allowed for a visual check and comparison of each firm's efforts in areas such as AMT adoption, layout, degree of worker empowerment and training, and level of technology relative to others in the industry. In general, these plant tours provided an opportunity for verification and clarification of survey and interview responses, as well as providing the researchers with a feel for the overall work environment and systems. A further example is a study by Hyer et al. (1998) of cell design. 'Data sources for the study included participant observation, structured and unstructured interviews of key participants, formal debriefing sessions following major design activities, and reviews of a wide array of relevant operational data and other documentation (meeting minutes, status reports, internal white papers, hard copies of electronic messages, and so forth). Although most of the data were qualitative in nature, quantitative data on organisational performance also were collected. This use of multiple measures drawn from different data sources is one way of improving both the validity and reliability of case study findings'.

5.6.3 Conducting interviews

Much, but not all field data will be collected through interviews. The effectiveness of case research will, in part, be dependent on the skills of the interviewer. Leonard-Barton (1990) compares the necessary interviewing skills with those of an investigative reporter. One needs to keep previous interviewee responses in mind while simultaneously probing with the current informant, and to be very aware of the significance of what is left unsaid as well as what is said, and so on. Yin (1994) lists a set of skill required by the field researcher:

- To be able to ask good questions and interpret the answers
- To be a good listener and not be trapped by preconceptions
- To be adaptable and flexible, to see newly encountered situations as opportunities not threats
- To have a firm grasp of the issues being studied
- To be unbiased by pre-conceived notions, and thus receptive and sensitive to contradictory evidence

There are many ways in which an interview can be conducted and evidence gathered. Interviews can be unstructured, focused with more structure or highly structured resembling a questionnaire. Alternatively evidence can also be gathered by direct observation of meetings, processes etc. This could be formal process analysis or casual observation. Another form of evidence collection is participant observation, also described as the clinical method; case research can evolve into clinical research, see

Chapter 8. Interviews may be with a single interviewee or with a group. The latter allows debate, but may also be dominated by one, possibly, senior individual.

5.6.3.1 *Single or multiple investigators*

Interviews are usually conducted by a single investigator, but as Eisenhardt (1989) points out, the use of multiple investigators can have advantages. They can enhance the creative potential of the teams and convergence of observations increases confidence in the findings. If interviews are done by two people or a team, investigators may either take notes independently or one may take the lead interview role, while the other takes a lead data collection role. In studies involving a large number of sites where multiple singe interviewers are used, it is important that early interviews are done in pairs or teams. This increases the probability of a common approach being used in all sites and allows inter-rater reliability to be checked. Inter-rater reliability can be defined in terms of the degree to which raters agree or disagree on the rating or interpretation of the evidence presented to them:

$$\text{Reliability} = \frac{\text{number of agreements}}{\text{total number of agreements} + \text{disagreements}}$$

For an example of the use of inter-rater reliability in Operations Management, see Ritzman et al. (1999). For a fuller discussion see Demaree and Wolf (1984).

5.6.3.2 *Collecting objective data*

The fact that case research is often associated with qualitative data should not deter the researcher from seeking out objective data. Indeed, case research provides the opportunity for researchers to collect such data with greater accuracy and reliability than in survey research, as they can have direct access to the original data sources on performance and operating data.

5.6.3.3 *Administering surveys*

As discussed earlier, triangulation through the use of different methods of data collection can strengthen the validity of research. It is not uncommon for researchers to administer questionnaires within organisations being studied. This can increase the efficiency of data collection and/or allow for data to be collected from a wider sample of respondents. For example Leonard-Barton (1990), in the case based research study mentioned earlier, conducted a telephone survey of 46 unit managers, and a series of questionnaires to about 100 sales representatives.

5.6.3.4 *Recording the data*

The research protocol should provide a strong foundation for documentation of the evidence gathered in case research. There are divided views on whether in interviews should be recorded. They certainly provide accurate rendition of what has been said. Where exactness of what people have said is important, then taping will be a benefit, on the negative side transcribing tapes can be time consuming, it often takes place some time after the interview, can be seen as a substitute for listening and may inhibit interviewees.

Whatever method is used to transcribe data, it is important there are good and accurate records and minutes of research interviews and meetings. In addition, that there is feedback and checking of the data. This is an important, if slow activity – 'obtaining agreement that the story had been accurately (and completely) presented was the most time consuming part of the studies' (Leonard-Barton, 1990). Feedback and checking typically involves presenting the case description or written up record of the data to the organisation for verification. Keeping additional field notes is an important part of field research. Field notes are a running commentary about what is happening in the research, involving both observation and analysis; – preferably separate from one another (Eisenhardt, 1989). Many researchers use field notes – writing down impressions when they occur – in order to push their thinking. Even prior to formal data analysis, it is important that the field researcher is sensitive to the emergence of patterns observed in the field. In case research, there is an overlap between data collection and data analysis. In addition to the formal collection of data, it is often useful to record ideas, impressions etc., as soon as they occur, and certainly before formal analysis takes place.

5.6.3.5 Seeking convergence and clarification

In the field there are a number of things that a researcher should be paying attention to. The first is looking for convergence of views and information about events and processes. It is not uncommon to find differing or incomplete views. In such cases, it is important to challenge, to revisit the issue and to seek other sources of data to clarify the information. Inevitably, on reflection and analysis there will be many uncertainties and gaps. In addition, during research in later cases it may become clear that some important areas of questioning may have been missed. There are a number of tactics for dealing with this. One is to revisit earlier cases and to review notes and evidence that may have been forgotten that could address the gaps. Another is to conduct interviews over a period of time, at least on two separate days. Prior to the final day all the data that has been collected can be reviewed to identify gaps and areas needing clarification. These can then be addressed.

5.6.3.6 Determining sequence (cause and effect)

One of the main advantages of case research is that it increases the chance of being able to determine the link between cause and effect, something that is difficult in survey research. It is therefore important to try and determine the sequence of events and the links between them. This is not always an easy task as interviewees often attribute a cause and effect after the event, which may not actually match the actual links. If historical data are being collected, rather than real-time observation, it is important to use multiple sources and cross-check carefully before attributing cause and effect. It can be very helpful to construct a timeline of key events being studied.

5.6.3.7 Challenges of observer bias

A researcher will enter the field, bringing with them a strong interest in an area and potentially strong biases. It is reported that students of innovation are notoriously prone to a strong 'pro-innovation' bias (Leonard-Barton, 1990). Similarly, it is likely that students of manufacturing strategy or JIT will have strong biases towards these areas as well. Personal biases can shape what you see hear and record. In addition, the researcher may become an advocate, not an observer. There are a number of ways of countering this. One is to use multiple interviewers. Each can then review what is observed by the other. If a structured research protocol is used, then inter-rater reliability can be assessed. It is important that researchers recognise their biases, but also that they do not overreact. The use of tape recording can contribute towards reduction of observer bias, especially if the evidence is presented verbatim rather than summarised.

5.6.3.8 *When to stop*

In case research, there is often the temptation to do 'just one more case' or 'just one more interview' to test some of the emerging theory or to get greater insight into the research questions. However this can lead to data saturation. Knowing when to stop is an important skill of a case researcher. It may be time to stop when you are in danger of not having enough time to complete the analysis and write up in the time available. It may also be when there are diminishing returns from incremental cases or interviews. Most importantly the time to stop is when you have enough cases and data to satisfactorily address the research questions.

5.6.3.9 *Summary*

Field research with case studies is an iterative approach, which frequently involves multiple methods of data collection, multiple researchers and an evolution of concepts and constructs. This can be illustrated in Operations Management research in a study of cell design by Hyer and Brown (1999).

> During the past two years, we have visited over 15 firms with the express purpose of exploring what works and what does not work in manufacturing cells. Using a standard set of questions, we asked operations managers to relate stories about cells they have implemented and to highlight the outcomes that have resulted from the changes they made. From this very rich set of stories, we uncovered consistent patterns that ultimately led us to reformulate our thinking about cells. Throughout the process, our definitions and their underpinnings evolved with each new or return plant visit, serving to reinforce or reshape our emerging theory. Our approach was consistent with the prescriptions for case study research of Eisenhardt (1989) in that we intentionally selected theoretically useful cases, used multiple (two) investigators, considered qualitative and quantitative data, and allowed the study to change course as themes emerged.

5.7 Reliability and validity in case research

As mentioned previously, it is particularly important to pay attention to reliability and validity in case study research. Reliability and validity have a number of dimensions.

Construct validity is the extent to which we establish correct operational measures for the concepts being studied. If the construct as measured can be differentiated from other constructs, it also possesses *discriminant validity* (Leonard-Barton, 1990). Construct validity can be tested by

- observing whether predictions made about relationships to other variables are confirmed.
- using multiple sources of evidence, (similar results are evidence of convergent validity)

Table 5.4 Reliability and validity in case research

Test	Case study tactic	Phase of research in which tactic occurs
Construct validity	use multiple sources of evidence establish chain of evidence have key informants review draft case study report	data collection data collection composition
Internal validity	do pattern matching or explanation building or time-series analysis	data analysis
External validity	use replication logic in multiple-case studies	research design
Reliability	use case study protocol develop case study data base	data collection data collection

Source: Yin, 1994, p. 33.

- seeing if a construct as measured can be differentiated from another, (evidence of discriminant validity)
- seeking triangulation that might strengthen construct validity

Internal validity is the extent to which we can establish a causal relationship, whereby certain conditions are shown to lead to other conditions, as distinguished from spurious relationships (Yin, 1994, p. 35) *External validity* is knowing whether a study's finding can be generalised beyond the immediate case study. *Reliability* is the extent to which a study's operations can be repeated, with the same results (Yin, 1994, p. 36).

Yin (1994) has outlined how some of these might be addressed as show in Table 5.4. In addition, qualitative data often provide a good understanding of the why, a key to establishing internal validity – what is the theoretical relationship and why this happens. Multiple cases have higher external validity than single cases.

5.8 Data documentation and coding

Once data are collected they should be documented and coded. A key issue in analysing case research is the volume of data.

5.8.1 Documentation

The necessary first step is a detailed write up of each site following the research protocol structure. Where appropriate this will involve transcription of tape recordings. Ideally this should be done as soon as possible after the case visit, both to maximise recall and to facilitate follow up and filling of gaps in the data.

An example in Operations Management research is a study of Just in Time manufacturing by McLachlin (1997).

for each site visited, the raw data, originally grouped by informant, was recorded electronically, coded with standard codes, and grouped by construct category. For each construct, summary paragraphs and associated ratings were derived using all available evidence, qualitative and quantitative. The condensed information was placed in a summary display for the particular plant.

Documentation can include typing up of notes and/or transcription of tapes. This produces a *case narrative*. Other documentation can include gathering together documents and other material collected in the field or through other sources. It should also include documenting ideas and insights that arose during or subsequent to the field visit. Accuracy of the documentation can be increased by letting key informants review draft reports. There are an increasing number of tools available for textual analysis of qualitative data. These allow on-screen coding of documents and exploration of patterns and relationships of words and phrases. These can be particularly useful when tape-recorded interviews are transcribed.

5.8.2 *Coding*

Central to effective case research is the coding of the observations and data collected in the field. It is important to try to reduce data into *categories* (Glaser and Strauss, 1967; Miles and Huberman, 1994). There are many manuals on coding, see for example Saldana (2009). The existence of good documentation of observations and multiple sources of evidence allows a chain of evidence to be established. *Incidents* of phenomena in the data are *coded* into *categories*. By comparing each incident with previous incidents in the same category, the researcher develops theoretical *properties* of categories and the *dimensions* of these properties.

Many researchers have followed the coding scheme suggested by Strauss and Corbin (1990). They propose three steps. The first step is open coding – data are fragmented or taken apart. Concepts are the basic building blocks of theory and open coding is an analytic process by which concepts are identified and are developed in terms of their properties and dimensions. Individual observations, sentences, ideas, events are given names, and then regrouped into *sub-categories* which in turn can be grouped as *categories*. The next step is axial coding – the putting together the data in new ways. The objective of this step is to regroup and link categories in to each other in a rational manner. The final step is selective coding – selecting a core category and relating it to other categories.

An example of this in Operations Management research is a study of black box engineering by Karlsson et al. (1998). One of the drivers of doing good data documentation and coding is to improve reliability. They state:

> In order to improve reliability, i.e., demonstrating that the data collection procedures can be repeated with the same results, data from interviews, open discussions, and observations exist in three forms:

- Directly taken field notes (from interviews and observations),
- Expanded typed notes made as soon as possible after the fieldwork. This includes comments on problems and ideas that arise during each stage of the fieldwork and that will guide further research),
- A running record of analysis and interpretation (open coding and axial coding).

When coding constructs based on case research, it is often prudent to limit the number of categories.

> For testing propositions, the magnitude of each construct was either the existence or the non-existence of a condition, based on high, neutral, and low ratings. The purpose

of having a neutral range, for which no conclusions would be drawn, was to avoid making mistakes between high and low ratings.

(McLachlin, 1997)

Miles and Huberman (1994) suggest three concurrent stages to be followed: data reduction, data display and conclusion drawing/verification. Having now addressed data reduction, we can examine the next two stages, which can be seen as the analysis stage.

5.8.3 Coding and analysing data using software packages

There are an increasing number of packages that can be very helpful in analyzing interviews, field notes, textual sources, and other types of qualitative data. These include NVivo and ATLAS.ti. Data can be coded using a pre-defined code list that can be expanded during the analysis to capture emerging themes. Coding interviews and using software can contribute to more systematic analysis procedures and guard against information-processing biases. Although these are valuable tools, it must remembered that they are tools are not a substitute for thought. There is always a danger of too much coding, not enough reflection. Each tool comes with comprehensive guides on their use and further understanding of how to use such software packages can be found in Friese (2014) and Lewins and Silver (2007).

A useful approach to organizing the data is that of Gioia et al. (2013). Initial codes can be developed into first order categories or concepts. These can be aggregated into second order themes. These can then be distilled into a limited number of aggregate dimensions. These provide the basis for building a data structure, an example is shown in Figure 5.2. The data structure not only allows us to configure our data into a sensible visual aid, it also provides a graphic representation of how we progressed from raw data to terms and themes in conducting the analyses (Gioia et al. 2013, p 20).

5.9 Analysis

Eisenhardt (1989) suggests two steps in analysis: analysis of within-case data, and searching for cross-case patterns.

5.9.1 Analysing data – within cases

Having developed detailed case descriptions and coded the data, the first step is to analyse the pattern of data within cases. A very useful and common starting point is to construct an array or display of the data, and with longitudinal cases construct an analysis of the sequence of events. A display is a visual format that presents information systematically so that the user can draw valid conclusions. Displays can be simple arrays, but might also be event listings, critical incident charts, networks, time ordered matrices, taxonomies etc. (Miles and Huberman, 1994). The overall idea is to become intimately familiar with each case as a stand alone entity, and to allow the unique patterns of each case to emerge before you seek to generalise across cases (Eisenhardt, 1989). This in turn gives the researcher the depth of understanding that is needed for cross-case analysis.

Once an array or display has been constructed, then the researcher should begin looking for explanation and causality. Miles and Huberman present a number of ways of analysing case data. One is the case dynamics matrix. This displays a set of forces for change and traces the consequential processes and outcomes. Another form of analysis is

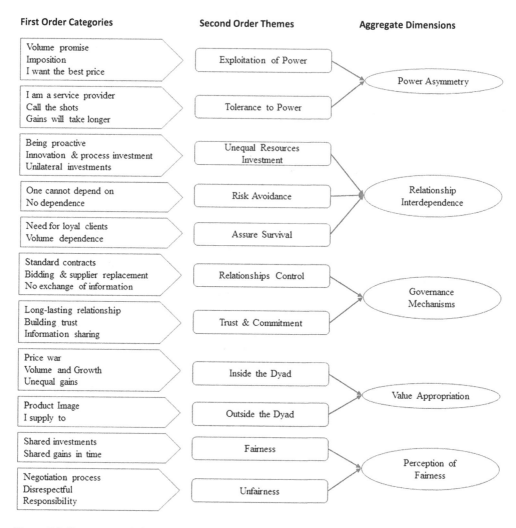

Figure 5.2 Category and theme analysis example.

Source: Brito and Miguel (2017).

making predictions and then using the case data to test them. This might consist of gathering, in tabular form, the evidence supporting and evidence working against a prediction and examining it. A third method is the causal network. A causal network is a 'display of the most important independent and dependent variables in a field study and of the relationships among them' (Miles and Huberman, 1994, p. 153). Causal networks are associated with analytic texts describing the meaning of the connections among factors. This has been used in Operations Management by Sousa (2000), following Miles and Huberman's (1994) guidelines:

> The working blocks were the codes, researcher comments, interim case summaries and the displays constructed in the data reduction stages. In the whole process, several

tactics for generating meaning were used such as noting patterns, seeing plausibility, clustering, counting, making contrasts/comparisons, subsuming particulars into the general, noting relations between variables, finding intervening variables, building a logical chain of evidence and making conceptual coherence (Miles and Huberman, 1994, pp. 245–262). As more knowledge became available during the course of the fieldwork and associated conceptualisation, recurrent patterns of interaction between variables within the orienting research framework started to emerge, both within and across cases. Some variables looked connected, while others looked random or unconnected. These patterns guided guesses about directions of influence among sets of variables. Initial versions of the causal networks were amended and refined as they were successively tested against the data collected in the field. During this process, I actively looked for negative evidence opposing the emerging relationships as well as rival explanations. In addition, I received feedback from informants on the networks' emerging relationships. In order to reduce the effect of the researcher on the behaviour of informants, this was done towards the later stages of the data collection when a certain rapport had already been established with the informants. At these later stages, the relationships to be tested were also clearer. This process led to five individual networks whose relationships received support from the data. In parallel, the five individual case networks were compared with each other in order to identify similarities and differences. These comparisons resulted in the extraction of relationships that were found to replicate across cases, abstracting from the peculiarities of individual cases and generalising them to a broader theory. This resulted in the building of general (cross-case) causal networks embodying generalisable explanations that were empirically grounded in the five individual case networks.

An example of one of Sousa's causal networks is shown in Figures 5.3.

5.9.2 Analysing data – searching for cross-case patterns

The systematic search for cross-case patterns is a key step in case research. It is also essential for enhancing the generalisability of conclusions drawn from cases.

There are a wide variety of methods and tools available for this. As with within-case analysis, the simplest and often most effective method is to construct an array. When visiting case-researchers, it is not uncommon to see a wall completely covered with charts that embody a full array of the summarised case data. Typically this involves the construction of very large spreadsheets or charts, and in turn refining these to two by two cells. Having constructed an array, a simple but very effective analytical approach is to pick a group or category and to search within for group similarities or differences. A similar approach is to select pairs of cases and to look for similarities and differences, including subtle ones. Miles and Huberman (1994) suggest a number of approaches to facilitate cross-case analysis. The first is partially ordered displays. These are appropriate for first-cut analysis 'to see what the general territory looks like'. They suggest that further displays can be constructed by organising by concept, by case or by time. Within these, they describe many ways of structuring the data including constructing and summing indices, two variable matrices, contrast tables that compare extreme cases or exemplars with other, scatterplots and sequence analysis.

With well-coded and quantified case data, continuous measures or data ordered in sequences can be developed. This lends itself to simple analysis such as graphing and

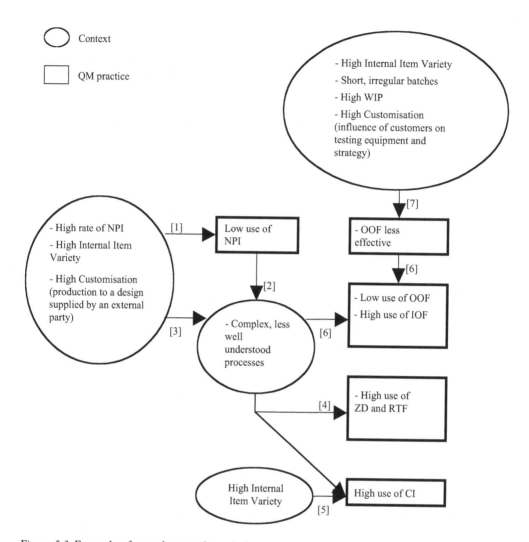

Figure 5.3 Example of causal network analysis.

Source: Adapted from Sousa and Voss (2001).

Note: The research variables are shown in boxes or circles and the relationships among them are shown by arrows. Each arrow (labelled 1 to 7) represents a different connection. The text below the figure describes the meaning of the connections among variables in the network. Constructs are: QM = Quality Management, OOF = Overall process off-line feedback , IOF = In process off-line feedback, NPI = Formalised New Product Introduction Process, ZD = Zero defects process, RTF = Real time feedback, CI = Changeover Inspection.

more sophisticated statistical tests. There are a number of non-parametric statistical tests that can be used to test and explore patterns, even with relatively small sample sizes. Where large numbers of cases have been used, then the standard analytic procedures of survey research can be used.

Cross-case analysis should also seek to increase the internal validity of the findings. As argued above, the use of multiple data sources or triangulation is important in case research. Deliberately seeking confirmation from multiple data sources leads to more reliable results. As Eisenhardt (1989) points out, we are poor processors of information.

We tend to leap to conclusions based on a limited set of data, be overly influenced by individuals such as elite respondents, ignore basic statistical properties and inadvertently drop conflicting evidence. Cross-case analysis is an attempt to counter this.

Case research must be both situationally grounded, that is there is a need to remain empirically disciplined and to pay attention to the contextual idiosyncrasies already in the data collection phase, and seek a sense of generality. 'Generality is not whether the results generalize to other empirical contexts or to other observational units. The question is rather about the extent to which a sense of generality can be found in terms of theory' Ketokivi and Choi, 2014, p. 234).

5.9.2.1 *Hypothesis development and testing*

Case research is used for both hypothesis testing and theory development. In most case research there will be some initial hypotheses, which can be tested directly using the case data, in particular with larger case sample sizes. However, in much case research the focus is also on theory development and on shaping and developing new propositions from the data as well as testing the initial ones. Typically, deductive research derive and test hypotheses, whilst inductive research will develop propositions from the analysis. Wacker (1998) puts forward a four step general procedure for theory building – Definition of variables, limiting the domain, relationship (model building) and finally theory prediction and empirical support. The process of theory testing involves measuring constructs and verifying relationships (Eisenhardt, 1989).

5.9.2.1.1 SHAPING HYPOTHESES

During the process of case research, overall themes, concepts and possibly relationships between variables will begin to emerge. This is an iterative process, whereby the emergent themes, frameworks or hypotheses are compared with data from each case. This will iterate towards theory that provides a close fit. During this there will be a parallel process of refining the definition of the constructs using evidence that measures the construct in each case. At this stage we are likely to have new or refined hypotheses and constructs that allow us to verify the emergent relationship. This can be done through examining the hypothesis in *each* case, treating each as part of a series of experiments.

5.9.2.1.2 TESTING HYPOTHESES

If replication logic has been used in case selection then cases that confirm an emergent relationship enhance confidence in the hypothesis or theory. Cases that disconfirm may at first seem problematical. However to the researcher seeking to develop and test theory, they provide the opportunity to refine and expand the theory. When the data seem to support hypotheses, case research allows the researcher to go one step further and examine the underlying reasons in each case as to why things are happening. What are the theoretical reasons for the observed relationships?

There are many different approaches. One is to propose alternate theories and use cases to test the fit of each theory. For example Orlikowski (1992) identified three alternative theoretical models relating technology to the organisation. She conducted depth case studies of five projects at various stages of their life cycles. She then ascertained the fit or lack of fit of each model to the case data. From this she was able to propose a revised theoretical model. A new approach to analysis of case data is first to frame the propositions to be tested as sufficient or necessary conditions. Then these propositions can be tested using set theoretic logic (Dul and Hak (2008). These methods, are yet to be applied in Operations Management research, but have the advantage of being able to address both the small samples often found in case research and to evaluate alternative paths (equifinality).

5.9.2.1.3 ENFOLDING LITERATURE

In theory development research, it is important to review the findings and any emergent theory against the existing literature. This research must be built on existing theory. It is not an excuse to say that 'this precise issue has not been studied before'. There is always some relevant literature to refer to. Reviewing emergent theory involves asking what is similar, what is different and why (Eisenhardt, 1989). It is very important to address literature that conflicts with the findings. Not to do so reduces confidence in the findings, and doing it may force you into more creative thinking and deeper insights. Literature discussing similar findings will help tie together underlying similarities. Overall effective enfolding of literature increases both the quality and the validity of the findings.

5.9.2.1.4 WRITING UP THE RESEARCH

Case research will ultimately only have a strong impact if it is written up well. First, it is important that the methodology is well defined and justified. This includes justification of the methods used, and the number of cases used, stating what is the unit of analysis, and clearly stating how the researcher got from their data and field notes to their conclusions (Barratt et al., 2011). Eisenhardt and Graebner (2007) present some valuable guidelines about theory building research. It is important to begin with strong grounding in related literature that identifies a research gap and to justify why theory building methods are more appropriate than theory testing methods. Next, a critical aspect is presenting the evidence from which the theory of interest was induced. In single cases this may be through a relatively complete rendering of the 'story' behind the case. In multi-case research, space limitations often mean that there is a trade-off between theory and empirical richness. One way to address this is to develop a theory in sections or by distinct propositions in such a way that each is supported by empirical evidence. The use of tables and other devices that summarize the related case evidence are central to signalling the depth and detail of empirical grounding. Their final guideline is about presenting the emergent theory. There is no one right way of doing this. They recommend sketching the emergent theory at the beginning of the paper, then in the body of the paper link each proposition to the supporting empirical evidence for each construct and the relationships between them. When this is done the propositions will mostly be consistent with the cases and is effectively pattern matching between theory and data. It is crucial to write the underlying theoretical arguments that provide the logical link between the constructs within a proposition. This should thus convey a clear theoretical argument to the reader.

A well-written and well-conducted case research should demonstrate the elements in Table 5.5. This shows – synthesized from the literature – the constituents of well-written case research.

Finally, in writing up case research, a valuable approach is to study how others have done this in OSCM.

Table 5.5 Constituents of well-written case research

Criteria	Overview
Justification for research approach	States why the case method was adopted in the research.
Case selection	Whether an inductive, deductive or abductive approach was used
Research Protocol	Explaining the logic for case selection and the number of cases.
Data collection	A proper research protocol been developed as the basis for data collection.
Research question	Clearly stated and linked to both theory and method
Theory	Shows how the research is grounded in existing theory and/or phenomenon
	The role of existing theory and constructs is made clear
Clarification of Unit of analysis	Provides an explicit statement of the unit of analysis.
Construct validity	The extent to which a study investigates what it claims to investigate.
Key informant review	Have the key informants review the study.
Data triangulation	Using different data collection strategies and data sources.
Chain of evidence	Allow reader go from the initial research questions to the final conclusions.
Data collection procedure	States how data were collected and the actual procedure.
Explanation of data analysis	Explains how the data were analysed.
Internal validity	Refers to the causal relationships between variables and results.
Research framework	Demonstrates the logical causal relationship.
Pattern matching	Compares the observed pattern with either the predicted ones or ones in previous studies.
Multiple perspectives	Verifies findings by adopting multiple perspectives.
External validity	The extent to which findings drawn from studying one case are applicable to other similar cases.
Theoretical basis	The research was framed by existing theory.
Rationale for sampling	The rationale for sampling the cases.
Reliability	Refers to the absence of random error, enabling subsequent researchers to arrive at the same insights if they conduct the study using the same steps.
Transparency	The transparency of the research process.
Careful documentation	All the necessary information in the research process is properly documented.
Clarification of research protocol	Provides information on detailing the research protocol.
Replication	The research allows subsequent researchers to replicate the research.

5.10 Conclusion

This chapter has set out a step-by-step approach for conducting case research in OSCM. Though these have been set out as sequential steps, anyone who has conducted case research will know that they are both parallel and iterative. The research question may be revisited during case analysis, constructs refined and redefined during field research and analysis and so on. It is important to recognise this, and also to have the courage to bring the research to a firm conclusion, and resist the temptation to continually and incrementally improve the findings. Having read the chapter you should be able to answer question such as those in the text box below:

---

1 What are the strengths and weaknesses of case research?
2 How can case research be used for theory development? Theory testing? Theory elaboration? And the relationship with inductive, deductive and abductive research?
3 What are the choices in case selection and on what basis should these choices be made?
4 What are sample controls in case research?
5 What are the skills required of a field researcher?
6 What is triangulation and when and how should it be used?
7 What is data coding and how can it be done?
8 What are the main methods of analysis of case data?

We hope that this chapter will help researchers conduct case research with the appropriate rigor, which when combined with relevance makes case-based research a very powerful methodology.

Notes

1 This chapter builds on Voss, C.A., Frohlich, M., and Tsikriktsis, N., (2002), Case research in operations management, *International Journal of Operations and Production Management,* 22(2) 195–219.
2 *Reliability* is the degree to which a measure is free from random error components (i.e., what you intended to measure is actually being measured). *Validity* is the extent to which a measure only reflects the desired construct without contamination from other systematically varying constructs (DeVellis, 1991).

References

Åhlström, P. A. Blackmon, K., & Voss, C. A. (1998). Diagnostic benchmarking and manufacturing improvement, in Coughlan, P., Dromgoole, T. & Peppard, J. (Eds), *Operations Management, Future Issues and Competitive Responses* . Dublin: University of Dublin, pp. 7–12.
Alvesson M. & Sandberg J. (2011). Generating research questions through problematization, *Academy of Management Review*, 36(2): 247–271.
Bacharach, S. (1989). Organizational theories: Some criteria some evaluation for evaluation, *Academy of Management Review*, 14(4): 496–515.
Baines, T., Bigdeli, A., Sousa, R., & Schroeder, A. (2020). Framing the servitization transformation process: A model that enables the description of servitization journey, *International Journal of Production Economics*, 221: 107463.
Benbasat, I., Goldstein, D. K., & Mead, M. (1987). The case research strategy in studies of information systems, *MIS Quarterly*, 11(3): 369–386.
Boer, H., Holweg, M., Pagell, M., Schmenner, R., & Voss, C. (2015). Making a meaningful contribution to theory, *International Journal of Production and Operations Management*, 35(9): 1231–1252.
Boyer, K. K., & McDermott, C. (1999). Strategic consensus in operations strategy. *Journal of Operations Management*, 17, 289–305.

Brito R. & Miguel P. L. S. (2017). Power, governance, and value in Collaboration: differences between buyer and Supplier perspectives, *Journal of Supply Chain Management*, 53(2): 61–87.

Busse, C., Meinlschmidt, J., & Foerstl, K. (2017). Managing information processing needs in global supply chains: A prerequisite to sustainable supply chain management, *Journal of Supply Chain Manag*, 53: 87–113.

Chandrasekaran, A., de Treville, S., & Browning, T. (2020). Editorial: Intervention-based research (IBR)—What, where, and how to use it in operations management, *Journal of Operations Management*, 66: 370–378.

Danese, P., Mocellin, R., & Romano P. (2021). Designing blockchain systems to prevent counterfeiting in wine supply chains: Aa multiple-case study, *International Journal of Operations & Production Management*, 41(13): 1–33.

Demaree R. G. & Wolf G. (1984). Estimating within-group inter-rater reliability with and without response bias, *Journal of Applied Psychology*, 69(1): 85–98.

DeVellis Robert, F. (1991). *Scale Development: Theory and Applications*. Newbury Park, CA: Sage Publications.

Done, A., Voss, C. A., & Gorm Rytter, N. (2011). Best practice interventions, short term impact and long term outcomes, *Journal of Operations Management*, 29(5): 500–513.

Drejer, A., Blackmon, K., & Voss, C. (1998). Worlds apart? – A look at the operations management area in the US, UK and Scandinavia, *Scandinavian Journal of Management*, 16: 45–66.

Dube, N., Van der Vaart, T., Teunter, R. H., & Van Wassenhove, L. N. (2016). Host government impact on the logistics performance of international humanitarian organisations, *Journal of Operations Management*, 47–48: 44–57.

Dubois, A. & Gadde, L. E. (2002). Systematic combining: An abductive approach to case research, *Journal of Business Research*, 55: 553–560.

Dul, J. & Hak, T. (2008). *Case Study Methodology in Business Research*. Oxford: Butterworth Heinemann.

Edmondson A. C. & McManus S. E. (2007). Methodological fit in management research, *Academy of Management Review*, 32(4): 1135–1179.

Foerstl, K., Azadegan, A., Leppelt, T., & Hartmann, E. (2015). Drivers of supplier sustainability: Moving beyond compliance to commitment, *Journal of Supply Chain Management*, 51: 67–92.

Friese, S. (2014). *Qualitative Data Analysis Using Atlas.ti*. London: Sage Publications.

Glaser, B. G. & Strauss, A. L. (1967). *The Discovery of Grounded Theory: Strategies for Qualitative Research*. New York: Aldine De Gruyter.

Handfield, R. S. & Melnyk S. A. (1998). The scientific theory-building process: A primer using the case of TQM. *Journal of Operations Management*, 16(19): 321–339.

Hyer, N. L. & Brown K. (1999). The discipline of real cells, *Journal of Operations*, 17(18): 557–574.

Hyer, N. L., Brown, K. A., & Zimmerman, S. (1998). A socio-technical systems approach to cell design: case study and analysis. *Journal of Operations Management*, 17, 179–203.

Ivanova, A., Gray, J., & Sinha, K. (2014). Towards a unifying theory of management standard Implementation, *International Journal of Operations and Production Management*, 34(10): 1269–1306.

Jick, T. D. (1979). Mixing qualitative and quantitative methods: Triangulation in action, *Administrative Science Quarterly*, 24: 602–611.

Journal of Operations Management (2015). Journal mission. Available at: http://www.journals.elsevier.com/journal-of-operations-management/. Accessed on 16 April 2015.

Kaipia, R., Holmström, J., Småros, J., & Rajala, R. (2017). Information sharing for sales and operations planning: Contextualized solutions and mechanisms. *Journal of Operations Management*, 52(1): 15–29.

Karlsson, C. & Åhlström, P. (1995). Change processes towards lean production: The role of the remuneration system, *International Journal of Operations and Production Management*, 15(11): 80–99.

Karlsson, C., Nellore, R., & Söderquist, K. (1998). Black box engineering: Redefining the role of product specifications, *Journal of Product Innovation Management*, 15: 534–549.

Kovács, G. & Spens, K. M. (2005). Abductive reasoning in logistics research, *International Journal of Physical Distribution & Logistics Management*, 35(2): 132–144.

Kreye, M. E. (2019). Does a more complex service offering increase uncertainty in operations?, *International Journal of Operations & Production Management*, 39(1): 75–93.

Lewins, A. & Silver, C. (2007). *Using Software in Qualitative Research: A Step-by-Step Guide.* London: Sage Publications.

Lewis, M. W. (1998). Iterative triangulation: A theory development process using existing case studies, *Journal of Operations Management*, 16(4): 455–469.

McLachlin, R. (1997). Management initiatives and just-in-time manufacturing. *Journal of Operations Management*, 15, 271–292.

Meredith, J., & Vineyard, M. (1993). A longitudinal study of the role of manufacturing technology in business strategy. *International Journal of Operations & Production Management*, 13, 3–14.

Mintzberg H. (1979). "An emerging strategy of "direct" research", *Administrative Science Quarterly*, 24: 590–601.

Mukherjee, A., Mitchell, W., & Talbot, F. B. (2000). The impact of new manufacturing technologies and strategically flexible production, *Journal of Operations Management*, 18(2): 139–168.

Narasimhan, R. & Jayaram, J. (1998). Reengineering service operations, a longitudinal case study, *Journal of Operations Management*, 17(1): 7–22.

Oliva, R. (2019). Intervention as a research strategy, *Journal of Operations Management*, 65(7): 710–724.

Oliveira, N., Argyres, N., & Lumineau, F. (2022). The role of communication style in adaptation to interorganizational project disruptions, *Journal of Operations Management*, 68(4): 353–384.

Orlikowski, W. (1992). The duality of technology, rethinking the concept of technology in organisations, *Organization Science*, 3(3): 398–447.

Pagell, M., & Krause, D.R. (1999). A multiple-method study of environmental uncertainty and manufacturing flexibility. *Journal of Operations Management*, 17, 307–325.

Polyviou, M., Croxton, K. L., & Knemeyer, M. A. (2020). Resilience of medium-sized firms to supply chain disruptions: The role of internal social capital, *International Journal of Operations & Production Management*, 40(1): 68–91.

Ritzman, L. P. & Safizadeh, M. H. (1999). Linking process choice with plant level decisions about capital and human resources, *Production and Operations Management*, 8(4): 374–392.

Sá, M. M.de, Miguel, P.L.d.S., Brito, R.P.d., & Pereira, S. C. F. (2020). Supply chain resilience: The whole is not the sum of the parts, *International Journal of Operations & Production Management*, 40(1): 92–115.

Saldaña, J. (2009). *The Coding Manual for Qualitative Researchers.* London: Sage Publications.

Schonberger, R. (1982). *Japanese Manufacturing Techniques.* New York: The Free Press, pp. 259.

Selviaridis, K. & van der Valk, W. (2019). Framing contractual performance incentives: Effects on supplier behaviour, *International Journal of Operations and Production Management*, 39 (2): 190–213.

Senot, C., Chandrasekaran, A., & Ward, P. (2016). Collaboration between service professionals during the delivery of health care: "Evidence from a multiple-case study in U.S. hospitals, *Journal of Operations Management*, 42–43: 62–79.

Sousa, R. (2000). Quality management practice: universal or context dependent? An empirical investigation.unpublished Ph.D. thesis. London Business School.

Sousa, R. & Voss, C. A. (2001). Quality management: Universal or context dependent, an empirical investigation across the manufacturing strategy spectrum, *Production and Operations Management*, 1(4): 383–404.

Smith, N. L. (1987). Towards a justification of claims in evaluation research, *Evaluation and Programme Planning*, 10: 209–314, quoted in Miles and Huberman (1994) op. cit.

Sting, F. & Loch, C. (2016). Implementing operations strategy: How vertical and horizontal coordination interact, *Production and Operations Management*, 25(7): 1177–1193.

Van de Ven, A. H. (1989). Nothing is quite as practical as a good theory, *Academy of Management Review*, 14(4): 486–489.

van der Valk, W. & Wynstra, F. (2014). Variety in business-to-business services and buyer-supplier interaction: The case of cleaning services, *International Journal of Operations & Production Management*, 34(2): 195–220.

Voss, C. A. (1984). Multiple independent invention and the process of technological innovation, *Technovation*, 2: 169–184.

Wacker, J. G. (1998). A definition of theory: Research guidelines for different theory building research methods in operations management, *Journal of Operations Management*, 16: 361–385.

Wu, Z. & Jia, J. (2018). Toward a theory of supply chain fields – Understanding the institutional process of supply chain localization. *Journal of Operations Management*, 58–59(1): 27–41.

Yin, R. (1994). *Case Study Research*. Beverly Hills, CA: Sage Publications.

Further reading

Barratt, M., Choi, T. Y., & Li, M. (2011). Qualitative case studies in operations management: Trends, research outcomes and future research implications, *Journal of Operations Management*, 29(4): 329–342.

Eisenhardt K. M. (1989). Building theory from case study research, *Academy of Management Review*, 14(4): 532–550.

Eisenhardt K. M., & Graebner M. E. (2007). Theory building from cases: Opportunities and challenges, *Academy of Management Journal*, 50(1): 25–32.

Gioia, D. A., Corley, K. G., & Hamilton, A. L. (2013). Seeking qualitative rigor in inductive research: Notes on the Gioia methodology. *Organizational Research Methods*, 16: 15–31.

Grodal, S., Anteby, M., & Holm, A. L. (2021). Achieving rigor in qualitative analysis: The role of active categorization in theory building, *Academy of Management Review*, 46: 591–612.

Ketokivi, M. & Choi, T. (2014). Renaissance of case research as a scientific method, *Journal of Operations Management*, 32(5): 232–240.

Leonard-Barton, D. (1990). A dual methodology for case studies: Synergistic use of a longitudinal single site with replicated multiple sites, *Organisation Science*, 1(1): 248–266.

Meredith, J. (1998). Building operations management theory through case and field research, *Journal of Operations Management*, 16(4): 441–454.

Miles, H. & Huberman, M. (1994). *Qualitative Data Analysis: A Sourcebook*. Beverly Hills CA: Sage Publications.

Saldaña, J. M. 2015. *The Coding Manual for Qualitative Researchers*. 3rd ed. London: SAGE Publications.

Strauss, A. & Corbin, J. (1990). *Basics of qualitative Research: Grounded Theory Procedures and Techniques*. Newbury Park, CA: Sage Publications.

Voss, C. A., Frohlich, M., & Tsikriktsis, N. (2002). Case research in operations management, *International Journal of Operations and Production Management*, 22(2) 195–219.

Yin, R. K. (2017). *Case Study Research and Applications: Design and Methods*. Thousand Oaks, California: Sage Publications.

6 Longitudinal field studies

Pär Åhlström and Christer Karlsson

Chapter overview

6.1 Introduction to the longitudinal field study – describing what the longitudinal field study is and how it is a special form of case research
6.2 Setting up the longitudinal field study – choosing the appropriate research questions, gaining access to data and setting up the study
6.3 Collecting data in the longitudinal field study – dealing with the peculiarities and challenges of collecting longitudinal data
6.4 Analysing longitudinal field data – developing ways of analysing the overwhelming amount of data often collected in longitudinal field studies
6.5 Building theory from longitudinal field studies – developing and reporting on the findings of the longitudinal field study
6.6 Evaluating longitudinal field studies – ensuring reliable and valid results from a longitudinal field study
References

Longitudinal field studies are in-depth studies of change processes. The longitudinal field study is a case study since it seeks to study a phenomenon in its natural setting. However, the longitudinal field study has several features that requires treating it separately from case research, which was covered in Chapter 5. As a research strategy, longitudinal field studies are best used for exploration and theory building. Longitudinal field studies are particularly useful for studying processes of change and development. This chapter explains the nature of longitudinal research, particularly focusing on how it is different from case research. The chapter also provides a description of how to design, execute and report longitudinal field studies.

6.1 Introduction to the longitudinal field study

Here we introduce the longitudinal field study, focusing particularly on its nature and why it can be considered a special type of case research.

6.1.1 Longitudinal versus cross-sectional research

In defining what we mean by a longitudinal field study, we first need to make a distinction between longitudinal and cross-sectional research. Cross-sectional research implies

DOI: 10.4324/9781003315001-6

studying a phenomenon at a specific point in time. For instance, we may conduct cross-sectional case studies to discern how companies use benchmarking to improve their manufacturing processes. The research concerns companies' current usage of benchmarking and thus refers to a specific point in time. Cross-sectional research can refer to history. For instance, we can use case research to investigate how companies make decisions regarding capacity extensions, by retrospectively studying the decision processes behind already conducted capacity extensions.

Conducting longitudinal research implies studying a phenomenon over time. Longitudinal research can be seen as several cross-sectional snapshots of a phenomenon, taken over time. Suppose we are using case studies to study how companies improve their manufacturing process over time. We visit a select number of companies every three months over two years. During each visit we inquire about various aspects of how the manufacturing process has been improved since our last visit and any future plans for manufacturing improvement.

With longitudinal research being the study of a phenomenon over time using multiple observations, then one could argue that we have a longitudinal study if we have two snapshots. However, we would normally require a bit more of a study for it to qualify as a longitudinal study. Exactly how many snapshots are required is not possible to say beforehand, since it depends on many different things, most importantly the research question.

6.1.2 *The difference of timing – The longitudinal field study is a real-time study*

Within the domain of longitudinal studies, what further characterises the longitudinal field study is timing. Timing is a choice along a continuum with two endpoints: retrospection or real-time (Perks and Roberts, 2013). In retrospective studies we attempt to discern what has happened by asking respondents to recollect historical events. In real-time studies we study current events. Longitudinal field studies imply studying change processes as they unfold, in real time. Real-time studies overcome a major weakness of retrospective research – the difficulty of determining cause and effect from reconstructed events (Leonard-Barton, 1990). In retrospective research, respondents tend to reinterpret things from a new perspective and can therefore not always give an accurate account of the past (Becker and Geer, 1957).

The difference in timing lies along a continuum. The purest form of a longitudinal field study would require be daily observation, which is seldom feasible for the researcher. Longitudinal field studies thus contain an element of retrospection. One of the key characteristics of longitudinal field studies remains – that the researchers are present in the organization. For instance, we may be in place in an organization every other week. Although part of the data collected during the time spent in the organization refers to past events, the error introduced by respondents interpreting events is likely to be smaller than if we visit the organization once every three months. A longitudinal field study involving a series of multiple interviews about recent events offers the benefit of proximity in time to current events. This increases the likelihood that the researcher can determine the sequence and nature of events accurately (Leonard-Barton, 1990).

Longitudinal field studies share important characteristics with ethnography, the study of cultures. The ethnographic approach is that of anthropology and sociology, using participant observation. This approach allows a fieldworker to use the culture of the setting to account for the observed patterns of human activity (Van Maanen, 1979). Crucial in ethnography is long residence and participant observation (Sanday, 1979).

Ethnographers become part of the situation being studied to feel what it is like for the people in that situation. They become immersed in the everyday life of the observed, for an extended period (Barley, 1990).

6.1.3 Longitudinal field studies – To generate process theory

Longitudinal field studies are particularly suitable for developing theory since they allow researchers to get close enough to the studied phenomena to discover the forces most crucial to the object of inquiry. Researchers can also remain close to the studied phenomena for long enough to discover the causal links among events and constructs, resulting in a very fertile basis for generating theory (Miller and Friesen, 1982). Longitudinal field studies offer an opportunity to determine causality; why and how things happen (Kuula and Putkiranta, 2012).

Longitudinal field studies are particularly useful for studying processes of change and development in organizations (Barley, 1990; Van de Ven, 1993). During processes of change, respondents' tendency to reinterpret things from a new perspective is highly prevalent. A change process almost by definition means that things are changing, meaning that so is probably also the perspective of people being interviewed. During transformations, organization members will find it difficult or impossible to remember former actions, outlooks, or feelings. Reinterpreting things from a new perspective, interviewees cannot give an accurate account of the past, for the concepts in which they think about the past have changed and with them perceptions and memories (Becker and Geer, 1957).

Contributions to scholarly knowledge resulting from longitudinal field studies are thus likely to focus on process and dynamic aspects. In the Minnesota Innovation Research Program, for instance, researchers developed a process theory of innovation, explaining the temporal order and sequence of steps that unfold as an innovative idea is transformed into a concrete reality (Van de Ven and Poole, 1990). Similarly, Leonard-Barton (1988) developed a theory on the nature of the innovation process during the internal development of equipment, processes, and software tools.

In operations and supply chain management, longitudinal research has been used for different purposes. Åhlström (1997) used a longitudinal field study to develop a framework on the sequence between different improvement initiatives whilst adopting lean production. Rytter et al. (2007) studied operations strategy processes, which they conceptualized as processes of dialogue and action occurring in an iterative manner over time. Rungtusanatham and Salvador (2008) employed a longitudinal research design to understand the challenges associated with implementing mass customization within an existing mass production environment. Akkermans et al. (2019), finally, employed longitudinal field research of three cases embedded in a single company to explore the process of ramping up and down digital services.

Although the dominant focus for longitudinal field studies tends to involve processes, it is possible to use them to gain deep insights into other phenomena. For instance, Trentin et al. (2015) used a longitudinal field study to investigate the interconnectedness of the capabilities needed by a firm to mass customize environmentally friendly products. Soundaararajan and Brammer (2018) employed a longitudinal multiple case study method to explore multiple intermediary – sub-supplier dyads in South India's knitwear garment industry. Their focus is on developing an in-depth understanding of the developing country sub-suppliers' perspectives and behaviours towards social sustainability demands and the micro-level interactions occurring between the intermediaries and the sub-suppliers. Meinlschmidt et al. (2016), finally, employed a longitudinal research design to identify the mechanisms that allow firms to acquire and share sustainability-related knowledge with suppliers and how these knowledge generation and desorption mechanisms support the evolution of their sustainable supply management capabilities.

6.2 Setting up the longitudinal field study

In designing a longitudinal field study, several issues are necessary to consider. First, defining an appropriate research question. Second, selecting organizations to study. After detailing these initial considerations, we present ways of gaining access to relevant data and putting together a framework for data collection. Finally, we discuss the demands that longitudinal field studies put on the researcher.

6.2.1 Defining an appropriate research question for longitudinal field studies

Longitudinal field studies are particularly suited for the following general research question: "How does organizational change emerge, develop, grow, or terminate over time?" (Van de Ven and Huber, 1990). This question is concerned with describing and explaining temporal sequences of events that unfolds as an organizational change occurs. The explanations may be sought in terms of some underlying mechanisms that cause events to happen and the circumstances or contingencies when these mechanisms operate.

This conceptualisation of research questions suited for longitudinal field studies rests on a specific definition of the process of change. The term "process" is here taken to mean: a sequence of incidents, stages, events, or activities that describe how things change over time (Van de Ven, 1993), which represents a development view of how change unfolds. The central focus is on progressions (i.e. the nature, sequence, and order) of activities or events that an organizational entity undergoes as it changes over time.

Within this view of change processes, it is possible to further specify the types of change processes that constitute good candidates for longitudinal field studies. First, the change process must be reasonably limited in time. In an ideal world, one would like to study a change process throughout its entire life, from beginning to end (Van de Ven and Poole, 1990). To permit the study to be conducted within a reasonable time frame, this requirement places restrictions on the process to be studied. The restrictions placed are particularly apparent for doctoral students who are under time pressure to finalize their thesis. All research involves compromises of different kinds, but it is always good to know what the ideal is (Czarniawska-Joerges, 1992).

In designing the study, it is important to ensure that the study is not dependent on the change process being studied having run its entire length, for two reasons. First, it is not always easy to determine exact end points for change processes. Since change is increasingly becoming an integral part of organizational life, determining when exactly a change process has ended, is not a trivial task. Second, it is not uncommon for change processes to be stretched out in time, beyond the point in time they were originally set out to end. Therefore, it is recommended to pose the research question in such a way that interesting results are yielded regardless of whether the change process has finished or not. In a similar vein, one may also want to avoid a situation where the research question relies on a particular outcome of the change process. The research question needs to be put in such a way that no matter what the outcome is, something valuable comes out of the research.

Another demand we can put on a change process for it to be amenable to a longitudinal field study is that the process needs to be observable. This requirement is related to the size of the organization. It is easier to observe change processes in reasonably small organizations. For instance, observing the process of adopting lean production at a company with four hundred employees is easier than observing it at a company with four thousand. The types of changes that can be more difficult to observe in a longitudinal field study are strategic changes, occurring at a higher level of abstraction, involving multiple organizational units. However, employing a team of researchers carrying out the study may be one way of addressing this difficulty. Note finally that size and unit of analysis are related to each other. The larger the organization, the more important it is to choose a unit of analysis that is observable. Conversely, in a smaller organization, even more strategic and high-level change processes can be possible to observe.

The choice of unit of analysis is thus an important choice in designing longitudinal field studies. The challenge here is to define it at such a way that it is amenable to observation. Various units of analysis are possible. For example, in her study, Leonard-Barton (1990) observed the internal development of equipment, processes and software tools. Soundaararajan and Brammer (2018) use the relationship in an intermediary-sub-supplier dyad as their unit of analysis. Lawrence et al. (2016) used professional service work as their unit of analysis whilst exploring the forces that drive the transition of professional service work from being completely new and innovative to becoming less customized and eventually commodified.

6.2.2 Demands on longitudinal field study cases

Two main considerations go into the selection of organizations to study when conducting longitudinal field studies. The first consideration concerns numbers. Conducting longitudinal field studies is very demanding in terms of the time researchers need to spend in the organization. The amount of time naturally depends on the extent of the researcher's engagement in the organization. However, in general, it is very difficult to manage to study more than one organization, at least for researchers who are not part of a team.

Studying only one organization obviously leads to disadvantages in terms of generalization. The properties of the chosen case will also have a profound impact on the outcome of the study. An important question therefore becomes whether the case is representative of the specific type of phenomenon that is studied? The answer to this question will affect the degree to which the findings can be considered to have general value (Berg, 1981). We will return to the topic of generalisation towards the end of the chapter.

Using a single case study is also subject to potential biases, such as misjudging the representativeness of a single event, exaggerating the salience of a datum because of its ready availability, or biasing estimates because of unconscious anchoring (Leonard-Barton, 1990). These are biases related to the observer, which need to be safeguarded against. We will later detail several practices to help achieve this safeguarding.

One way of avoiding the shortcomings of having only one organization to study is to combine a longitudinal field study with retrospective case studies. In her landmark study on the implementation of technology, Leonard-Barton (1988) combined a longitudinal field study and several retrospective case studies. The benefits of employing the research design are described in Leonard-Barton (1990).

However, it is important to note that within one single organization, it is possible to study different cases, depending on how we define the unit of analysis. Assume that we are interested in studying the innovation process when developing new products. We may choose to follow several product development projects within the same organization. Thus, although we study only one organization, our study includes several cases. This was the design that Akkermans et al. (2019) employed in their study of ramp ups and ramp downs in the context of digital services, through studying three cases embedded in a single company.

Furthermore, it is also possible to identify several cases within one organization by following a strategy of "temporal bracketing" (Langley et al., 2013), identifying comparative unts of analysis within a stream of longitudinal data. This enables the identification of specific theoretical mechanisms recurring over time. In attempting to understand the process of digital servitization in a manufacturing company, Chen et al. (2021) used temporal bracketing to structure the process into three distinct stages that emerged from the data analysis.

The second consideration when selecting organizations to study is to choose organizations where the phenomenon of interest is likely to be transparently observable. This is particularly important if only one organization is chosen. This recommendation is linked to the more general idea that in case research one may choose cases where the phenomenon of interest is most likely to appear, such as extreme situations and polar types (Eisenhardt, 1989).

For example, in our own research, we were interested in studying manufacturing companies' adoption of lean production (Åhlström, 1997). We were particularly interested in the issues (or problems) that arose as companies changed their operations in accordance with lean production principles. Since only one company could be chosen for the study, due to reasons of time constraints, it was important to choose a case where the adoption process was likely to be transparently observable. The chosen company provided such an opportunity as its operations at the outset of the study were very traditional and thus provided an opportunity to study a radical reorganization, where issues were likely to occur.

To these two considerations when choosing cases to study, we want to add the role of serendipity. For instance, Rungtusanatham and Salvador (2008) had an opportunity to study a manufacturing plant that had failed to adapt appropriately to environmental changes, resulting in a production shutdown. This allowed for observations and interviews to unobtrusively build a understanding of the factors that hindered the transition from mass production to mass customization.

Researchers interested in performing longitudinal field studies often face limited possibilities for strategic choice (Berg, 1981). Research opportunities are not abundant and if one is given the possibility to conduct a longitudinal field study, one may have to seize the opportunity (Czarniawska-Joerges, 1992), even if the opportunity does not fit completely into an à priori developed sampling design. When the purpose of the study is theory building, the opportunities for careful sampling are also made difficult by the fact that the dimensions that could be said to govern sample choice have not yet been explored.

6.2.3 *Gaining access to relevant data*

A major obstacle towards conducting longitudinal field studies is the problem of gaining access to organizations. Organizations often have a need to keep their inner functioning hidden from observers. Observers may also get in the way or organization members do not want to share personal conflicts, stress, and setbacks (Sofer, 1961). Gaining access to an organization is likely to be more of a problem the longer the study of the organization is. Researchers who wish to conduct a longitudinal field study thus face a problem of access, which is not to be underestimated (Leonard-Barton, 1990; Van de Ven, 1993). One way of dealing with the access problem to set up the longitudinal field study as clinical research, which is discussed at length in Chapter 8. Akkermans et al. (2019), for instance, employed a clinical approach as the case company invited one of the co-authors to study and address the problems associated with the ramp up of a new service.

Once access has been granted, the next important step in the research design is to find a suitable vantage point from where to gather data. In operations and supply chain management, it often means taking a managerial perspective since research questions often concern how various change processes can be managed (Van de Ven, 1993). With an interest in how to manage the implementation of new technology, Leonard-Barton (1988) had to place herself within the managers' temporal and contextual frames of references. The focus was then primarily on the actions and perceptions of managers over time.

A general guiding principle for fieldwork is that the researchers' account of the studied scene should build on information provided by the most knowledgeable members of that scene (Van Maanen, 1979). The aim for the researcher is to collect data from the change process to promote a rich, full understanding of the context and the process from the perspective of someone who has lived through the events (Leonard-Barton, 1990). There is often a need to find ways of gaining access to the relevant management level of the company. Access to the management levels of the organization gives the researcher a chance to assess the impact of high-level decisions on a lower level (Schein, 1987). A researcher who only gains access to the lower levels of the organization must infer decisions taken higher up in the organization.

On a more practical level, project meetings are often good places to gain access to relevant data. In investigating the nature of functional involvement in the cross-functional make or buy decision process, Moses and Åhlström (2009) attended the monthly make or buy decision board meeting for over two years in the manufacturing company they studied. Under the assumption that the study concerns a change process, participating in project meetings associated with the change process is an economical way of gaining access to data. The key is to gain the access which permits the researcher to be kept informed when events occur that affect the study (Leonard-Barton, 1990).

Data can also be collected through interaction with managers at relevant levels and in relevant functional areas, depending on the research focus. The study of organizational change processes often needs to consider the organizational context of the change process (Pettigrew, 1985). There is therefore a need to collect data from a broad array of organizational functions and levels, not focusing too narrowly. The research design needs to slice vertically though the organization, enabling the researcher to obtain data from multiple levels and perspectives (Leonard-Barton, 1990).

6.2.4 The importance of a framework for data gathering

Before entering the field, longitudinal field researchers need a research framework, as does any case researcher, as pointed out in Chapter 5. The risk of starting without a framework is also that the data collected will not be relevant for the final analysis (Miles, 1979). The framework is not to be taken for pre-formulated theoretical propositions, which may bias and limit the findings (Eisenhardt, 1989). The framework is more like a telescope, pointed towards the organization to direct the researcher's attention towards some aspects of the organization (Berg, 1974). It is important to remember that any research framework specified beforehand needs to be flexible, as both constructs and research question may shift during the research (Eisenhardt, 1989). It can also be tempting to beforehand divide the research process into neat stages. However, when researchers use a priori stages or phases to design their research and collect data, their results can easily become self-fulfilling prophesies (Van de Ven, 1993).

It is of course impossible to say anything general on the content of the research framework since it is entirely dependent on the research question. However, a distinction can be made between the conceptual part of the framework and the more practical part. The following examples illustrate the point. Let us start by illustrating two examples of the conceptual part of a framework for data collection:

Researchers in the Minnesota Innovation Research Program (Van de Ven et al., 1989) were interested in studying innovation processes. To this end, they used a framework consisting of a set of categories or variables to describe innovation development. These categories were viewed as sensitising categories. Assumptions and definitions of these concepts changed substantially and become progressively clearer with field observations over time.

In our study, we were interested in studying the adoption of lean production (Åhlström, 1997). The basis for the research framework as a definition of lean production. With this definition as the starting point, our framework directed our attention towards the adoption process: the order and sequence of events as the organization adopted lean production.

The starting point in both examples is the research question, which is used to focus data collection. The research question is used to form a conceptual framework. The concepts in this framework are seldom directly observable. A more practical part therefore needs to be added to the research framework, where concepts are operationalized, to help the researcher to know what exactly to look for while in the field.

Knowing more exactly what to look for while conducting the fieldwork as spending a significant amount of time in the field compounds the need for having limited the range of behaviour to observe (Turner, 1981). Observation needs to be systematic, selecting aspects of behaviour to observe (Scott, 1965). We also need to choose a unit of observation (Leonard-Barton, 1990). For instance, are we interested in observing comments of individuals involved in the change process or are we focusing on the major outcomes of various project meetings held in the change process?

Longitudinal field researchers are often interested in events. Events require careful definition and vary with the subject being investigated. Only by being clear about the subject and conceptual categories does the researcher know "what" events/activities to record, and "where" to look for them. This is particularly important since it is often difficult to identify critical data in a longitudinal field study, whilst one is in the midst of the research (Leonard-Barton, 1990). What turns out to be critical events when the analysis is being done, after the fact, is not necessarily apparent while the events are unfolding.

Please note here that events are constructs; conceptual categories that are not directly observable but are indicated by observable incidents (Van de Ven and Poole, 1990). Exactly how these observable incidents are defined, will depend on the research question. In studying the interconnectedness of the capabilities needed by a firm to mass customize environmentally friendly products, Trentin et al. (2015) defined events as "variations in the capabilities of interest" and incidents as "variations in their underlying routines".

We have ourselves found it fruitful to use as a modified version of the critical incident technique (Flanagan, 1954). In this technique, an incident is defined as: "any observable human activity that is sufficiently complete in itself to permit inferences and predictions to be made about the person performing the act" (Flanagan, 1954: 327). A few modifications of this definition can be made:

- Speech acts can be included in the definition of acts. Acts are not confined to something being done; acts also refer to something being said.
- Incidents can include non-acts. This is in line with Leonard-Barton (1990) who found it necessary to inquire "about critical individuals' lack of action as well as about their overt actions" (p. 258).

How do we know that incidents are critical, being worthy of observation? Again, the research question is an important indicator. But the original definition of the critical incident technique serves as a useful starting point, where critical incidents are "effective or in-effective with respect to attaining the general aims of the activity" (Flanagan, 1954: 338).

In our own research, incidents were considered critical when they indicated events that either facilitated or impeded the process of adopting lean production. With the process view of manufacturing improvement taken in the study, the factors influencing the success and failure of the adoption process were of essence (Voss, 1988). When looking for the critical incidents two major types of questions were used:

1 For the observable incidents, we asked ourselves: "does it affect the adoption of lean production? If it does, then how?" The observable incidents comprised both acts (something which was done) and remarks (something which was said).
2 When searching for the covert incidents, we asked ourselves: "if something should be done, why isn't it?"

These two questions cover most of the decision rules used for observing critical incidents. To the decision rules were added some "subjective judgements" (Van de Ven and Poole, 1990). Some personal judgements were necessary to decide whether an incident was to be classified as critical or not. Thus, it is not possible to give an exact account of the types of incidents that were noted down. Having observed a critical incident, it is important to note down the relevant information concerning the incident as quickly as possible (Van de Ven and Poole, 1990).

6.2.5 Demands on the researcher conducting longitudinal field studies

Longitudinal field studies are not for everyone, as the demands they place on the researcher do not fit everyone. Before considering conducting a longitudinal field study, the researcher is well advised to consider the following (see also Leonard-Barton, 1990).

- The research skills needed are those resembling an investigative reporter. Attention to detail is paramount. One needs to listen attentively while simultaneously asking the right questions, keeping the previous interview or observation in mind. One also needs to be very aware of the significance of what is left unsaid as well as what is said. These observations must then be recorded, categorised, and later coded.

- One must really enjoy fieldwork. The longitudinal field study may require as much time on fostering and maintaining relationships with organizations as on the actual data gathering. Further, to observe critical events, one must often spend an inordinate amount of time observing non-critical events. The researcher therefore needs to enjoy spending time in organizations. It is easier to make remote interviews, than having to confront the same people, day after day.
- The analysis of data collected in a longitudinal field study is a particularly challenging task. Process data are messy and making sense of them is a constant challenge (Langley, 1999). The analysis starts already during the fieldwork, when deciding which observations to record. The observations must then be categorised and later coded. The data analysis task requires the researcher having a high tolerance for ambiguity, to be able to systematically iterate from a huge amount of qualitative data towards clarity.

6.3 Collecting data in the longitudinal field study

Longitudinal field researchers have at their disposal the same methods for data collection as case researchers, which are well described in Chapter 5. However, the longitudinal field researcher is likely to rely heavily on participant observation. This method is often complemented by formal and informal interviews and studies of documents, as using different data collection methods can help the researcher triangulate evidence; using the strength of one method to compensate for the weaknesses of another (Jick, 1979).

6.3.1 Main method for collecting data is participant observation

The participant observer collects data by participating in the organization. Participant observation allows the researcher to record action as it occurs, without relying on the willingness or ability of respondents to describe their actions (Scott, 1965). As participant observer, researchers gather data by participating in the daily life of the organization being studied. By entering conversations with some of the participants in the observed events, researchers can discover participants' interpretations of the observed events (Becker, 1958).

Participant observation gives the researcher a possibility to learn the language of the group under study (Becker and Geer, 1957). Any social group will to some degree have a culture differing from that of other groups. These differences will find expression in a language whose nuances are peculiar to that group and fully understood only by its members. In interviewing we cannot fully understand this language, and we often do not understand that we do not understand and are thus likely to make errors in interpreting what is said to us. Participant observation provides a situation in which the meaning of words can be learned with great precision through the study of their use in context.

When researchers participate in the daily activities of the people in the organization, they can become aware of the full meaning of hints. Participant observation is thus helpful in reading the cues that are an important part of communication (Czarniawska-Joerges, 1992). The quality of the observations that are made tend to increase if the researcher can gain the informal status of an employee. The rapport gained through being seen as an employee is valuable, since information is not withheld from the researcher for being an outsider. This may facilitate acquiring the kind of knowledge required to communicate about a domain without necessarily being able to practice in that domain (Langley et al., 2013).

The role a participant observer can take in the field can be seen as positions on a continuum (Schwartz and Schwartz, 1955). At one end of the continuum is the passive observer and at the other end the active observer. The passive participant observer attempts not to interact with the organization's members. Just by spending time at the company, the researcher will be able to collect data that can prove useful for the analysis. Conversations can be overheard, non-verbal cues read, and who spoke to whom, about what, can be observed. This has benefits in terms of maintaining objectivity. However, passive participant observation may exclude the researcher from some arenas, for being an outsider.

Active participant observers use themselves as the principal instrument of observation and interpretation (Sanday, 1979). Participating actively in the organization, the researcher builds an ever-growing fund of impressions that give an extensive base for interpretation and analysis (Becker and Geer, 1957). By experiencing the life of and sharing the perspectives of the subject group, researchers can use their own feelings and attitudes as clues in interpreting the behaviour of those observed (Scott, 1965). The researcher's experiences of the situation can also be used in the analysis (Smircich, 1983). What is important when active participation is used is to meticulously note down in the field notes one's own actions and any observable effects on the organization and its members. These notes then need to be considered in the analysis.

The choice of being an active or passive participant observer in part depends on the employed research approach. But any researcher who participates in an organization over an extended time, will find it is difficult not to participate actively in the organization (Schwartz and Schwartz, 1955).

6.3.2 Dealing with the risks associated with participant observation

The main risk of participant observation as a data collection method is the danger of "going native". The participant observer who has gone native gets totally immersed in the studied organization and loses the perspective necessary for a researcher. Losing the perspective means the researcher finds little that requires explanation (Scott, 1965).

One way of dealing with the risk of going native is to temporarily withdraw from the field. By allowing the researcher to withdraw regularly from the field back to the academic environment, the risk of going native can to some extent be avoided. During the periods in the academic environment, the researcher reads literature, writes up field notes, and discusses with colleagues. These activities help raise the level of abstraction on what has been observed while in the field, which helps to avoid the risk of losing perspective.

The researcher remaining cognisant of being a researcher can also reduce the risk of going native. This may sound like a truism, but our experience is that that the difference between working in an organization and studying it, is large enough that the risk of going native is not to be overstated.

Participant observation is also associated with emotional difficulties. These kinds of problems accompany all methods but are especially salient when researchers use themselves as research tools in longitudinal participant observation (Barley, 1990). Meeting respondents day after day is more difficult than making a few visits. Conducting a longitudinal field study is like moving into a new culture with accompanying feelings of alienation (Czarniawska-Joerges, 1993).

Apart from affecting the researcher, the emotional difficulties associated with participant observation may have effects on the data that are collected. If you work long enough in one place, you tend to become involved with the observed emotional life (Schwartz and Schwartz, 1955). One negative effect of this involvement is that the researcher's concern with protecting and developing good relations with people in the organization interferes with the collection of data (Scott, 1965). The best advice here to try and be aware of the risk and to withdraw from the field at regular intervals.

6.3.3 Complementing data gathering using interviews and documents

The longitudinal field researcher is also likely to use interviews as a data collection method. These interviews may be informal, bordering on conversations, part of the process of observation (Zelditch, 1962). For instance, by engaging in conversations with organization members the researcher can gain a deeper understanding of the change process being studied. During interaction with organization members, the researcher can probe for what they feel of their current situation and the changes that are taking place.

There will be occasions when the conversations are more formalised and are more like informant interviews. These can, for instance, be used to collect data from the periods researchers are not present in the organization. Interviews can also be valuable in finding explanations to observed behaviour. The informants used for interviews can be seen as "surrogate observers": people who were in a situation that enabled them to observe significant events (Scott, 1965). The researchers cannot possible be everywhere, all the time (Zelditch, 1962). Selviaridis and Spring (2018), for instance, in their longitudinal study of the process of supply chain alignment used retrospective interviewee accounts of early phases of the contracting process that was their focus, as a complement to the high volume of contemporaneous data as the process of negotiating pay-for-performance provisions was tracked in real time.

More formalised interviews, using a structured interview protocol can of course be used. The same type of guidelines for conducting these applies in longitudinal field studies as they do in any case study. A major reason for not conducting more formalised interviews can be that they may interrupt the rapport the researcher has achieved. Being seen as an employee, rather than as a researcher, is of importance for the quality of the data obtained. Using more formalised interviews may threaten the rapport gained.

A final source of data for the longitudinal field researcher is documents, such as meeting minutes, official statements, webpages, leaflets, and newsletters. Documents can be useful for many types of data, but particularly to keep track of events taking place before the start of the study and events that the researcher was not able to observe. Rytter et al. (2007), for instance, investigated relevant documents from time periods before and after they were engaged with the case company. The danger with documents is that they cannot always be taken at face value (Scott, 1965). Documents may not contain enough information to be of any real value or be biased in the sense they do not reflect what was said in a meeting. Documents are also subject to the dangers of selective survival (Pettigrew, 1990). The content of documents therefore needs to be crosschecked with informant interviews whenever possible.

6.3.4 Keeping field notes and other data records

Participant observation requires diaries (Czarniawska-Joerges, 1992). The participant observer needs to note what is observed as accurately as possible (Van Maanen, 1979).

Good notes are rich in detail and provide full or complete explanations. Good notes describe and explain the context of a comment or event and identify all actors, preferably by position, role, and location in the organization under study (Martin and Turner, 1986).

Pen and paper are likely to be used for taking field notes, which later must be transcribed, a potentially time-consuming task. The need for transcribing notes as quickly as possible after the observation is perhaps self-evident. Despite this need, the transcription can at times not be done immediately. The researcher in the field always faces a fear of having missed something important. To overcome this fear, emphasis tends to be put on data collection. Unfortunately, as more data are collected, the easier it is to become late with transcription (Miles, 1979).

The more covert observations that the participant observer makes should not be noted down immediately. There is a great risk in the researcher jeopardises the rapport achieved by constantly taking notes of what people say. Instead, the researcher needs to memorise the most important points of what was said and write these points down as quickly as possible. The longitudinal field researcher is likely to notice that the skill in memorising observations increases over time, since one is often forced to practise the skill of observing without taking notes.

The rapport gained with organization members is also the reason why pen and paper are likely to be most useful in taking field notes. Using a computer may work but could act against the rapport the researcher has achieved with the organization's members. It is hard to make general recommendations; researchers are advised to rely on their own judgement here. The rapport is also the reason using a recording device during data collection may not be a good idea. The risk of missing something must be weighed against the advantage of not disturbing too much. There is also a more pragmatic side to the choice of using a recording device. Transcribing recordings of an extended period of interaction with organization members is potentially a huge task, particularly if the researchers themselves must do it.

To facilitate the analysis task, it is advisable to set up a good system for keeping track of all the documents that tend to accumulate during longitudinal field studies. Field notes, diaries, meeting protocols and other types of documents that the researcher is likely to hoard as part of the study tend to accumulate over time, creating vast amounts of data. Our own experience shows that a good way of organizing the field notes and other data records is to keep them in the order of observation date, possibly using databases or software dedicated to the analysis of qualitative data.

6.4 Analysing longitudinal field data

Analysing qualitative data is a challenging task (Huberman and Miles, 1983). The challenge is to order and analyse an overwhelming amount of descriptive data (Barley, 1990). For some, the result is "death by data asphyxiation – the slow and inexorable sinking into the swimming pool which started so cool, clear and inviting and now has become a clinging mass of maple syrup" (Pettigrew, 1990: 281). The central difficulty in analysing qualitative data is that methods are not well formulated (Miles, 1979). Methods for analysis are particularly lacking for researchers interested in processes of change in organizations (Langley, 1999). Researchers undertaking process studies have therefore been forced to develop their own methods through trial and error (Van de Ven and Huber, 1990).

In the following, we describe a few examples of activities that take place when the fieldwork is completed. The exact nature of the analysis activities will depend on the research design. For a fuller description of various approaches to analysing longitudinal data, please see Langley (1999). The analysis activities described below constitute the mechanics of the analysis process, the time-consuming and more mechanical part that precedes the more creative theory-building part. The mechanics of analysing longitudinal field data is in essence a question of data reduction.

6.4.1 Data reduction as analysis

Data reduction is at the core of the task of analyzing qualitative data (Miles and Huberman, 1984). To help the longitudinal field researcher cope with data overload, qualitative data need to be reduced for any analysis to occur. Data reduction not only allows analysis, it also is analysis, since the choice of a reduction strategy or heuristic will determine what kind of analysis is possible. We therefore need to put two demands on the data reduction methods (Huberman and Miles, 1983):

1 They need to reduce the data without unduly distorting or oversimplifying them.
2 They need to leave room for a wide range of alternative analytic approaches, not locking in the researcher.

The activities described below are guidelines to help the longitudinal field researcher with the task of analyzing data. They have proved fruitful in earlier studies. Note, however, that researchers will probably have to develop their own analysis methods depending on the circumstances of the study.

6.4.2 Writing a narrative of the change process

The starting point for the analysis is a story that narrates the sequence of events in the change process (Langley, 1999). Rytter et al. (2007), for instance, we wrote a case narrative on the operations strategy intervention they focused on in their study and the operational changes that took place following this intervention. Before writing the narrative, it is very useful to read through all the collected material to gain familiarity with it. The material needs to be read with an open mind at this stage, trying not to single out different aspects of the material for further elaboration. However, the material needs to be read with the research question in mind. Having read the material several times, it can be typed up as a narrative, compiling field notes, documents, and interview protocols. Having all the collected material as one document will give researchers a better grasp of the change process before starting the more detailed analysis.

If the researcher has been careful in recording the observations made during the study, the narrative will basically be a compilation of all field notes and documents, sorted in chronological order. The narrative needs to include all events that took place in the studied change process, transcribed as closely from the original sources as possible. Whatever interpretation the researcher makes of the material at this stage of the analysis needs to be kept out of the narrative and be added as comments.

6.4.3 Dividing the narrative for further analysis

As second analysis activity is to divide up the narrative exposing the studied change process to permit further analysis. The division is done to arrive at the basic element of information - the datum. A datum can be entered into a data file for analysing temporal event sequences in the change process (Van de Ven and Poole, 1990). A qualitative datum can be defined as:

1 A bracketed string of words capturing the basic elements of information,
2 about a discrete incident or occurrence (the unit of analysis),
3 that happened on a specific date, which is
4 entered as a unique record in a qualitative data file, and
5 is subsequently coded and classified as an indicator of a theoretical event.

The qualitative datum in a process study can be termed "incident". It is here important to distinguish between an incident (which is a raw datum) and an event (which is a theoretical construct). Whereas an incident is an empirical observation, an event is not directly observed; it is a conceptual construct that explains the occurrence of incidents. For each event one can choose any number of incidents as indicators that the event has happened.

Thus, a qualitative datum is a bracketed string of words about a discrete incident. Explicit decision rules are needed to bracket raw words. These decision rules of course need to reflect the purpose and focus of the research. A few examples will illustrate. As with many decision rules in qualitative research, some further subjective judgements are involved in defining incidents in an operationally consistent manner.

Researchers in the Minnesota Innovation Research Program used as a rule to bracket words using their definition of incident: a major recurrent activity or change in any of the five core concepts (Van de Ven and Poole, 1990):

- People – the people involved in an incident, the roles, and activities they perform at a given point in time.
- Ideas – the ideas or strategies used by innovation group members to describe the content of an innovation.
- Transactions – the informal and formal relationships among innovation group members, other firms and groups involved in the incident.
- Context – exogenous events outside of the innovation unit in the larger organization and industry, which affected the innovation.
- Outcomes – evidence of results of the innovation, being positive, negative, or mixed/ neutral.

When each incident was identified, the bracketed string of words required to describe it included: date of occurrence, the actor(s) or object(s) involved, the action or behaviour that occurred, the consequence (if any) of the action, and the source of the information.

In our own research, an incident was defined as an occurrence that either facilitated or impeded the process of adopting lean production. The starting point for defining the incidents was the narrative and in particular the experiences of the actors involved in the adoption process, expressed through their language. The incidents were defined by reading the narrative several times and bracketing the incidents each time a transition in meaning in the narrative was experienced. An incident was therefore not necessarily equal to one sentence in the narrative. The number of sentences could vary, and it was the basic meaning of the incident that was of interest.

Trentin et al. (2015) defined an incident as the "establishment of a new organizational routine, or a change in an existing one, which supported mass customization and/or green management" (p. 256). When deciding whether an occurrence mentioned in the case narrative was to be considered an incident, they asked themselves the following two questions:

1 Did the occurrence represent a change in the organizational routines of the company?
2 Did it support mass customization and or green management at the company?

Only in the case of a positive answer to both questions, the occurrence was considered an incident.

6.4.4 Coding incidents

The bracketed incidents then need to be coded into qualitative event constructs, as a list of incidents is not particularly useful for further analysis. The incidents need to be coded into theoretically meaningful events. Important here is to note the nature of codes:

> A code is an abbreviation or symbol applied to a segment of words [---] in order to classify the words. Codes are categories. [---] They are retrieval and organizing devices.
>
> (Miles and Huberman, 1984: 56)

Providing explicit recommendations on how to create codes is impossible. However, a few guidelines on the nature of codes are possible to outline. The codes can at one extreme be taken from theory or at the other extreme derived from the data. Where along this continuum the researchers position their codes depends on the nature of the research and particularly the role of existing theory in the research. Given that longitudinal field studies tend to be conducted to build theory, an approach where codes are derived from data is likely to be used.

Even though the data is used as a starting point for creating codes, it is of course the researchers who create the codes. When using data to create codes, the starting point for devising codes is the experiences of the individuals - what actors perceived as being important - expressed through their language. The terms individuals used comprised the fundamental material and the coding task is that of meaningfully abstracting from this material (Normann, 1980).

It is also possible to use a combination of the data and theory to create codes. Trentin et al. (2015), for example, had an initial coding scheme consisting of eleven coding rules that were based on the definitions of capabilities included in their initial research protocol. However, they also drew on the data to create several sub-codes capturing specific aspects of some of the capabilities. Thus, the researchers are still creating the codes, using the data as an important source of inspiration, but also employing existing theory. This approach lies within the nature of theory building research.

Since researchers design the coding system, codes used for incidents do not necessarily correspond to the way in which participants see the incidents. It is still necessary to test empirically whether the researcher's classifications are consistent with practitioners' common perceptions of events. If the evidence indicates inconsistency, researchers can still sustain claims about the meaning of the incident from their theoretical position, but no claims about the social reality of the event are appropriate (Van de Ven and Poole, 1990).

6.4.5 *Using software to keep track of incidents*

To include the full meaning of an incident, each incident can be coded on more than one dimension of an event (Van de Ven and Poole, 1990). One way to organize these multidimensional data into a format to analyse change processes is to array them on multiple tracks that correspond to conceptually meaningful categories. Within each conceptual track several more specific codes are possible, depending on the questions being addressed by the researcher.

It is useful for the further analysis to code and enter the incidents in a database or using a software such as NVivo (O'Kane et al., 2021). Using software gives researchers the opportunity to keep track of all incidents in an efficient manner. It is useful to describe the incidents fully enough to avoid the need for backtracking to the notes to recall details (Martin and Turner, 1986). Using software will enable the researcher to search for all incidents with a certain code, to see how the code was used.

The definition of the codes used for the coding process needs to be kept separate, to facilitate going back to the codes' definition when necessary. It may also be necessary to modify the definition to take into account new information. This is in line with the inductive way in which most longitudinal field studies are designed. We are interested in building theory, not testing theory.

6.4.6 *Sorting and recoding to separate important events*

With the coded incidents as a basis, the analysis of the data can now continue. Before coming to the stage of the analysis where patterns are sought, inferences made and cause and effect are determined, an intermediate activity may be necessary. In this activity, the list of incidents is scrutinized, and incidents are sorted and perhaps recoded. The aim is to separate out the important events from the less important.

Whether this activity is necessary, and its exact nature, depends on several things. The research question that the research is trying to answer will have a big impact on whether the sorting and recoding of incidents is needed or not. How focused the data collection was in the first place will also matter. The importance of focusing data collection was stressed earlier in the chapter. It is at this stage of the analysis the researcher will start getting the benefit of a focused data collection. Or conversely, if the data collection has not been that focused, using a conceptual framework as a starting point, the sorting and recoding activity can become very cumbersome indeed.

However, what particularly determines whether sorting and recoding is necessary or not, is the complexity inherent in the coded incidents. This complexity is partly a function of both the research question and how focused data collection was. The complexity is also determined by the amount of time the researcher spent in the organization and how much data that were collected. The number of incidents is one indicator of the complexity inherent in the coded incidents.

The activity of sorting and recoding aims at separating out the important events from the less important. This can be done in different ways. A fruitful way of working can be to start by sorting the incidents in various ways, reading, and re-coding them. This process essentially means that the researcher switches between the whole and the parts; between a string of incidents and an individual incident. The rationale for switching between the whole and the parts is that coding an incident is easier when each incident is seen in relation to other incidents.

One possible tool in this activity is to use printouts of all the incidents sorted in different ways. Several different rounds of recoding are probably necessary, each round with the incidents sorted in different ways, depending on the research question. Each round needs to share two characteristics: it should involve a search for incidents indicating recurring events and an elimination of those incidents that do not indicate recurring events. At least one of the rounds should have the incidents sorted in chronological order.

The importance of separating out important events retrospectively should not be underestimated. What may have seemed important during data collection is not necessarily important in the retrospective analysis: "time itself sets a frame of reference that directly affects our perceptions of change" (Van de Ven, 1993: 318). Therefore, the retrospective analysis is often to be trusted more than the initial assessment of an incident's importance. This does not invalidate the initial judgement made during data collection, but the whole picture is needed to be able to relate the details to it. For instance, not all incidents that are collected may turn out to have a significant effect. Perhaps it transpires out that some incidents were related to individuals that turned out to have only ephemeral roles in the studied change process (Leonard-Barton, 1990).

Graphical techniques are also useful tools here. After several rounds of sorting and recoding, the researcher may still have hundreds or even thousands of incidents left for further analysis. With this number of incidents, it is easy to get lost in detail if only text is used. Remember the adage: "a picture says more than a thousand words". Exactly how graphical techniques can be used is of course highly dependent on the research question. One way of working is to convert lists of incidents to graphical displays consisting of a timeline with an "X" marking each incident. These timelines often need to be created at different levels of analysis, for instance for each event. The displays are useful for assessing the importance of different events, since the displays give an overview of the change process. It is important to note that it is not simply a matter of assessing the importance of an event and excluding incidents based on simple counting. Both the graphical displays and printouts of the incidents need to be used, together with the researchers' judgement and insights gained during the fieldwork.

Regardless of what tools are used, this part of the analysis is likely to lead to reduced complexity in the further analysis. Incidents are recoded; events may be taken out or merged. It is here useful to exclude incidents from analysis technically through a code in the database or software program used. The actual incidents should still be kept for reference in the further analysis.

6.5 Building theory from longitudinal field studies

After the more mechanical side of the analysis task, follows the more creative side, where the collected data are used as the basis to develop theory. The researcher should not expect to proceed in a linear fashion from raw data to final theory. The process is self-consciously and intentionally non-linear and iterative (Martin and Turner, 1986). Providing general recommendations exactly on how to proceed in building theory is very difficult. What we can offer are some general guidelines. The difficulty of explicitly describing exactly how analysis takes place is compounded by the fact that interpretation and analysis begins already during the fieldwork (Berg, 1981).

As will all field research, an important part of the analysis is going on when data are still being collected (Barley, 1990). The researcher conducting a longitudinal field study builds an overgrowing fund of impressions, many of them at the subliminal level, which give an extensive base for the interpretation and analytic use of data (Becker and Geer, 1957). While collecting data, the researcher needs to write down whatever impressions occur; to react to rather than to sift out what may seem important (Eisenhardt, 1989). When noting down the impressions it is useful to let them stand out in the field notes, so that impressions are not mixed with observations.

6.5.1 Seeking underlying mechanisms through sequences and patterns

In building theory from longitudinal field studies, the basis for the theory is the events indicated by the incidents. Thus, the incidents are the raw material for the analysis, but what we are interested in are the events underlying the incidents. Concerning the level of analysis and interpretation, a differentiation can be made between surface and in-depth interpretations (Berg, 1981). Surface interpretations deal with the easily apparent and observable, whereas in-depth interpretations deal with the underlying mechanisms, structures, and processes. Process theorization needs to go beyond surface description to penetrate the logic behind observed temporal progressions (Langley, 1999).

Key to identifying underlying mechanisms in longitudinal field data is sequence analysis (Van de Ven and Poole, 1990). Sequence analysis is concerned with determining temporal order, relationships, and patterns among events. This pattern will gradually evolve during the analysis process, not suddenly emerge (Berg, 1981). The coded data that was the outcome of the previous, more mechanical, stage of the analysis is scanned for sequences. The pattern is, in a sense, generated as the researchers work with the data. Once a sequence or patterns of events is identified, one can turn to questions about what the causes or consequences are of the events within the process pattern (Van de Ven and Huber, 1990). These are the underlying mechanisms, the in-depth interpretations.

6.5.2 Techniques for identifying sequences and patterns

In determining sequences and patterns, the researcher is greatly helped by using different techniques for data analysis. The objective should be for the longitudinal field researcher to avoid relying exclusively on subjective eye-balling and anecdotal information in qualitative data (Van de Ven and Poole, 1990). The intention is not to make the analysis process standardised and mechanical, but to combine the rich insights that are gained during the fieldwork with more systematic techniques. Two types of techniques are highly useful for the longitudinal field researcher – graphical and quantitative techniques.

Graphical techniques are simply visual models that help the researcher visualize data, patterns, and sequences (Berg, 1981). These can range from simple figures to complex displays of relationships between events and constructs, covering several square meters. Visual graphical representations are particularly attractive for the analysis of process data because they allow the simultaneous representation of several dimensions, and they can easily be used to show precedence (Langley, 1999). Exactly how these figures and displays are constructed will of course vary. Regardless, graphical displays are an indispensable way for the researcher to gain an overview over large amounts of qualitative data. Regardless of how the displays are made, the display modes chosen will inevitably condition the conclusions of the analysis (Huberman and Miles, 1983). One piece of advice is therefore to use a variety of display modes.

The longitudinal field researcher can also make good use of quantitative analytical methods to find regularities or patterns that might be hidden in the material. One method is simple counting, which enables researchers to remove nagging doubts about the accuracy of their impressions about the data (Silverman, 1993). The data can also be subjected to more rigorous statistical treatment. Van de Ven and Poole (1990) recommends transforming qualitative codes into quantitative dichotomous categories, using one for presence or zero for absence of a qualitative incident. This will permit applying various statistical methods to examine time-dependent patterns of relation among event constructs. Regardless of method chosen, our position is that quantitative methods should be seen as tools by means of which hidden information might be washed out of the data, information that makes sense only when related to the researchers' interpretation.

6.5.3 Comparing the emerging theory with literature

When the longitudinal field researcher is analysing the data, the concepts that are used to describe and explain the process of change are generally derived from and grounded in the data, and not from a preconceived theoretical framework. However, this does not deny the value of theoretical concepts derived from existing frameworks. On the contrary, existing theories and concepts are very valuable for connecting the developing theory with a wider theoretical framework. Most important of all, existing theories can be used as creative devices in the search for sequences and patterns (Berg, 1981).

An essential feature of theory building is comparison of the emergent theory and its concepts with existing literature (Eisenhardt, 1989). This involves asking what is this similar to, what does it contradict, and why. A key to theory building from longitudinal field studies, is to consider a broad range of literature as it helps strengthen the general nature of the theory:

- Literature that discusses similar findings in different contexts is important since it ties together underlying similarities in phenomena normally not associated with each other. The result is often a theory with stronger internal validity and wider generalizability.
- Literature which conflicts with the emergent theory is equally important to consider. Taking conflicting literature into account strengthens the confidence in the findings and forces the researcher into more creative thinking.

The importance here of creative thinking cannot be underestimated. Building theory is not only a mechanical process, which takes the researcher from raw data to theory. There is no homogenous recipe for theorizing from process data (Langley, 1999). When building theory, researchers design, conduct, and interpret imaginary experiments (Weick, 1989). If we are to develop new knowledge, then we do not know the answer in advance. The significant discovery requires a high degree of uncertainty and ambiguity at the outset (Daft, 1983). Theory building involves a significant degree of guess work, the making up and revising of hypotheses in disciplined thought experiments.

The way theory is developed from longitudinal field studies shares an important characteristic with all case research – it is subjected to the myth that the theory building process is limited by the researcher's preconceptions. In general, just the opposite tends to be true:

> The constant juxtaposition of conflicting realities tends to "unfreeze" thinking, and so the process has the potential to generate theory with less researcher bias than theory built from incremental studies or armchair, axiomatic deduction.
>
> (Eisenhardt, 1989: 546)

However, there are also some weaknesses and dangers to theory building from longitudinal field studies, most importantly that researchers get stuck in details and is unable to raise the level of generality of the theory. The researcher must also avoid overinterpreting the idiosyncrasies of a particular case.

6.5.4 Presenting the developed theory

The final challenge for longitudinal field researchers is to present the large amount of rich data that have been collected, so that the presentation provides evidence for the developed theory (Huberman and Miles, 1983). The challenge includes ensuring that the longitudinality of findings is properly represented in the presentation of the theory (Perks and Roberts, 2013). In one respect, the challenges in presenting the developed theory are similar in all case research, see Chapter 5. The challenges are, however, often compounded due to the large amounts of data that are often collected in longitudinal field studies.

Critical in writing up longitudinal field studies is to illustrate how the researchers arrived at the conclusions (Åhlström, 2007). Few general recommendations can be made here. Researchers need to use their judgement and inventive abilities to find ways to present their findings and the data underlying them. Just as they are helpful in the analysis process, the use of graphical techniques can be strongly recommended in presenting the findings. Instead of taking the researcher's word for it, the reader has a chance to gain a sense of the data (Silverman, 1993). Although it is not an easy task to represent the dynamics of change processes onto a static two-dimensional page, visual representations are often crucial in describing and communication the results of longitudinal field studies (Langley et al., 2013).

The graphs can be complemented with illustrations from the rich qualitative data the researcher is likely to have collected. The main purpose of the illustrations should be to introduce to the reader parts of the researcher's own learning process, in reaching the conclusions, to facilitate the reader's learning process (Normann, 1980). The use of excerpts should not be seen as a way of proving a point. All usage of interview excerpts is subject to subjective choice. The use of shorter excerpts can be a complement to presenting findings in a detailed narrative style, focused on a theorized storyline (Lawrence et al., 2016).

6.6 Evaluating longitudinal field studies

In evaluating the research findings derived from longitudinal field studies, we first need to discuss the qualitative nature of the inquiry that characterizes the longitudinal field study. Qualitative research is normally contrasted with quantitative research based on which techniques have been used for data collection and analysis. In this technique-based view, we tend to stress the importance of reliability, validity, and accurate measurement before research outcomes can contribute to scholarly knowledge (Daft, 1983). Objectivity is another concept celebrated by quantitative researchers (Kirk and Miller, 1986).

However, distinguishing qualitative from quantitative research, based on which techniques are used for data collection and analysis, cannot absorb the diversity of uses to which the qualitative label applies (Van Maanen, 1979). Qualitative researchers are more interested in the meaning, rather than the measurement, of organizational phenomena (Daft, 1983). Qualitative research is best seen as an approach rather than a set of techniques

(Morgan and Smircich, 1980). Nothing excludes the qualitative researcher from using data collection and analysis techniques considered "quantitative", such as statistical techniques (Daft, 1983).

The standards used for judging quantitative studies are inappropriate for judging qualitative studies (Agar, 1986). This does not mean that no standards are applicable to qualitative research; qualitative research is not less scientific than quantitative research (Silverman, 1993). It is a matter of using different ways of ensuring reliability and validity in qualitative research. We must ensure that the longitudinal field study is not done as "industrial tourism". Rigour must be applied both in research design, data collection and analysis.

The description of reliability and validity ordinarily provided by quantitative researchers needs to be modified to fit qualitative research (Kirk and Miller, 1986). A qualitative approach requires the reader to be able to make judgements about components of the research process leading to the final product (Strauss and Corbin, 1990). Qualitative research is scientific in that the collection, analysis, and reporting of data are done systematically, with care and discipline (Smircich, 1983). The researcher's task is in no small part to convince the reader the findings are trustworthy (Pratt et al., 2020), drawn from material that has been processed by methods that can be explicitly described.

6.6.1 *Increasing reliability through a systematic research process*

In longitudinal field studies, reliability translates to demands on the research process: "reliability depends essentially on explicitly described observational procedures" (Kirk and Miller, 1986: 41). Two aspects of data collection are particularly relevant: making the observations and writing up field notes.

While collecting data, researchers need to pay continual and careful attention to the details of their adventures in the field (Van Maanen, 1979). There is a need to separate first- and second-order concepts. First-order concepts are the facts of the investigation and second-order concepts are the theories the researcher uses to organize and explain the facts. During data collection, the researcher needs to be careful not to mix the observations with the interpretation of the observations. In the field notes this may for example be done through using different typefaces. During the analysis process, the interpretation of coded incidents needs to be kept away from the actual observations.

During the fieldwork there is also a need to pay constant attention to the distinction between observational and presentational data (Van Maanen, 1979). Observational data refer to observed activity. Presentational data concern those appearances informants strive to maintain or enhance. Making the separation between the two types of data is an analytic task to be carried out while in the field, although the line separating the two types is not always distinct. Both types of data are useful, since the intentionally subjective picture given by presentational data can be an extremely important asset, since it provides the researcher with additional information on the organization being studied (Berg, 1981).

Longitudinal observation facilitates the task of separating observational data from presentational data, since people will find it difficult to monitor their behaviour for a long period of time (Barley, 1990). Through spending a significant amount of time in the field, and participating in daily interaction, the longitudinal field researcher will gain knowledge of how to read the cues that are part of communication, which helps in separating observational from presentational data.

A final detail to pay attention to while conducting the fieldwork is whether informants speak the truth, as they know it (Van Maanen, 1979). There may be different reasons why false information is given. Informants may want to mislead the researcher. Informants may also themselves be misled or wrong about their own matters. To overcome both these reasons for not speaking the truth, the researcher needs to rely on the information provided by the most knowledgeable members of the organization (Van Maanen, 1979). Who these informants are is linked to the research question. A benefit of setting up the longitudinal field study in the form of clinical research, is that informants are less likely to conceal the truth since the researcher is there to help (Argyris, 1968). For more details, please see Chapter 8.

The reliability of longitudinal field studies is also increased through proper field notes (Kirk and Miller, 1986). There is a need to "conduct research as if someone were always looking over your shoulder" (Yin, 1989: 45). Information on how and in what contexts field notes were recorded is needed (Silverman, 1993). Apart from the observation, the following information needs to be noted, at a minimum: when the observation was made, in what forum, and which actors were present. Furthermore, field notes must conform to two requirements (Kirk and Miller, 1986). First, they must be legible and chronologically ordered. Second, although the field notes do intrinsically involve the observer, the field notes must differentiate between what people said and the researcher's interpretation.

Finally, the researcher needs to be able to demonstrate as clearly as possible how the conclusions were reached. This requires the researcher to as carefully and accurately as possible document and describe the analytical processes that lead from data to final analysis (Huberman and Miles, 1983). The description particularly needs to be of the data reduction procedures described earlier, the more mechanical side of the analysis task. This will allow the reader to follow how the researchers arrived at the conclusions.

6.6.2 Increasing validity through the research design and coding process

There are several ways to increase the validity of longitudinal field studies. In fact, the research design itself is a way of increasing validity. Given that longitudinal field studies are used for researching change processes in organizations, the research design increases validity as making real-time observations increases the validity of a study compared with retrospective research (Leonard-Barton, 1990).

Longitudinal field studies can be validated by triangulation: using multiple methods and sources of data (Silverman, 1993). When collecting data using multiple methods, one way of increasing validity is to transcribe the field notes as quickly as possible (Schwartz and Schwartz, 1955). Apart from participant observation, interviews, and documents, studies within operations and supply chain management can often benefit from using quantitative measures of performance outcomes. These measures can be used to help determine effects of the processes that are being studied.

For the qualitative observation, the issue of validity is to a certain degree a question of whether the researcher is calling what is measured by the right name (Kirk and Miller, 1986). This means that the coding process employed in the longitudinal field study has implications for validity. Codes developed after data collection are less likely to be biased by the researcher's own fantasies, since the categories emerge from and remain closer to the data (Barley, 1990). Participant observation helps increase the validity of the coding procedure. The participant observer has tested partial analyses during the fieldwork, prior to the actual coding (Glaser and Strauss, 1967). During data collection, researchers act on tentative conclusions based on their current understanding of the situation. If this understanding is invalid, the researcher will sooner or later find out about it (Kirk and Miller, 1986).

Validity can also be increased by respondent validation; feeding back the research findings to the studied organization's members research and see whether it provides them with a meaningful explanation (Berg, 1981). However, there are risks associated with respondent validation. One risk is that individuals recognise themselves in the material, despite necessary attempts to cover up identities. It can also be that the respondents do not agree with the researcher's interpretation. This can lead to demands on the researcher to change the interpretation. At the very least, this process is time-consuming and can in some environments lead to threats of legal action (compare Miles, 1979).

Related to respondent validation is whether the research results can be communicated to and understood by other people (Normann, 1980). Are the findings understandable to individuals who have some familiarity with the phenomena under study (Turner, 1983)? One way of validating the research findings is by letting colleagues experienced in the study's focus read and comment on the research results.

To complement these more traditional ways of validating qualitative research, simple counting procedures or statistical techniques can be used (Silverman, 1993). The methods of generalising to a larger population are a way of increasing the validity of a study's findings.

6.6.3 Generalizing from longitudinal field studies

As discussed in Chapter 5, the ability to generalise has widely been considered a barrier for case studies, particularly for single case studies (Yin, 1989). Single case studies resulting from longitudinal field studies can obviously not be generalised in the statistical sense. Statistical generalisation is, however, not the aim. The ability to generalise is related to the way in which corroboration takes place (Spencer and Dale, 1979). Quantitative studies rely on multiplicative corroboration; a multiplication of evidence (Pepper, 1942). Qualitative studies, on the other hand, rely on a structure of evidence; structural corroboration (Spencer and Dale, 1979). The persuasive force in structural corroboration comes from assembling a mass of evidence converging on the same point (Pepper, 1942). An example illustrates the difference between the two methods of corroboration.

Suppose I want to find out if a chair is strong enough to hold my weight. I can ask several people of my approximate weight to sit on the chair, one at a time. If the chair holds these people, it should be strong enough to hold my weight. The problem has been solved through multiplicative corroboration. Another way of solving the problem of the chair's strength is by examining the relevant facts about the chair. What kind of material is it made of? Are the chair's legs thick enough? How is the chair joined together? Have the makers of the chair got a reputation for making solid chairs? Putting all this evidence together, it is possible to conclude whether the chair is strong enough to hold my weight. This process of giving evidence is structural corroboration.

Using structural corroboration to generalise from a longitudinal field study can be done by comparing the findings with something outside the study (Berg, 1981). The general value of the findings will increase if they can be supported by observations from other organizations or from literature. It is here that the comparison with existing theory plays an important role, a comparison taking place during the analysis of data.

When discussing generalisation, one need to bear in mind that generalisation from case studies takes place towards theory, not towards samples and universes (Yin, 1989). The value of in-depth single case studies lies in their capability to be used for developing and refining concepts and frameworks, which can be generalised (Pettigrew, 1985). Results of in-depth studies of single organizations can also be cumulative (Miller and Mintzberg, 1983).

6.7 Summary

6.7.1 Introduction to the longitudinal field study

Longitudinal field studies are in-depth studies of change processes. They are case studies, with two distinguishing features. First, longitudinal research implies studying a phenomenon over time. Second, the longitudinal field study is a real-time study of an organizational phenomenon, often with the research being present in the organization for periods of time. Longitudinal field studies are often used for building theories of change processes, since they enable researchers to better observe cause and effect.

6.7.2 Setting up the longitudinal field study

Research questions suitable for longitudinal field studies concern how organizational change emerge, develop, grow, or terminate over time. Organizations suitable for longitudinal field studies are those where the change process is likely to be transparently observable, but they are not always easy to find. Before entering the field, a framework for data gathering is critical. Data need to be gathered from a position in the organization, where organization members are likely to be most knowledgeable about the change process being studied. Because of the nature of longitudinal field studies, the researcher attempting them needs skills resembling that of an investigative reporter, where attention to detail is paramount.

6.7.3 Collecting data in the longitudinal field study

Longitudinal field researchers have at their disposal the same toolbox of methods for data collection as any case researcher. However, the longitudinal field researcher is likely to rely heavily on participant observation. To deal with the risk of going native, it is important to regularly withdraw from the field back to the academic environment. Participant observation requires careful and meticulous note taking, together with a system to organize the collected data. Participant observation is often complemented by more informal interviews and studies of documents.

6.7.4 Analysing longitudinal field data

Analysing longitudinal field data is a challenging task due to the large amounts of data being collected and the lack of well-defined methods for data analysis, making a certain amount of invention critical. Central to data analysis is a process of data reduction. The more mechanical side of the analysis process starts with the writing of a narrative of the change process. The narrative is then divided into basic units of information, using explicit decision rules. The third step of the analysis process is to code incidents, for retrieval and organizing purposes. To help keep track of the coded incidents, databases or software are useful tools. The incidents are finally sorted and recoded, for instance using graphical techniques.

6.7.5 Building theory from longitudinal field studies

The more creative part of the analysis process, the generation of theory, starts while the researcher is still in the field. Therefore, field notes should distinguish observations from the interpretation of them. The starting point for building theory is the incidents, but we are interested in the mechanisms underlying them. The analysis requires identifying sequences and patterns in the events, using for instance graphical techniques. The theory developed needs to be constantly compared with existing theory. Finally, presenting longitudinal field studies is a real challenge, requiring a certain amount of innovation from the researcher.

6.7.6 Evaluating theory from longitudinal field studies

The evaluation of longitudinal field studies needs to be made in relation to how the findings are derived. Although the longitudinal field researcher may be more interested in the meaning of phenomena, rather than their measurement; rigour is still very important. To increase the reliability, the researcher needs to adhere to a systematic research process. Validity is enhanced through the research design and through a systematic coding process. Generalization in longitudinal field studies is always towards theory, not samples, since they tend to build on one or a few cases.

References

Agar, M. H. (1986), *Speaking of Ethnography*, Sage University Paper series on Qualitative Research Methods, Volume 2, Sage, Beverly Hills, California.

Akkermans, H., Voss, C., and van Oers, R. (2019), "Ramp Up and Ramp Down Dynamics in Digital Services", *Journal of Supply Chain Management*, Vol. 55, No. 3, pp. 3–23, 10.1111/jscm.12189

Åhlström, P. (1997), *Sequences in the Process of Adopting Lean Production*, EFI, Stockholm.

Åhlström, P. (2007), "Presenting Qualitative Research: Convincing through Illustrating the Analysis Process", *Journal of Purchasing and Supply Management*, Vol. 13, No. 3, pp. 216–218.

Argyris, C. (1968), "Some Unintended Consequences of Rigorous Research", *Psychological Bulletin*, Vol. 70, No. 3, pp. 185–197.

Barley, S. R. (1990), "Images of Imaging: Notes on Doing Longitudinal Field Work", *Organization Science*, Vol. 1, No. 3, pp. 220–247.

Becker, H. S. (1958), "Problems of Inference and Proof in Participant Observation", *American Sociological Review*, Vol. 23, pp. 652–660.

Becker, H. S. and Geer, B. (1957), "Participant Observation and Interviewing: A Comparison", *Human Organization*, Vol. 16, No. 3, pp. 28–32.

Berg, C. (1974), *Samrådssystemet: En klinisk undersökning i ett växande företag* (The Participation System: A Clinical Study of a Growing Company. in Swedish), EFI, Stockholm.

Berg, P-O. (1981), *Emotional Structures in Organizations: A Study of the Process of Change in a Swedish Company*, Studentlitteratur, Lund.

Chen, Y., Visnjic, I., Parida, V., and Zhang, Z. (2021), "On the Road to Digital Servitization – The (Dis)continuous Interplay between Business Model and).Digital Technology", *International Journal of Operations and Production Management*, Vol. 41, No. 5, pp. 694–722. 10.1108/IJOPM-08-2020-0544

Czarniawska-Joerges, B. (1992), *Exploring Complex Organizations: A Cultural Perspective*, Sage, Newbury Park, California.

Czarniawska-Joerges, B. (1993), *The Three-Dimensional Organization: A Constructionist View*, Studentlitteratur, Lund.

Daft, R. L. (1983), "Learning the Craft of Organizational Research", *Academy of Management Review*, Vol. 8, No. 4, pp. 539–546.

Eisenhardt, K. M. (1989), "Building Theories from Case Study Research", *Academy of Management Review*, Vol. 14, No. 4, pp. 532–550.

Flanagan, J. C. (1954), "The Critical Incident Technique", *Psychological Bulletin*, Vol. 51, No. 4, pp. 327–358.

Glaser, B. G. and Strauss, A. L. (1967), *The Discovery of Grounded Theory: Strategies for Qualitative Research*, Aldine de Gruyter, New York.

Huberman, A. M. and Miles, M. B. (1983), "Drawing Valid Meaning from Qualitative Data: Some Techniques of Data Reduction and Display", *Quality and Quantity*, Vol. 17, pp. 281–339.

Jick, T. D. (1979), "Mixing Qualitative and Quantitative Methods: Triangulation in Action", *Administrative Science Quarterly*, Vol. 24, No. 4, pp. 602–611.

Kirk, J. and Miller, M. L. (1986), *Reliability and Validity in Qualitative Research*, Sage, Beverly Hills, California.

Kuula, M., and Putkiranta, A. (2012), "Longitudinal Benchmarking Studies in Operations Management: Lessons Learned", *Benchmarking*, Vol. 19, No. 3, pp. 358–373. 10.1108/14635 771211243003

Langley, A. (1999), "Strategies for Theorizing from Process Data". *Academy of Management Review*, Vol. 24, No. 4, pp. 691–710. http://www.jstor.org/stable/259349

Langley, A., Smallman, C., Tsoukas, H., and van de Ven, A. H. (2013), "Process Studies of Change in Organization and Management: Unveiling Temporality, Change, and Flow", *Academy of Management Journal*, Vol. 56, No. 1, pp. 1–13.

Lawrence, B., Zhang, J. J., and Heineke, J. (2016), "A Life-Cycle Perspective of Professionalism in Services", *Journal of Operations Management*, Vol. 42–43, pp. 25–38. 10.1016/j.jom.2016.03.003

Leonard-Barton, D. (1988), "Implementation as Mutual Adaptation of Techonology and Organization", *Research Policy*, Vol. 17, pp. 251–267.

Leonard-Barton, D. (1990), "A Dual Methodology for Case Studies: Synergistic Use of a Longitudinal Single Site With Replicated Multiple Sites", *Organization Science*, Vol. 1, No. 1, pp. 248–266.

Martin, P. Y. and Turner, B. A. (1986), "Grounded Theory and Organizational Research", *The Journal of Applied Behavioral Science*, Vol. 22, No. 2, pp. 141–157.

Meinlschmidt, J., Foerstl, K., and Kirchoff, J. F. (2016), "The Role of Absorptive and Desorptive Capacity (ACDC) in Sustainable Supply Management: A Longitudinal Analysis". *International Journal of Physical Distribution and Logistics Management*, Vol. 46, No. 2, pp. 177–211. 10.1108/ IJPDLM-05-2015-0138

Miles, M. B. (1979), "Qualitative Data as an Attractive Nuisance: The Problem of Analysis", *Administrative Science Quarterly*, Vol. 24, No. 4, pp. 590–601.

Miles, M. B. and Huberman, A. M. (1984), *Qualitative Data Analysis: A Sourcebook of New Methods*, Sage, Beverly Hills, California.

Miller, D. and Friesen, P. H. (1982), "The Longitudinal Analysis of Organizations: A Methodological Perspective", *Management Science*, Vol. 28, No. 9, pp. 1013–1034.

Miller, D. and Mintzberg, H. (1983), "The Case for Configuration", in Morgan, G. (Ed.), *Beyond Method: Strategies for Social Research*, Sage, Newbury Park, California, pp. 57–73.

Morgan, G. and Smircich, L. (1980), "The Case for Qualitative Research", *Academy of Management Review*, Vol. 5, No. 4, pp. 491–500.

Moses, A., and Åhlström, P. (2009). "Nature of Functional Involvement in Make or Buy Decision Processes", *International Journal of Operations and Production Management*, Vol. 29, No. 9, pp. 894–920. 10.1108/01443570910986210

Normann, R. (1980), *A Personal Quest for Methodology* (Fourth Edition), SIAR Dokumentation, Stockholm.

O'Kane, P., Smith, A., and Lerman, M. P. (2021), "Building Transparency and Trustworthiness in Inductive Research through Computer-Aided Qualitative Data Analysis Software". *Organizational Research Methods*, Vol. 24, No. 1, pp. 104–139. 10.1177/1094428119865016

Pepper, S. C. (1942), *World Hypotheses*, University of California Press, Berkeley, California.

Perks, H., and Roberts, D. (2013), "A Review of Longitudinal Research in the Product Innovation Field, with Discussion of Utility and Conduct of Sequence Analysis", *Journal of Product Innovation Management*, Vol. 30, No. 6, pp. 1099–1111. 10.1111/jpim.12048

Pettigrew, A. M. (1985), "Contextualist Research and the Study of Organisational Change Processes", in Mumford, E. et al. (Eds.), *Research Methods in Information Systems*, North Holland, Amsterdam, pp. 53–78.

Pettigrew, A. M. (1990), "Longitudinal Field Research on Change: Theory and Practice", *Organization Science*, Vol. 1, No. 3, pp. 267–292.

Pratt, M. G., Kaplan, S., and Whittington, R. (2020), "The Tumult over Transparency: Decoupling Transparency from Replication in Establishing Trustworthy Qualitative Research", *Administrative Science Quarterly*, Vol. 65, No. 1, pp. 1–19. 10.1177/0001839219887663

Rungtusanatham, M. J., and Salvador, F. (2008), "From Mass Production to Mass Customization: Hindrance Factors, Structural Inertia, and Transition Hazard", *Production and Operations Management*, Vol. 17, No. 3, pp. 385–396. 10.3401/poms.1080.0025

Rytter, N. G., Boer, H., and Koch, C. (2007), "Conceptualizing Operations Strategy Processes", *International Journal of Operations and Production Management*, Vol. 27, No. 10, pp. 1093–1114. 10.1108/01443570710820648

Sanday, P. R. (1979), "The Ethnographic Paradigm(s)", *Administrative Science Quarterly*, Vol. 24, No. 4, pp. 527–538.

Schein, E. H. (1987), *The Clinical Perspective in Fieldwork*, Sage, Newbury Park, California.

Schwartz, M. S. and Schwartz, C. G. (1955), "Problems in Participant Observation", *American Journal of Sociology*, Vol. 60, pp. 343–353.

Scott, W. R. (1965), "Field Methods in the Study of Organizations", in March, J. G. (Ed.), *Handbook of Organizations*, Rand McNally, Chicago, Illinois, pp. 261–304.

Selviaridis, K., and Spring, M. (2018), "Supply Chain Alignment as Process: Contracting, Learning and Pay-for-Performance", *International Journal of Operations and Production Management*, Vol. 38, No. 3, pp. 732–755. 10.1108/IJOPM-01-2017-0059

Silverman, D. (1993), *Interpreting Qualitative Data*, Sage, London.

Smircich, L. (1983), "Studying Organizations as Cultures", in Morgan, G. (Ed.), *Beyond Method: Strategies for Social Research*, Sage, Newbury Park, California, pp. 160–172.

Sofer, C. (1961), *The Organization from within: A Comparative Study of Social Institutions Based on a Sociotherapetuic Approach*, Tavistock, London.

Soundaararajan, V., and Brammer, S. (2018), "Developing Country Sub-Supplier Responses to Social Sustainability Requirements of Intermediaries: Exploring the Influence of Framing on Fairness Perceptions and Reciprocity", *Journal of Operations Management*, Vol. 58–59, pp. 42–58. 10.1016/j.jom.2018.04.001

Spencer, L. and Dale, A. (1979), "Integration and Regulation in Organizations: A Contextual Approach", *Sociological Review*, Vol. 27, No. 4, pp. 679–702.

Strauss, A. and Corbin, J. (1990), *Basics of Qualitative Research: Grounded Theory Procedures and Techniques*, Sage, Newbury Park, California.

Trentin, A., Forza, C., and Perin, E. (2015), "Embeddedness and Path Dependence of Organizational Capabilities for Mass Customization and Green Management: A Longitudinal Case Study in the Machinery Industry", *International Journal of Production Economics*, Vol. 169, pp. 253–276.

Turner, B. A. (1981), "Some Practical Aspects of Qualitative Data Analysis: One Way of Organising the Cognitive Processes Associated With the Generation of Grounded Theory", *Quality and Quantity*, Vol. 15, pp. 225–247.

Turner, B. A. (1983), "The Use of Grounded Theory for the Qualitative Analysis of Organizational Behaviour", *Journal of Management Studies*, Vol. 20, No. 3, pp. 333–348.

Van de Ven, A. H. (1993), "An Assessment of Perspectives on Strategic Change", in Zan, L., Zambon, S. and Pettigrew, A. M. (Eds.), *Perspectives on Strategic Change*, Kluwer Academic Press, Dordrecht, pp. 313–325.

Van de Ven, A. H., Angle, H. L. and Poole, M. S. (1989), *Research on the Management of Innovation*, Ballinger, Cambridge, MA.

Van de Ven, A. H. and Huber, G. P. (1990), "Longitudinal Field Research Methods for Studying Processes of Organizational Change", *Organization Science*, Vol. 1, No. 3, pp. 213–219.

Van de Ven, A. H. and Poole, M. S. (1990), "Methods for Studying Innovation Development in the Minnesota Innovation Research Program", *Organization Science*, Vol. 1, No. 3, pp. 313–335.

Van Maanen, J. (1979), "The Fact of Fiction in Organizational Ethnography", *Administrative Science Quarterly*, Vol. 24, No. 4, pp. 539–550.

Voss, C. A. (1988), "Implementation: A Key Issue in Manufacturing Technology: The Need for a Field of Study", *Research Policy*, Vol. 17, pp. 53–63.

Weick, K. E. (1989), "Theory Construction as Disciplined Imagination", *Academy of Management Review*, Vol. 14, No 4, pp. 516–531.

Yin, R. K. (1989), *Case Study Research: Design and Methods* (Revised Edition), Sage, London.

Zelditch, M. Jr. (1962), "Some Methodological Problems of Field Studies", *American Journal of Sociology*, Vol. 67, pp. 566–576.

7 Action research

Paul Coughlan and David Coghlan

Chapter overview

7.1 Introduction

Action research is a generic term, which covers many forms of action-oriented research. It acknowledges diversity in theory and practice among action researchers, so providing a wide choice for potential action researchers as to what approach might be appropriate for their research question. Action research (AR) is an established and active field of scholarly activity and practice, constantly developing. The *Sage Encyclopaedia of Action Research* (Coghlan and Brydon-Miller, 2014) includes 300+ contributions, each of contemporary and historical applications of action research. It joins (and is joined by) academic journals, handbooks (Reason and Bradbury, 2001, 2008; Bradbury, 2015) and a four-volume series titled *Action Research in Business and Management* (Coghlan and Shani, 2016). In contemporary action research there is a wide diversity in both practice and in the discourse on action research practice. Action research has come to be understood as a family of practices expressed through modalities which emphasise

DOI: 10.4324/9781003315001-7

different assumptions, contexts and starting points (Coghlan, 2010). The outcomes of action research are both an action and research-based knowledge which contrast with traditional positivist science, which aims at creating knowledge only. Action research has applicability to unstructured or integrative issues. It has broad relevance to practitioners where it can contribute actionable knowledge and it can contribute to theory. This chapter explores the themes, challenges and layers of choice facing operations management and supply chain management (OSCM) researchers as they attempt to enquire into the practice of designing, running, evaluating and improving operating systems. We introduce AR at two levels: a broad and generic set of principles and characteristics; and application of those principles in the context of the operation within the firm or network. The distinction is of value. The field of AR is evolving and, as scholars focus their efforts on the further development of the methodology or its application in new and different contexts (situations and disciplines), so also the range and depth of choice available to the OSCM researcher expands (Shani and Coghlan, 2021a).

7.2 Action in operations and supply chains

In operations and supply chains, something happens. Inputs are converted into outputs and there is an interconnection between the operating model, the business model and the social model. The operation to be managed may focus on achieving a market share, a cost target, community acceptance, a quality outcome, an environmental impact or some combination of objectives. Regardless, the operations and supply chain manager has a role as an actor in directing, developing and deploying the operating model where achievement of outputs, operational improvements and learning from experience depend upon on the manager's experience-based understanding of the system. The learning here is key to the achievement of both the next order cycle and the systematic improvements in the way in which the operation is designed, run and evaluated. This learning and improvement through action casts the operations manager as a researcher from the inside who may collaborate with suppliers, customers and academic researchers.

7.3 What is action research?

Action research may be defined as:

> … an emergent inquiry process in which applied behavioural science knowledge is integrated with existing organizational knowledge and applied to address real organizational issues. It is simultaneously concerned with bringing about change in organizations, and developing self-help competencies in organizational members and adding to scientific knowledge. Finally, it is an evolving process that is undertaken in a spirit of collaboration and co-inquiry.
>
> (Coghlan and Shani, 2018: 4)

7.3.1 Critical themes

Critical themes constitute action research: as an emergent inquiry process it engages in an unfolding narrative, where data shift as a consequence of intervention and where it is not possible to predict or to control what takes place. It focuses on real operations issues or problems, rather than issues created particularly for the purposes of research. It is applied in multiple organizational settings and disciplines and engages with applied behavioural and organisational science knowledge (Shani and Coghlan, 2021a).

Coghlan and Shani (2018) present a comprehensive framework in terms of four factors.

- *Context*: These factors set the context of the action research project. Environmental factors in the global and local economies provide the larger context that drives the imperative for action and within which action research takes place. Internally organizational characteristics, such as resources, history, formal and informal organizations and the degrees of congruence between them affect the readiness and capability for participating in action research.
- *Quality of relationships:* The quality of relationship between members of the system and researchers in collaborating to address the issue and to cogenerate knowledge is paramount. Hence the relationships need to be managed through trust, concern for other, equality of influence and common language.
- *Quality of the action research process:* The quality of the process is grounded in the dual focus on both the inquiry process and the implementation process.
- *Outcomes:* The dual outcomes of action research are some level of sustainability (human, social, economic ecological) and the development of self-help and competencies out of the action and the creation of actionable theory through the action and inquiry.

7.3.2 Philosophy of action research

Kurt Lewin (1891–1947) is considered to be one of the founders of action research. For Lewin, it was not enough to try to explain things; one also had to try to change them. This insight led to the development of action research and the powerful notion that human systems could only be understood and changed if one involved the members of the system in the inquiry process itself. Action research was based on two assumptions: involving the clients or learners in their own learning, not only produces better learning but more valid data about how the system really works; and, one only understands a system when one tries to change it, as changing human systems often involves variables which cannot be controlled by traditional research methods (Schein, 2010).

Susman and Evered (1978) argue that the conditions from which people try to learn in everyday life are better explored through a range of philosophical viewpoints: Aristotelian praxis, hermeneutics, existentialism, pragmatism, process philosophies and phenomenology. They proposed that action research provides a corrective to the deficiencies of positivist science by being future-oriented, collaborative, agnostic and situational implying system development and, so, generating theory grounded in action. Coghlan (2011, 2016) grounds action research in a philosophy of practical knowing which was neglected by philosophers and the academy when they turned to problems of the objectivity of knowing.

An added dimension to the engagement in practical knowing as a philosophy of research is that it involves researching in the present tense (Coghlan and Shani, 2017). Much of what we refer to as qualitative research is focused on the past. Action research builds on the past and takes place in the present with a view to shaping the future. Accordingly, engagement in the cycles of action and reflection perform both practical and philosophical functions in its attentiveness and reflexivity as to what is going on at any given moment and how that attentiveness yields purposeful action.

Action research shares features of transdisciplinary collaboration, reflexivity and an orientation to cogenerating actionable knowledge, that is, knowledge which is both useful to practitioners, theoretically robust for scholars and that can serve simultaneously the needs of a living system and the scientific community (Adler and Shani, 2005). These features contrast with what Gibbons, Limoges, Nowotny, Schartzman, Scott and Trow (1994) call Mode 1 research which is characterised by explanatory knowledge generated in a disciplinary context, which for many is 'identical with what is meant by science'. The canons of Mode 1 science aim to create of universal knowledge or covering law within a disciplinary field. Findings are validated by logic, measurement and the consistency achieved by the consistency of prediction and control. The scientist's relationship to the setting is one of neutrality and detachment. MacLean, MacIntosh and Grant (2002) locate action research in Mode 2. Gibbons et al. describe Mode 2 research as 'the new production of knowledge' as a network activity, where knowledge is created in the context of application and is transdisciplinary and reflexive,. As Gustavsen (2003) has argued, action research has been enacting Mode 2 knowledge production long before the term was articulated.

7.3.3 Characteristics of action research

The distinctive characteristic of action research is that it addresses the twin tasks of bringing about change in organisations and in generating robust, actionable knowledge, in an evolving process that is undertaken in a spirit of collaboration and co-inquiry, whereby research is constructed with people, rather than on or for them. Further characteristics are that it seeks to contribute to the realm of practical knowing including decisions and actions by practitioners in order to improve situations and that it involves researching in the present tense.

Coghlan and Shani (2018) lay out ten major characteristics of action research, each of which has implications for the execution of action research and the action researcher. We present and discuss each in the context of operations management.

- *Action researchers take action.* Action researchers are not merely observing something happening; they are actively working at making it happen. In OSCM, the actions, for example, may be in such areas as process modification, methods improvement, workforce organisation, capital-for-labour substitution, product modification, materials substitution or supplier change.
- *Action research always involves two goals*: to address a practical issue and to contribute to science. Action research is about research in action and does not postulate a distinction between theory and action. Hence the challenge for action researchers is to engage in taking action and contributing to practice, in standing back from the action and reflecting on it as it happens in order to contribute theory to the body of knowledge. In OSCM, for example, the practical issue may be to exploit digital technologies as digitization to replace discrete processes or tools with digital analogues, or as digitalization through using digital information to revisit intra and inter-organizational decision-making, processes and architectures (Holmström, Holweg, Lawson, Pil, and Wagner, 2019). The contribution to practice may be to encapsulate OSCM information digitally for transfer across actors, and to permit control of open and interactive systems. The contribution to knowledge may be an understanding of impact on processes over the product life cycle.

- *Action research is interactive.* In action research, the action researcher and the firm's personnel are co-researchers working to resolve or to improve the firm's issue, and to contribute to the body of knowledge (Shani, Mohrman, Pasmore, Stymne and Adler, 2008; Shani and Coghlan, 2021b). As action research is a series of unfolding and unpredictable events, the co-researchers need to work together and to be able to adapt to the contingencies of the unfolding story.
- *Action research aims at developing holistic understanding* during a project and recognising complexity. As organizations are dynamic socio-technical systems, action researchers need to have a broad view of how the system works and to be able to move between formal structural, technical and informal people subsystems (Pasmore, 2001). In OSCM, the action researcher works with organizational systems and requires an ability to work with dynamic complexity (Senge, 1990) arising from multiple causes and effects over time.
- *Action research is fundamentally about change.* Action research is applicable to the understanding, planning and implementation of change in operations. Over time, an operation in a competitive environment has to improve along many competitive dimensions including quality, speed, dependability, flexibility and cost (Slack and Lewis, 2015). As action research is fundamentally about change, knowledge of and skill in the dynamics of organizational change are necessary. Such knowledge informs how an operation, as a large system, recognises the need for change, articulates a desired outcome from the change and actively plans and implements how to achieve that desired future (Coghlan, 2019).
- *Action research requires an understanding of the ethical framework*, values and norms within which it is used in a particular context (Coghlan and Shani. 2005; Holian and Coghlan, 2013; Coghlan, 2019). In action research, ethics is grounded in the authentic relationships between the action researcher and the members of the firm as to how they understand the process and take significant action Coghlan and Shani, 2018. Values and norms that flow from such ethical principles typically focus on how the action researcher works with the members of the organisation. In OSCM, people, and not just systems and procedures, are the focus of managerial attention. For example, actions taken towards socially sustainable sourcing (Benstead, Hendry and Stevenson, 2018) may impact directly and indirectly on the roles, responsibilities, relationships, accountabilities and actionabilities of people and, so, raise ethical dilemmas. Inquiring into such dilemmas through action research carries the challenge of acting so as not to increase the power of the more powerful over the less powerful.
- *Action research can include all types of data gathering methods.* Action research does not preclude the use of data gathering methods applied in traditional research. Qualitative and quantitative tools, such as interviews and surveys (as developed in Chapter 4 are commonly used. However, it must be noted that data gathering methods are themselves interventions and generate data. For example, a survey or interview may generate feelings of anxiety, suspicion, apathy and hostility or create expectations among staff. If action researchers do not attend to this and focus only on the collection of data, they may miss significant data that may be critical to the success of the project, or they may confront the data they think that they are gathering. What is important, then, in action research is that the planning and use of these methods be thought through in advance with the members of the organization and be clearly integrated into the collaborative action research design. In OSCM, differing kinds of data emerge in such decision areas as capacity, supply networks, process technology and product development, requiring inclusion of different methods. For example, in relation to capacity, relevant data may

include not just how fast capacity expansion or reduction might be pursued, but also the potential knock-on effects for staff motivation of such changes.

- *Action research requires a breadth of pre-understanding* of the corporate environment, the conditions of business, the structure and dynamics of operating systems and the theoretical underpinnings of such systems. Pre-understanding refers to the knowledge the action researcher brings to the research project. Action researchers in OSCM, therefore, need to have knowledge of operations and the level of contribution of operations to the competitive strategy of the firm, complemented by an appreciation of organisational systems and the dynamics of the operation in its contemporary business, social and environmental context. Such a need for pre-understanding signals that an action research approach is inappropriate for researchers who, for example, think that all they have to do to develop theory is just to go out into the field and look narrowly.

- *Action research should be conducted in real time,* or as Coghlan and Shani (2017) express it, in the present tense, though retrospective action research is also acceptable. While action research is being written as it unfolds, it can also take the form of a traditional case study (as discussed in Chapter 5 written in retrospect, when the written case is used as an intervention into the organization in the present. This expression of action research is called learning history (Bradbury, Roth and Gearty, 2015).

- *The action research paradigm requires its own quality criteria.* Action research should not be judged by the criteria of positivist science, but rather within the criteria of its own terms. Levin (2003) argues that the contribution of action research to scientific discourse is not a matter of sticking to the rigour-relevance polarity but of focusing on vital arguments relating to participation, real-life problems, joint-meaning construction and workable solutions. In OSCM, for example, quality research into how horizontal collaboration aids organisations in responding to modern slavery legislation may demand the participation of manufacturers, retailers and non-government organisation staff (Benstead, Hendry and Stevenson, 2018). To the extent that their collaborative efforts towards a workable solution – social sustainability improvements to enhance ethical trade and benefit vulnerable workers – are integrated and joint-meaning construction is facilitated, then the research may be deemed of high quality. We develop the notion of quality in action research later in this paper.

7.3.4 The origins of action research

Action research has many roots, some of which are in the tradition of organisational renewal that developed in western industrial economy over the past fifty years (Pasmore, 2001; Bradbury, 2015). Other roots lie outside of this setting and are grounded in emancipatory movements (Greenwood and Levin, 2007). Action research is seen now as a family of approaches, rather than as a single unitary concept where there is only one way of conducting it. For instance, action research in the context of organizational improvement necessarily embodies different emphases than action research undertaken in the context of social exclusion. The family of approaches is grounded in the ten major characteristics presented above and variation occurs through context and emphasis.

As noted earlier, action research originates primarily in the work of Kurt Lewin and his colleagues and associates. In the mid-1940s, Lewin and his associates conducted action research projects in different social settings. Through the following decades, action research in organisations grew into what became recognised as organization development

(OD), particularly in the United States (Coghlan and Shani, 2018). One of the best-known organizational action research studies explored the problems a manufacturing plant was having with employee injuries and how, through action research, the issues were addressed through employee participation (Pasmore and Friedlander, 1982).

The socio-technical work of the Tavistock Institute originated in the United Kingdom in the field of coal mining and then extended to other industries in India, Sweden and the United States (Trist and Murray, 1993; Pasmore 2001; Weisbord, 2012). The learning from these research initiatives is that social and technical perspectives on work are interdependent and that organisational and work design needs to optimise both.

7.3.5 *What action research is not*

Action research is based on collaboration between the researcher and the client on intervening in the organization (the action), exploring issues and generating data on the development of the organization (the research activity). They construct the meaning of the issues at hand and co-develop action plans to address these issues and implement change. Together they evaluate the outcomes of the actions, both intended and unintended. This evaluation may then lead to further cycles of examining issues, planning action, taking action and evaluation. Cyclical-sequential phases may be identified that capture the movements of collaboration through planning and action to evaluation and to theory development or generation.

The action research process of engaging in cycles of action and reflection parallels similar processes in the fields of experiential learning, project management, prototyping and quality improvement. But they should not be confused. Action research may be conducted in such fields and may use their methods (Whitehead, 2005; Coghlan, Shani & Coughlan, 2022). The fundamental difference is in the use of the term research. Action research has intended implications beyond those involved directly in it and has an explicit aim to develop or generate theory as well as to be useful to the organization. A similar contrast may be made with consulting. Action research has many characteristics that are found in consulting, particularly in what is called organization development (OD) but as noted above, action research is also researching the organization and is aiming to develop or generate theory. Typically, theory generation is not the focus for consulting.

Design Science Research (DSR) merits mention also. Design science is an approach to knowledge production aimed primarily at discovery and problem solving as opposed to accumulation of theoretical knowledge (Holmström and Hameri, 2009). DSR is "a domain-independent research strategy focused on developing knowledge on generic actions, processes and systems to address field problems or to exploit promising opportunities. It aims at improvements based on a thorough understanding of these problems or opportunities" (van Aken, Chandrasekaran and Halman, 2016: 8). The roots of DSR are in design activities aimed at solving problems and testing original solutions in engineering and architecture settings. In contrast, the roots of action research are in organizational renewal and development. DSR may describe a new method for artefact design, intervene to change an organization by designing a solution to a perceived (sometimes artificial) organizational problem, or build design capability in an organization. In contrast, action research focuses on solving a practical problem while contributing to science. Collaboration, intervention, inquiry and co-creation of meaning characterise the action research process. DSR often addresses a specific organizational issue or process, frames the study in terms of design theory, investigates the issue using specific research methods (such as observation, simulation or intervention), and tests the emerging research results. Further, the design research scientist must be able both to generalise the findings and demonstrate a theoretical contribution (Holmström and Hameri, 2009). Finally, DSR seeks to develop generic knowledge to support organizational improvement actions. In contrast, action research aims for situation specific actionable knowledge.

7.4 What is needed before selecting action research

Before selecting action research, the researcher needs to consider the practical needs of the operation in relation to the expectations of the academic research education programme, as a potential research opportunity.

7.4.1 Positioning in relation to the needs of the operation

Essentially, three things are needed to position the action research in relation to the needs of the operation: a real issue, access and a contract. A *real issue*, such as integrating sustainability issues with lean operations and supply chains (Piercy and Rich, 2015), must be of managerial significance. It must have an uncertain outcome and the group or organization must be willing to subject their action on the issue to rigorous inquiry, particularly the analysis and implementation of action. Finally, it must have research significance for the researcher. Study of this issue cannot be carried out from a distance (or, indeed, the researcher's office). Rather, the action researcher has to *gain physical access* to the operation and to be contracted as an action researcher. The access may result from a request by the researcher (or supervisor) to inquire into a practice within the operation. Alternatively, this access may result from an invitation from the organization to the academic supervisor to help. Developing the *contract*, a key element of the pre-step (defined in the following section), and execution of the contract requires recognition of the different stakeholders in the issue, their differing expectations of interrelationships, process and outcomes; interaction with the stakeholders in real time; data gathering and data generating opportunities; and confidence that stakeholders can be relied upon to engage in joint-exploration of the issue. The stakeholders (as parties to this contract) include the key members of the organization who recognise the value of the action research approach and are willing (and, indeed, tolerant) to have the action researcher working with them through inquiring into the real issue, reflecting on it and generating shared insights as they progress towards workable solutions. The acknowledgement of this willingness and tolerance forms the basis for how the collaborative relationships unfold ethically.

7.4.2 Positioning in relation to the academic research education programme

When the action researcher is enrolled in an academic education programme, such as one leading to a masters or a doctorate, it is useful to note that two action research projects co-exist in parallel (Zuber-Skerritt and Perry, 2002). First, there is the *core* action research project which is the project on which the student researcher is working within the operation. This project has its own identity and may proceed, irrespective of whether or not it is being studied. As this project addresses a real issue within the organization and is driven by organisational needs, it may represent an opportunity for the student researcher to tap into an already active agenda for action and change. The project may also be funded externally and carry with it a timescale and deliverables which are independent of the academic research programme. Second, there is also the *thesis* action research project.

This project involves the action researcher's inquiry into the core project and is the opportunity to demonstrate his/her doctorateness through synergy across:

- Deep discipline knowledge with a clear contribution
- High levels of competence in research skills with appropriate choice of methodology and explicit research design.
- Competence in presentation of argument with engagement with theory and conceptual conclusions (Coghlan, Coughlan, and Shani, 2019).

This distinction is useful as it is the thesis project which will be submitted for examination, rather than the core project. While the core project may be successful or unsuccessful, it is the researcher's inquiry into the process (rather than the outcome) and the associated contribution to OSCM knowledge which merits the academic award the student researcher is pursuing.

7.5 Designing the thesis action research project

The previous section positioned the action research project in relation to the academic programme and the needs of the organisation. As with any research, designing the thesis project confronts the researcher with challenges of framing the issue, determining its scope, gaining access, contracting and building collaborative relationships.

7.5.1 Framing the thesis research issue

Framing and selecting the thesis research issue from the core issue is a complex process (Coghlan, 2019). To frame the issue is to categorise it within a field. An initial framing may not reflect the conceptual breadth or depth of the issue and, so, re-framing follows. Finally, the scale, scope and temporal nature of the issue may extend beyond the boundaries of a single thesis research project and may even support a number of thesis researchers at the same time.

In OSCM, there are many and complex connections between inputs, transformations and outputs. There may appear to be a wide and diverse set of issues all vying for management attention. Some issues may be obvious, such as cost overruns, while others may go unnoticed, such as waste from inflexible response capability, unless attempts are made to uncover organisational members' perceptions of these core issues. Not every issue will volunteer itself automatically for resolution or, indeed, research. It is human construction that makes the difference thus leading us to conclude that organisational actors' interpretations are pivotal. Further, the organization may have framed the issue sufficiently to invite the academic supervisor to provide help. A researcher's response to this invitation brings the research into the category of clinical research. Alternatively, the organization may respond to the offer of the researcher to enquire into an issue. An organisation's response to this latter invitation brings the research into the category of traditional action research.

7.5.2 Determining the scope

For the action researcher, the questions of who selects the scope of the thesis project, who provides access and who is involved in it are important, as they are in any thesis research. In this sense, determining the scope is through and part of an ongoing conversation, not just with the managers in the organisation, but also with the supervisor who has a mentoring relationship with the researcher, or with the team members in a funded research project who may be engaged in their own thesis research. It is in the conversation with supervisor that the distinction between the master's and doctoral scope may be evident. For the master's thesis, the scope should enable the identification of a phenomenon and replication of an intervention, perhaps in a new context. In contrast, for the doctoral researcher, the scope should enable an original contribution to knowledge.

7.5.3 Gaining access

For the action researcher working towards a masters or a doctorate, access may come through the university and more specifically through the academic supervisor. Such access may fit with the notion of clinical inquiry where the organization may invite the experienced professor to help it and pay the university department, and the professor supervises the doctoral student to facilitate and engage with the operation. Two types of access are relevant: primary and secondary. Primary access refers to the ability to get into the operation and to contract to undertake action research. Secondary access refers to access to specific areas within the operation or specific levels of information and activity.

Action researchers may play one of two roles in an action research project: outside agent and insider. Roles are patterns of behaviour which individuals expect of others performing specific functions or tasks. The two roles are related but different. More commonly, action researchers are outside agents who act as facilitators of the action and reflection within an organisation. In this role, the action researcher is acting as an external helper, working in a facilitative manner to help the managers or staff to inquire into their own issues and create and implement solutions (Schein, 1995, 2008). This role contrasts with the expert model as in the doctor-patient model (Schein, 2009) where patients go to doctors for expert diagnosis and prescriptive direction.

There is also a growing incidence of action research being done from within organisations by insiders, as when practising managers undertake action research projects in and on their own organisations (Coghlan, 2001; Coghlan, 2019). This role is increasingly common in the context of managers participating in academic programmes. For example, Powell and Coughlan (2020) explored how suppliers can learn to learn as part of a buyer-led collaborative lean transformation initiative over a three year period. Access was assured as one of the authors was responsible for developing and deploying the global lean production program in the focal organization. The quality of access enabled the researchers to distinguish between learning about and implementing lean best practices and adopting a learning-to-learn perspective to build organisational capabilities, consistent with lean thinking and practice. In such contexts, where the manager takes on the role of researcher in addition to regular organisational roles, he/she should find access, both primary and secondary, easier. The other participants are likely to include subordinates, partners and colleagues whose buy-in to the project is necessary. In addition, the manager is likely to have a personal stake in the outcome of the project.

7.5.4 Contracting

For the action researcher, there is potential role ambiguity and role conflict as different expectations from the organization and the university may make different and conflicting demands on the action researcher (Coghlan and Shani, 2005). In operations, the typical focus is on delivering a product or service to today's customer, while considering also the possible requirements of tomorrow's customer. In that sense, the orientation is towards the task, the individual operators or managers, and the formal and informal systems which enable the individuals to carry out the task. What may not be so typical is reflection on the task and even inquiry into the integration opportunities derived from the task where the aim, priority, rationale, resourcing or achievement may be of interest. For example, Ellwood, Williams and Egan (2022) explored medical technology development across the often called "Valley of Death". Their action research involved working over a period of eighteen months with programme-level managers, as well as project managers who co-ordinated teams of scientists, clinicians, and commercial partners. Engagement brought together different threads of activity in order to articulate a clinical value proposition. The researchers became a resource that project teams could exploit to integrate knowledge that otherwise might not have been possible.

This then is the world into which the aspiring (or seasoned) action researcher steps. Here, the invitation, if there is one, or the acceptance of an offer to research, may be associated with the development of an agenda for some individual or group and, so, expectations of the researcher may be set even before the first visit. Accordingly, negotiating a role whereby the action researcher can engage in the thesis project, while engaging in the core project, is a necessary early step – and one to which the researcher will need to return. The role may be misunderstood, there may be conflict and ambiguity. In addition, the university may have its expectations. Further, there may be events or episodes which challenge the originally-negotiated role and lead to re-negotiation. There is no assurance that the original role may be salvaged and, so, the research may end.

7.6 Implementing action research

Action research is research *with* rather than *on* or *for* the organisation. Accordingly, implementing the action research design developed through the preceding steps requires building collaborative relationships in order to engage in cycles of planning, action and evaluation for both the core and thesis research projects is central.

7.6.1 Building collaborative relationships

Within the organisation, change projects of a strategic or operational nature may be ongoing in many domains of activity, and in parallel. One, some or all of these projects may be of interest or relevance to the action researcher. These projects may be directed by a senior management group that develops the focus and priority while deploying resources to implement the desired changes. Central to maintaining the researcher's role is building collaborative relationships with these key members of the organisation. These relationships help to identify the learning mechanisms that led to and house the change project. Learning mechanisms typically refer to planned organisational structures and processes that encourage dynamic learning, particularly to enhance organisational capabilities. The mechanisms can apply at individual, group, organisational or inter-organisational levels and can aim to initiate, facilitate, monitor and reward learning. Shani and Docherty (2008) present three types of learning mechanism: cognitive, structural and procedural. As such, the building of relationships occurs within the learning mechanisms and the organisation, and between the learning mechanisms and the organisation.

Within the firm, the action researcher works with teams or groups of insiders that both own the core AR project issue or process and also are engaged in new knowledge creation. In addition, the action researcher may work with a project steering group or other task force or team with a controlling interest in the project. In the core AR project, the action researcher participates in the steering group that is established by senior management and led by managers designated to be project leaders. These groups are essential for the action researcher as they drive the core project and provide the researcher with valuable insider knowledge. The action researcher's role in such a group is to assist the group in advancing the assigned tasks. This is a subordinate role; the action researcher is not running this agenda and is not in control of it.

In contrast, the action researcher should have a thesis action research project group that can assist the researcher in reflecting on the emerging insights, knowledge and learning. In this latter group, the action researcher is the leader or convener; the action researcher is running this agenda and is in control of it. The members are both interested in the reflection and learning, are well connected across the organization or university, value both their own judgements and that of the action researcher and understand the process of action research.

For example, Le Dain, Calvi and Cheriti (2011) focused on the evaluation of the supplier's performance in collaborative design. Their main research questions were:

- What should the customer firms that involve suppliers in their NPD phases evaluate to achieve and sustain the suppliers' co-design effort?
- How can the dynamic (nature) of customers' requirements during the project be taken into account in this performance assessment?

Their goal was to build generic actionable knowledge, that is, knowledge taking the form of generic propositional statements and/ or principles that are mutually consistent for both researchers and practitioners. Because action research addressed the theme of research in action, they adopted this approach in the co-construction by researchers and practitioners of actionable knowledge on a supplier performance evaluation. They conducted the research over two phases:

- Phase I: construction of a preliminary supplier performance evaluation framework: cycles of literature review, data gathering and data analysis, leading to a preliminary framework
- Phase II: development of the framework: they sought feedback on the functionality and the completeness of the framework with the objective of improving it. Working sessions discussed and built user understanding and insights were shared. An action researcher was present at each workshop to host the discussions and to collect feedback. All remarks were taken into account for the elaboration of the framework.

7.6.2 *The action research cycle*

Implementing action research involves implementing two related but different projects: the core action project and the thesis research project. Each goes through cycles of planning, action and evaluation.

For the researcher, the core project is located in the world of practice and may be understood in terms of key concepts and relationships drawn from the literature of OSCM.

Familiarity with this literature and knowledge of operations practice are pre-requisites for engaging in the thesis action research based upon the core project. Research-based inquiry into the core project through action research (the thesis project) may be framed as cycles of action and reflection matching the core project as it develops iteratively. Engaging in such cycles places action at the heart of the research process and thereby marks action research as fundamentally distinct from research approaches that are typically referred to as 'applied'. In action research, the managers/operators and the thesis researcher are co-researchers. It is through the collaborative study of cycles of action and reflection that the actionable knowledge from the core project is generated, and the thesis project develops.

The concept of cycle has an intellectual heritage. Practitioners think and talk about product life cycles, operations improvement cycles involving plan-do-check-act, and operations improvement cycles of co-direct – co-develop – co-deploy (Coughlan and Coghlan, 2011). Correspondingly in action research, in its original Lewinian and simplest form (Lewin, 1997) the action research cycle comprises a pre-step and three core activities: planning action, taking action and fact-finding:

- The pre-step involves naming the general objective and questions the rationale for the action and for the research.
- Planning comprises having an overall plan and a decision regarding what the first step to take is.
- Action involves taking that first step
- Fact-finding involves evaluating the first step, seeing what was learned and creating the basis for correcting the next step.

So there is a continuing 'spiral of steps, each of which is composed of a circle of planning, action and fact-finding about the result of the action' (Lewin, 1997: 146). While these cycles may be presented differently (e.g. Coghlan, 2019; Stringer and Ortiz Aragon, 2020), any presentation captures the essential elements of the original Lewinian framework. In working within the realm of practical knowing where knowing is always incomplete, engaging in and paying attention to these cycles is paramount.

Integral to the engagement in cycles of action and reflection is the process of abductive reasoning. The American philosopher, Charles Peirce describes three forms of reasoning: deductive, inductive and abductive. Deductive reasoning draws on generalizable theory to craft particular arguments whereas inductive reasoning proceeds from particular observations to clarify more generalizable theory. Abductive reasoning expresses the form of reasoning that takes place as the action research progresses through the collaborative cycles of action and reflection as they unfold in the present tense in anticipation of more definite answers when the research is completed (Shani, Coghlan and Alexander, 2020); Saetre and Van de Ven, 2021).

Figure 7.1 presents an action research cycle comprising a pre-step and four main steps - constructing, planning action, taking action and evaluating action (Coghlan and Shani, 2018; Coghlan, 2019). The thesis research project involves a series of such cycles.

Although such cycles of action and reflection are central to the practice of action research, they need not be enacted in a rigid manner but may find expression in an imaginative and expressive approach (Heron, 1996). Coghlan (2019) present the outcomes of the cycles of action and reflection as generating content, process and premise learning, the third area being the fruit of critical thinking.

We discuss each of the steps in turn.

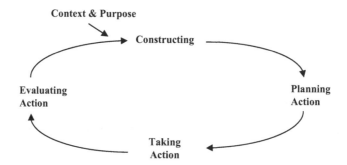

Figure 7.1 The action research cycle.

Source: Coghlan, 2019: 9.

7.7 Pre-step: Context and purpose

The pre-step may coincide with the preparation of the thesis proposal and, so, forms the basis for the research which follows. The thesis action research cycle unfolds in real time and begins with an understanding of the context. The pre-step is characterised by two questions:

• What is the rationale for the core action?
• What is the rationale for the thesis research?

The sequence of these questions illustrates the essential link: without the core action, there is no opportunity for the thesis research in that context.

7.7.1 What is the rationale for the core action?

The core project unfolds in real time and requires a clear rationale for action. The firm may be clear in its own terms on why it needs to engage in the action and why now. The action may be grounded in a strategic operations orientation to improve the competitive positioning of the firm through developing the economics, innovativeness, responsiveness or lean nature of its operations. The firm may be embarking on a process that involves the directing of the change, the development of capabilities to implement and embed the change, and the deployment of those capabilities in the market. The process may involve customers or suppliers, introducing a layer of organisational complexity to the core action. At the same time, the researcher needs to interact with key members of the organization to develop a practical knowing and understanding of the context of the core action project, in particular the necessity and desirability of the project. In preparation for that, the researcher needs to become familiar with the industry in which the firm is competing and the position of the firm within that industry. An outcome of the pre-step is securing access and consolidating a recognised role for the action researcher.

7.7.2 What is the rationale for the thesis research?

Just because it is necessary for the firm to engage in the proposed action does not mean that it holds the potential to contribute new knowledge of value in thesis research terms.

The complementary question is to ask what the rationale for the research is and, in particular, the rationale for the thesis action research project. So, for example, the researcher might ask:

- Why is the core action project worth studying?
- Is there a thesis research project in prospect and at what level – master's or doctorate?
- What is the underlying research question?
- How is action research an appropriate methodology to adopt? What is my philosophical position?
- What is the level of existing knowledge of topic, what is the role of existing theory, and what contribution to knowledge is the thesis project expected to make?
- What might be suitable levels of analysis?
- Are there likely to be problems of access?
- What will my involvement be in the research setting?
- What level of control will I have over the research process?
- How will I achieve research that is rigorous, reflective, relevant and ethical?
- As a researcher, what skills will I need?

7.8 Main steps

There are four main steps. We introduce each in turn.

7.8.1 Constructing

Constructing involves naming the issues, however provisionally, as a working theme – such as improving supplier collaboration - on the basis of which action will be planned and taken. It involves articulating the theoretical foundations of action – such as seeing collaboration as a process in its own right - it needs to be done carefully and thoroughly. While the construction may change in later iterations of the action research cycle, any such changes need to be recorded and articulated clearly, showing how events in practice have led to the alternative construction (on which further action is to be based) and presenting the evidence and rationale for the new construction. It is important that the constructing step be collaborative where the action researcher engages relevant others– such as the supply chain managers, suppliers and customers – in the process of constructing and does not act as the expert who does the constructing apart from others.

Data are central to constructing. There are what are sometimes referred to as "hard" data. These data are gathered through performance statistics such as frequency of engineering engagement, improvement in development interval, or reduction of waste. Then there are "soft" data, such as supplier expectations of trust and perceptions of sustainability in the supply relationship. The supposed "softness" lies in the often subjective nature of these data and, consequently, may be more difficult to interpret.

While some data are gathered through established systems of performance measurement, data are also generated through the process of inquiry itself. For the action researcher, data generation comes through active involvement in the day-to-day organisational and operational processes relating to the core project. Not only are data generated through participation in and observation of individuals and teams at work, through problems being solved and decisions being made, but also through interventions made to advance the core project. People's responses to these interventions generate further data. For example, hesitancy to adopt a particular course of action may illustrate reticence to novelty or an underlying attitude that hitherto was hidden. Accordingly, the action researcher has to be sensitive to and able to work in the context of, and even to address, such hesitancy. Some of these observations and interventions are made in formal settings – meetings and interviews; others are made in informal settings – over coffee, lunch and other recreational settings. The data are always available.

The critical aspect of data review and analysis in the constructing step is that it is collaborative - both the researcher and, for example, the core project team, the supplier, a customer group, do it together. This collaborative approach is based on the assumption that the team knows their organization best, knows what will work, and, ultimately, will be the ones to implement, own and follow-through on whatever actions will be taken. Hence, their involvement in the analysis is critical. The criteria and tools for analysis need to be talked through openly, critiqued and linked directly to the purpose of the thesis research and the aim of the core project.

7.8.2 Planning action

Planning the action to be taken in the core project follows from the construction of the issue in the context and purpose of the project. A key question is where to start. It may be that this action planning focuses on a first step or a series of steps. The managers and project leaders are the key actors in this action planning. As Coghlan and Shani (2018)) advise, their key questions may focus on:

- What needs to change?
- In what parts of the organization?
- What types of change are required?
- On what timescale?
- Whose support is needed?
- How commitment is to be built?
- How resistance is to be managed?

These questions are critical and need to be answered as part of the core project change plan. For example, for an organization planning to develop its lean capabilities, it may identify the timescale over which relevant processes need to change, schedule contact with the relevant stakeholders, anticipate the enablers and barriers to change, and identify potential sources of human and financial resources. The planning step may end with a workshop for key stakeholders at which the plan is introduced, debated and, ultimately, signed off.

In a complementary way, the thesis project requires a planning step. Planning to research while engaged in the core project develops with and follows from the core project plan. Key questions may focus on:

- What kinds of data?
- How might the data emerge and be captured? What access will be required to whom, when and on what terms?
- On what timescale?

- What will my involvement be? What meetings will I participate in? What will I do? Who can I meet within and outside of the firm?
- Whose support is needed?
- How will research and data integrity be maintained? How will I maintain trust and confidentiality?

Given the development of the two plans for the core and thesis projects, the planning step ends with the integration of the plans demonstrating agreed commitments to action and to research. The integration prepares the ground for the following step, taking action, so that research and action can proceed in a complementary way: the core action will not be held up by the research focus, while the research will be protected and both projects accommodated to each other.

7.8.3 *Taking action*

The firm takes or implements the planned core action. This action involves making the desired changes and following through on the plans in collaboration with relevant key members of the organisation. For example, in the context of collaborative improvement in the supply network, the initial action may focus on defining and setting up the project (Coughlan and Coghlan, 2011), including:

- Identify broadly-defined improvement needs
- Recruit, select and invite appropriate firms who, as suppliers to the system integrator, share or contribute to the initiative.
- Establish initial contact, explaining the purpose of the project and secure commitment to participation.
- Identify and select team members with the authority, knowledge and commitment to implement solutions.
- Identify and select a facilitator to assist with the discussion and to provide a structured approach towards reflection on progress evaluation.

The selection of the particular focus, suppliers and team may be with a view to providing the greatest insight into how the system integrator and the suppliers, individually and interactively deal with the issues and each other, while not putting the whole development project at risk of delay or non-completion. The term of the planned action may extend over one or more iterations, taking some weeks or months.

For the researcher, this is both an exciting and potentially confusing step – the "heat of battle". The core action will generate minutes of meetings, revised specifications, performance evaluations and discussion documents. In addition, the researcher will converse both socially and formally with key stakeholders. However, much of the raw data emerging from the core action may not come neatly packaged in sound-bites or summary documents. Instead, it may be evident in changing alliances, ideas expressed in firm-specific acronyms and reflections couched in nuances. The action researcher must be respectful of the political context within which the action is taking place – so "you never know who you are talking to. You are not sure if you can believe them. And, you don't know if you are getting the real story". Data sufficiency and traceability are challenges while separation of reflection from observation demand a disciplined approach to the developing theory.

7.8.4 Evaluating action

Evaluation means appraising some aspect of a change situation. "To evaluate an idea or concept or product means to judge any aspect of it that helps determine its bottom-line payoff" (Crawford, 1986: 48). It is a system and not an act characterised by a continuing flow of decisions, assessments and measurements, which are all designed to lead ultimately to a successful outcome. Such evaluation is the key to learning. Without evaluation, actions can go on and on regardless of success or failure; errors can proliferate and ineffectiveness and frustration increase. And, yet, many firms do not take the time to carry out and to learn from, for example, post-project reviews (Koners and Goffin, 2007). As Figure 7.2 illustrates, the cyclical process continues as the project moves from cycle to cycle. Evaluation at the end of a cycle feeds into the cycle following and, in particular cycles, may intensify and emphasise particular metrics over others.

For the researcher, evaluation involves reflecting on the outcomes of the core action, both intended and unintended, against the planned core purpose as a basis for a response to the underlying thesis research question. In the thesis project, reviews involve questioning what took place in the core project, how and what meanings the outcomes and process have in terms of the research project.

- Was the original constructing useful, enabling and relevant – looking back was I on the right track?
- Was the content of the action taken appropriate?
- Was the action was taken in a timely, efficient and ethical manner?
- What feeds into the next cycle of constructing, planning and action?

So, a problematic or disappointing outcome for the core project may be rich in insight from the perspective of the thesis project.

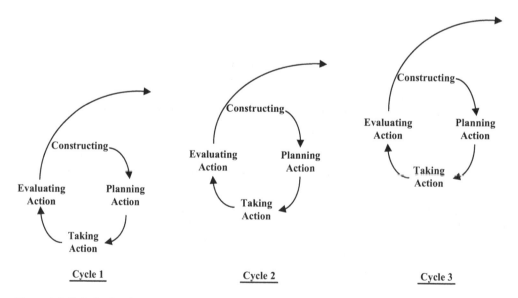

Figure 7.2 Spiral of action research cycles.

Source: Coghlan, 2019: 11.

7.9 Meta learning

The notion of meta learning, that is learning about learning, is central to the two action research projects which we discussed earlier and which are operating in parallel – the core action research project and the thesis action research project. We discuss the role of meta learning in relation to these two projects.

7.9.1 Meta learning in the core action research project

Meta learning is grounded in the process of reflection of which there are many forms. Reflection is the process of stepping back from experience to process what the experience means, with a view to planning further action. Of relevance here are Coghlan's (2019) three forms of reflection – content, process and premise – in an action research context. *Content* reflection is where the researchers think about the issues, what is happening. *Process* reflection is where they think about strategies, procedures and how things are being done. *Premise* reflection is where they critique underlying assumptions and perspectives. In action research, all three forms of reflection are critical. When content, process and premise reflections are applied to the action research cycle, they form the meta cycle of inquiry (Figure 7.3). Argyris (2003) argues that such inquiry into the steps of the cycles themselves is central to the development of actionable knowledge. It is the dynamic of this reflection on reflection that incorporates the learning process of the action research cycle and enables action research to be more than everyday problem solving. Hence it is learning about learning, in other words, meta learning.

While the stakeholders in the firm are engaging in the cycles of the core project, they need to be constructing, planning, taking action and evaluating about how the core project itself is going and what they are learning. They need to be inquiring continually into each of the four main steps in a cycle, asking how these steps are being conducted

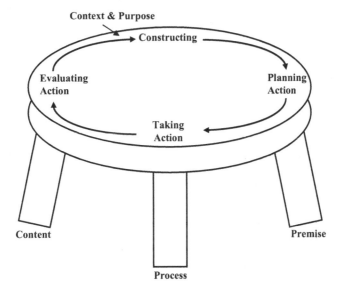

Figure 7.3 Meta-cycle of action research.

Source: Coghlan, 2019: 14.

and how they are consistent with each other, with the original purpose and, so, shaping how the subsequent steps are conducted.

The *process* of how constructing is undertaken, how action planning flows from that diagnosis and is conducted, how actions follow and are an implementation of the stated plans and how evaluation is conducted are critical foci for inquiry. In prototyping, for example, the way in which the stakeholders work together in evolving cycles of experimentation are of interest. The process may begin as a pilot concentrating on a specific product module, selected for its representation of the breadth of issues faced at the broader product level. This pilot may engage upstream and downstream groups and suppliers with the potential to inform the redesign of the broader prototyping process.

There is also *premise* reflection, which is inquiry into the unstated, and often taken for granted, underlying assumptions which govern attitudes and behaviour. Here, through action research, Bogers and Horst (2014), explored the transformative effect of collaborative prototyping on the act of prototyping. Rather than seeing the process as a set of discrete steps at the managerial level, they identified a continuous process of iterative problem solving at the designer level, which allowed participants from with and outside of the organization to see their suggestions implemented and exposing them to the design constraints.

7.9.2 Meta learning in the thesis action research project

For those action researchers who are writing a dissertation, the meta cycle is the focus of the dissertation. The dissertation is an inquiry into the core action project and, hence, action researchers need to describe both the core and thesis action research projects in a way that demonstrates the quality of rigour of the inquiry and the linkages between the two projects.

Returning to the three forms of reflection, described earlier, *content* reflection would articulate and challenge the contribution of the work to the academic and managerial communities. Implications for managerial practice might describe the locus and focus of the problematic issue(s) being tackled, the specific audience(s) to which implications are relevant, a small number of reflections on what the audience might/might not do based on the research insights and experience of the research, and lessons learned.

The *process* reflection is where the action researchers think about the research strategies, data generation procedures and how the researchers have dealt with the inevitable difficulties and opportunities which can arise in the course of an action research project. Such reflection, while different from that on content, is also a contribution to actionable knowledge.

Premise reflection is where the action researchers critique their underlying assumptions on the role of research in action on the development of actionable knowledge and outcomes for managers and researchers. Part of the basis for the underlying assumptions may include a perception of the domain of OSCM and of the boundaries of that domain. Let us return one last time to the prototyping example. If, as part of the core action initiative to improve the prototyping process, the researcher had called a meeting of stakeholders and that few of those who had accepted the invitation showed up, what assumptions would this situation challenge? Action research takes a holistic view of the operation and, so, the assumption of the isolation of the prototyping process from the political and cultural dynamics of the operation is challenged by the non-attendance. There may be a shared view among stakeholders that, as past attempts to manage this issue had failed, the issue was, essentially, intractable. Or, there may have been a reluctance to engage in an attempt to address the issue, given the likely "political" fallout from the honesty required. In this situation, the premise that the change initiative could be studied only within its own technical terms is disconfirmed and the premise broadens to include political and cultural dynamics of the operation, with implications for the researcher's perception of the OSCM domain.

7.10 Generating theory through action research

Theory is fundamental to OSCM research. Theory may or may not be the starting point for the research. However, it is intended that OSCM research can contribute to theories which are domain-specific, at least, to OSCM. The way in which theory is built from experience remains elusive. How is it done? It seems that frameworks are useful in making sense of the world. But which frameworks? What do they leave out? How accessible are they to participants? What effect does that have on participation, and in turn on actions? Action research intentionally merges theory with practice on the grounds that actionable knowledge can result from the interplay of knowledge with action. Action research demands an explicit concern with theory that is generated from the conceptualisation of the actionable knowledge associated with the particular experience in ways that are intended to be meaningful to others. Accordingly, OSCM theory generated through action research has three characteristics: it is situation specific, emergent and incremental:

- Action research does not lend itself to repeatable experimentation – each intervention will be different to the last. So, action research projects are *situation specific* and do not aim to create universal knowledge.
- Action research generates *emergent* theory, in which the theory develops from a synthesis of the understanding which emerges from reflection on the core project data and from the use in practice of the body of OSCM theory which informed the research purpose. In contrast to positivist science, where a hypothesis is defined in advance, theoretical understanding in action research unfolds through the meta learning step and the reflection on content, process and premise.
- Theory generation in the core action research project is *incremental*, moving from the individual action to the situation specific theory in small steps. A core action research project unfolds through cycles as the problematic issue(s) being tackled is confronted (or the opportunity exploited) and members of the organization attempt resolution with the help of the action researcher. The enactment of the cycles of planning, taking action and evaluating can be anticipated but cannot be designed or planned in detail in advance. The philosophy underlying action research is that the stated aims of the project lead to planning and implementing the first action, which is then evaluated. Through learning about learning, the meta step, the second action cannot be planned in detail until evaluation of the first action has taken place. Demonstrating how the theoretical outcome is trustworthy depends on the transparency of how the cycles are enacted and described.

For example, Rytter, Boer and Koch (2007) explored how to reduce problems with the ideas of manufacturing strategy – a key obstacle to the penetration of operations strategy models and methods into industrial practice and the mindsets of practitioners. The theoretical context of the research objective was an established literature in operations strategy. The research process featured a combination of action research and ethnography. The research team comprised two researchers and two representatives from industrial organisations sponsoring the project. A core strategy intervention took place over a period of nine months on a part-time basis in collaboration with managers and employees. Researchers led, conducted and participated in activities leading to the development and initial implementation of a strategy. One researcher acted as core process and work force facilitator, while conducting research in and on the core strategy process through the intervention. During the intervention period, technical-rational data were collected. In addition, researchers became aware of critical cultural and political issues that surfaced. They observed and documented actions, conducted interviews and informal conversations, and collected archival data. After the intervention period, researchers wrote an intervention narrative, identified plots and addressed technical, sociopolitical processes and performance. Developing the emerging strategy process theory would have been difficult with other less intensive case-oriented methods.

A further dimension of OMSC theorizing is how it takes places within the OM community. Scholars are formed in an academic community (or family), where senior and junior scholars and doctoral students engage through publications, conferences and seminars to build the field (Hansen and Madsen, 2019).

7.11 Quality in action research

The action research paradigm requires its own quality criteria, taking quality to mean a grade of excellence. The argument is that action research should *not* be judged by the criteria of positivist science, but rather within the criteria of its own terms. Reason (2006) argues that action research is characteristically full of choices. As action research is conducted in practice, conscious attentiveness to these choices and their consequences, and being transparent about them are significant for considering the quality of action research. Reason argues that action researchers need to be aware of the choices they face and make them clear and transparent to themselves and to those with whom they are engaging in inquiry, and to those to whom they present their research in writing or presentations. The explicit attention to these questions takes action research beyond the mere narration of events, described as "anecdotalism", to rigorous and critical questioning of experience leading to actionable knowledge for both scholarly and practitioner communities.

There are several typologies of quality. For example, Eden and Huxham (2006) list of fifteen characteristics of good action research while Levin (2003) identifies four criteria for judging the quality of action research. Pasmore, Woodman and Simmons (2008) postulate that action research needs to be *rigorous, reflective* and *relevant*. Under the *rigorous* criterion, they group: data-driven, multiple methods, reliability across settings, co-evaluation, causality, underlying mechanisms and publishability. Under r*eflection* they group: historical impact, referential, co-interpretation, community of practice, collection and repeated application. Under *relevant* they group: practical, codetermined, re-applicable, teachable, face-valid, interesting, true significance and specific. Coghlan and Shani (2018) apply these quality criteria at seven critical control (process choice) points:

1 Where the *purpose and rationale* for the core action and the thesis research, as described in the Pre-step, are firmly established to form the basis for the intended contribution to both situation specific theory and practice.
2 Where the operational, organisational and academic *context* of the research is chosen.

3 Where the *methodology and methods of inquiry* define the roles played by the researchers, how they contract with the organisation, and identify ethical issues.

4 Where the *design* of data collection and generation methods inform how cycles of action and reflection are planned and how collaborative relationships are built.

5 Where the *narrative* of events is described, including intended and unintended *outcomes*.

6 Where *reflection* on and analysis of the narrative (or story) is undertaken in the light of experience gained, judgments made and the theory.

7 Where the *discussion extrapolates* to a broader context and *articulates* the proposed contributions to both situation specific theory and practice: "Action research projects are situation specific and do not always aim to create universal knowledge. At the same time, extrapolation from a local situation to more general situations is of utmost importance. Action researchers are not claiming that every organization will behave as the one studied. But they can focus on some significant factors, consideration of which is useful for other organizations, perhaps like organizations or organizations undergoing similar types of change processes or offer a contribution to methodology.

Managing quality in action research requires foresight and a mechanism to address quality criteria continuously. Table 7.1 provides a template for managing the three quality criteria at each of the seven critical control points. The template is built around a set of illustrative questions which the researcher may pose or use as prompts designing in and assuring quality.

Depending on the focus of the core action project, exploring these dimensions involves different cycles of engagement with multiple stakeholders, such as project teams, suppliers or customers. In order to maintain quality, action researchers must consciously and deliberately enact these action research cycles, testing their own assumptions and subjecting their assumptions to public testing. Correspondingly, for the thesis project, the process of gathering, generation and reflection on the data must demonstrate an explicit method and orderliness in order to generate the theoretical content of each episode and the process whereby issues are planned and implemented. Furthermore, managing quality involves being attentive as the core action project is initiated and unfolds, and engaging in shared inquiry into the planned and unanticipated events that occur throughout the implementation.

In sum and in general, action researchers need to show how they engaged in cycles of action and reflection in collaboration with others, how they accessed multiple data sources to provide contradictory and confirming interpretations, what choices were made along the way and how they were made, provide evidence of how they challenged and tested their assumptions and interpretations continuously throughout the project and how their interpretations and outcomes were challenged, supported or disconfirmed from existing literature.

In particular, the expectation of thesis research quality, against which the actual thesis may be evaluated depends upon the level of the programme in which the researcher is registered. As a doctoral student, the expectations are higher. In line with the first Salzburg Principle, the goal of doctoral education includes the nurturing of flexibility of thought, creativity and intellectual autonomy through an original, concrete research project. It is the practice of research that creates this mind-set. In contrast, the goal of master's level education, while similar, may be achieved without an original research project. As such, the purpose and rationale may be to replicate rather than to initiate action, the research design may respect the shorter time interval available for the research,

Table 7.1 Action research as rigorous, reflective and relevant. [Coghlan and Shani 2014: 529–30]

	The Essence	Rigor	Reflective	Relevant
Purpose and Rationale for Action and Inquiry	*Case for why action and research are necessary or desirable? *What contribution is intended	*Does it provide a clear rationale for inquiry and action? *To what extent the focus addresses a gap in the scientific literature? *Does it display the data to justify the purpose and rationale for the study?	*Is it linked to past research and scientific literature? *Is it linked to contemporary business and organisational issues?	Does it describe why action is necessary or desirable? (to achieve what for whom)
Context	Understanding the business, organisational and academic context	Is the contextual data captured in a scientific, systematic and holistic way?	*Does it build on past and present scientific research that is central to the focus of the study? *Does it build on past and present organisational experience that is central to the issue studied?	To what extent relevant analytical frameworks applied to understand the context?
Methodology and Method of Inquiry	*The role of the action researcher *Ethical issues *Contracting *Establish learning mechanisms	*To what extent is the process of contracting, selection of methods of action and inquiry collaborative? *To what extent are the methods and inquiry process described with sufficient details? *To what extent are alternative LMs tapestries explored? *Are appropriate modes of AR selected and justified?	*To what extent are the action and research cycles described? *To what extent is the LMs tapestry involved in the development of the methodology and inquiry method?	To what extent are the methods of action and inquiry driven by the organisation's needs and scholarly criteria?
Design	*Data collection and generation *Cycles of action research *Building relationships	*To what extent is the project designed and implemented to ensure rigor? *To what extent the data is collaboratively and rigorously generated, collected and explored?	*To what extent is the project designed and implemented collaboratively? *To what extent attention is paid to the development of the quality of the relationship?	To what extent is the research design directed to meet the organisation's needs, as well as those of academic rigor?

Narrative and Outcomes,	*Describe the story and outcomes, (intended and unintended)	*How well is the story told, with an appropriate level of detail? *To what extent are facts and values distinguished?	*To what extent does the story demonstrate collaborative inquiry and action in the present tense?	*To what extent does it captures what happened? *What were the outcomes, both intended and unintended?
Reflection on the Story and Outcomes	*Analyse story and reflection *Make judgments on the process and outcomes	*To what extent do the narrative and description of outcomes meet the standards/criteria of research?	*To what extent is the story reflected on collaboratively? *To what extent is shared meaning created? *To what extent did dialogue about meaning and possible actions among different organisational groups/units/communities of practice take place?	*To what extent are story and outcomes' meaning focused on the organisation's needs? *To what extent are story and outcomes' meaning focused on addressing the scientific needs?
Discussion • **Extrapolation to a broader context** • **Articulation of actionable knowledge.**	*Link story to theory (existing and emerging theory) *Discuss the story and outcomes *Discuss the action research process, quality of relationships and sustainability of the outcomes *Articulate contribution to both situation specific theory and practice	To what extent does the entire account (purpose/rationale, methodology and methods, design, narrative and outcomes, reflection, the quality of the action research process, the quality of relationships) contribute to knowledge and practice?	*To what extent does the entire account (purpose/rationale, methodology and methods, design, narrative, outcomes, sustainability of the outcomes and, reflection) fit the quality of the action research process and the quality of relationships?	*To what extent does the entire account (purpose/ rationale, methodology and methods, design, narrative and outcomes, reflection) contribute to actionable knowledge and sustainable outcomes for the organization and situation specific and emergent theory for scholars? *To what extent does the AR approach demonstrate returns that make the process and effort worthwhile?

and extrapolation to a broader context may not be expected. So, in summary, there are principles of action research quality, a template for managing the achievement of that quality and a contingent character to the evaluation of the resulting thesis quality depending upon the programme level – Master's or PhD.

Shani and Coghlan (2021a), in their review of action research in business and management, reflect that, in their view, published accounts have not realised action research's potential for generating robust actionable knowledge. This is because, they argue, the accounts do not demonstrate rigorous reflection on how choices were made in relation to contextual analysis, design, degrees of collaboration, implementation, review and so on. They invite readers of the article to question how the context is framed, how collaborative relationships are formed, built and sustained, how the cycles of action and reflection are enacted and how both forms of outcomes are presented.

7.12 Action research skills

Action research is a challenging approach to research because it requires confident and experienced researchers to work collaboratively in the context of the uncertainty of the unfolding story of the core project and the expectations of scholarship in the thesis project. To work as an action researcher in organisations, the researcher needs to be able to *contribute* to the core project when exposed to the reality of organisational change in real time. The researcher's collaboration with the management teams is at the heart of this contribution and the quality of the learning mechanisms developed is what can have the most impact on the organisation. In contrast, to develop the thesis project as an action researcher, the researcher needs to be able to take the *lead* in uncovering meaning, framing theoretical understanding and explanation, and communicating the emerging insights. Fulfilling these expectations requires skills in collaborating with others, in analysing data, in learning in action.

7.12.1 Collaborating with others

In the core project, the action researcher helps the project teams to identify issues, construct what they think is causing the issues, plan, implement and evaluate action and learn from the experience. Such key inter-personal inquiry and helping skills may be developed through explicit training and education. Shani and Coghlan (2021b) provide a framework for inquiry and intervention from which action researchers may draw for skill development in this area:

- Pure inquiry promotes the elicitation of the story carefully and neutrally
- Exploratory/diagnostic inquiry explores the project team's reasoning, emotions and actions as to how the team is managing the project
- Confrontive inquiry shares the researcher's own thoughts about content and process and challenges the project team to think from a new perspective

To develop the thesis project, collaboration with the thesis supervisor is of relevance. While the supervisor may not engage directly in the core project, he/she will help in guiding the inquiry to achieve at an appropriate academic level. This expectation requires skills on the part of both the student and supervisor in analysing emergent data, following the story while maintaining the research focus, interpreting political barriers and maintaining access to the core project, and learning in action.

7.12.2 *Analysing*

Analysing draws on concepts, models and methods in order to make sense of the current state of an organisation, to help find ways to solve problems, to enhance organisational effectiveness, and to contribute to theory. Correspondingly, OSCM action researchers need to have a basic knowledge of the theory and practice of operations management. From this knowledge, they need be able to select, adapt and operationalise suitable frameworks and instruments to contribute practically to the core project. In addition, the researchers need to extend theoretical knowledge at a level appropriate to their programme of study – master's or doctorate. Throughout, and with the awareness that their underlying assumptions may be challenged as the research progresses, they need to be aware that frameworks and instruments from other domains or areas of research may become relevant.

7.12.3 *Learning in action*

Learning in action is grounded in the inquiry-reflection process. It is the key to learning as it enables action researchers to develop an ability to uncover and make explicit to themselves what they planned, discovered, and achieved in practice. They need to learn how they are themselves instruments in the generation of data. Here, some of the core skills of the action researcher are in the areas of self-awareness and sensitivity to what they observe, supported by the conceptual analytic frameworks on which they base their observations and interpretations. Their inquiry can be focused outward (e.g. what is going on in the organisation, in the team?) or inward (e.g. what is going on in me?). When they inquire into what is going on, when they show people their train of thought and put forward hypotheses to be tested, when they make suggestions for action, they are generating data. People's responses (as organisational team members, fellow researchers or supervisor) to these interventions generate further data.

In action research, reflection is the activity that integrates action and research. Reflection on content, process and premise must be brought into the open so that it goes beyond the action researchers' privately-held taken-for-granted assumptions and helps them to see how their knowledge is constructed. Accordingly, action researchers need to combine advocacy with inquiry, that is, to present their inferences, attributions, opinions, viewpoints as open to testing and critique. This combination involves illustrating inferences with more directly observable data and making reasoning both explicit and publicly testable in the service of learning.

The inquiry-reflection process at the heart of learning in action, is enabled by journal keeping (Moon, 1999). A research journal keeps a systematic and regularly kept record of events, dates and people and is a record of the researcher's interpretative, self-evaluative personal experiences thoughts and feelings, with a view to trying to understand their own actions. Journals may be used as an analytic tool where data can be examined and analysed and also act as a reflective account where the researchers can tease out their interpretations of what is taking place. Throughout the core and thesis research projects, action researchers note their observations and experiences in their journal and, over time, learn to differentiate between different experiences and ways of dealing with them. Journal keeping enables integration of information and experiences which, when understood, help the action researchers to understand their reasoning processes and consequent behaviour and, so, anticipate experiences before embarking on them. Regular journal keeping imposes a discipline on the action researchers and captures their experience of key events close to when they happen and before the passage of time intervenes to change perception. While the learning journal will be a critical source of data and reflection, not everything in the journal may merit inclusion in the dissertation.

7.13 Writing an action research dissertation

For action researchers, the thesis or dissertation is an inquiry into the core action project. As a document, it is a structured, scholarly piece of writing which should describe the thesis action research cycle and demonstrate the quality of the action research. As a basis for the award of a PhD, it needs to capture and to demonstrate a philosophical perspective consistent with the intervention undertaken in the core action project; the voice of the researcher as an engaged actor, rather than a detached observer needs to be heard.

There are many elements of the structure of the action research dissertation (Coghlan, 2019; Herr and Anderson, 2014). For example, the structure may deal with the purpose and rationale of the research, the context, methodology and methods of inquiry, story and outcomes, self-reflection and learning of the action researcher, reflection on the story in the light of the experience and, finally, the extrapolation of the emergent situation specific theory and methodology to a broader context, and articulation of usable knowledge. Each of these elements needs to be treated clearly and formally. In the dissertation, some may merit a chapter, while others, like the narrative, might be spread over several chapters, depending on duration, complexity and the contribution to cycles in the research process. Of course, not every incident in the narrative may merit inclusion in the dissertation and, so, as with all such writing, maintaining a clear focus will be an ongoing concern. At the conclusion, the dissertation needs to locate the achievements as contributions to situation specific theory and practice.

7.14 Publishing/dissemination

Two books published in the past few years provide a lens through which action research publications may be viewed and presented. In one, Mirvis, Mohrman and Worley (2021) describe designing and conducting relevant research as studying the real issues, problems and demands facing organizations and the people that work in and manage them. This means generating knowledge that is a) applicable to practice, b) useful to practitioners, and c) actionable. They further advance the need to integrate the concepts of theory-driven, practice-driven, and "sweet spot" management research. A sweet spot is viewed as "[...] an ideal or most favorable location, level, area, or combination of factors for a particular activity or purpose" (p. 23). In the framework of this chapter, the context expresses the sweet spot where the imperative for action and for knowledge generation is located and where the dual outcomes of change and actionable knowledge has an impact. Creating research for impact is the topic of the second book. Here, MacIntosh, Mason, Beech and Bartunek (2021) have proposed a model of impact in management research that is "processual, contextual and that incorporates different impact types that enable the actors to make choices about how they proceed" (p.81). Action research's emphasis on the processes of addressing a real issue, of building collaborative relationships, of engaging in cycles of action and reflection the combination of which lead to dual outcomes of change and actionable knowledge as an active response to the demands of the context has the potential to create impact.

There is a growing acceptance of action research as a scholarly approach to addressing certain kinds of research question. Underpinning this acceptance is a recognition of a fundamental difference between action research and consulting: an aim to elaborate or develop theory. In OSCM, the numbers of action research-based dissertations, conference papers and journal articles are increasing. In addition, the commitment to improving the quality of action research in OSCM is evident in the methodology citations drawn from within and outside of the domain. Journals in the OSCM domain are accepting and publishing substantive content and research insights enabled by action research. Between 1986 and 2022, the *InternationalJournal of Operations and Production Management* has published forty-one papers relating to action research. Among these papers, eight have action research in the title. Of these eight papers, that by Coughlan and Coghlan (2002) explored and developed the usefulness and usability of action research in operations management and has had over twenty-two hundred citations since its publication. Of specific note is that 40 per cent of these citations have been made in the most recent five years, suggesting a continuing and increasing engagement in action research. In contrast, while JOM identified action research as an alternative research paradigm in 1989 (Meredith, Raturi, Amoako-Gyampah and Kaplan, 1989), it has published just four papers subsequently, including two based upon intervention as a research strategy. While identifying opportunities for new research directions, multi-methodological research and enhancing the practical relevance of research, Production & Operations Management has not published an action research paper. As a meeting of the OSCM community (or family), the EurOMA annual conference continues to provide an opportunity for presentation of action research-based studies. More generally, there are action research-specific journals outside of the OSCM domain where the focus is more on the action research process. Here, the OSCM content forms the setting or background for a methodological exploration. Each type of publication opportunity offers a different writing and communication challenge to the researcher, and each may be valued differently by readers. Regardless, there is a market for well-done research and action research is no different.

It is a common expectation that the doctoral dissertation will be the basis of one or more published articles. Indeed, in some institutions, the dissertation may comprise a set of already-published articles. An action research thesis may offer the prospect of articles written by the researcher, in conjunction with the supervisor or with members of the core action project team. All may be possible; the question is what to publish and where?

The thesis project is rich in publication possibilities. The central question and the new insights derived from the research is an easily recognised theme. As interesting, however, is the possibility to contribute to the process through which the focal firms or organisations engaged in the various cycles of action, the barriers they encountered and the learning achieved. In addition, the reflections of the researcher on his/her growing development in relation to the substantive content of the action project, the process engaged in and the premises challenged may be of interest to those concerned with the development of the researcher's mind-set.

7.15 Conclusions

This chapter has presented an in-depth articulation of action research as a rigorous, reflective and relevant methodology for research in OSCM. It has highlighted the need, nature and process of collaborative inquiry by managers and researchers into operational realities that are both intellectually interesting and managerially challenging. Inquiry into these realities requires a methodology respectful of the emergent nature of the data and of the active involvement of key actors, including the thesis researcher. The set of iterative action research cycles yields unique insights that can deepen understanding, improve practice and extend theory.

Action research, then, is an approach to research that does not distinguish between research and action; it addresses the theme of *research in action*. Accordingly, compared with other approaches to research it accommodates the imprecise, uncertain and sometimes unstable activity that characterises operations in practice. It works at gathering and generating data with practitioners who want to improve their organisations. Action research is a form of science, which differs from experimental physics but is genuinely scientific in its emphasis on careful observation and study of behaviour in human systems engaging in change. Quality action research is characterised by rigorous, relevant and reflective research. Achieving that quality demands a holistic attention to the enactment of the cycles of action and reflection, the quality of participation in the core action project, the development of emergent theory from the action in the thesis project, and the co-generation of actionable knowledge.

References

Adler, N. and Shani, A.B. (Rami). (2005), 'In search of an alternative framework for the creation of actionable knowledge: table-tennis research at Ericsson'. In W. A. Pasmore and R. Woodman (eds.) *Research in Organizational Change and Development*. Greenwich, CT: JAI, Vol. 13, pp. 13–79

Argyris, C. (2003), 'Actionable knowledge'. In T. Tsoukas and C. Knudsen (eds.) *The Oxford Handbook of OrganizationTheory*. Oxford: Oxford University Press, pp. 423–452.

Benstead, A. V., Hendry. L. C. and Stevenson, M., (2018), 'Horizontal collaboration in response to modern slavery legislation: An action research project', *International Journal of Operations & Production Management*, Vol. 38, No. 12, pp. 2286–2312

Bogers, M. and Horst. W., (2014), 'Collaborative Prototyping: Cross-Fertilization of Knowledge in Prototype-Driven Problem Solving', *Journal of Product Innovation Management*, Vol. 31, No. 4, pp. 744–764.

Bradbury, H. (2015), *The Sage Handbook of Action Research* 3rd ed. London: Sage.

Bradbury, H., Roth, G., and Gearty, M. R. (2015), 'The practice of learning history'. In H. Bradbury (ed.) *The Sage Handbook of Action Research*. 3rd ed. London: Sage, pp. 17–30.

Coghlan, D. (2001), 'Insider action research: Implications for practising managers', *Management Learning*, Vol. 32, No. 1, pp. 49–60.

Coghlan, D. (2010), 'Seeking common ground in the diversity and diffusion of action research and collaborative management research action modalities: Toward a general empirical method'. In W. A. Pasmore, A. B. (Rami) Shani and R. W. Woodman. (eds.) *Research in Organizational Change and Development*, Vol. 18, Bingley: Emerald, pp. 149 181.

Coghlan, D. (2011), 'Action research: Exploring perspective on a philosophy of practical knowing'. *Academy of Management Annals*, Vol. 5, pp. 53–87.

Coghlan D. (2016), 'Retrieving the philosophy of practical knowing for action research', *International Journal of Action Research*, Vol. 12, pp. 84–107.

Coghlan, D. (2019), *Doing Action Research in Your Own Organization*. 5th ed. London: Sage.

Coghlan, D. and Brydon-Miller, M. (2014), *The Sage Encyclopedia of Action Research*, London: Sage.

Coghlan, D. and   Shani, A.B (Rami)   (2014). Creating action research quality in organization development: Rigorous, reflective and relevant. *Systemic Practice and Action Research*, Vol. 27, pp. 523–536.

Coghlan, D., Coughlan, P. and Shani, A.B. (Rami) (2019), 'Exploring doctorateness in insider action research'. *International Journal of Action Research*, Vol. 15, No 1, pp. 47–61.

Coghlan, D. and Shani, A.B. (Rami) (2005), 'Roles, politics and ethics in action research design', *Systemic Practice and Action Research*, Vol. 18, No. 6, pp. 533–546.

Coghlan, D. and Shani, A.B. (Rami) eds. (2016), *Action Research in Business and Management*. 4 volumes. London: Sage.

Coghlan, D. and Shani, A.B. (Rami). (2017), 'Inquiring in the present tense: The dynamic mechanism of action research'. *Journal of Change Management*, Vol 17, No 2, pp. 121–137.

Coghlan, D., and Shani, A.B. (Rami) (2018). *Conducting Action Research for Business and Management Students*. London: Sage.

Coghlan, D., Shani, A.B. (Rami) and Coughlan, P. (2022), 'Enhancing the quality of project management through action research'. *International Journal for Managing Projects in Business*, 10.1108/IJMPB-10-2021-0291

Coughlan, P. and Coghlan, D. (2002), 'Action research for Operations Management', *International Journal of Operations Management*, Vol. 22, No. 2, pp. 220–240.

Coughlan, P. and Coghlan, D. (2011), *Collaborative Strategic Improvement Through Network Action Learning*. Cheltenham: Edward Elgar.

Crawford, C. M. (1986), 'Evaluating new products: a system, not an act', *Business Horizons*, Vol. 29, No. 6, pp.48–55.

Eden, C. and Huxham, C. (2006), 'Researching organizations using action research'. In S. Clegg, C. Hardy, T. Lawrence and W. Nord (eds.) *The Sage Handbook of Organization Studies*. Thousand Oaks: Sage.

Ellwood, P., Williams, C. and Egan, J., (2022), 'Crossing the valley of death: Five underlying innovation processes', *Technovation*, Vol. 109, 10.1016/j.technovation.2020.102162

Gibbons, M., Limoges, C., Nowotny, H., Schwartzman, S., Scott, P. and Trow, M. (1994), *The New Production of Knowledge*. London: Sage.

Greenwood, D. and Levin, M. (2007), *Introduction to Action Research*, 2nd ed. Thousand Oaks, CA: Sage.

Gustavsen, B. (2003), 'New forms of knowledge production and the role of action research', *Action Research*, Vol. 1, No. 2, pp.153–164.

Hansen, A. V. and Madsen, S. (2019). *Theorizing in Organizational Studies*. Edward Elgar, Cheltenham.

Heron, J. (1996), *Co-operative Inquiry*. London: Sage.

Herr, K. and Anderson, G. (2014), *The Action Research Dissertation*, 2nd edition, Thousand Oaks, CA: SAGE.

Holian, R. and Coghlan, D. (2013), 'Ethical issues and role duality in insider action research: Challenges for action research degree programmes', *Systemic Practice and Action Research*, Vol. 26, pp.399–418.

Holmström, J. and Hameri, M. (2009), 'Bridging practice and theory: A design science approach', *Decision Sciences*, Vol. 40, No. 1, pp. 65–87.

Holmström, J., Holweg, M., Lawson, B., Pil, F. K., and Wagner, S. M. (2019), 'The digitalization of operations and supply chain management: Theoretical and methodological implications', *Journal of Operations Management*, Vol. 65, pp. 728–734.

Koners, U. and Goffin, K. (2007), 'Learning from post-project reviews: A cross-case analysis', *Journal of Product Innovation Management*, Vol. 24, No. 3, pp.242–258.

Le Dain, M.-A., Calvi, R. and Cheriti, S. (2011) 'Measuring supplier performance in collaborative design: proposition of a framework', *R&D Management*, Vol.41, No. 1, pp.61–79.

Levin, M. (2003), 'Action research and the research community', *Concepts and Transformation*, Vol. 8, No. 3, pp.275–280.

Lewin, K. (1997), 'Action research and minority problems'. In K. Lewin (ed.), *Resolving Social Conflicts*. Washington, DC: American Psychological Association, pp. 143–154. (Original publication, 1946).

MacIntosh, R., Mason, K., Beech, N., and Bartunek J. (2021), *Delivering Impact in Management Research*,. Abingdon: Routledge.

MacLean, D., MacIntosh, R. and Grant S. (2002), 'Mode 2 management research', *British Journal of Management*, Vol.13, No. 2, pp.189–207.

Meredith, J. R., Raturi, A., Amoako-Gyampah, K. and Kaplan, B. (1989), Alternative Research Paradigms in Operations', *Journal Of Operations Management*, Vol. 8, No. 4, pp.297–326

Mirvis, P., Mohrman, S. A. and Worley, C. (2021), *Doing Relevant Research: From the Ivory Tower to the Real World*. Cheltenham UK & & Northampton MA: Edward Elgar.

Moon, J. (1999), *Journal Keeping*, London: Routledge.

Pasmore, W. A. (2001), 'Action research in the workplace: The socio-technical perspective'. In P. Reason and H. Bradbury (eds.) *Handbook of Action Research*. London: SAGE, pp. 38–47.

Pasmore, W. A. and Friedlander, F. (1982), 'An action research program for increasing employee involvement in problem solving', *Administrative Science Quarterly*, Vol.27, pp.343–362.

Pasmore, W.A., Woodman, R.W. and Simmons, A.L. (2008), Toward a more rigorous, reflective and relevant science of collaborative management research, in A.B. (Rami) Shani , S.A. Mohrman , W.A. Pasmore , B. Stymne and N. Adler (eds.) *Handbook of Collaborative Management Research*, Thousand Oaks, CA: Sage. pp. 567–582.

Piercy, N. and Rich, N. (2015),'The relationship between lean operations and sustainable operations', *International Journal of Operations & Production Management*, Vol. 35, No. 2, pp. 282–315.

Powell, D. J. and Coughlan, P. (2020), 'Rethinking lean supplier development as a learning system', *International Journal of Operations & Production Management*, Vol. 40 No. 7/8, pp. 921–943

Reason. P. (2006), 'Choice and quality in action research practice', *Journal of Management Inquiry*, Vol. 15, pp.187–203.

Reason, P. and Bradbury, H. (2001), *The Handbook of Action Research*. London: Sage.

Reason, P. and Bradbury, H. (2008), *The Sage Handbook of Action Research*, 2nd edition. London: Sage.

Rytter, N. G., Boer, H. and Koch, C. (2007) 'Conceptualizing operations strategy processes', *International Journal of Operations & Production Management*, Vol.27, No. 10, pp.1093–1114.

Saetre, A. S., and Van de Ven, A. (2021). 'Generating theory by abduction'. *Academy of Management Review*, Vol. 46, No. 4, pp. 684–701.

Schein, E. H. (1995), 'Process consultation, action research and clinical inquiry, are they the same?' *Journal of Managerial Psychology*, Vol. 10, No. 6, pp. 14–19.

Schein, E. H. (2008), 'Clinical Inquiry/Research'. In P. Reason and H. Bradbury (eds.) *The SAGE Handbook of Action Research*, 2nd edition, London: Sage, pp. 266–279.

Schein, E. H. (2009), *Helping*. San Francisco: Berrett-Kohler.

Schein, E. H. (2010), 'Organization development: Science, technology or philosophy?' In D. Coghlan and A. B. (Rami) Shani (Eds.), *Fundamentals of organization development*. SAGE Publications, Vol 1, pp. 91–100

Senge, P. (1990), *The Fifth Discipline*. New York: Doubleday.

Shani, A. B. (Rami) and Coghlan, D. (2021a), 'Action research in business and management: A reflective review', *Action Research*, Vol 19, No 3, pp. 518–541.

Shani, A .B. (Rami), and Coghlan D. (2021b), *Collaborative Inquiry for Organization Development and Change*. Cheltenham, UK & Northampton MA: Edward Elgar.

Shani, A. B. (Rami), Coghlan, D. and Alexander, B. (2020), 'Rediscovering abductive reasoning in organization development and change research'. *Journal of Applied Behavioral Science*, Vol. 56, No. 1, pp. 60–72.

Shani, A .B (Rami), Mohrman, S. A., Pasmore, W. A., Stymne, B. and Adler, N. (2008), *Handbook of Collaborative Management Research*, Thousand Oaks, CA: SAGE.

Shani, A. B. (Rami) and Docherty, P. (2008). Learning by design: Key mechanisms in organization development. in T. Cummings, (ed.) *Handbook of Organization Development*, Thousand Oaks, CA: SAGE, pp. 499–518.

Slack, N. and Lewis, M. (2015), *Operations Strategy*, 4th edition, Harlow: Pearson Education.

Stringer, E. and Argon Ortiz, A. (2020), *Action Research*, 5th b edition, Thousand Oaks, CA: SAGE.

Susman, G. I. and Evered, R. D. (1978), 'An assessment of the scientific merits of action research'. *Administrative Science Quarterly*, Vol. 23, pp.582–601.

Trist, E. and Murray, H. (1993), *The Social Engagement of Social Science. A Tavistock Anthology. Volume II, The Socio-Technical Perspective*. Philadelphia: University of Pennsylvania Press.

van Aken, J., Chandrasekaran, A. and Halman, J. (2016), 'Conducting and publishing design science research: Inaugural essay of the design science department of the Journal of Operations Management', *Journal of Operations Management*, Vol. 47–48, pp.1–8

Weisbord, M. R. (2012), *Productive Workplaces*, 3rd edition. Jossey-Bass-San Francisco.

Whitehead, D. (2005), 'Project management and action research: Two sides of the same coin?' *Journal of Health Organization and Management*, Vol. 19, pp.519–531.

Zuber-Skerritt, O. and Perry, C. (2002), 'Action research within organisations and university thesis writing', *The Learning Organisation*, Vol. 9, pp.171–179.

8 Clinical management research – Interventionist and collaborative approaches

Christer Karlsson

Chapter overview

DOI: 10.4324/9781003315001-8

8.1 Introduction

8.1.1 Clinical research approaches

This chapter describes clinical approaches to management research and positions them in relation to other field research approaches. The key characteristics of the clinical approaches are that the researcher is asked to intervene in a diagnostic relationship and its concurrent development of the researched object, that is, a company or other organization, and the research field. It is not only observation, but also intervention. The researcher intervenes to help and perhaps cure the organizational patient and concurrently does research on that organization, just as a clinical doctor does in a university hospital. The history of this approach goes back to the very significant early work of Schein (1969, 1987, 1991, 1995).

In a typical management consulting process, the CEO or other executive will contact the consultant, who will then interview organizational members, analyse the situation and make recommendations. The consultant may be available for planning and implementation. The clinical research has a similar process, but in a clinical research project there is a continuous dialogue and exchange of information in which the researcher concurrently gives information to the organization and receives information for the research aimed at developing general knowledge for the academic field (Schein, 1995).

In this chapter, clinical research approaches are analysed in comparison with other approaches, such as case and action research, regarding appropriate research questions, the research process, potential contributions and how to report them. Some examples from clinical research identify how the approaches have been used and developed to make contributions in publications in major journals in the field. Applicability and comparative strengths and weaknesses are discussed.

The chapter builds on the preceding approaches of case, longitudinal field and action research. A clinical perspective can be taken when doing case, longitudinal field and action research and the organization in which the research is done finds the research and researcher interesting and asks for some help. The distinguishing dimension is clinical inquiry and intervention. Therefore, the description of some practical activities such as data gathering, and generation are reduced in this chapter to focus on the ways in which they are special and different in the clinical approaches.

8.1.2 Variants and adjacent approaches

Clinical research is not a homogenous concept in the literature. There are different versions and concepts that are overlapping or very similar, such as interventionist and collaborative research.

A categorization of the variants is provided in Schein (2001) (see tables). The first table contains versions of researcher involvement where the researcher has contacted the organization for conducting research, this is dealt with in other chapters. The second table contains versions of researcher involvement where the research object has contacted the researcher to get some kind of help. The low involvement versions Internship and Educative are of a knowledge transfer type. In this chapter, we deal with the high involvement by the researcher versions as clinical research approaches.

Table 8.1 Researcher initiated research approaches

External project initiation – for example researcher			
		Object involvement	
Researcher involvement		Low	High
	Low	Demographic	Experiments
	High	Participatory	Action research

Table 8.2 Client initiated research approaches

Project initiation from Subject organization = Research object			
		Object involvement	
Researcher involvement		Low	High
	Low	Internship	Educative
	High	Contract research and consulting	Process consulting & Clinical inquiry

We describe briefly the variants and adjacent approaches. Some are detailed and developed in other chapters.

8.1.2.1 Clinical research

Clinical research is a response to a problem encountered by a client who wants help in dealing with it. This is the perspective in this chapter, but we will first overview adjacent approaches to identify some fine differences in the approaches' concepts.

Clinical research can also be carried out in the case, longitudinal, and action research formats. We will come back to how these relate to each other in the next section but start here with very comprehensive descriptions.

8.1.2.2 Action research

Action research is where the researcher is an interventionist with the client exploring and testing an approach to change. The researcher intervenes in repeated cycles of constructing, planning action, taking action and evaluating action, continuously challenges and tests assumptions and interpretations and then reflects on the outcomes of the actions, both intended and unintended (see Chapter 7). The practical and theoretical outcomes of the action research are related to the type of intervention and are context specific.

Organization Development (OD) is deeply embedded in action research. The OD aims to improve an organization's processes of renewal resonates with the opportunities that arise in operations and supply chain management and which is dealt with in Chapter 7 on action research.

8.1.2.3 Clinical inquiry

Clinical inquiry is synonymous with process consultation. It is where the observation, elicitation and reporting of data that are available when the researcher is engaged in helping organizations manage change (Coghlan, 2000, citing Schein). The collaborative process engages the clinical researcher and organizational members in perceiving and understanding the practical setting in order to use that knowledge to take action (Coghlan and Brydon-Miller, 2014). See also Chapter 7 on action research. This method is discussed later in this chapter.

8.1.2.4 Case research

Case research in its traditional form is where the research objective is often explorative, and the researcher explores an issue with the aim of generating hypotheses or theory. The researcher collects in-depth data through interviews, documents and often through participative observation. The generated hypotheses are tested against theory, aiming at generalizations that relate to an issue rather than to a population. Case research is not by itself clinical but single cases over a long time may turn clinical when the case company management asks for advice. See chapter 5.

8.1.2.5 Collaborative research

Collaborative management research is viewed as 'an emergent systematic inquiry process, embedded in a true partnership between researchers and members of a living system for the purpose of generating actionable scientific knowledge' (Shani et al., 2004: 83–84). Scholars and their managerial partners work together to define the research focus, develop the methods to be used for data collection, participate equally in the analysis of data and work together in the application and dissemination of knowledge. Applications include individual development, organizational development, regional development efforts and economic policy (Shani et al., 2008).

8.1.2.6 *Intervention research*

Intervention research entails the empirical study of professional intervention behaviour in human services. There are three facets of intervention research: knowledge development, knowledge utilization and design and development (Rothman and Thomas, 1994). Knowledge development seeks to acquire knowledge that is practical, instrumental and closely related to the problems of intervention. Knowledge utilization involves the purposive transformation of theory and data into a form that has strong implications for intervention, both for practice and policy. In design and development, researchers seek and use a systematic methodology for constructing effective operational tools of practice.

8.1.2.7 *Interactive research*

Yet another concept that has emerged is Interactive research (e.g. Svensson et al. (2007), Introduction – on Interactive Research, International Journal of Action Research 3(3):233–233). Interactive and iterative research brings members of a client organization into direct contact with stakeholders such as customers in order to explore issues, develop solutions to organizational issues and learn jointly. This approach to research has become popular in Scandinavia and stakeholders are increasingly seen as collaborative members of a research process rather than research subjects who are studied but kept in the dark about the task in hand.

8.1.2.8 *Participatory research*

There are also approaches with much similarity such as participatory research but although the research objects participate it is not necessarily on their demand and with a consulting and helping aim.

Participatory research focuses on a process of sequential reflection and action, earned out with and by local people (particularly in the developing world) rather than on them. Local knowledge and perspectives are not only acknowledged but form the basis for research and planning. (Cornwall and Jewkes, 1995), (Bergold, J. & Thomas, S., 2012).

Participatory Action Research (PAR) describes a community-based approach to knowledge creation which combines social investigation, education and action. (Chevalier, J.M. and Buckles, D.J., 2013; Coghlan and Brydon-Miller, 2014).

8.2 Characteristics of clinical research approaches

8.2.1 *Deep and rich insights*

Clinical research approaches offer an opportunity to organizations and their management to achieve deeper and richer insights into particular issues, and for researchers to study causal relations. The reason for this is that the project is concurrently both research and response to a problem encountered by a client who wants help in dealing with it. It can be claimed that both the client organization and the researcher gain considerable advantages. The researcher has a strong position for making inquiries in the organization and obtaining rich but confidential insights. This is especially true and valuable for research objectives that go beyond the descriptive and analytical and that want to explore contextual and causal relations and how causal effects can be dealt with. The research results can include a deep understanding of the causal relations between issues, strategic choices and effects of interventions. That is why the clinical approach offers unique potential relevance for practice. In no other approach can the researcher be so certain of finding the actual issues that organizations are confronted by, must deal with and have to work with. It is these issues that organizations have themselves given priority to and are prepared to spend considerable internal and external resources on, rather than those defined in an external research project. Hence, the opportunities for collaboration and intervention are unique and, consequently, so is the potential for valid actionable knowledge.

8.2.2 Issues and results interesting for both theory and practice

Clinical research enables the researcher to define research issues that are of interest both to the company and the researcher from among the issues identified by the company. In clinical research there will naturally be a change process that the researcher will be involved in; change processes are often of interest both in theory and in practice.

The field of Operations and Supply Chain management (OSCM) lacks studies of the process of implementing new tools and practices. Existing literature tends to focus on the content of the tools and practices and ignores the problems associated with implementing new tools and practices. Thus, studying change processes associated with OSCM is a fruitful area for clinical research as well as longitudinal field studies (see Chapter 6).

In clinical research the company does not only get a final report; the company wants practical and actionable knowing benefits from the relationship with the researcher. The combination of the researcher's aim of contribution to knowledge and the company's quest for short-term benefits can be provided in several different ways in the clinical research design, for instance in the form of:

- A research question that reflects the interest of the company and is actionable by the researcher. Co-developing such a research question helps to ensure that the time the researcher spends in the organization is of benefit to both the company and the researcher.
- Analyses of current practices at the company. The researcher can make investigations of current practices at the company and analyses which can be used as input to the unfolding change process.
- Theoretical input into the change process. The researcher can often provide input from the literature into the change process. Even if the change and the change processes are the object of study in clinical research, there are often many opportunities to provide theoretical input to a company.
- Support in the change process. In clinical research the researcher will take on the role of providing support in the change process, for instance diagnostic information when problems arise or when actions are taken as part of the unfolding change process.

An example will illustrate what we mean by a research question that fits the description of being of interest both to the company and to the researcher (see Åhlström, 1997, and Chapter 6). In this study, both parties were interested in the process of adopting lean production. The company was interested in keeping the adoption process as smooth as possible and the researchers' interest was in the issues that arose in the implementation process.

8.2.3 Concurrent collaborative knowledge development

A requirement of the clinical research project is that the researcher gets the opportunity to develop knowledge as the clinical problem-solving is unfolding. As such, clinical research entails a balancing act between the scientific and the practical aspects of the collaboration. The balancing act concerns the researcher's interest in studying and the company's interest in receiving support with the problem diagnosis and solving. The following are examples of measures that can be taken to help the researcher in this balancing act:

- Make the dual expectations explicit in the contract between the researcher and the company; that is, make sure to include the need for time for the researcher to conduct concurrent theoretical development.
- Choose a research design that allows the researcher to regularly spend time away from the organization. This is necessary for the researcher to be able to analyse data and read up on theory on the phenomenon being studied. Time away from the company also gives the researcher the necessary distance to avoid the dangers of getting too close to the studied organization.

8.2.4 The researcher as a collaborative interventionist

A requirement in the design of a clinical research project is that the researcher becomes involved in the organization in a way that enables the researcher to act as a helping clinician and concurrently do the research. There is a need to find a role in the organization that increases the chances of observations being made in line with the research question while also permitting the researcher to contribute to the organization.

A clinical researcher will affect the studied organization since it is the nature of the methodology. In fact, all forms of inquiry into organizations entail intervention. Just by asking people questions we start to make them think, possibly about things they had not thought of before (Schein, 1987). At the outset of the clinical research relationship, it is the other way round: the researcher is asked to intervene and will then inquire.

The interaction between the observer and the observed is compounded in organizational inquiry: 'in the organizational context, the quest for objectivity, in the sense of freedom from influence by the research process, is probably hopeless' (Schön, 1983: 127). An appropriate kind of objectivity has to do with the researcher's awareness of his or her effect on others. As a clinical researcher, you need to be aware of what you do in the organization and how this is received. Such awareness is 'the best remedy against self-confirming hypotheses and irresponsible interventions' (Czarniawska-Joerges, 1992). The researcher must also reflect and attempt to assess the nature and extent of his or her effect on the studied phenomena (Sofer, 1961).

8.3 How to do clinical management research - Process

8.3.1 Interventionist and collaborative processes

A key characteristic of clinical management research is that the consultative role and actions with the aim of helping the client are going on in parallel with the research role and actions, with the aim of knowledge creation and development. Although many activities can serve both aims, the researcher should be aware of, and attentive to, what is

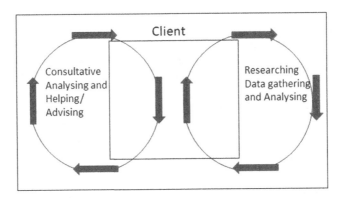

Figure 8.1 Clinical parallel research processes.

Table 8.3 Clinical research activities

Consulting, analysing and helping		Researching, knowledge development	
Home	In client	In client	Home
Approaching	Sponsor contract	Clinical inquiry	Staffing, Co-researcher
Contract	Issues exploration	Critical incidents	Data documentation
Interview guides	Relation building	Data documentation	Coding
Data points	Data gathering	Steering group	Interpretation
Data documentation	Liaison roles	Analysis versus theory	Generalizing
Coding	Building trust	Validity test	Conclusion
Interpretation	Analysis versus theory		

what. Both processes go on with activities that take place inside and outside of the client organization. An illustration of this is found in Figure 8.1. In consultative mode, the researcher is there to analyse the issue in the organization and iteratively withdraws to analyse. In clinical mode, the researcher is there to gather and generate data by clinical inquiry and iteratively withdraws to do the scientific analyses.

All the activities in these continuous processes will now be described. To provide an overview they are inserted with keywords in Table 8.3. The table is not intended to provide a correct process but to indicate what can and should happen in different relations and settings.

8.3.2 *Data gathering – intervention and diagnosis*

The researcher doing clinical research is said to inquire. Inquiry is a process of creating or refining knowledge driven by a search for insight. There is a difference between intervening and other data gathering methods. In clinical research, all interventions count, from the very first contact to recommendations and implementation. When we in clinical research gather and generate data we intervene, and every time we intervene we are data gathering and generating. In addition, data gathering, generation and analysis are simultaneous and integrated. In relation to interventions, Schein stated that intervention precedes or is simultaneous with diagnosis and that improved diagnosis results from early efforts to intervene (1987).

8.3.3 *Defining data sources*

The important data sources in clinical research will be key individuals, and also some documents, for example from meetings where important decisions are made. The definition process of identifying data sources is initially guided by the client/sponsor pointing out members of the organization to participate as members of the steering group. These members, with their personal contact networks within the organization, are then critically important for identifying and gaining access to data points. Then, data points define new data points.

There is often a need to find ways to gain access to the relevant management level of the company. Access to the management levels of the organization gives the researcher the chance to triangulate and assess the impact of high-level decisions on a lower level. A researcher who only gains access to the lower levels of the organization has to infer the decisions taken higher up in the organization (Schein, 1987).

8.3.4 *Interview guides and types of question (the why, why, why approach)*

Clinical management research consists of digging for data rather than only data gathering. This means that we do not only collect data that is available through questions of a descriptive nature, but we also dig into the data with analytical and causal questions using a causal why, why, why approach or asking, 'Why is something happening?', 'What are the alternatives?', and so on, to understand the elements causing the client's disease. Causal relations are the focus and the strength of clinical research. Interview guides are less frequently used. In clinical research, the client has taken the initiative while the researcher continuously probes the client to understand what is causing the problem.

8.3.5 *Clinical inquiry*

There are several ways to intervene, from an observing style with a descriptive purpose to a reason-digging style looking for causalities. Schein differentiated between four levels of inquiry.

8.3.5.1 *Pure inquiry*

This is the first level of intervention, and it has a mapping purpose. It is the typical interview situation. The researcher will ask questions such as 'What is going on?'. Pure questions are also followed up by further pushing for more details and further considerations, for example by saying 'Tell me more'.

The idea with pure inquiry is to interfere minimally with the client's own efforts to get their story out in their own way.

8.3.5.2 *Diagnostic inquiry*

This is the second level of intervention, and it has the purpose of searching for causalities. It is a characteristic of clinical research with its philosophy of a diagnostic relationship and the view that diagnosis takes place simultaneously with data gathering. The researcher will typically ask questions such as 'Why did that happen?', 'Why did you do that?' and 'How did that make you feel?'. The questions are causally related. The root finding sequence of why, why, why questions, going backwards on causations and reasons, is effective here.

The idea with diagnostic inquiry is to interfere with the client's thought process and make the client think about reasons and causal linkages. The researcher may influence the client's thought process and inquire about feelings and reactions.

8.3.5.3 *Action-oriented inquiry*

This is the third level of intervention, and it has the purpose of searching for both past and future causalities. The focus is on activities and especially those that have had a significant or critical effect on what has happened or may happen. This approach can be seen as the critical incident technique (CIT) (Flanagan, 1954). It is important in clinical research and is developed below. The researcher will typically ask questions such as 'What did you do?', 'What will you do about that?', 'What was decided?' and 'What were the reasons for that?'. The idea with action-oriented inquiry is to interfere with the client's thought process by forcing the client to think about prior, present, and future actions and other incidents. The researcher is influencing the thought process towards actions and other incidents in the past, present and future.

8.3.5.4 *Confrontive inquiry*

This is the fourth level of intervention and now it has the purpose of influencing not only the thought process but also the actual content of the dialogue. The idea is to confront the client with concepts, constructs, explanations, analyses, suggestions, recommendations and more interventions that are direct. This intervention is confrontive because it forces the client to think about what may not have been thought about before. The researcher will typically ask questions such as 'Could this have happened for the following reason?', 'Could it be that you were the cause?', 'Could it be that they did that because?', 'What do you think about it?' and 'What would happen if you did that?'. The client must now consider some thoughts, analyses, suggestions, or other ideas the researcher has.

In a dialogue situation, it may be natural to go through all the four interventions styles in turn. If one occasion is not appropriate for this, it may be that a series of interventions will move through these steps. The complete clinical research project can also be seen as going through these different levels of inquiry in consequent steps.

8.3.6 Critical incidents

As in case and longitudinal research, it may be relevant to apply the Critical Incident Technique (CIT) (Flanagan, 1954). It is especially relevant in clinical research since it will focus activities that have had an impact on the performance of the organization and hence will help identify what we are looking for here; that is, causal relations. CIT is used as a data gathering technique in interviews and document analysis where unusual

organizational incidents are identified. CIT is a set of procedures for collecting observations of activities to understand their potential usefulness in solving problems and
developing principles. For a more extensive description, see Chapter 6.

It should be emphasized that CIT does not consist of a single rigid set of rules governing such data collection. One practical device for obtaining specific data is to obtain
records of 'critical incidents' observed by the reporter from the organization.

Such incidents are defined as extreme behaviour, either outstandingly effective or
ineffective with respect to attaining the general aims of the activity. The procedure has
considerable efficiency because of the use of only the extremes of behaviour. It is known
that extreme incidents can be more accurately identified than behaviour which is closer to
average in character (Flanagan, 1954).

An incident means any specifiable human activity that is sufficiently complete in
itself to permit inferences and predictions to be made about the performance of the
act. To be critical, the incident must occur in a situation where the purpose or intent
of the act seems clear to the observer and where its consequences leave little doubt
concerning its effects. For further information and instructions see the article by
Flanagan (1954).

8.3.7 Data documentation

How to document data is another important topic involving participant observations and
various kinds of field study techniques such as clinical inquiry. Participant observation
requires diaries. For this discussion, see the chapters on case and action research and
longitudinal field studies.

8.3.8 Coding

Data are coded based on transcripts, interviews, meeting notes and secondary data.
Coding follows the same principles and steps as those in case and action research and
longitudinal field studies.

8.3.9 The interpretation

Issues identified in the critical incidents are taken apart, organized and classified into
recurrent topics and categories. A first part of the coding process can be accomplished by
the researcher and, in a subsequent step, collaboratively at steering group meetings with
managers. This interpretation part of the research process aims to assess the validity of
the identified issues and to secure reliability. In this way, the results from the coding are
checked for consistency through collaboration between practitioners and researchers. In
the following step, each category is compared with the literature to increase the internal
validity and to shape hypotheses. As the final step, patterns are searched for within and
between categories to synthesize the emerging patterns of concepts. See the chapters on
case and action research for details.

8.3.10 Analysis versus theory

Analysis is an integrated part of clinical management research. Analysis occurs in
interviews and participation in meetings using the why, why, why causal data mining
approach as well as in steering group meetings that discuss and interpret the collected

data and make comparisons with existing theory. This analytical approach exemplifies the continuous analysis constantly present within the clinical approach. The interplay forms a bridge between instant valuable feedback to the client and longer-term value as the foundation for solving the client's problem and as input for research.

8.3.11 Theoretical generalization and model building

Having undergone the more mechanical side of the analysis task, the more creative part follows. It is during this stage that the collected and generated data are used as the basis for the development of theory, hypotheses or models. Being close to data enhances the possibility of discovering the forces most crucial to the inquiry, which provides a fertile basis for generating theory (Miller and Friesen, 1982). Giving general recommendations on exactly how to proceed here is naturally impossible. What we can offer are some general guidelines. The difficulty of explicitly describing exactly how analysis takes place is compounded by the fact that the interpretation and analysis have already begun in the field and continue throughout the whole process (Berg, 1981). The researcher should not expect to proceed in a linear fashion from raw data to final theory. The process is self-consciously and intentionally non-linear and iterative (see Chapter 6 and Martin and Turner, 1986).

8.3.12 Results and generalizable conclusions

The results from clinical management research often stem from one organization. However, this organization might be a large global company that is active in multiple business areas, with many employees and driven by initiatives to implement various types of change. For the CEO or other representative of the client, the whole organization is in focus and constitutes the boundary for the project. However, the researcher may have an opportunity to see the specific issue that is present in different subsections, such as product or regional business units, and to observe them as units with their own boundaries within the same context. Within such an organization several cases can be identified and addressed, which means that clinical management research within one large company may yield more than a single-case study. Because of the agreement to help the client, and because of commissions that are often very long, clinical management research often ends up in truly longitudinal approaches within one company.

8.3.13 Validity

The format of clinical research is supposed to offer high validity. The invited and in-depth nature of the access achieved in clinical research will increase the familiarity and collaboration the researcher achieves with the company. This familiarity will help the researcher to make assessments of the effects of any interventions and facilitate discussions with organization members regarding the effects the researcher has on the organization.

For clinical researchers, the ultimate validation test is whether they can predict the results of a given intervention. This test is relevant because the aim of clinical research is to understand causal relations and effects and be able to make recommendations. The value of the result is how it can be generalized in a certain problem situation and not the existence of the problem in a significant population.

8.4 How to do clinical management research – organization

8.4.1 Approaching the organization and vice versa

Approaching the organization consists of several steps when conducting clinical management research. A clinical research project begins when the client contacts the researcher. The inquiry begins immediately when the researcher tries to understand the characteristics of the 'disease'. Physical follow-up meetings with the client, typically the sponsor, initiate continuous inquiries. The formation of the steering group and further meetings are also mechanisms for intervention.

8.4.2 'What are the issues?' versus 'How is it done?'

A frequent and natural process in the early part of the clinical research project is the redefinition of the problem or issue. The project may start out from observations internal to the organization regarding the problems or challenges to be dealt with. When the clinical researcher enters and starts the dialogue on problem definition, the clinical research process is already in progress. The researcher adds to the understanding in the organization by contributing conceptual and analytical frameworks as well as theories and restating the problem definition. In the following process, the problem is gradually transformed into topics. From the start the problem experienced by the organization may be complex and difficult for members of the organization to structure. Here the experienced clinical researcher can help by analysing the issue with theoretical frameworks and managerial models so the organization can better understand the issues and the researcher can identify topics for research.

8.4.3 Relation roles: Sponsor, contact, researcher, but not consultant

Conducting clinical management research contains some distinguishing roles. In general, six types of roles are involved: the client, the sponsor, the liaison officer, the steering group, the senior researcher and the research assistant. Their roles and characteristics are presented in Table 8.4.

8.4.4 The client and the sponsor

To be able to balance the dual interests of helping a client while conducting research, it is important to identify a sponsor within the client's organization. A sponsor is typically an

Table 8.4 Roles and their characteristics in clinical management research

Roles	Characteristics
The client	Typically, a company, or an organization within a company
The sponsor	A top-executive manager with the mandate and resources to initiate a study
The liaison officer	An internal gatekeeper who helps to identify data sources and makes reservations for interviews and meetings
The steering group	A group of senior managers influenced by the problem, and with an organizational mandate to act on the knowledge development evolving from the study
The senior researcher	A knowledgeable researcher with recognized knowledge about a problem topic
The research assistant	A young/junior researcher, e.g. a PhD candidate

executive manager in a high-level strategic position with an organizational mandate covering a problem topic. Normally the request for consultancy and help will come from the top executive of a company or business unit and that person will be the sponsor.

The sponsor must be able to open doors and should put together a steering group, thereby framing and creating initial structures around problem topics. In this way, the sponsor creates a foundation for building trust by blessing the clinical researchers. A foundation for creating a mutual research plan and a design for the study is established.

8.4.5 The steering group

An essential objective for undertaking clinical management research projects is obtaining rich data to understand the essence of a problem topic as deeply as possible. To obtain rich in-depth data it is important to secure valuable mechanisms for knowledge transfer. One valuable method is to use a steering group. See also Chapter 7 on action research.

Steering groups are typically formed by a sponsor. They consist of a handful of managers affected by the problem topic in focus. It is advantageous if the participating steering group members have complementary organizational perspectives and mandates that enable them and the researchers to see problem topics from multiple angles. It is beneficial to hold meetings with steering groups on a regular basis to secure continuity. The agenda for steering group meetings could vary between several topics: data feedback meetings in which the researchers discuss observations with organization members, theoretical feedback meetings in which the researchers provide organizational members with theories and tools to analyse their situation and analytical meetings with joint analyses of causal relations. Meetings with steering groups are also highly important for validating data and for identifying new sources for the collection of data.

8.4.6 The researchers

Clinical management research is labour and time consuming and therefore needs to be managed in terms of roles, tasks and activities. Two roles are essential from a research point of view: the senior and the younger/junior researcher. The senior researcher is typically the person who was contacted by the client. That senior researcher needs an assistant who can collect data from daily interventions with clients. Younger researchers in their initial research careers, for example, PhD candidates and post-docs, are ideal and may get a unique dissertation project. The use of two researchers with slightly different roles in the company can facilitate the assessment of the effects of the researchers' interventions. The senior clinician can focus on the role of clinician, while the younger researcher will get opportunities to study in depth and assess the effects of the interventions.

In a clinical research project, which resulted in a new production system and a PhD thesis (Åhlström, 1997), the agreement with the company was that the researchers would be given access to the adoption process in return for providing help in developing and implementing a new lean production system with input from research into the process. The roles as researchers were:

- The more senior researcher would visit the company approximately one day per month to give various forms of input on the adoption process, in communication with the CEO and other executives, and conduct seminars with staff.

- The more junior researcher would participate in the daily activities of the projects that were part of the adoption of lean production and was therefore appointed secretary for these projects.

8.4.7 The contract

A requirement for the clinical research project is that the researcher receives the opportunity to develop knowledge during the project process. Clinical research entails a balancing act between the scientific and the practical aspects of the collaboration. The balancing act concerns the researcher's interest in studying a problem-solving process and the company's interest in receiving support during the treatment. The following are examples of measures that can be taken to help the researcher in this balancing act:

- Frame a research question that is of interest to both the client and the researcher. A research question that interests both parties help to ensure that the time the researcher spends in the organization is of benefit to both the client and the researcher.
- And as said in 8.2.3:
- Make the dual expectations explicit in the contract between the researcher and the client. That is, make sure to include the need for time for the researcher to conduct concurrent theoretical development.
- Choose a research design that allows the researcher to spend time away from the organization regularly. This is necessary for the researcher to be able to analyse the data and read up on the theory relating to the phenomenon being studied. Time away from the organization also gives the researcher the necessary distance to avoid the danger of becoming too close to the studied organization.

8.4.8 Building trust

This is initially handled when the client contacts the researcher because of the researcher's known knowledge about a problem topic. Typically, the client has sufficient knowledge about the researcher's personality, behaviours and other determining skills to manifest a condensed level of trust and belief in the researcher's abilities to help. Once again, clinical research starts when the client makes the initial contact with the researcher, describing the symptoms of the illness, and an interpretative exchange of information inevitably advances the problem topic.

8.5 The Outcome – potential contributions to knowledge

8.5.1 Conclusions: Applicability, strengths and weaknesses

It should be clear that action research and clinical research are closely related but not the same, even if clinical research is sometimes referred to as a branch of action research (see Tables 8.1 and 8.2 in Section 8.1.2). Action research involves the client in the data gathering but is driven by the researcher's agenda. Clinical research involves the consulting researcher in inquiry in the client's process and the process is driven by the client's needs.

8.5.2 The strengths

A foundation for clinical management research is the mutual benefits of the intervention. The client has asked for help from the knowledgeable researcher and therefore has no reason to hide any potentially relevant data. Hence, the researcher does not have to beg to access the data. On the contrary, based on the client's desire to recover from the disease, the researcher can request data, directly and indirectly, from steering group members and other influential people in the organization. In conclusion, based on a contract to solve a problem, clinical management research offers benefits to both the organization and the researcher.

8.5.3 The weaknesses

Unfortunately, there are also some important drawbacks for the researcher. First, it is more or less impossible that the client will allow publication either of the detailed information or of the name of the organization. The other main drawback is the request for generalization based on more cases. The second problem can be dealt with if the reviewer understands the idea of theoretical generalization and case-based hypothesis generalization, although this is not always the possible. The first problem is worse. Even if a 'single-case study' is accepted with its aims, the necessary degree of confidentiality is a hurdle close to a block. When there are no data tables, there is a demand for concrete data in the forms of activities and quotes. The main way to deal with this is generalization of the issues rather than generalization across populations. An important way to deal with this drawback to clinical research is through an extensive description of the process and publication of a research protocol.

8.5.4 Contemporary published clinical operations management research

There are not that many examples of clinical research in OSCM. The field of organizational change and development is much richer. It is true that clinical management research is hidden under other headings. Action research is one, but probably even more often under case research and the single, in depth, longitudinal or applied categories. It is very difficult to see through; action research publications often say they participated in implementation, but whether the researchers were clinicians or not is hard to say. Experience shows that action research and longitudinal research can often turn into a clinical relation.

Below follow some examples of clinical research by the present author. They are published in well-established journals, and they demonstrate how the approach has been used to contribute to knowledge in major journals in the field. They are used as examples not to be egocentric, but because I know they are based on clinical research. Some are:

- Åhlström, P. and Karlsson, C. (1996) Change processes towards lean production: The role of the management accounting system. *International Jour- nil of Operations & Production Management*, 16(11): 42–5
- Karlsson, C. and Sköld, M. (2007) Counteracting forces in multi-branded product platform development. *Creativity and Innovation Management*, 16(2): 133–141.
- Sköld, M. and Karlsson, C. (2007) Multibranded platform development: A corporate strategy with multimanagerial challenges. *Journal of Product Innovation Management*, 24(6): 554–566.
- Sköld, M. and Karlsson, C. (2011) Product platform development in industrial networks. *International Journal of Automotive Technology and Management*, 11(3): 205–220.
- Sköld, M. and Karlsson, C. (2012) Technology sharing in manufacturing business groups. *Journal of Product Innovation Management*, 29(1) 113–124.
- Sköld, M. and Karlsson, C. (2012) Product platform replacements: Challenges to managers. *International Journal of Operations & Production Management*, 32(6): 746–766.

- Karlsson, C. and Sköld, M. (2013) Forms of innovation openness in global automotive groups. *International Journal of Automotive Technology and Management*, 13(1): 1–17.
- Sköld, M. and Karlsson, C. (2013) Stratifying the development of product platforms: Requirements for resources, organization and management styles. *Journal of Product Innovation Management*, 30(S1): 62–76.

Some other examples of articles that are based on clinical inquiry, collaborative research, participatory research and where the researchers seem to have had some kind of clinical effects, although which are not referred to as clinical research:

- Browning, T. R. and Heath, R. D. (2009) Reconceptualizing the effects of lean on production costs with evidence from the F-22 program. *Journal of Operations Management*, 27(1) 23–44.
- Jacobs, G. (2010) Conflicting demands and the power of defensive routines in participatory action research. *Action Research*, 8(4): 367–386.
- Godsell, J., Diefenbach, T., Clemmow, C., Towill, D. and Christopher, M. (2011) Enabling supply chain segmentation through demand profiling. *International Journal of Physical Distribution & Logistics Management*, 41(3) 296–314.
- Cirella, S., Guerci, M. and Shani,A. B. (2012) A process model of collaborative management research: The study of collective creativity in the luxury industry. *Systematic Practice and Action Research*, 25(3): 281–300.

8.5.5 Implications for clinical research in operations and supply chain management

In a publication situation, there are two alternatives. We either follow the request for context information that reveals the case (if we are allowed to at all) and then generalize data to a degree of very abstract discussions, or, as in the clinical alternative, keep the context very general, such as the type of industry or product, and use in-depth data on issues, critical incidents, alternatives, choices and reasons.

8.6 The clinical research approach in summary

8.6.1 Clinical management research and adjacent approaches

The essence of the clinical perspective can be summarized in the following points:

- The process is client initiated.
- The inquiry is client- and problem-centred.
- The inquiry is oriented towards a state of disease in the organization.
- The process and relation involve services for fees.
- Much data come from client needs and perspectives.
- Inquiry comes from the clinician's theory of organizational health.
- Data are deep, but not broad.
- Data involve matters that must be kept confidential.
- Data are validated through predicting responses to interventions.
- Data are analyzed in workshops and collective meetings as data feedback sessions.
- The ethical/legal responsibility is to avoid malpractice.
- Implementation and training are focused on developing skills and supported by internship.

- Scientific results are developed in parallel processes, although they are secondary to the researcher helping the client.
- Clinical data are one valid basis for doing organizational research.
- Clinical research may be the best way to learn about what goes on in the power centres of organizations and to understand causal relations.

To better understand clinical research, it is here positioned in relation to case and action research. Characteristics of each are summarized in Tables 8.5–8.8.

Table 8.5 Type of project

Perspective	Case research	Clinical research	Action research
Problem	Wish to explore an issue	Experienced problem in a company	Wish to address a practical problem and generate knowledge for action
Initiation	Researcher	Company rep or researcher inquiry	Researcher together with an organization
Problem owner	Researcher	Company representative	Researcher
Purpose	Exploration and theory generation	Solving a problem and exploring tools	Address a practical problem
Research aim	Finding issues and variables, additions to theories	Deep, may be causal understanding of issues and cures	Finding out about change mechanisms and address a practical problem
Researcher– object relation	Observer	Helper Feeder	Interventionist
Knowledge classification	Explorative and analytical	Analytical and normative	Relevant, reflective and situational

Table 8.6 Research process

Perspective	Case research	Clinical research	Action research
Problem definition	An identified issue, exploring it in reality	An experienced problem or challenge, may be to be restated	A problem in practice
Project start	Identification of earlier research	Company representative contacts researcher	Action researcher approaches company, this may be an insider
Data gathering	Interviews, documents	Inquiry, client and problem focused	Observations and data generation through intervention
Data	Inside data May be confidential	Pathology oriented, illness and cures Confidential	Situational Probably confidential
Analysis	Within-case and across-case analysis and pattern finding	Clinician's theory perspective Symptoms, reasons, cures, effects	Continuing co-inquiry with the people in the system
Analytical process	Transcripts Text analysis Data feedback	In case of data feedback meetings, sharing with colleagues	Continuous iteration between acting and reflecting
Concluding	Proposed variables Hypotheses	Reasons for problems and potential cures	Impacts of intervention

Table 8.7 Contributions

Perspective	Case research	Clinical research	Action research
Type	Context-specific analyses	Client perspective	Experiences from interventions
Target	Researchers Some practitioners	Client, practitioners, researchers	Managers, practitioners of OD, researchers
Validation	In relation to earlier literature	Through predicting responses to interventions	Joint processes and solutions. Relation to earlier research
Reliability	Several sources Triangulation	Data depth and detail Reliability of data points	Participation, real-life problems
Generalization	In relation to issue Tested against theory	In issue Nothing in numbers	Situational in relation to problem situation
Strengths	Context and problem related Recognizable situations	Thorough problem understanding Normative propositions	Development of self-help competencies and creation of actionable theory.
Weaknesses	Limited generalizability Seldom exceeds exploratory	Resource demanding Low accessibility	Generalization hardly identifiable

Table 8.8 Reporting

Perspective	Case research	Clinical research	Action research
Products	Case-based research articles in academic journals Teaching material	Report to client Cases in teaching Case-based research in academic journals	Actionable knowledge Articles in academic and practitioner journals Cases in teaching
Product types	Research articles	Clinical pathological reports	Process reflective reports
Product characteristics	Analytical frameworks Managerial tools	Deep understanding of causes and normative proposals	A narrative and reflection on an intervention experience
Value	Base for further research Tools for consultants and other practitioners	Potential high for client Causal hypotheses for researchers	Issues related experience and knowledge

The characteristics are expressed in brief statements, which will assist comparisons and analysis toward understanding and positioning clinical research in management. The characteristics are typologies describing the basic concept. This should not rule out that both a case research project and an action research project can become clinical research. The key characteristic and difference from the others are that clinical research is based on a request from the client for help.

Reading the columns vertically is meant to provide a definition of each approach. The action and case research columns are there for comparisons and draw upon the preceding chapters on case research and action research and for more detailed descriptions the reader should refer to those chapters. Following the structure of the analysis, the tables are divided into type of project, research process, contributions and reporting.

The tables enable an overview of the approaches, but also across approaches. Following the content in each table we can summarize the characteristics of the methods as follows. Case research typically explores an issue with the aim of generating theory. In case research, in-depth data are analyzed in within- and cross-case analyses. The generated hypotheses are tested against theory, aiming at generalizations that relate to the issue rather than a large population. In action research, the researcher is an interventionist exploring and testing an approach to change. The researcher tests interventions in repeated cycles and studies the process and outcomes in context. The results are related to the tool or type of intervention and are context specific. For clinical research the researcher has a strong position for making inquiries in the organization and obtaining rich but confidential insights, since clinical research is a response to a problem encountered by a client who wants help in dealing with it. The results are deep in causal understanding of issues and strategic choices, but difficult to report.

Looking across the approaches, they have similarities that often lead to them being categorized to one group, at least in rough characterizations such as case and action research. However, the differences are considerable and important with respect to the data and results they generate and the kinds of contributions they can offer.

References

Åhlström, P. (1997) *Sequences in the Process of Adopting Lean Production.* Stockholm: EFI.

Berg, P. -O. (1981) *Emotional Structures in Organizations: A Study of the Process of Change in a Swedish Company.* Lund: Studentlitteratur.

Bergold, J. and Thomas, S. (2012) Participatory Research Methods: A Methodological Approach in Motion, http://www.qualitative-research.net/

Coghlan, D. (2000) Interlevel dynamics in clinical inquiry. *Journal of Organizational Change Management*, 13(2): 190–200.

Coghlan, D. and Brydon-Miller, M. (eds) (2014). *The SAGE Encyclopedia of Action Research*, Thousand Oaks, CA: SAGE Publications

Cornwall, A. and Jewkes, R. (1995) What is participatory research? *Social Science Medicine*, 41(12), 1667–1676. 10.1016/0277-9536(95)00127-S

Czarniawska-Joerges, B. (1992) *Exploring Complex Organizations: A Cultural Perspective.* Newbury Park, CA: SAGE Publications.

Flanagan, J. C. (1954) The critical incident technique. *Psychological Bulletin*, 51(4): 327–358.

Martin, P. Y. and Turner, B. A. (1986) Grounded theory and organizational research. *Journal of Applied Behavioral Science*, 22(2): 141–157.

Miller, D. and Friesen, P. H. (1982) The longitudinal analysis of organizations: A methodological perspective. *Management Science*, 28(9): 1,013–1,034.

Rothman, J. and Thomas, E. J. (eds) (1994) *Intervention Research: Design and Development for Human Services.* Binghamton, NY: The Haworth Press.

Schein, E. H. (1969) *Process Consultation: Its Role in Organization Development.* Reading, MA: Addison-Wesley.

Schein, E. H. (1987) *The Clinical Perspective in Fieldwork*: *Professional and Ethical Issues in Clinical Versus Ethnographic Work.* Newbury Park, CA: SAGE Publications.

Schein, E. H. (1991) Legitimating clinical research in the study of organizational culture. *Working Paper No. 3288-91-BPS.* Hoboken, NJ: Stevens Institute.

Schein, E. H. (1995) Process consultation, action research and clinical inquiry: Are they the same? *Journal of Managerial Psychology*, 10(6): 14–19.

Schein, E. H. (2001) *Clinical Inquiry Research, SAGE Handbook of Action Research.* Thousand Oaks, CA: SAGE Publications.

Shani, A.B. (R.), David, A. and Willson, C. (2004) Collaborative Research: Alternative Roadmaps. In Adler, N. Shani, A. B. (R.) and Styhre, A. (eds) *Collaborative Research in Organizations: Foundations for learning, change and theoretical development*, 83–100. Thousand Oaks, CA: SAGE Publications.

Schön, D. A. (1983) Organizational learning. In: Morgan, G. (ed.) *Beyond Method: Strategies for Social Research*, 114–128. Beverly Hills, CA: SAGE Publications.

Sofer, C. (1961) *The Organization From Within: A Comparative Study of Social Institutions Based on a Sociotherapetuic Approach*. London:Tavistoc.

Svensson et al. (2007) Introduction on Interactive Research. *International Journal of Action Research*. 3(3): 233–233.

Further reading

Åhlström, P. and Karlsson, C. (1996) Change processes towards lean production: The role of the management accounting system. *International Journal of Operations & Production Management*, 16(11): 42–56.

Barley, S. R. (1990) Images of imaging: Notes on doing longitudinal field work. *Organization Science*, 1(3): 220–247.

Chevalier, J. M. and Buckles, D. J. (2013) *Participatory Action Research: Theory and Methods for Engaged Inquiry*. Routledge UK. ISBN 978-0415540315.

Drejer, A., Blackmon, K., and Voss, C. (2000) Worlds apart? A look at the operations management area in the US, UK and Scandinavia. *Scandinavian Journal of Management*, 16(1): 45–66.

Eisenhardt, K. M. (1989) Building theories from case study research. *The Academy of Management Review*, 14(4): 532–550.

Johnson, P., Duberley, J., Close, P. and Cassell, C. (1999) Negotiating field roles in manufacturing management research: The need for reflexivity. *International Journal of Operations & Production Management*, 19(12): 1,234–1,253.

Karlsson, C. (1992) Knowledge and material flow in future industrial networks. *International Journal of Operations & Production Management*, 12(7/8): 10–23.

Karlsson, C. (2013) Relevance above all: Knowledge creation from clinical research in operations strategy and management. 20th International Conference of the European Operations Management Association (EurOMA), Dublin, Ireland.

Karlsson, C. and Åhlström, P. (1997) Perspective: Changing product development strategy – A managerial challenge. *The Journal of Product Innovation Management*, 14(6): 473–484.

Karlsson, C. and Åhlström, P. (1999) Technological level and product development cycle time. *Journal of Product Innovation Management*, 16(4) 352–362.

Karlsson, C. and Sköld, M. (2007a) Counteracting forces in multi-branded product platform development. *Creativity and Innovation Management*, 16(2): 133–141.

Karlsson, C. and Sköld, M. (2007b) The manufacturing extraprise: An emerging production network paradigm. *Journal of Manufacturing Technology Management*, 18(8): 912–932.

Karlsson, C. and Sköld, M. (2012) Knowledge creation in clinical product development management research. 19th International Product Development Management Conference of the European Institute for Advanced Studies in Management (EIASM), Manchester, UK.

Karlsson, C. and Sköld, M. (2013) *Forms of Inovation Openess in Global Automotive Groups*, International Journal of Automotive Technology Management; 13 (1): 1 – 17.

Kemmis, S. and McTaggart, R. (1990) *The Action Research Planner: Doing Critical Participatory Action Research*. Geelong: Deakin University Press.

Leonard-Barton, D. (1990) A dual methodology for case studies: Synergistic use of a longitudinal single site with replicated multiple sites. *Organization Science*, 1(3): 248–266.

Nielsen, K. A. and Svensson, L. (eds) (2006) *Action Research and Interactive Research: Beyond Theory and Practice*. Maastricht: Shaker Publishing.

Schein, E. H. (1999) *Process Consultation Revisited: Building the Helping Relationship*. Reading, MA: Addison-Wesley.

Shani, A. B. (R.), Mohrman, S. A., Pasmore, W. A., Stymne, B. and Adler, N. (eds) (2008) *Handbook of Collaborative Management Research*. Thousand Oaks, CA: SAGE Publications.

Sköld, M. and Karlsson, C. (2007) Multibranded platform development: A corporate strategy with multimanagerial challenges. *Journal of Product Innovation Management*, 24(6): 554–566.

Sköld, M. and Karlsson, C. (2011) Product platform development in industrial networks. *International Journal of Automotive Technology and Management*, 11(3): 205–220.

Sköld, M. and Karlsson, C. (2012) Product platform replacements: Challenges to operations managers. *International Journal of Operations & Production Management*, 32(6): 746–766.

Sköld, M. and Karlsson, C. (2013) Stratifying the development of product of platforms: Requirement for resources, organization, and management style. *Journal of Product Innovation Management*, 30 (S1): 62–76.

9 Model-based research

J. Will M. Bertrand, Jan C. Fransoo, and Maximiliano Udenio

Chapter overview

9.1 Introduction
9.2 Origins and development of model-based research in OM

   9.2.1 Scientific management
   9.2.2 Business schools and idealized problems: operations research
   9.2.3 Complex and multidisciplinary problem instances: operational research
   9.2.4 Influential work from quantitative modelling
   9.2.5 Analysis of industry breakthroughs in relation to quantitative models
   9.2.6 Implications for current model-based research in OSCM

9.3 Methodologies in model-based research

   9.3.1 Method and methodology
   9.3.2 Axiomatic research
   9.3.3 Empirical research
   9.3.4 General differences between axiomatic and empirical research

9.4 How to conduct quantitative research in OM

   9.4.1 Background
   9.4.2 Axiomatic research – descriptive and prescriptive
   9.4.3 Demonstration of axiomatic descriptive research - analytical
   9.4.4 Axiomatic prescriptive research – decision rules
   9.4.5 Model-based empirical research
   9.4.6 Demonstration of model-based empirical research

9.5 Summary
References

9.1 Introduction

Quantitative Modelling has been the basis of most of the research in operations ever since its inception. This was labelled as Operational Research in Europe, and was the basis of initial management consulting and of Operations Research in the United States. Initially, quantitative modelling in Operational Research was oriented very much towards solving

DOI: 10.4324/9781003315001-9

real-life problems in operations management rather than towards developing scientific knowledge. Later however, especially in the United States a strong academic research line in operations research has emerged in the 1960s, working on more stylized problems and using these to build scientific knowledge in operations management. During that same period, much of this research lost its empirical foundations, and research methods have been primarily developed for these more or less theoretical research lines, leaving the more empirically oriented research lines for more than thirty years in the blue with regard to research methodology. Only since the 1990s empirical research has started to grow again in Operations Management; initially much of this empirical renaissance had a qualitative nature. The access to more digitally available data, and the inclusion of laboratory experiments in the set of research methodologies in the 2000s has substantially enhanced the empirical nature of – quantitative – model-based research in Operations Management. Moreover, the scope of research has been enlarged from a single company across the entire supply chain, such that the model-based paradigms in Operations Management have been extended to the the broader field of Supply Chain Management.

The need to develop explanatory and predictive model-based theory regarding operational processes, operations management, and supply chain management became apparent in the late 1990s. Initially, this development started with articles that formulated requirements for theory development in operations management (Schmenner and Swink 1998; Amundson 1998; Wacker 1998) or that tried to connect the knowledge generated along the various research lines into a more general theoretical framework (Melnyk and Handfield 1998). Starting in the 2000s, these ideas became fully embedded in the research philosophy of the operations and supply chain management field; with the consequence that considering real-life oberservations and applications – both as motivation for research as well as validation of results – are once again at the forefront of the field. The ideas in this chapter are based on Bertrand and Fransoo (2002) and thoroughly revised to include developments in research trends in the twenty years since.

In this chapter, we give an overview of quantitative model-based research in Operations and Supply Chain Management (OSCM), focusing on research paradigms and associated methodologies. Operations Management is defined as the process of design, planning, controlling, and executing operations in manufacturing and service industries, with Supply Chain Management extending the scope beyond a single company. Our emphasis is on model-based quantitative research, i.e., research where models of causal relationships between (independent) control variables and (dependent) performance variables are developed, analyzed, or tested. Performance variables can be either physical variables, such as inventory position, utilization rate, and carbon emissions, or economic variables such as profits, costs, or revenues. Currently emerging work also includes wider performance variables, such as those in the social responsibility domain, like worker well-being. We distinguish between empirical and axiomatic research, and furthermore between descriptive and prescriptive research. We address the problem of assessing the academic quality of research work in this arena and present guidelines for doing so. In this context, academic quality is defined as the rigor with which the standard for good academic research for the type of research conducted has been adhered to. It is important to note that academic quality does not only relate to rigor, but also to relevance. In particular in OSCM, there is a long-standing tradition of industry-academia cooperation and interaction, and much of the most influential research in OSCM is not only characterized by rigor, but also by relevance. However, the rigor/relevance debate is beyond the scope of this chapter, and we focus primarily on rigor; we do this however from a perspective of the value of empiricism in OSCM research, in particular in relation to the development in model-based research over the past two decades to substantially engage in empirical validation, experimentation, and implementation of quantitative models.

To distinguish between axiomatic and empirical research, we present a typology of model-based quantitative OSCM research, and present research guidelines for each of these types. In constructing our arguments, we build on learnings from Operations Research and Operations Management research from the past century and on research from a selected number of other academic disciplines.

In this chapter, we use the following working definition to distinguish quantitative model-based research in OSCM from other research in OSCM:

Quantitative models are based on a set of variables that vary over a specific domain, with *quantitative and causal* relationships between these variables having been defined explicitly.

Having the relationship defined in a quantitative manner means that the effect size of a relationship is meaningful and related to actual values of variables in the real world. This sets quantitative relationships apart from relationships between variables based on other observations such as surveys deploying Likert or similar scales. Further, having the relationship defined causally implies that the model makes the relationship between the independent and the dependent variable so explicit that a change in the independent variable leads to a change in the dependent variable *by definition*. The (estimated) parameter in the quantitative and causal relationship is meaningful in the sense that the model can be used to predict quantitatively the change in the dependent variable based on a change in the independent variable. Traditionally, this holds in models that are grounded in Operations Research, but also novel empirical methods from the field of econometrics, such as structural estimation, have this property.

The rest of this chapter is organized as follows. In section 2, we give a short overview of the origins and historical development of quantitative model-based research in Operations Management, highlighting the strong and weak points of this type of research. Next, in section 3, we give the major characteristics of model-based empirical and axiomatic research. Section 4 discusses in detail how the various types of quantitative model-based research in OM can be conducted. We conclude in section 5.

9.2 Origins and development of model-based research in OM

9.2.1 Scientific management

Scientific management (Taylor 1911) can be considered as the origin of the development of quantitative operations management. The essence of scientific management was the analysis of instances of real life operational processes, based on systematic observations and measurements of these process instances, and the redesign of these processes in order to improve quality and productivity. As such, scientific management did not produce generic scientific knowledge about real life operational processes. Its claim was that applying the methods of scientific management to existing operational processes would improve their performance. Scientific management therefore was not a science but an engineering profession; it was a systematic working method to achieve something. However, unlike engineering professions such as mechanical engineering and chemical engineering, scientific management lacked the underlying generic scientific knowledge about operational processes. Nevertheless, despite this lack of scientific foundations, the scientific management approach was extremely successful in improving operational processes. This illustrates the power of learning by doing and copying; a method of working facilitated by the emergence of the consultancy profession.

9.2.2 *Business schools and idealized problems: Operations research*

Scientific management laid the basis of the profession of management consultancy in the United States during the interbellum. Simultaneously, business school education emerged and quantitative models were introduced in these educational programs. In order to teach the methods and techniques from scientific management and management consultancy at these schools, the type of problems encountered in real life were simplified and formulated in general terms. Only those aspects of the problems were included that were assumed relevant from the perspective of the method and technique dealt with, and the problem was formulated independently of any particular instance of the problem in industry.

These are what we call *stylized problems*. Examples of such stylized operations management problems are the Economic Order Quantity problem (Harris 1913) and the Newsvendor problem (Arrow, Harris, and Marshak 1951), in inventory theory; wholesale price contracting (Lariviere and Porteus 2001), in supply chain coordination; or pooling systems (Liu, Nain, and Towsley 1992), in queuing theory. Note that a model is always an abstraction from reality in the sense that it is not possible to include the complete reality within it. An stylized model is a model where, in addition, the abstraction from reality has been further extended so that essential trade-offs become very explicit, functions become one- or two-dimensional, differentiable, continuous, etc, in order to make the model tractable for mathematical analysis.

It is clear from this description that these stylized OSCM problems were not intended as scientific models of real-life managerial problems, in the sense that the models could be used to explain or predict the behaviour or performance of real-life operational processes. They were just partial models of problems that operations and supply chain managers may encounter. The models were partial because all aspects of the problem that were not related to the method or technique used were left out, the implicit assumption being that these aspects would not affect the effectiveness of the problem solutions based on these models. It was left to the practitioner to include these aspects into the solution based on their knowledge of reality and of the partial model of the problem. Operational processes can be very complex systems that are difficult to model scientifically from a performance point of view. This is because the performance of an operational process – generally measured in terms such as product quality, production efficiency, cost, environmental impact, and in delivering speed, flexibility, and service – can be affected by many different elements in the process. For instance, machine conditions in a factory may affect quality and volume of output; however the actual impact of machine conditions on the factory output may also depend on the knowledge, motivation and training of the personnel, and on the information systems and performance measurement systems used by management. An important shortcoming of the stylized problems is therefore that the effect of the human factor on the performance of the operational process is largely neglected. Moreover, many stylized models deliberately relax specific constraints that are typically present in a more complex reality. As a result, implementing problem solutions based on these models often turned out to be a tedious process, and frequently failed.

It is important to realize that the models that were (and in fact are still) taught in the business school were aimed at creating insights and not at direct application. Neither were the models developed as scientific models of operational processes, i.e., models that can be used to explain or predict the output or performance of the process as a function of process characteristics, process states and inputs to the process. The professors teaching these models however conducted research, Operations Research, to further study the models, and increase their complexity. Analysis of these stylized operations and supply chain management problems has generated valuable knowledge about and insight into its solution, and can inform managers about the fundamental trade-offs in their complex decisions, and directionally provide guidance towards making such decisions. However, in academia, more and more research was conducted on analyzing such problems and finding optimal or near optimal solutions, or tractable problem properties. Stylized problems are formulated in mathematical terms, and mathematical techniques are used for analysis and solution. Gradually the complexity of the problem formulations studied was increased, making use of progress made in mathematics, statistics and computing science, leading to the development of Operations Research as a branch of applied mathematics and computer science. These stylized models have provided us with valuable insights in basic trade-offs, at a managerial level, but cannot be characterized as explanatory or predictive models of operational processes.

Some may consider Operations Research as conducting quantitative research in operations management. However, the scientific aspect of Operations Research does not pertain to the modelling of operational processes, but to the analysis of the mathematical aspect-models of the process and the quality of the mathematical solutions. In Operations Research hardly any attention is paid to the actual scientific modelling of operational processes, that is, describing the statics and dynamics of the processes that are the object of study in Operations and Supply Chain Management. Instead, an OR-methodology has been developed mainly dealing with technique oriented modelling of problem instances and implementing of solutions derived from the model. An example of this OR methodology is the well-known hierarchical planning approach (Bitran and Hax 1977), where the problem is formulated in terms of a set of hierarchically positioned mathematical programming models. Only twenty-five years later, de Kok and Fransoo (2003) described in detail the conceptual foundations of planning hierarchies, documenting in detail the actual modeling process, and building on the principal-agent paradigm in planning developed earlier by Schneeweiss (2003).

9.2.3 Complex and multidisciplinary problem instances: Operational research

Independent from the development of Operations Research in the United States, during World War II in the United Kingdom, Operational Research developed as another branch of quantitative modelling in operations management (see, e.g., Keys 1991, for an excellent overview of this development). In Operational Research, teams of researchers with different disciplinary backgrounds, in close co-operation with the problem owner, work on developing a simple but sufficiently externally valid model of the problem, derive solutions to the problem based on this simple model, and test and implement the solution under problem-owner leadership. The Operational Research approach intends to include all aspects of operational processes that are relevant for explaining the behaviour and actual performance of the process, including the knowledge, views and attitudes of the people at the operational level and the managerial level (see, e.g., Ackoff 1957, for an explanation of this phenomenon). However, also the Operational Research approach does not produce scientific knowledge about operational processes, since it is only interested in explaining and improving the performance of one specific operational process instance. Operational Research studies are rich in terms of modelling the various aspects and details that are considered relevant for the problem at issue. This relevance is determined exclusively by the team consisting of problem owner(s) and researchers. Operational Research studies generally lack in construct validity (for definitions and a discussion on construct validity in Operations Management we refer to O'Leary-Kelly and Vokurka 1998). Operational Research can be viewed as a straightforward extension to Taylor's scientific management approach to solving operational process problems. The extension that Operational Research provides is the concept of working in multi-disciplinary teams in close cooperation with and reporting to the problem owner(s) and in making more extensive use of mathematical and simulation models as tooling.

9.2.4 Influential work from quantitative modelling

Because of the developments described above in the United States and in the United Kingdom, which roughly took place between 1920 and 1960, quantitative scientific models of operational processes were virtually non-existent. With scientific models, we mean models which can be used to predict the behaviour or performance of operational processes, and which can be validated empirically in an objective way. However, the Operations Research literature contains valuable knowledge about aspects of operational processes through their analysis of stylized models, and the Operational Research literature contains valuable knowledge about problem instances. In addition, the fact that models were either particular to a specific problem instance (as in Operational Research) or not validated in reality (as in Operations Research) does not imply that the work conducted by these researchers has not been used. Two examples of work from the Operations Research community that developed in the research tradition outlined in 9.2.2 have had a significant impact in industry. The first example of such impact is the development of powerful short-term forecasting techniques, based on statistical analyses of historical data of the variables to be forecasted. These results have been consolidated in the work of Box and Jenkins (1976). It is interesting to note that their approach is based on discerning patterns in historical data that can be used to predict future data. This approach does not seek causal relationships to explain past behaviour or predict future behaviour, but considers the process that generates the data as a black box. The second example is in the area of inventory control where a large amount of stylized inventory control problems have been studied and solved to optimality or good approximate solutions have been found. This work has been consolidated in the work by Zipkin (2000). Inventory control theory may well be the most frequently applied part of stylized models in operations research.

Despite the rather underdeveloped scientific state of the field, in the last two decades of the twentieth century methods and techniques developed by Operations Research have been starting to make a serious impact on the design and control of operational processes. This especially pertains to highly automated operational processes, or operational processes and operational decision problems where the impact of the human factor is negligible. A prominent field of successful application of mathematical optimization techniques is in the general area of static allocation problems. In those problems the objective is to optimize the allocation of a resource, such as in bin-packing and cutting-stock problems (see Delorme, Iori, and Martello 2016, for an overview) and vehicle routing problems (see Toth and Vigo 2014, for an overview).

Apart from the impact of the work in forecasting, inventory modelling, and mathematical optimization, three other streams of work have had significant impact in real life. They can be distinguished from the work mentioned above by the fact that the work has been validated extensively within the research process. These three exceptions are industrial (system) dynamics, queuing theory, and pricing and revenue management.

In the 1950s, Jay Forrester at MIT developed a theoretical model of the interactions between flows of resources, materials, and information in operational processes, which was able to explain the dynamic behaviour of these processes. The Industrial Dynamics models of Forrester are scientific theoretical models of operational processes, as they can explain and predict the dynamic behaviour and performance of the processes, and can be validated empirically (Forrester 1961). In this respect, the work of Forrester was a major breakthrough, which has led to a general methodology for modelling dynamic systems known as System Dynamics (Sterman 2000).

The second important major impact in theoretical model-based research in OR was achieved by the field of Queuing Theory (see Buzacott and Shantikumar 1993, for a comprehensive overview of queuing models for manufacturing systems). Queuing Theory provides us with a firm basis for understanding the performance of an operational process from its resource structure and the variability in order arrivals and resource availability (e.g., Hopp and Spearman 2013). Just like Industrial Dynamics provides a theoretical framework for understanding the dynamic or non-stationary behaviour of industrial systems from the feedback characteristics of the system, Queuing Theory provides a theoretical framework for understanding the steady-state or stationary behaviour of the system from the variability in orders and resources.

Revenue management in the airline industry, as a third example, has a rich history of scientific development, which has resulted in advanced models for optimizing pricing and capacity (overbooking) decisions. The initial ideas of revenue management can be traced back to the 1960s and 1970s, when researchers first started exploring the mathematical foundations of optimizing pricing and capacity decisions. Over time, these early theories were refined and expanded, leading to the development of sophisticated optimization algorithms and decision-making models. The implementation of these models in the airline industry allowed companies to optimize their revenue, taking into account factors such as demand forecasts, capacity constraints, and competition. We refer to McGill and Van Ryzin (1999) for a complete historic overview of this important field and its joint development with applications in the airline industry.

9.2.5 Analysis of industry breakthroughs in relation to quantitative models

In the 1980s OR was a mature and well-established field as far as mathematical analysis was concerned. Major theoretical contributions had been made in the field of mathematical programming and other areas of discrete optimization. However, in those days, apart from the exceptions discussed above, its impact on the design and control of real-life operational processes was very limited. In the early seventies, articles were published stating that the OR research community was mainly talking to itself. In the late seventies, one of the founding fathers of OR, Russell Ackoff, wrote an article stating that "the future of OR is past" (Ackoff 1979), expressing his frustration over the tremendous amounts of resources spent on analysis of problems that had only a weak relation to real-life operational processes. Their lack of impact on the management of operational processes could be attributed to the fact that many of the models and solutions provided were not recognized by managers as having close correspondence to the problems they struggled with. Therefore, the real breakthrough developments took place in industry and were not driven by theoretical findings. We will give three examples of such industry breakthroughs to elaborate on this statement.

In the 1970s, in industry much time was spent on introducing information technology for the control of manufacturing processes, especially MRP (Material Requirements Planning) systems (Wight 1974). At the first instance, the OR research community did not consider these systems to be of any importance. Even more so, it was demonstrated that MRP systems from a modeling perspective were actually wrong; leading to extensive "exception messages" in industrial practice. However, the MRP systems evolution was a carrying wave for APICS, the American Production and Inventory Control Society, to start a real crusade to reduce inventories, increase efficiency, and increase delivering performance in the American industry. The Society organized professional education, launched its own journals, and was highly successful in terms of membership and getting the profession (production and inventory control) to a higher level. Initially, scientists did not play an important role in this development. Eventually, however, the MRP system was adopted as a "way of working" and OR theorists started to analyze MRP related problems, thereby creating insights into the working of MRP systems, but again without much impact on the profession.

A similar phenomenon was observed in response to the introduction of Japanese manufacturing techniques, as in the Toyota Production System (Schonberger 1982). In the Toyota factories in Japan, in the 1950s and 1960s a way of organizing manufacturing processes had evolved which was quite different from the processes used in the West. The Japanese put an emphasis on reliable machines, reliable products (quality) and flexibility, both in terms of machine set-ups and resource flexibility. The result was a manufacturing system that was not only more efficient than those used in the West, but at the same time more flexible, more easy to control, and could deliver high quality products. In short, their operational processes were superior to those used in the West. Studying the Toyota Production System the West has learned the lessons, and consequently used Just-in-Time techniques, Total Quality Management, and Total Productive Maintenance. In response, the OR research community has shifted its attention to new operational process problems, including elements of e.g., Just-in-Time manufacturing, and started to analyze these new problems, producing insight into the characteristics of these new manufacturing techniques.

Another example is the use of workload control to manage throughput time in complex production systems. Workload control was already advocated as "input-output control" by Wight in his book on MRP (Wight 1974) and is now widely known as CONWIP (Hopp and Spearman 2013). In the 1970s and 1980s, two research groups involved in empirical research in industry observed independently that workload control dramatically improved both throughput and throughput time (Bertrand and Wortmann 1981; Wiendahl 1987). The observed improvements could not be explained by conventional OR models. The conventional way for OR to model a complex production system is an open queuing network model. Analysis of open queuing network models reveals no improvement when applying workload control; on the contrary, the performance deteriorates if workload control is applied. However, in many real-life production situations workload control was adopted as an effective management tool and eventually OR theorists have picked it up as a research topic. Later research showed that workload control does improve performance under the assumption that management can influence the arrival of new orders to the system (Hopp and Spearman 2013), thus closing the queuing network. However, the improvements observed in industry by Wiendahl (1987) were obtained without such control on new customer orders. Subsequent survey and field study research (Schmenner 1988; Holmström 1994; Lieberman and Demeester 1999) developed indications that one of the assumptions underlying the conventional queuing network models might be wrong. This lead to other types of queuing network models to explain what is observed in real-life operational processes (Bertrand and Van Ooijen 2002).

9.2.6 Implications for current model-based research in OSCM

In current model-based research in Operations Management, the clear impact of both Operations Research and Operational Research can still be observed. Much of the model-based research has a strong focus on deriving managerial insights from simplified models and solution methodologies for complex but single-aspect formalized models. Within those studies, validation of the models is typically not addressed. Below, we will further discuss this axiomatic type of research. Also, more case-oriented model development is published in a selective number of journals. In such studies, validation in the methodological sense is not conducted, but models are implemented and performance differences are measured.

The discussion above suggests that model-based research could become more effective by becoming more empirical. Model-based empirical research studies models that are closer to real-life operational processes. In fact, models which can be validated within real-life processes are developed, and in some cases even the results of the analysis are tested in real-life. In such a way, feedback is obtained regarding the quality of the model used for and the quality of the solutions obtained from the analysis. In this way, axiomatic model-based research is combined with empirical quantitative research. For early examples of such research, we refer to Inman (1999) and DeHoratius and Raman (2008).

In the past twenty years, researchers have widely joined this approach, under extensive encouragement of the editors of the leading journals in the field; for instance, in a recent editorial, (Treville, Browning, and Oliva 2023) appeal to authors to fill the gap between *"the [analytical] model's insights and what implementation in practice will entail"*. They call this approach Empirically Grounding Analytics (EGA) and offer multiple examples of how empirical work can contribute to the development or revision of analytical models (e.g., Gray et al. 2017; Serrano, Oliva, and Kraiselburd 2018; Chuang, Oliva, and Kumar 2022) as well as to the assessment of the performance of analytical models in real-life contexts (e.g., Gaur and Kesavan 2007; De Treville et al. 2014; Saunders, Merrick, and Holcomb 2021).

An important component in these recent trends in OSCM empirical research is the adoption of supportive methods from other disciplines, in particular from economics. Both experiments, primarily in the lab (see, e.g., Katok, Leider, and Donohue 2018, for an excellent overview) and increasingly in the field (Ibanez and Staats 2018), and (structural) econometric analyses (Olivares, Terwiesch, and Cassorla 2008) have enriched the axiomatic model-based research with methods to conduct validation in a quantitative and explicit manner, while maintaining the formal characteristics and associated structural strength of mathematical models. The laboratory experiments have allowed for explicit estimation of the structure of human behavior, such as cognitive biases and bounded rationality. Such estimations have been used to adapt formal models to explicitly incorporate such human behavior into their structure. This has enabled the establishment of managerial interventions to correct for or take advantage of such behaviors. Structural econometric models have allowed for explicit estimation of parameters in formal models such as in the newsvendor and queuing models. Empirically estimating the parameters allows to capture richer behavior. In particular, unobservable human behavioral estimates can hence be made explicitly.

In the next section, we discuss both axiomatic and empirical model-based research more extensively and explicitly and positioned these in a general quantitative modelling OSCM research framework.

9.3 Methodologies in model-based research

9.3.1 Method and methodology

Research methodology in model-based research in OSCM has traditionally not been perceived as an issue. This is likely due to the grounding of OR in engineering. Since engineers have a tradition of iteratively developing solutions and solving problems, the research work typically documents the problem, the solution, and the evidence that "it works". Moreover, since – as discussed earlier – more and more of the OR work had become disconnected from industrial practice, the discipline from a method perspective started reflecting more and more the traditions of mathematics, where problems were explicitly defined in a paper, and subsequently analyzed and solved. Since in mathematics the analysis – if fully transparent and verifiable – is formally complete, typical issues in research methodology such as verification, external validation, generalizability, and reproducibility were not an issue, as they were obvious in the papers.

Quantitative model-based research can be classified as a rational knowledge generation approach (Meredith et al. 1989). It is based on the presumption that we can build objective models that explain (part of) the behaviour of real life operational processes or that can capture (part of) the decision making problems that are faced by managers in real-life operational processes. Note that this presumption obviously is not "true" in the philosophical sense. However, model-based researchers are explicit about this in the way that they capture and describe reality (when they abstract from and coneptualize that reality), and by explicitly listing "assumptions" underlying their models. Since models are usually captured in the language of mathematics or in computer code, the models themselves are completely transparent and unambiguous. Quantitative models consist of explicitly defined variables and the causal relationships between them. Hence, it is explicitly recognized that a change of value x in one variable will lead to a change of $f(x)$ in another variable. Variables can be both *state variables* capturing the state of a system that is being modeled, and *decision variables* of which the decision maker would like to determine the value. Typically, this value is determined at the hand of an *objective function* that determines the performance objectives of the decision maker.

In other types of quantitative research, such as survey research, relationships between the variables that are under study are also defined. However, generally in survey research the range over which the variables vary is not always defined explicitly, and the relationship between the variables is usually not causal, and in most cases not quantitative. With "quantitative" in this observation, we refer to the "effect size": the extent to which the dependent variable changes, when a specified change in the independent variable occurs, is quantitative. An important consequence of the fact that relationships are causal and quantitative, is that the models can be used to predict the future state of the modelled processes rather than be restricted to explaining the observations made. These include a wide range of models, such as formal mathematical models – such as stylized models, dynamic programming models, and discrete optimization models –, models combined with experimental outcomes – such as is common in much of the laboratory-experiment-based models in behavioral operations management (Katok, Leider, and Donohue 2018) –, and econometric models that incorporate specific structure – in particular so-called structural econometric models (Low and Meghir 2017). Recently, with the increasing availability and accessibility of computer-science-based models under a common denominator of *artificial intelligence models*, in particular variants of machine learning (ML), a debate has emerged whether such techniques can be seen as model-based research. The challenge of ML models is that, in general, the models are not first defined and then tested, but rather the models emerge from applying ML techniques to very large datasets. In that sense, the approach departs from the common positivistic and deductive nature of model-based research, and instead can be conceived to be of a more inductive nature. Consequently, such results typically cannot be interpreted as causal by themselves, although they are often able to do forecasts in the very specific settings for which the models have been tuned. However, in those cases it is not clear *why* the models perform so well in terms of forecasting, and hence it remains unclear under which specific conditions the models could be applied to other cases and datasets. It has been argued (Kesavan and Olivares 2019) that when more extensive "what-if analyses" are conducted, where the tuned model is tested on other data, claims regarding causality could potentially be made. Recently, supervised learning has also been proposed as an exploratory theory-development tool (Chou et al. 2022). In this chapter, however, we limit ourselves to a purely deductive perspective of model-based research, and this implies that any such ML-model would need to be properly validated and/or tested using conventional techniques such as simulation experiments or econometric analyses.

Within the model, all claims are therefore unambiguous and verifiable. It is important to realize that this is not valid for claims that pertain to the world outside the model. For the world outside, unambiguous and verifiable predictions are more difficult to make. In line with this, we distinguish two distinct classes of model-based OM research: axiomatic model-based research and empirical model-based research.

9.3.2 Axiomatic research

Axiomatic research (Meredith et al. 1989) is primarily driven by the (often styilized) model itself. In this class of research, the primary concern of the researcher is to obtain solutions within the defined model and make sure that these solutions provide insights into the structure of the problem as defined within the model. Axiomatic research produces knowledge about the behaviour of certain variables in the model, based on assumptions about the behaviour of other variables in the model. It may also produce knowledge about how to manipulate certain variables in the model, assuming desired behaviour of other variables in the model, and assuming knowledge about the behaviour of still other variables in the model. Formal methods are used to produce this knowledge. These formal methods are developed in other disciplines. In fact, theoretical model-based OM research heavily leans on results obtained in mathematics, statistics, and computer science. As a result, the types of models that are studied in this line of research are largely determined by the available methods and techniques in mathematics, statistics, and computer science, such as combinatorial optimization, markov decision processes, and queuing theory. In fact, the researchers look at the operational process or the operational decision problem, through the looking glass of the mathematical models that can be analyzed. Researchers in this line have received training in (applied) mathematics or related disciplines.

Axiomatic research can be both descriptive or prescriptive. Descriptive research is primarily targeted at understanding a modelled system, for instance by demonstrating certain behavioral properties. Prescriptive axiomatic research is primarily aimed at developing policies, strategies, and actions, to improve over the results available in the existing literature, to find an optimal solution for a newly defined problem, or to compare various strategies for addressing a specific problem. Much of the inventory literature is prescriptive in nature, as is much of the literature in OR using mathematical programming or related combinatorial techniques modeling allocation problems. The latter include, for example, the vast bodies of literature on production scheduling, network design, and vehcile routing. Research in the area of queuing theory and game theory typically is descriptive in nature and in most cases model-based. Descriptive research is primarily interested in analyzing a model, which leads to understanding and explanation of the characteristics of the model, such as equilibria in game theory, or performance evaluation in queuing theory.

The axiomatic model-based research line has been very productive and a vast body of model-based knowledge has been developed over the last fifty years. Regularly this knowledge is consolidated in monographs and books. Well-established examples of such books are:

- Stochastic Models of Manufacturing Systems (Buzacott and Shantikumar 1993),
- Supply Chain Management (Graves and de Kok 2003)
- Foundations of Inventory Management (Zipkin 2000),
- Vehicle Routing (Toth and Vigo 2014)

9.3.3 Empirical research

The second class of model-based research is primarily driven by empirical findings and measurements. In this class of research, the primary concern of the researcher is to ensure that there is a model fit between observations and actions in reality and the model made of that reality. This type of research can also be both descriptive and prescriptive. Descriptive empirical research is primarily interested in creating a model that adequately describes the causal relationships that may exist in reality, which leads to understanding of the processes going on. Examples of this type of research is the Industrial Dynamics research conducted by Forrester in the 1950s (Forrester 1961), the research on clock speed in industrial systems by Fine, Mendelson, and Pillai in the 1990s (Fine 2000; Mendelson and Pillai 1998), and the research dedicated to finding evidence of the bullwhip effect in real-life (e.g., Cachon, Randall, and Schmidt 2007; Bray and Mendelson 2012; Udenio, Fransoo, and Peels 2015, among others).

A development that has been widely adopted since the early 2000s is to make use of laboratory experiments to develop and validate models that explicitly incorporate human behavior. For instance, in their seminal paper, Schweitzer and Cachon (2000) show in an experiment that human decision makers tend to place orders in a newsvendor setting that are closer to the mean than would be optimal, i.e., smaller orders for high-margin products and larger orders for low-margin products. Subsequently, through formal modeling, researchers have argued for various explanations for this phenomenon. For instance, Su (2008) builds a model arguing this behavior is driven by bounded rationality, and shows his model is consistent with earlier experimental findings. In forecasting, Tong and Feiler (2017) develop a mathematical model that can explain certain forecasting biases based on behavioral experimental findings. Many other examples exist (Katok, Leider, and Donohue 2018). The power of the laboratory experiment is that due to the manipulation in the experimental design, cause and effect can be established, although it might not be possible to always find the exact mechanism. Combining formal models with experiments, as Su (2008) and Tong and Feiler (2017) show, may hence enhance understanding of actual operations and supply chain decision making.

Prescriptive empirical quantitative research is primarily interested in developing policies, strategies, and actions, to improve the current situation.

Historically, purely empirical prescriptive research has been rare, some prescriptive claims have been made within quantitative empirical articles (e.g., Blocher, Garrett, and Schmenner 1999), but the validation is usually not very rigorous. As with any research with a longitudinal design where a change action is made during the research, it is very hard to assess which changes in performance are due to the specific action and which are due to other changing circumstances. In empirical Operations Management research, controlling all relevant variables is impossible. Hence, "simply" implementing a model and subsequently measuring the change in performance does not lead to valid claims regarding the cause and effect between the model implementation and empirical performance. Still, such implementation can be informative in terms of documenting the actual implementation process. The journal *INFORMS Journal of Applied Analytics* documents such implementations in detail and hence creates valuable insights. However, it generally cannot lead to a valid scientific claim unless extreme care is taken at the design stage, and interventions are conducted with the express aims of theory testing or development.

In the most recent two decades, however, prescriptive insights have become commonplace in OSCM research – and certainly required if one is to publish in one of the field's top journals. To reconcile the difficulty of conducting purely empirical-prescriptive research with the need of developing relevant managerial insights, several practices have emerged.

A powerful example of such practice is the use of structural estimation models. These econometric models leverage the formal structure of (mathematical) micro-economic models with the power of advanced regression models. Structural estimation models in economics are based on microeconomic formal mathematical models and are designed to capture the underlying mechanisms and processes that determine economic behavior; taking into account various factors such as market structure, individual preferences, and policy interventions. The models are used in microeconomics to study individual behavior and decision-making in markets, explicitly estimating the values of unobservable – often behavioral – parameters of the models. Here, the models retain the explicit formal structure of the underlying mathematical formulation of the micro-economic model. This allows for the model to be used to conduct counterfactual analysis, i.e., to predict outcomes under specific values of the state variables in the system that may not be part of the actual data set that was used for the estimation. As this is factually a causal and quantitative relationship, we consider the use structural econometric models to be model-based research, unlike the use of reduced-form models (which do not have such causal structure) and unlike structural equations models (which do not have this quantitative characteristic).

In OSCM, the first application of structural estimation models is the work by Olivares, Terwiesch, and Cassorla (2008). They study the trade-off that surgeons in a hospital make when reserving time for the operating room for clinical operations that have stochastic duration. If they would reserve too much time, they would be paying relatively too high fees, while reserving too little time would lead to extensive hassle and potentially undue time pressure. Using a large operational dataset of actual bookings and realizations of operating time, they can estimate the parameters of the behavioral trade-off that surgeons make. The counterfactual could then estimate the consequences of interventions such as changes in the fees.

One of the main challenges with structural econometric models is their computational difficulty. These models often require complex mathematical algorithms to estimate parameters, and this can be a time-consuming and resource-intensive process. Additionally, the models may be subject to overfitting or other forms of estimation bias, which can impact the validity of the results.

Despite these difficulties, the power of the large availability of (micro-) transactional data in operations and supply chains has the potential to greatly enhance the use of structural econometric models. By having access to large amounts of data, more complex models can be more accurately estimated, providing greater insights into the underlying mechanisms that determine performance outcomes. These models can be applied to a wide range of fundamental models in areas such as in queuing and in inventory management, offering new ways of understanding and predicting performance outcomes in these domains based on actual behavior.

Apart from structural models, also reduced-form models have been used to empirically enhance the findings of formal (axiomatic) models, hence basing the causal argument on the formal model, and empirically testing its external validity using a reduced-form econometric model. Most of this work is descriptive in nature rather than prescriptive, although it is commonly accepted to discuss managerial implications and sometimes even recommendations; strictly speaking, such recommendations are of a speculative nature; only if field experimentation is conducted, research can be considered prescriptive. An example of such work is Rumyantsev and Netessine (2007), who use secondary data to test whether the insights based on causal relationships in simplified inventory models extend from the product level (for which they were originally developed) to the aggregate firm level. The reasoning behind this type of research is that establishing and extending the external validity of the (axiomatic) predictions enables the authors to explain inventory performance at the firm level. One point of attention here is that extreme care needs to be given to the experimental design so that the causality from the axiomatic model is maintained in the reduced-form econometric model. This is typically addressed either theoretically (e.g., by demonstrating in the theoretical model that an increase in variable X rationally leads to an increase in variable Y, but not the other way around) or econometrically (e.g., by using lagged variables).

Both the development of structural estimations models and the combination of axiomatic models with reduced-form econometric models rely extensively on combining insights from formal (axiomatic) models with (oftentimes novel) econometric techniques. Indeed, the last twenty years has seen a growth in empirical model-based work, much of which is grounded in earlier axiomatic work. Top journals are increasingly publishing work which embed axiomatic research in an empirical context and vice-versa (Terwiesch et al. 2020). One interesting consequence of this trend is that extensive understanding across research methods is now needed, leading to larger and more multi-disciplinary author teams.

A different way in which empirical research leads to prescriptive insights is with the adoption of field experiments. These typically use primary data (collected specifically for research purposes) and can vary in their set-up, according to the degree with which the researcher is able to design the boundaries of the setting (Ibanez and Staats 2018). The least hands-on field experiment is quasi-experimental research, which exploits natural experiments (where different entities experience different contexts outside the control of the researcher) using econometric matching procedures to test the effect of a "treatment" vs a control; following this, experimental research increases the control that the researchers have over the setting, for example by explicitly deciding (beforehand) upon changes to the treatment group; finally, randomized control trials offer the strongest causality proof of the effect of treatments, at the cost of generalizability issues (beyond the context of the experiments). Much of the methodology in such research builds on developments in economics, where the various styles of field experimentation are increasingly seen to reinforce each other, as discussed by Imbens (2022) in his Nobel lecture.

Field experiments are becoming more common in OM research, partly driven by the increase in availability of transactional data. This, a consequence of the digitalization of all aspects of business in the past decades, carries a risk: research topics being driven by the availability of data. Without belittling its importance, it's interesting to note that (for such availability reasons) online retail is typically over-represented in this type of research.

Independent of the context, validation in empirical research is challenging because, by definition, such research is conducted using a specific dataset; thus generalizability in the formal sense is mostly questionable. Therefore validation in empirical OSCM research is very much dominated by qualitative arguments that rely on domain knowledge (for example arguing that, due to similar incentives for decision-makers, behavior observed in US public firms can be extended to firms in other parts of the world). Similarly, the maturity of the theory being tested has an influence on the research questions and methods required of the work; open-ended research questions that suggest new connections are sufficient "validation" for nascent (novel) theories, whereas precise research questions –and models supported by extensive evidence– are required to elaborate on, or challenge, mature (accepted) theories (Edmondson and McManus 2007).

9.3.4 General differences between axiomatic and empirical research

The discussion above leads to a classification as shown in Table 9.1.

Each of these four research types leads to different contributions to the general research questions in OSCM. Note that in large-scale research projects, several of these research types could be combined; for instance, a doctoral dissertation may include chapters that are axiomatic prescriptive to develop formal policies and empirical descriptive to establish external validity. In addition, research methodology varies across the different types of quantitative model-based research.

In the axiomatic domain, the discussion on methodology is largely absent. Instructions for referees in journals publishing this type of work do not mention the methodology issue. Rather, they focus on mathematical correctness (referring to the earlier mentioned

Table 9.1 Classification of quantitative (model-based) research types.

	Descriptive	Prescriptive
Empirical	ED	EP
Axiomatic	AD	AP

fact that the line of reasoning must be unambiguous). Arguments around the relevance and external validity of the model are qualitative, and relate in particular to the assumptions made in the model formulation, and oftentimes required to be able to conduct formal mathematical analysis. In the leading OSCM journals, such extensive qualitative arguments are provided in the introductory section of the paper. In numerical studies or computer simulations of richer model formulations following the sections where the formal results are obtained, authors provide evidence that the theoretical results are likely to hold under less restrictive assumptions. While such work is usually conducted using synthetic data, increasingly authors also calibrate their models with actual data. Axiomatic research that makes use of computer simulation as the primary method of analysis generally does address methodology issues explicitly. The methodology in computer simulation relies largely on statistics theory in experimental design and analysis and has been well established in books such as Kleijnen (2018) and Law and Kelton (2007).

An early contribution to the methodology discussion in OSCM is the seminal article by Mitroff et al. (1974). Their model is presented in Figure 9.1.

Mitroff et al. (1974)'s model is based on the initial approaches used when operational research emerged as a field. In his model, the operational research approach consists of a number of phases:

- conceptualization
- modelling
- model solving
- implementation

It is important to note that the "reality" as included in Mitroff et al. (1974)'s model cannot be observed. A researcher conceptualizing that reality always views reality through a specific lens. While the rational knowledge generation approach discussed earlier in this chapter assumes that a model can be constructed from reality in an objective manner, different researchers observing the same reality will likely also conceive that reality in a different way. Hence, the "conceptualization" phase is critical in the model building

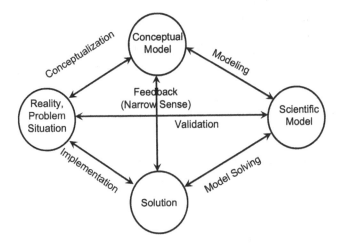

Figure 9.1 Research model.

Source: Mitroff et al. (1974).

process. In the conceptualization phase, the researcher makes a conceptual model of the problem and system they are studying. The researcher makes decisions about the variables that need to be included in the model, and the scope of the problem and model to be addressed. More importantly, the researcher also makes explicit decisions about what *not* to include in the model. Many researchers underestimate the importance of a conscious conceptualization. When the conceptualization is documented well, this is a sound basis not only for developing the scientific model, but also provides the scope for the validation and for the eventual scientific claims resulting from the analysis. Unless a field experiment is conducted, scientific claims must be restricted to the scope of he conceptualization, and cannot be claimed to have been validated in reality.

In the next phase, the researcher actually builds the quantitative model, thus defining causal relationships between the variables. Different from survey models or reduced form econometric models, these causal relationships have specific mathematical shapes (such as linear, convex, concave, or polynomial) that also are parameterized such that the parameters have a meaning in relation to reality. Due to this quantitative specification, validation may be conducted with actual data from reality. Such data in OSCM are increasingly taken from (corporate) transactional databases. As discussed above, structural or reduced-form econometrics can be deployed in this validation.

After the scientific model has been established (and potentially validated), the model solving process takes place, in which mathematics usually plays a dominant role. This may be through formal mathematical analysis. However, if the structure of the model does not allow for formal analysis, researchers may resort to numerical analysis or computer simulation. Note that generally the results are considered more parsimonious ("stronger") if the results are obtained through formal analysis, even if the model might need to be simplified to obtain such results. Results obtained through mathematical analysis are the most explicit in terms of their correctness and scope.

Finally, the results of the model are implemented, after which a new cycle may start. Mitroff et al. (1974) argue that a research cycle can arguably begin and end at any of the phases in the cycle, if the researcher is aware of the specific parts of the solution process that he is addressing and, consequently, of the claims he can make based on the results of his research. Additionally, they put forward the notion of shortcuts in the research cycle that are often applied and that lead to less-than-desirable research designs. For instance, they distinguish the cycle, and comment that many researchers following this cycle tend to mistake the model solving process for implementation. Note that this is not necessarily a problem, as long as the researchers recognize the scope of their claims. Alternatively, they name the cycle, which tends to mistake conceptualization for modelling, and thus distinguishing a flaw that characterizes some of the non-quantitative research. Mitroff et al. (1974)'s model is very helpful in identifying a specific methodological path that a specific article is following, and relating it to the validity of the claims that are made in the article.

As such, each of the four research types identified in the previous section can be positioned in this model. Since we are discussing quantitative model-based research, the "scientific model" is a central issue in all four types.

In axiomatic descriptive research, the modelling process is central. The researcher takes a conceptual model – mostly from the literature – and makes a scientific model of this. Furthermore, the researcher does some analyses on this scientific model to gain insight into the behaviour of this model. The researcher typically does not move into the model solving phase. This extension is made in axiomatic prescriptive research, where the model solving process is the central research process reported. In many AP articles, the modelling process is also included, and the results of the model are fed back to the conceptual model. This leads to the shortcut discussed above.

In empirical descriptive research, the researcher typically follows a cycle. It is interesting to note that the main risk that Mitroff et al. (1974) notice is an over-concern with validation, i.e., the researcher wants to make a perfect fit between the model and reality. Above, we noticed that reality in operations management cannot be fully captured and an over-axiomatic approach in empirical research should therefore be avoided. Finally, the most complete form of research is empirical prescriptive, where the entire cycle is conducted. As discussed above, in many cases, this research builds upon earlier published research that is in the AD category and has already developed paths for the stages, and furthermore relies on formal methods for field experimentation.

9.4 How to conduct quantitative research in OM

In this section, we discuss how to conduct axiomatic and empirical quantitative research in OSCM. In the axiomatic research domain. For each of the research types, we present an example that demonstrates the methodology in more detail. These examples are taken from the domain of inventory theory. Therefore we first explain some basics of inventory theory and inventory research.

9.4.1 Background

In this section, we look at different aspects of a particular problem area in OSCM to demonstrate the different types of model-based research. The problem area we chose to highlight is the control of production-inventory systems.

It is impossible to overstate the importance of managing production and inventory systems for society. Even when, for the last fifty-plus years, the trend in the developed world has been towards globalization and the shifting of the main economic drivers from manufacturing to service industries, inventory management remains crucial for the functioning of society. Indeed, the past few years have highlighted that, perhaps precisely because of globalization, inventory management has only grown in importance. Since the outbreak of the global COVID-19 pandemic at the start of 2020, issues related to supply chains in general and inventory management, in particular, started to become trending news items — from shortages in PPE material and consumer staples in the first half of 2020, largely attributed to lockdowns, sudden border closures, and the need for entire industries to adapt to the new reality, to the great semiconductor shortage that rippled through global supply chains, causing production stops and automobile shortages as late as early 2022.

The performance of supply chains, both global and local, is primarily impacted by their inventory management. The incentive for firms to avoid running out of product is obvious: shortages lead to revenue, customer, and reputation losses. The opposite, however, is also highly undesirable: keeping excess inventory is wasteful in the best of cases and can lead, in the worst of cases, to significant write-offs and financial distress.

Already in the early days of operations management research, correctly navigating this trade-off (between too much and too little inventory) has been recognized as the key to successful inventory management, and mathematical models have been used to explain the steady state and dynamic behavior of production-inventory systems.

Inventory theory adopts methodologies from several applied mathematics techniques (among others, dynamic programming, stochastic programming, applied statistics, and control theory) and is one of the tools in the toolbox of researchers that conduct model-based research. OM researchers doing model-based research generally do not contribute to developing the theory behind the mathematical techniques, but instead apply their results to improve their understanding of the behaviour of production-inventory systems, and to find ways to improve the performance of these systems. Over the past century, inventory theory has developed into a very rich body of knowledge with many application areas. In this chapter, we do not assume the reader to have any foreknowledge about inventory theory, and our only aim is to demonstrate the nature of model-based research at the hand of OSCM systems and OSCM problems based on inventory modeling. Therefore, we only scratch the surface of this fascinating field. Readers interested in inventory theory we refer to, e.g., Zipkin (2000), and readers interested in the application of inventory theory to strategic supply chain and operations processes we refer to, e.g., Graves and de Kok (2003) and Van Mieghem and Allon (2008). Before demonstrating the different types of model-based research at the hand of research on production-inventory systems, we therefore first present a few basic concepts for the benefit of the unfamiliar reader.

Inventories are the natural consequence of two conditions: 1) the fact that firms do not generally know with certainty what their customers will require of them in the future, and 2) that it takes time to produce (or procure) products. Formally, we denote these conditions as 1) stochastic (or uncertain) demand and 2) positive lead time. Under these (realistic) conditions, the only way to satisfy customer demands is to, at some stage in the supply chain, build up inventory ahead of time. This is obviously true in make-to-stock supply chains, where the final product is produced ahead of time (think about your latest trip to the supermarket, everything there is produced ahead of time and is available in quantities that the store considers optimal, not too much nor too little). However, the need for inventory is also true in assemble-to-order, make-to-order, or just-in-time supply chains, where the final product is only produced after a firm customer order is received (think about products that are customizable to varying degrees, e.g., automobiles or bespoke hand-made musical instruments). In such processes, even when there is no inventory of the finished product, intermediate components or raw materials are typically stored based on the expectations of such customer demands.

Basic concepts in inventory theory, from the standpoint of a focal firm, are:

- Order quantity: the amount of products requested from a focal firm's upstream partner (i.e., its supplier).
- Demand quantity: the amount of products requested by a focal firm's downstream partner (i.e., its customer).
- On-hand inventory: inventory that is physically held by the focal firm.
- Pipeline inventory: everything that has been ordered but has not yet arrived (also called in-transit stock).
- Backorder: when a customer demand arrives, there isn't enough inventory to fulfill the order and the customer agrees to wait until the firm is able to deliver the product.
- Lost sale: when a customer demand arrives, there isn't enough inventory to fulfill the order and the customer decides to purchase something else or go elsewhere.

- Inventory position: a "virtual" inventory consisting of everything that has been ordered but not yet sold; i.e., the on-hand inventory plus the pipeline inventory, minus backorders.
- Lead time: the time elapsed between placing an order and receiving said order.

When dealing with stochastic demands, inventory theory generally defines these concepts in probabilistic terms; that is, given the probability density function of the demand and a set of ordering decisions, it defines the probability density functions of inventory and backorders (or eventually lost sales). One important characteristic of an inventory system, which needs to be explicitly defined, is the question of how often is the inventory status determined and replenishment orders generated. Here we typically distinguish between continuous and periodic review systems. In continuous review systems, the status of the inventory is always known and orders are generated when the inventory falls below a pre-determined threshold. In periodic review systems, the status of the inventory is only known in discrete periodic intervals (e.g., every Monday morning all existing stock is counted). Orders can be generated every period, or only when the actual inventory falls below a pre-determined threshold. Another important characteristic of an inventory system is the type of orders that are generated. Order quantities are either fixed (where every order placed is equally as large) or variable (where the firm typically orders the necessary amount required to bring the inventory position to a predetermined, Order-Up-To, level).

9.4.2 Axiomatic research – descriptive and prescriptive

As discussed above, we distinguish two types of analytical research in OSCM. The first type of research, axiomatic descriptive, aims at creating managerial insights into the behaviour of operational processes and their control. The second type of research, axiomatic prescriptive, aims at developing rules and tools for managerial decision making. The borderline between these two types is not always very sharp, since insights into how to control a process may directly lead to decision rules. We first discuss axiomatic descriptive research aiming at creating managerial insights; a demonstration of this type of research is given in section 9.4.3. Section 9.4.4 contains some comments that indicate research elements that are specific to prescriptive research.

9.4.2.1 Conceptual modelling

Axiomatic quantitative OSCM research starts with a condensed description of the characteristics of the operational process or the operational decision problem that is going to be studied. This corresponds with the conceptual model in Figure 9.1.

The conceptual model description should use, as much as possible, concepts and terms that are accepted as standards published in scientific OSCM literature on the subject under study. Generally, what is studied is a variant of a process or a problem that has been studied before. Therefore, in the conceptual model description reference is given to generally accepted anchor articles that contain descriptions of the general characteristics of the process or problem studied in the research line in which the current research fits (e.g., economic lot sizing, queuing, or inventory control). In addition, references are given to the recent articles that study processes or problems that are closely related to the process or problem under study. In this way, the process or problem under study is clearly positioned in the scientific literature. Note that studying a process can be considered as descriptive, whereas studying a problem can be considered as prescriptive research. In axiomatic research, it is also required to describe all assumptions that underlie the conceptual model.

The scientific relevance of the research is mainly determined by what the research intends to contribute by the existing literature. We can distinguish two types of contribution. The first type of contribution is the study of a new variant of the process or problem, using well-known solution techniques. The second type of contribution is to study a process or problem that has been studied before, but provides a new, or in some respects better solution to the problem, either by applying new types of solution techniques to the problem or by achieving better results with accepted solution techniques.

9.4.2.2 Scientific modelling

The second phase in axiomatic quantitative research is the specification of the scientific model of the process or problem. The scientific model must be presented in formal, mathematical terms, such that either mathematical or numerical analysis is possible, or computer simulation can be carried out. In addition, the relationships in the model should be explained, and possibly related to earlier work in which similar relations have been developed. The scientific quality of the model is determined by various characteristics, including its innovative formulation, the compactness of the model, and the degree to which the model can be studied analytically. Any description of a scientific model should discuss the additional assumptions that are introduced when developing the scientific model from the conceptual model.

Analytical research aimed at managerial insights does not try to provide the manager with a direct answer to his question; instead, it constructs an idealized model of the problem, ensuring that an answer for the idealized problem can be found with the analytical methods and tools available. At this point, the analytical OSCM researcher has to answer the validity questions regarding his modelling assumptions. Since he deals with idealized models, validity in this context does not mean that his model needs to be a true representation of any real life occurrence of the model of system that he is studying. Validity here means that the model captures some of the characteristics of each of the real life occurrences of the model that is being studied.

Validity can be claimed in three ways. First, the researcher may refer to scientifically accepted axiomatic descriptions of the system studied that contain evidence of the occurrence of the characteristics in real life. Second, the researcher may refer to published empirical research that shows the existence in real life of the characteristics captured in the model. Third, the researcher may simply refer to earlier published research that uses the same modelling assumptions. The idea behind this is that, once a modelling assumption has been accepted as being valid for a certain class of production systems, this assumption can be used in all future research about this class of production systems.

Models used in analytical research are most of the times small-scaled, that is, the characteristics of the system are studied at a small-scale model. The reason for this can be twofold: First, problems may exist where results obtained for a small scale can be scaled up to larger models. In this case, it is efficient to study a small-scale model. Second, high dimensional models may be analytically intractable; therefore, results can be obtained only for small-scale models. The difficulty with the obtained results is of course that it is uncertain to what extent the managerial insight from the small-scale model also applies at a larger scale.

9.4.2.3 Analysis, solution, and proofs

Researchers analyze the scientific model using algebraic techniques, numerical techniques, or use computer simulation. Thus researchers in this field must be well educated in mathematical analysis, numerical analysis, or computer science. The objective of using algebraic techniques is to develop so-called "closed-form solutions". Closed-form solutions are expressions in which all variables can be related and only simple mathematical functions can be included. For more complex problems, this is oftentimes not possible, but an expression can be developed which can be computed numerically (for instance by using a computer algorithm). For many problems, even this is not possible, and in those cases, computer simulation is used as a research tool. In case computer simulation is used, knowledge about experimental design and statistical analysis is also needed. The scientific quality of the research is mainly determined by the "optimality" of the result, given the scientific model. In case of prescriptive research, "optimality" pertains to the extent to which the result can be proven the best possible solution for the problem given. In case of descriptive research, "optimality" pertains to the extent to which the results can be proven to provide exact characteristics of the process given.

Proofs generally can only be delivered with mathematical analysis. Therefore, in axiomatic research a strong mathematical background is needed for doing high quality research. This is also needed to be able to judge which scientific problem formulations, given the current state of mathematical knowledge, are good problems; that is, problems for which high quality results can be obtained. High quality solutions result from insight into what might be a solution, in combination with a mathematical proof of the quality of the solution. Criteria for the correctness of the proof are found in the branch of mathematics used in the research. This is not discussed in this chapter. Both in finding a solution and in proving the correctness of the solution, intuition plays an important role. Thus, good research is not just the result of analytic skills or applying a methodology, but also the result of good intuition in combination with analytical skills and a good methodology.

9.4.2.4 Insights

After providing the analysis and developing the solution, the researcher needs to deduce managerial insights from the analysis, solution, and proofs. This requires the researcher to relate the scientific model to the conceptual model, and develop insights within the conceptual model assumptions. In many cases, these insights will be somewhat speculative, since the conceptual model assumptions are generally less strict than the assumptions in the scientific model. An example would be that to construct a specific proof, an additional assumption may be needed about the probability density function of demand. Strictly speaking, the results from the analysis can then only be applied to managerial insights under the same restrictive assumption. In most journals, it has however been accepted that some degree of speculation on assessing the impact of assumptions is applied.

9.4.3 Demonstration of axiomatic descriptive research - analytical

Throughout this chapter, we demonstrate different aspects of research in OM by means of analysing a production-inventory system. In such a system, a decision-maker controls the amount of a certain product that is kept in stock waiting for a customer to purchase it, or (in a make-to-order setting) for a customer order to trigger a production request that requires it. Typical research questions are:

- Given a certain inventory level, what is the probability that an arbitrary demand or production request is met from inventory, i.e., what is the service level? (conversely, what is the probability of a stock-out?)
- What would be the effect on the service level, if the inventory was increased by x per cent?
- What would be the effect on the service level, if the variability of demand increased by y per cent?

These questions ultimately relate to the main decisions that the manager of an inventory-point needs to deal with: How much inventory should one attempt to maintain? And consequently, when and how should replenishment orders be placed?

9.4.3.1 Axiomatic descriptive

How would an analytical researcher tackle the questions posed above? First, assuming familiarity with inventory theory, they may postulate that (for example) a periodic-review, single-echelon, production-inventory model with uncertain demand, and fixed replenishment lead-time is a good representation of the behavior of the system. Moreover, they can argue that a simple decision-rule, such as an order-up-to (OUT) policy, can be used to control the system, i.e., to decide when to place a replenishment order and how large this order should be. This postulate implies that if the parameters of the model (the review period, the replenishment lead time, and the demand distribution function) can be determined, then the expected evolution of the inventory can be calculated as a function of the decision variable, the OUT level.

Descriptive research is not interested in optimizing the system. Rather, given a set of parameters and decision variables, descriptive research is concerned in showing how the system behaves when these parameters and decision variables change. To understand the evolution of a system's inventory in time, we start by defining a sequence of events. This sequence of events can be arbitrary or based on observations of the real-life system we are modeling.

For the purposes of illustration we consider a single-product inventory system where a firm can place an order to its single supplier every period. (The model can be extended to other situations, such as multiple products and suppliers, different review periods, or manufacturing –rather than material procurement– settings. The insights here discussed hold in general.) Lets define the following formal sequence of events for our inventory system: at the beginning of each period (t) a replenishment order (o_t) is placed with the supplier. Following this, orders that were placed L periods prior are received. Next, the demand for the period (d_t) is observed and served from the available inventory. At the end of the period, the on-hand inventory (i_t) is computed and excess demand is back-ordered. Based on this sequence of events, we can write down an explicit relationship between the different variables –the inventory balance equation– that is defined as:

$$i_t = i_{t-1} + o_{t-L} - d_t$$

A first, relatively obvious, managerial insight to be gained from describing the system in this way is that the only reason to invest in inventory is uncertainty. If demand was known ahead of time and orders always arrived in time, inventory would not be needed; the system could be controlled by simply anticipating demand, i.e., by setting $o_{t-L} = d_t$.

When L is positive (i.e., when there is a delay between placing and receiving an order) and demand is uncertain, orders are placed in advance of the demand and thus rely on the decision-maker anticipating the demand, i.e., on a demand forecast. Given that no forecast is ever 100 per cent accurate, inventory always fluctuates — it increases when $o_{t-L} > d_t$ and it decreases when $o_{t-L} < d_t$.

Notice that inventory is only affected by the orders that were placed L periods before. When L is larger than one, this implies that at any given moment there could be orders that were placed in some previous period(s) but that have not yet arrived. These orders are in-transit; they will not affect the on-hand inventory until they arrive but they represent inventory that exists in some capacity and cannot be changed. We can define this pipeline inventory (P_t) mathematically by computing everything that has already been ordered but has not yet arrived, $p_t = \Sigma_{i=t-L+1}^{t} o_i$.

Also note that if demand at any given period is larger than the sum of the initial inventory and order receipts (i.e., $d_t > i_{t-1} + o_{t-L}$) then the inventory becomes negative. In a backlogging system, this means that customers are "owed" inventory, which will eventually be delivered with a delay. Mathematically, we can distinguish on-hand inventory from a backlogs by using the *positive part* and *negative part* of the inventory parameter. Hence, on-hand inventory and backlogs are represented by i_t^+ and i_t^- respectively.

To be able to properly control our inventory, both in-transit and backordered inventory need to be explicitly taken into account in our models. To do so, we introduce the concept of "inventory position". The inventory position is the sum of the on-hand and pipeline inventory minus any eventual backorders, $ip_t = i_t^+ + p_t - i_t^-$.

A simple decision-rule that can be used to control such a system is the order-up-to (OUT) policy. The OUT policy consists of placing replenishment orders such that, every time an order is placed, the inventory position is brought up to a certain quantity, called the order-up-to level (OUT level, typically denoted as S). Mathematically, this implies that $o_t = [S - ip_t]^+$.

An important performance metric of a production/inventory system is its service level (SL). There are multiple ways to define the service level in an inventory system, all revolving around the concept of somehow quantifying the level of satisfaction of customers. In this chapter, we explore two popular definitions: the cycle service level (also called Type I SL) and the fill rate (also called Type II SL). The cycle service level is defined as *the probability that any arbitrary demand can be satisfied directly from the on-hand inventory*; the fill rate is defined as *the fraction of customer orders that are satisfied directly*. Notice how these two metrics provide different information to the decision-maker. The cycle service level communicates the fraction of periods in which a firm experiences *any* type of stock-out without any insights regarding their severity — which the fill rate fully describes. Using our inventory model, calculating the expected cycle service level of an inventory system is reduced to calculating the probability that backorders in a given period are equal to zero. In other words, the probability that the demand in a given period is smaller or equal to the on-hand inventory at the moment said demand is observed; mathematically, $SL = 1 - Prob(d_t \leq i_{t-1} + o_{t-L})$.

If the decision-maker knows the mathematical characterization of the demand (its distribution, mean, and standard deviation), this probability can be estimated. (It's intuitive to see that the calculation of the fill rate is more complex because it requires, in addition to the characterization of the overall demand, a mathematical description of the size of the customer orders. In other words, to calculate the cycle service level it suffices to know that the total demand in a period is, say, one hundred units but to calculate the fill rate we need to know whether these one hundred units are the consequence of, for example, one order of a hundred units, or ten orders of ten units each. We discuss the calculation of the fill rate in section 9.4.4.) If lead times are deterministic, the estimation of the cycle service level over the lead time (SL^L, the expected fraction of the demand *during a length of time equal to* L that is satisfied from inventory) can be simplified: $SL^L = 1 - Prob(d^L \leq S)$, with d^L representing the lead-time demand. Thus, a second important managerial insight to be gained from this model is that customer satisfaction is directly related to the OUT level. This comes at a cost: high service levels can be achieved through large inventories, which are costly to maintain. As a corollary, we can add that, all else equal, lower lead times (L) lead to lower inventory requirements for a given cycle service level.

It is clear that this type of modeling can make management better aware of the nature of the processes that they manage. However, it is left to the decision-maker to integrate this knowledge into their mental model of the operational process as a whole, and to use it in making decisions of all kinds. This requires them to be sufficiently familiar with the basic concepts of inventory theory. They need this knowledge in order to be able to interpret their own operational process in term of inventory theory concepts, and to translate the insights gained from the model analysis into action to be taken.

9.4.4 *Axiomatic prescriptive research – decision rules*

Decision-rule oriented research is more ambitious than managerial-insight oriented research. Its goal is to provide the manager with recommendations that, when applied, would allow for optimal or near optimal performance with respect to some objective function. These recommendations are in the form of explicit decision-rules (e.g., a formula to set the OUT level to achieve minimum costs). Results in this field are more difficult to obtain and, specially when providing decision-rules, modelling assumptions are often less strict. In particular, the results must be obtained for realistic large-scale models, or must be easily scalable to a realistic size.

Well-known examples of this type of research are the determination of the optimal order quantity under constant demand, fixed ordering costs and linear inventory holding costs (see e.g., chapter 5 of Silver, Pyke, and Peterson 1998). Another famous example of this type of analytical research is the study of Holt et al. (1960) into the simultaneous determination of aggregate capacity levels, aggregate production levels and aggregate inventory levels for a plant. In order to achieve analytical results they assumed quadratic cost functions for changing capacity levels, for operating at a production level different from the capacity level, and for deviating from an aggregate inventory target level. Assuming knowledge about future aggregate demand over a long horizon, they could derive the decision rules for the future period capacity levels and the future period production levels that minimize total costs over the horizon. Quadratic costs functions were assumed because taking the derivative of a quadratic cost function to the future production levels and future capacity levels leads to a system of linear equalities that, with some mathematical manipulation, can be solved to optimality.

A well known decision rule for the production/inventory system we have been discussing is, under the assumption of normally distributed demand, to set the OUT level as

$S = (L + 1)\bar{d} + z \times \sigma_d\sqrt{(L + 1)}$, where L is the lead time, $\bar{d}$ is the expected demand per period, σ_d is the variability of demand, and z is a safety factor that depends on the desired service level to be achieved (see, for example, Nahmias and Olsen 2015, for a detailed derivation of the decision-rule). A decision-maker can, therefore, use this rule to find the optimal OUT level for any given desired service level. If, for example, a certain cycle service level is desired, then the service factor z can be directly set as the percentile that achieves the desired cycle service level. For instance, if the decision-maker desires a cycle service level of 0.95, then the z-value that corresponds to the 95th percentile of the unit normal is $z = 1.65$, and thus the optimal OUT level is set as $S = (L + 1)\bar{d} + (1.65) \times \sigma_d\sqrt{(L + 1)}$. If, however, the decision-maker desires a fill rate of 0.95, setting the service factor z is more complicated because, in addition to the probabilistic characterization of the total demand, the decision-maker needs to model the distribution of the order size of each customer. In the simplest case, when every order is of size 1, then the service factor z that guarantees a fill rate of $\beta = 0.95$ can be calculated using the standard normal loss function such that $L(z) = (1 - \beta)(L + 1)\bar{d}/(\sigma_d\sqrt{(L + 1)})$. For illustration purposes, if $L = 2$; $\bar{d} = 100$; and $\sigma = 25$, then the OUT to guarantee a cycle service level of $\alpha = 0.95$ is $S_1 \simeq 305$ units. With identical parameters, and assuming orders of size 1 the OUT to guarantee a fill rate of $\beta = 0.95$ is $S_2 \simeq 286$ units.

The resulting decision rules give optimal results within the assumptions of the model, but are not easy to "understand" by the decision-maker. Not in the least because the difference in the definition of the different service levels, which can appear semantic at first *(ensure that 95 per cent of the periods end without stockouts vs. ensure that 95 per cent of orders are satisfied)*, results in a really significant difference in the resulting optimal decision.

In general, interpreting the rationality of the decision rules requires the manager to understand the way in which the decision problem has been modelled, which is not provided by the decision rule as such. The impact of decision-rule oriented model-based research on managerial decision making is very similar to that of insight-oriented model-based research. Full-fledged implementations of decision rules derived from models do occur, but are rare; for an example of an implementation of decision rules derived from an OUT inventory model, we refer to Disney et al. (2013). However, studying both the model and its resulting decision rules may lead to new managerial insights that can help the manager in his actual decision making, even if the decision rules themselves are not directly used.

9.4.5 Model-based empirical research

As discussed in Section 9.3.3, the main concern of the empirical modeler is to ensure there is a fit between real-life observations of a particular process and the model made of that process. Empirical modeling is therefore used to test the (construct) validity of scientific models used in quantitative theoretical research, to make estimates of the parameters governing explicit causal mathematical relationships of said scientific models, or to test the (real-life) usability and performance of problem solutions obtained from prescriptive theoretical research. Empirical modeling is thus naturally suited as a descriptive research tool. In recent years, however, the adoption of advanced econometric methodologies, as well as (field) experiments, has resulted in an increase in prescriptive insights derived from empirical research in OSCM.

Empirical scientific research tests the validity of theoretical models and challenges the usability and performance of the solutions of theoretical problems. Empirical scientific research should be therefore carefully distinguished from the use of axiomatic research results in improvement projects conducted by consultants. The latter aim at improving the performance of an operational process by either changing its structure or its control. The use of theoretical research results in such projects is based on the belief that the underlying process models are valid and the theoretical solutions are useable and will perform well. Yet, this belief is not usually validated during the project, although the methodological rules for the practice of operational research prescribe that the model assumptions should be checked (see, e.g., Ackoff and Sasieni 1968). It is not surprising that the assumptions in operational research projects are seldom checked, because doing so would be very time consuming and costly, due to the effort involved in collecting all the data needed for checking all the underlying model assumptions. This explains why real life operational process improvement projects rarely produce scientific knowledge about operational processes.

As stated before, quantitative empirical research must be designed to test the validity of quantitative theoretical models or quantitative theoretical problem solutions, with respect to real-life operational processes. This is in line with the more general concept of theory-driven empirical research in Operations Management (Handfield and Melnyk 1998; Melnyk and Handfield 1998; Terwiesch et al. 2020). Model-driven empirical research takes advantage of the large body of axiomatic quantitative research in OSCM, and designs the empirical research accordingly. We can identify four main research strategies: primary research, secondary research, experiments, and field experiments — which one to use depends on the problem context and the research question. Conceptually, it's important to note that it is the choice of research strategy which should inform the time-horizon and the source of the data and not the other way around. (i.e., a certain data should be used because it is appropriate for the research design; a research design should not be adopted just because the researcher has access to some data.) Secondary research uses secondary data (i.e., data that is not specifically collected for the purposes of the study) and primary research, experiments, and field experiments use primary data (i.e., data collected specifically for the study). The time-horizon of the data can be a time-series (one variable is measured multiple times), a cross-section (several variables are measured one time), or a panel (several variables are measured multiple times).

Some examples of empirical modeling in OSCM, spanning the full range of research strategies, are the work by Zoryk-Schalla, Fransoo, and de Kok (2004, Primary Research), Eroglu and Hofer (2011, Secondary Research), Olivares, Terwiesch, and Cassorla (2008, Structural Modeling), Schweitzer and Cachon (2000, Experimental), Kesavan and Kushwaha (2020, Field Experiment). Even though the approaches are methodologically different, the essence of their work is always to validate either the conceptual model or the solution proposed by axiomatic research results. Zoryk-Schalla, Fransoo, and de Kok (2004) analyze the decision modelling process in advanced planning software, and compare the theoretical assessment to the empirical observations they make. Their empirical observations are driven by hypotheses that are based on the theories developed earlier in primarily axiomatic research settings. Eroglu and Hofer (2011) analyze whether firm inventories have become leaner in the prior decades and whether – as results from axiomatic research indicate – the relationship between firm performance and leanness has an "inverted U" shape, i.e., leaner inventories are beneficial, but only up to a point. Olivares, Terwiesch, and Cassorla (2008) develop a structural model of the decision-making process behind operating-room reservations based on the well-known newsvendor model. They used secondary data related to the reserved and actual time-requirements of surgical operations that had taken place through the span of a year at a university hospital. By developing a structural model, which explicitly specifies the decision process that generates the data used in the estimation, they are able to make inferences about the unobservable parameters that would generate the outcome observed in the data. With this, they can go further than "just" validating the axiomatic model; they perform a what-if/counterfactual analysis that predicts how the outcome would change if the unobservable parameters changed. Schweitzer and Cachon (2000) conduct an experiment based on the newsvendor model, where subjects need to make ordering decisions for a single-period inventory model under different financial settings. They show the "pull to centre" effect, which causes players under high-margin settings to under-order and players under low-margin setting to over-order. They validate the theory-based explanations derived from prior axiomatic research. Kesavan and Kushwaha (2020) conduct a field experiment at an automobile replacement parts retailer that examines the profit implications of providing discretionary power to merchants. They find that over-riding the decisions made by the automated systems causes the profitability of merchants to decrease.

A major issue faced by empirical OSCM research is that real-life operational processes are all different, although there are structural similarities within classes of operational processes. The similarities are often due to the use of relatively standardized manufacturing technologies and decision support systems. Well-known classes of operational processes are for instance the continuous flow shop (e.g., assembly line), for high volume production of similar products, the job shop for low volume production of a large variety of different products, and batch processing of bulk raw materials into intermediate or finished products (e.g., in the process industry). Even though every different process encountered in real life will, to some extent, exhibit unique characteristics – due to, e.g., work organization, the information system used, the level of education of the work force, etc. – the type of operational process will necessarily define a certain structure behind the control requirements of the system. Therefore empirical quantitative research should aim at validating the basic assumptions about the operational processes and problem characteristics for well defined classes of operational processes, underlying the theoretical models and problems.

From these observations, we can derive the steps that need to be taken when doing empirical quantitative research.

9.4.5.1 *Identification of process or problem assumptions*

The first step is the identification of the basic assumptions regarding the operational process underlying the theoretical models or problems. In the OM literature, we can distinguish different research streams that share common assumptions about the operations process or operational decision problem. For instance, there exists a research stream that is based on a queuing model view of the production process, a behavioral research stream that is dedicated to model the processes behind human decision-making and how they affect operations, and a research stream that imposes statistical assumptions on demand generating processes to be able to optimize firms' inventory management. We call this a basic assumption.

9.4.5.2 *Identification of process and problem types*

The second step is that researchers should identify the type of operational process and the type of decision problem regarding this operational process, to which the basic assumptions are assumed to apply. For instance, it is assumed that decisions about the resource structure of a job shop production system should be based on a queuing model of the flow or orders along the work centres; that humans apply certain (well-known) mental models to make decisions; or that inventory control should be based upon the assumption that the demand stream follows a certain statistical distribution — typically associated with the specific industry/problem setting.

9.4.5.3 Development of operational definitions of the process

The third step is that operational, objective criteria must be developed for deciding whether or not a real-life operational process belongs to the class of operational processes considered (e.g., a manufacturing, behavioral, or inventory setting) and for identifying the decision system in the operational process that represents the decision problem considered. These criteria should be objective, that is, any researcher in OSCM using these criteria would come to the same decision regarding the process and the decision system.

9.4.5.4 Hypotheses development

The fourth step is to derive, from the basic assumptions, hypotheses regarding the behaviour of the operational process. This behaviour refers to variables or phenomena that can be measured or observed at the operational process in an objective way. The more different testable hypotheses are derived from the basic assumptions, the stronger the research is. Hypotheses are typically developed based on insights from axiomatic research and must be testable.

9.4.5.5 Metric development

The fifth step is to develop an objective way to define the metrics required by the research, and eventually how to make the observations. This very crucial step requires documentation. The reason for this is that, in operational process research, there often exists no formalized construct for certain variables (e.g., processing time, machine capacity, production output, etc.), nor do generally accepted ways of measuring these variables exist. Moreover, researchers performing secondary research often rely on metrics based upon transforming observed variables (e.g., to calculate inventory days, a very common metric in OSCM, one must transform the observed variables inventory value and cost of goods sold) as well as in proxy metrics, where a certain observed variable is used as an approximation of a variable of interest that is not defined, observed, or collected (e.g., researchers typically use the total assets as a proxy for the size of a given company; a metric that is not formally defined). The above illustrates a weak spot of quantitative empirical research in OSCM. The situation being as it is, empirical OSCM researchers must carefully document the way in which metrics are defined (and in the case of primary research, measured). This requires that the researcher knows how to identify the relevant characteristics of the operational process, and knows how these can be measured. Thus, model based empirical research cannot be done without a systematic approach for identifying and measuring real-life operational processes. This is what is called by Mitroff et al. (1974) the conceptual modelling of a system. Conceptual models define the relevant variables of a system under study, the nature of their relationships and their measurements.

9.4.5.6 Data collection

The sixth step consists of applying the measurement and observation systems, collecting, and documenting the resulting data. A variety of data collection methods and sources can be used, including surveys, public economic or finance data (e.g., Hendricks and Singhal 2003), private company transactional data (e.g., Fransoo and Wiers 2006), or observational studies (e.g., Van Zelst et al. 2009). In the case of (field) experiments, the data collection phase is crucial and inextricably linked to the full experimental design. There are therefore specific methodological characteristics behind designing and conducting empirical experiments (see Katok 2011, for an introduction to the topic).

9.4.5.7 Data analysis

The seventh step is the processing of the data, which generally includes the use of econometric analysis. Here, it's important to differentiate between data resulting of a laboratory experiment where variables in the system can be manipulated at will, and data from observations on a real life system that cannot be manipulated in an arbitrary way. The latter typically require cleaning and pre-processing that must be carefully documented. Sophisticated statistical techniques have been developed for this type of research in some branches of research in social sciences and microeconomics and later adopted by the OSCM field (Terwiesch et al. 2020). When developing the hypotheses regarding the behaviour of the operational process in step 4, it should be taken into account what type of behaviour can be expected of the process under the given real-life circumstances; the hypotheses should be restricted to behavior in the expected range and time frame. Developing effective hypotheses and an efficient operational measurement system require that the researcher is quite familiar with the type of operational process and the type of decision problem concerned, and is very familiar with the statistical techniques available for analysis of the data.

9.4.5.8 Interpretation of results

Finally, the last step in quantitative empirical research consists of the interpretation of the research results related to the theoretical models or problems that gave rise to the hypotheses that were tested. This step completes the validation process and may result in confirmation of (parts of) the theoretical model in relation to the decision problem and in relation to the operational process considered, but may also lead to (partial) rejections and suggestions for improving the theoretical models.

9.4.6 Demonstration of model-based empirical research

In this section, we demonstrate two different approaches to empirical modeling in OSCM based on the same underlying axiomatic model: the newsvendor model. Specifically, we demonstrate secondary research using structural estimation as the econometric approach (Olivares, Terwiesch, and Cassorla 2008) and research using laboratory experiments using human subjects (Schweitzer and Cachon 2000). The purpose of this demonstration is to briefly discuss some different methodological approaches and the type of insights that can be obtained through empirical modeling. Furthermore, by describing very different methodologies based however on the same analytical inventory model, we display the enormous area of application that empirical modeling has within OSCM. Therefore, in the interest of brevity, we focus on a few key points of each approach. We refer the interested reader to the original studies for in-depth discussions.

9.4.6.1 The newsvendor problem

The newsvendor problem abstracts the situation in which a decision-maker faces a single-period uncertain demand that they need to fulfill by anticipating it with inventory. In this setting, the decision-maker must procure (or produce) products before observing the demand and, crucially, cannot carry left-over inventory for later periods. The trade-off here is between building too small an inventory (and not being able to fulfill all demand) and building too large an inventory (and thus being left with "useless" products that they already paid for). The newsvendor problem has a long history. The usage of "news-vendor" or "newsboy" to refer to this problem dates from the early 1950s and is based on the observation that such a setting is a very good description of the problem of a newsboy deciding how many newspapers to stock, for newspaper demand is inherently single-period (Chen et al. 2016). The earliest mention of such a problem, however, appears to be from the late 19th century. Edgeworth (1888) introduces the "parable" of a London gentleman's club owner having to decide beforehand how much food to stock, knowing that the number of members staying for dinner follows a certain probability distribution. What we recognize as the modern formulation of the newsvendor, and the critical fractile solution, comes from a seminal paper by Arrow, Harris, and Marschak (1951). In the seventy-plus years since, the newsvendor has become one of the most written-about inventory models, and it's easy to see why: it is very simple, it captures a very clear (and realistic) trade-off, and it has (in its basic form) a closed-form optimal solution. A large body of axiomatic research exists, extending the formulation of the newsvendor model to more and more realistic settings (e.g., the multi-period newsvendor). In empirical research, the newsvendor is often used to explain observed behavior at the firm- as well as the individual-level; the later mostly in lab experiments.

Defining the costs for the decision maker as C_o, the marginal cost of overage (i.e., the cost associated with having one unit left over at the end of the period), and C_U the marginal cost of underage (i.e., the cost of having ordered one unit less than the demand realization), and assuming that these costs are linear, the solution to the newsvendor model can be represented via the concept of the critical fractile or critical ratio. The critical ratio depends uniquely on the above-mentioned costs is defined as $CR = \frac{C_U}{C_U + C_O}$. The decision that minimizes the total expected costs of the newsvendor is to order such that the probability that the demand (D) is smaller or equal to the order quantity is equal to the critical ratio. In other words, it's optimal for the decision-maker to place an order of size Q^* such that $Pr(D \leq Q^*) = CR$. The calculation of the probability depends on the statistical characterization of the demand. However, for most common distributions these probabilities are tabulated or easily computed.

9.4.6.2 A structural modeling application

Olivares, Terwiesch, and Cassorla (2008) use the newsvendor model to conceptualize a problem found in operating room management: prior to planned surgical operations, a reservation must be placed to lock the required capacity (the operating room itself, as well as the staff). However, even planned surgeries have stochastic duration. The trade-off, in this case, is between reserving too much time, with the consequence of unnecessary blocking of operating rooms and the associated idle costs for staff, and reserving too little time, which would result in surgeries extending into other reserved blocks, complicating scheduling, and negatively impacting the service.

The authors make the assumption that the decision made when reserving the operating room time can be modeled by the newsvendor logic. Notice that in this study the authors do not perform any hypothesis testing regarding this; they start with the prior that the newsvendor model is indeed used in practice. They support this claim through prior literature and the fact that decision support tools currently used in hospitals incorporate the newsvendor logic. The objective of this study is then to use historical data on reservations and actual surgery duration to estimate the critical ratio used by the decision makers. Looking at the axiomatic newsvendor model formulation, in this study the researchers observe the realizations of D and Q^* and use these to try to estimate the CR used by each decision-maker. (Given that they use data on past operations that was collected for other purposes, this constitutes an example of secondary research.)

One interesting aspect of this study is that, even though they posit that decisions follow the newsvendor logic, the researchers allow for some unexplained variability in the data (i.e., they expect that the same decision-maker may make slightly different decisions when confronted with identical observations). They do this through two different models. In the first model, the researchers do not claim to have full knowledge about every factor that can potentially affect the optimal decision. Therefore, they assume that, even though the decision-makers are rational, there are some factors available to them but unobservable by the researcher (i.e., the researchers do not have full visibility on the factors constituting C_U and C_o). With the second model, they assume that the decision-makers are *approximately* rational, that is, the decision has itself a random component such that the observed reservation, Q, is of the form $Q = Q^* + \epsilon$, where ϵ is a random error component.

Methodologically, these models require quite complex multi-step estimation procedures. The estimates of both models are consistent, estimating a median CR of 0.39 and 0.36 respectively. Even though the models offer a good fit with the data, the CR results imply that the idle cost is taken to be larger than the overtime costs. The authors recognize that the operating room management literature suggests otherwise; specifically, that staffing costs (especially overtime costs) are the main drivers for operating room allocation decisions. This discrepancy between their results and prior research can be caused because the hospital they studied indeed used a CR different from what the literature suggests (i.e., the model is valid and the discrepancy is caused by the variation in methods used by the hospital), or because the models themselves are not fully capturing the complexities of the decisions.

To account for the latter, and based upon observations from the data, the authors extend the model to allow for bias in the forecasting. Specifically, the new models allow for the possibility of systematic biases caused by "surgeons underestimating their case duration to get their cases to fit in their allocated operating room time", i.e., the observed reservations, Q, are consistently low. The estimation results of the models with forecasting bias imply an average CR of approximately 0.67, which is in line with the literature. Moreover, these estimates suggest that surgeons intentionally underestimate the duration of their operations to be able to get them programmed sooner in the schedule.

9.4.6.3 *A lab experiment application*

Schweitzer and Cachon (2000) set up a laboratory experiment to be able to better understand how behavioral biases affect newsvendor-type decisions. The motivating observation of this study is that, often, decisions made by human decision-makers differ from the profit maximizing optimum suggested by the critical ratio. Thus, the objective of this study is to identify whether choices made by human decision-makers systematically deviate from the optimum, and if so, to establish behavioral mechanisms that are consistent with the observations.

The authors identify nine different behavioral mechanisms that could cause orders to deviate from the optimal. They develop axiomatic models for each of them to predict the direction of the deviation that is expected. The behavioral mechanisms and expected deviations are:

1 Risk aversion. A risk-averse decision-maker will order less than the optimal.
2 Risk seeking. A risk-seeking decision-maker will order more than the optimal.
3 Prospect theory. When both gains and losses are possible, orders larger or smaller than the optimal are possible.
4 Loss aversion. A loss-averse decision-maker will order less than the optimal.
5 Waste aversion. A waste-averse decision-maker will order less than the optimal.
6 Stockout aversion. A stockout-averse decision-maker will order more than the optimal.
7 Underestimating opportunity costs. When a decision-maker underestimates opportunity costs, they will order less than the optimal.
8 Minimizing ex-post inventory error. Such a decision-maker will strive to minimize the deviation between orders and realized demand. They will order less than the optimal for high profit products and they will order more than the optimal for low profit products.
9 Anchor and insufficient adjustment. Such a decision-maker will use a heuristic where they anchor on a known quantity and then adjust away from this quantity. Possible anchors in the newsvendor setting are the mean demand and the last demand realization. The insufficient adjustment heuristic predicts the same too low/high pattern as minimizing ex-post inventory error.

The advantage of conducting laboratory experiments is that the researchers can control every aspect and thus are able to design experiments that can disentangle different potential explanations. In this case, the authors designed two sets of experiments to test the behavioral mechanisms above. In the first set of experiments they recruited first year M.B.A students following an operations management course to make repeated ordering decisions in both high profit and low profit newsvendor settings. The game was played for fifteen rounds in each of the high/low profit settings; the demand was random and identical for every subject. The subjects received full information of the demand distribution, the costs of overage/underage, their profits, and the history of their performance throughout the experiment. The subjects consistently ordered more than the mean but less than the optimal order quantity in the high-profit setting, and less than the mean bu more than the optimal order quantity in the low-profit setting. This pattern is consistent with the predictions from the behavioral mechanisms of prospect theory, minimization of ex-post inventory errors, and anchor and insufficient adjustment. The second set of experiments was designed to further refine these insights. Prospect theory only predicts the high/low order pattern in the case that profits can be both positive and negative whereas if minimizing ex-post inventory error or an anchor and insufficient adjustment were driving the behavior, the high/low pattern would appear even if only gains were possible. Thus, in this set of experiments the demand was adjusted such that every decision taken by the subjects would result in a positive profit. Otherwise, the experiment is conducted in almost identical manner as the first. Subjects were recruited from the second year of the same MBA program (and thus had already learned about the newsvendor model in their operations management course) and were asked, again, to make consecutive ordering decisions for fifteen rounds in each of a high/low profit setting. The results of this experiment exhibit the same too high/too low pattern as the first experiment. This, the authors argue, rules out the prospect theory explanation and is consistent with both minimizing ex-post inventory errors and an anchoring an incomplete adjustment heuristic.

This study was the first to investigate newsvendor decision-making in a laboratory setting. The results were replicated multiple times and the experimental design refined over the years to test different potential explanations and put forward more complex behavioral models, including ways of reconciling prospect theory with the observations (Long and Nasiry 2015; Uppari and Hasija 2019).

9.5 Summary

- The use of analytical and empirical modelling for researching Operations and Supply Chain Management issues were discussed.
- Operations and Supply Chain Management was defined and the quantitative modelling process that underlies the modelling research approach was characterized.
- How modelling evolved out of scientific management and developed into a distinctive research approach having specific strength and weaknesses relative to other OSCM research approaches such as survey research, case research, action research, and operational research as a special instance of action research was described.
- Inventory control, forecasting, mathematical optimization and queuing theory were mentioned as examples of influential results produced by modelling research, and the major breakthroughs in industry relative to the contribution of modelling were positioned.
- A trend in top OSCM research was identified, the past twenty years have seen a growth in publications that embed axiomatic work in an empirical context and vice-versa. As a consequence, understanding both facets of research becomes increasingly more important.
- Analytical and empirical modelling were characterized as descriptive or prescriptive research and identified in their positions in the Operations Management research model of Mitroff et al. (1974)
- Guidelines on how to conduct analytical model-based research were given, and the guidelines were demonstrated with an example.
- Finally, guidelines for doing model-based empirical research were given and also this research approach was demonstrated with two examples.

References

Ackoff, R. L. 1957. "A Comparison of Operational Research in the USA and in Great Britain." *Journal of the Operational Research Society* 8 (2): 88–100.

Ackoff, R. L. 1979. "The Future of Operational Research Is Past." *Journal of the Operational Research Society* 30 (2): 93–104.

Ackoff, R. L., and M. W. Sasieni. 1968. "Fundamental Considerations in Systems Behavior." *Management Science* 14 (7): 395–403.

Amundson, S. D. 1998. "Relationships Between Theory-Driven Empirical Research in Operations Management and Other Disciplines." *Journal of Operations Management* 16 (4): 341–359.

Arrow, K. J., T. Harris, and J. Marschak. 1951. "Optimal Inventory Policy." *Econometrica* 19 (3): 250–272.

Bertrand, J. W. M., and J. C. Fransoo. 2002. "Operations Management Research Methodologies Using Quantitative Modeling." *International Journal of Operations & Production Management* 22 (2): 241–264.

Bertrand, J. W. M., and J. C. Wortmann. 1981. *Production Control and Information Systems for Component-Manufacturing Shops*. Elsevier.

Bertrand, J. Will M., and H. P. G. Van Ooijen. 2002. "Workload Based Order Release and Productivity: A Missing Link." *Production Planning & Control* 13 (7): 665–678.

Bitran, G. R., and A. C. Hax. 1977. "On the Design of Hierarchical Production Planning Systems." *Decision Sciences* 8 (1): 28–55.

Blocher, J. D., R. W. Garrett, and R. W. Schmenner. 1999. "Throughput Time Reduction: Taking One's Medicine." *Production and Operations Management* 8 (4): 357–373.

Box, G. E. P., and G. M. Jenkins. 1976. *Time Series Analysis: Forecasting and Control*. Holden-Day.

Bray, R. L., and H. Mendelson. 2012. "Information Transmission and the Bullwhip Effect: An Empirical Investigation." *Management Science* 58 (5): 860–875.

Buzacott, J. A., and G. Shantikumar. 1993. *Stochastic Models of Manufacturing Systems*. Prentice Hall.

Cachon, G. P., T. Randall, and G. M. Schmidt. 2007. "In Search of the Bullwhip Effect." *Manufacturing & Service Operations Management* 9 (4): 457.

Chen, R. R., T. C. E. Cheng, T.-M. Choi, and Y. Wang. 2016. "Novel Advances in Applications of the Newsvendor Model." *Decision Sciences* 47 (1): 8–10.

Chou, Y.-C., H. H.-C. Chuang, P. Chou, and R. Oliva. 2022. "Supervised Machine Learning for Theory Building and Testing: Opportunities in Operations Management." *Journal of Operations Management* 69 (4): 643-675.

Chuang, H. H.-C., R. Oliva, and S. Kumar. 2022. "Group-Level Information Decay and Inventory Inspection: An Empirical-Analytical Approach." *Journal of Operations Management* 68 (2): 130–152.

De Kok, A. G., and J. C. Fransoo. 2003. "Planning Supply Chain Operations: Definition and Comparison of Planning Concepts." In *Supply Chain Management: Design, Coordination and Operation*, edited by S. C. Graves and A. G. de Kok, 11:597–675. Handbooks in Operations Research and Management Science. Elsevier.

De Treville, S., I. Bicer, V. Chavez-Demoulin, V. Hagspiel, N. Schürhoff, C. Tasserit, and S. Wager. 2014. "Valuing Lead Time." *Journal of Operations Management* 32 (6): 337–346.

De Treville, S., T. R. Browning, and R. Oliva. 2023. "Empirically Grounding Analytics (EGA) Research in the Journal of Operations Management." *Journal of Operations Management* 69: 337–348.

DeHoratius, N., and A. Raman. 2008. "Inventory Record Inaccuracy: An Empirical Analysis." *Management Science* 54 (4): 627–641.

Delorme, M., M. Iori, and S. Martello. 2016. "Bin Packing and Cutting Stock Problems: Mathematical Models and Exact Algorithms." *European Journal of Operational Research* 255 (1): 1–20.

Disney, S. M., L. Hoshiko, L. Polley, and C. Weigel. 2013. "Removing Bullwhip from Lexmark's Toner Operations." *Production and Operations Management Society Annual Conference*, 3–6.

Edgeworth, F. Y. 1888. "The Mathematical Theory of Banking." *Journal of the Royal Statistical Society* 51 (1): 113–127.

Edmondson, A. C., and S. E. McManus. 2007. "Methodological Fit in Management Field Research." *Academy of Management Review* 32 (4): 1246–1264.

Eroglu, C., and C. Hofer. 2011. "Lean, Leaner, Too Lean? The Inventory-Performance Link Revisited." *Journal of Operations Management* 29 (4): 356–369.

Fine, C. H. 2000. "Clockspeed-Based Strategies for Supply Chain Design." *Production and Operations Management* 9 (3): 213–221.

Forrester, J. W. 1961. *Industrial Dynamics.* MIT Press.

Fransoo, J. C., and V. C. S. Wiers. 2006. "Action Variety of Planners: Cognitive Load and Requisite Variety." *Journal of Operations Management* 24 (6): 813–821.

Gaur, V., and S. Kesavan. 2007. "The Effects of Firm Size and Sales Growth Rate on Inventory Turnover Performance in the U.S. Retail Sector."

Graves, S. C., and A. G. de Kok, eds. 2003. *Supply Chain Management: Design, Coordination and Operation.* Vol. 11. Handbooks in Operations Research and Management Science. Amsterdam: Elsevier.

Gray, J. V., G. Esenduran, M. J. Rungtusanatham, and K. Skowronski. 2017. "Why in the World Did They Reshore? Examining Small to Medium-Sized Manufacturer Decisions." *Journal of Operations Management* 49: 37–51.

Handfield, R. B., and S. A. Melnyk. 1998. "The Scientific Theory-Building Process: A Primer Using the Case of TQM." *Journal of Operations Management* 16 (4): 321–339.

Harris, F. W. 1913. "The Economic Order Quantity as a Deterministic Problem." *Journal of the Royal Statistical Society* 76 (1): 2–23.

Hendricks, K. B., and V. R. Singhal. 2003. "The Effect of Supply Chain Glitches on Shareholder Wealth." *Journal of Operations Management* 21 (5): 501–522.

Holmström, Jan. 1994. "The Relationship Between Speed and Productivity in Industry Networks: A Study of Industrial Statistics." *International Journal of Production Economics* 34 (1): 91–97.

Holt, C. C., F. Modigliani, J. F. Muth, and H. A. Simon. 1960. *Planning Production, Inventory and Work Force.* Englewood Cliffs, NJ: Prentice Hall.

Hopp, Wallace J., and Mark L. Spearman. 2013. *Factory Physics: Foundations of Manufacturing and Engineering.* 3rd ed. McGraw-Hill Education.

Ibanez, M. R., and B. R. Staats. 2018. "Behavioral Empirics and Field Experiments." In *The Handbook of Behavioral Operations,* edited by E. Katok, S. Leider, and K. Donohue, 121–147. John Wiley & Sons Hoboken, NJ.

Imbens, G. W. 2022. "Causality in Econometrics: Choice Vs Chance." *Econometrica* 90 (6): 2541–2566.

Inman, R. R. 1999. "Empirical Evaluation of Exponential and Independence Assumptions in Queueing Models of Manufacturing Systems." *Production and Operations Management* 8 (4): 409–432.

Katok, E. 2011. "Laboratory Experiments in Operations Management." In *Transforming Research into Action,* 15–35. INFORMS.

Katok, E., S. Leider, and K. Donohue, eds. 2018. *The Handbook of Behavioral Operations.* John Wiley & Sons.

Kesavan, S., and T. Kushwaha. 2020. "Field Experiment on the Profit Implications of Merchants' Discretionary Power to Override Data-Driven Decision-Making Tools." *Management Science* 66 (11): 5182–5190.

Kesavan, S., and M. Olivares. 2019. "Endogeneity and Related Concerns That Keep an Empirical Researcher up at Night." https://www.informs.org/Blogs/M-SOM-Blogs/M-SOM-Review/Endogeneity-and-Related-Concerns-that-Keep-an-Empirical-Researcher-Up-at-Night.

Keys, P. 1991. "Operational Research in Organizations: A Metaphorical Analysis." *Journal of the Operational Research Society* 42 (6): 435–446.

Kleijnen, J. P. C. 2018. *Design and Analysis of Simulation Experiments.* Springer.

Lariviere, M. A., and E. L. Porteus. 2001. "Selling to the Newsvendor: An Analysis of Price-Only Contracts." *Manufacturing & Service Operations Management* 3 (4): 293–305.

Law, A. M., and W. D. Kelton. 2007. *Simulation Modeling and Analysis.* Mcgraw-hill New York.

Lieberman, M. B., and L. Demeester. 1999. "Inventory Reduction and Productivity Growth: Linkages in the Japanese Automotive Industry." *Management Science* 45 (4): 466–485.

Liu, Z., P. Nain, and D. Towsley. 1992. "On Optimal Polling Policies." *Queueing Systems* 11: 59–83.

Long, X., and J. Nasiry. 2015. "Prospect Theory Explains Newsvendor Behavior: The Role of Reference Points." *Management Science* 61 (12): 3009–3012.

Low, H., and C. Meghir. 2017. "The Use of Structural Models in Econometrics." *Journal of Economic Perspectives* 31 (2): 33–58.

McGill, J. I., and G. J. Van Ryzin. 1999. "Revenue Management: Research Overview and Prospects." *Transportation Science* 33 (2): 233–256.

Melnyk, S. A., and R. B. Handfield. 1998. "May You Live in Interesting Times … the Emergence of Theory-Driven Empirical Research." *Journal of Operations Management* 16 (4): 311–319.

Mendelson, H., and R. R. Pillai. 1998. "Clockspeed and Informational Response: Evidence from the Information Technology Industry." *Information Systems Research* 9 (4): 415–433.

Meredith, J. R., A. Raturi, K. Amoako-Gyampah, and B. Kaplan. 1989. "Alternative Research Paradigms in Operations." *Journal of Operations Management* 8 (4): 297–326.

Mitroff, I. I., F. Betz, L. R. Pondy, and F. Sagasti. 1974. "On Managing Science in the Systems Age: Two Schemas for the Study of Science as a Whole Systems Phenomenon." *Interfaces* 4 (3): 46–58.

Nahmias, S., and T. L. Olsen. 2015. *Production and Operations Analysis.* Waveland Press.

O'Leary-Kelly, S. W., and R. J. Vokurka. 1998. "The Empirical Assessment of Construct Validity." *Journal of Operations Management* 16 (4): 387–405.

Olivares, M., C. Terwiesch, and L. Cassorla. 2008. "Structural Estimation of the Newsvendor Model: An Application to Reserving Operating Room Time." *Management Science* 54 (1): 41–55. 10.1287/mnsc.1070.0756.

Rumyantsev, S., and S. Netessine. 2007. "What Can Be Learned from Classical Inventory Models? A Cross-Industry Exploratory Investigation." *Manufacturing & Service Operations Management* 9 (4): 409–429.

Saunders, L. W., J. R. W. Merrick, and M. C. Holcomb. 2021. "Microdosing Flexibility in an Efficient Supply Chain." *Journal of Operations Management* 67 (3): 407–416.

Schmenner, R. W. 1988. "The Merit of Making Things Fast." *MIT Sloan Management Review* 30 (1): 11.

Schmenner, R. W., and M. L. Swink. 1998. "On Theory in Operations Management." *Journal of Operations Management* 17 (1): 97–113.

Schneeweiss, C. 2003. "Distributed Decision Making—a Unified Approach." *European Journal of Operational Research* 150 (2): 237–252.

Schonberger, R. J. 1982. *Japanese Manufacturing Techniques: Nine Hidden Lessons in Simplicity.* Simon & Schuster.

Schweitzer, M. E., and G. P. Cachon. 2000. "Decision Bias in the Newsvendor Problem with a Known Demand Distribution: Experimental Evidence." *Management Science* 46 (3): 404–420.

Serrano, A., R. Oliva, and S. Kraiselburd. 2018. "Risk Propagation Through Payment Distortion in Supply Chains." *Journal of Operations Management* 58: 1–14.

Silver, E. A., D. F. Pyke, and R. Peterson. 1998. *Inventory Management and Production Planning and Scheduling.* 3rd ed. John Wiley & Sons.

Sterman, J. D. 2000. *Business Dynamics: Systems Thinking and Modeling for a Complex World.* Irwin/McGraw-Hill.

Su, X. 2008. "Bounded Rationality in Newsvendor Models." *Manufacturing & Service Operations Management* 10 (4): 566–589.

Taylor, F. W. 1911. *The Principles of Scientific Management.* New York: Harper; Ro2.

Terwiesch, C., M. Olivares, B. R. Staats, and V. Gaur. 2020. "OM Forum—a Review of Empirical Operations Management over the Last Two Decades." *Manufacturing & Service Operations Management* 22 (4): 656–668.

Tong, J., and D. Feiler. 2017. "A Behavioral Model of Forecasting: Naive Statistics on Mental Samples." *Management Science* 63 (11): 3609–3627.

Toth, P., and D. Vigo. 2014. *Vehicle Routing: Problems, Methods, and Applications.* 2nd ed. Society for Industrial; Applied Mathematics.

Udenio, M., J. C. Fransoo, and R. Peels. 2015. "Destocking, the Bullwhip Effect, and the Credit Crisis: Empirical Modeling of Supply Chain Dynamics." *International Journal of Production Economics* 160 (0): 34–46. 10.1016/j.ijpe.2014.09.008.

Uppari, B. S., and S. Hasija. 2019. "Modeling Newsvendor Behavior: A Prospect Theory Approach." *Manufacturing & Service Operations Management* 21 (3): 481–500.

Van Mieghem, J. A., and G. Allon. 2008. *Operations Strategy*. Belmont, MA: Dynamic Ideas.

Van Zelst, S., K. van Donselaar, T. van Woensel, R. Broekmeulen, and J. Fransoo. 2009. "Logistics Drivers for Shelf Stacking in Grocery Retail Stores: Potential for Efficiency Improvement." *International Journal of Production Economics* 121 (2): 620–632.

Wacker, J. G. 1998. "A Definition of Theory: Research Guidelines for Different Theory-Building Research Methods in Operations Management." *Journal of Operations Management* 16 (4): 361–385.

Wiendahl, H.-P.. 1987. *Load Oriented Production Control*. Munich: Hanser.

Wight, O. W. 1974. *Production and Inventory Management in the Computer Age*. Cahners Books.

Zipkin, P. H. 2000. *Foundations of Inventory Management*. McGraw-Hill.

Zoryk-Schalla, A. J., J. C. Fransoo, and T. G. de Kok. 2004. "Modeling the Planning Process in Advanced Planning Systems." *Information & Management* 42 (1): 75–87.

Index

Note: *Italicized* and **bold** page numbers refer to figures and tables. Page numbers followed by "n" refer to notes.

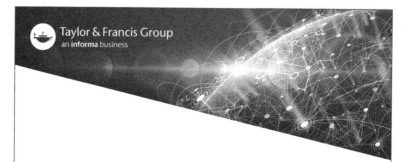

Taylor & Francis eBooks

www.taylorfrancis.com

A single destination for eBooks from Taylor & Francis
with increased functionality and an improved user
experience to meet the needs of our customers.

90,000+ eBooks of award-winning academic content in
Humanities, Social Science, Science, Technology, Engineering,
and Medical written by a global network of editors and authors.

TAYLOR & FRANCIS EBOOKS OFFERS:

A streamlined
experience for
our library
customers

A single point
of discovery
for all of our
eBook content

Improved
search and
discovery of
content at both
book and
chapter level

REQUEST A FREE TRIAL
support@taylorfrancis.com

Printed in the United States
by Baker & Taylor Publisher Services